# MORE ABOUT JUSTIFYING VIOLENCE:

## METHODOLOGICAL STUDIES OF ATTITUDES AND BEHAVIOR

# MORE ABOUT JUSTIFYING VIOLENCE:

## METHODOLOGICAL STUDIES OF ATTITUDES AND BEHAVIOR

MONICA D. BLUMENTHAL

LETHA B. CHADIHA

GERALD A. COLE

TOBY EPSTEIN JAYARATNE

Survey Research Center ● Institute for Social Research
The University of Michigan
Ann Arbor, Michigan

Library of Congress Catalog Card No. 74-620136
ISBN 0-87944-191-7 paperbound
ISBN 0-87944-192-5 clothbound

Published by the Institute for Social Research
The University of Michigan, Ann Arbor, Michigan 48106

First Published 1975

# PREFACE

Research on contemporary social problems has not yielded impressive solutions to those problems nor even prospects of palliating them. Social scientists have not learned how to cure crime or control poverty. Indeed, it is not clear that we are significantly closer to understanding the great social issues of our time than we were several decades ago. Theories have changed and new research techniques have been invented, but it is not always certain that the newer theories have more predictive power than the old, or that the new instruments and measurements represent improvements over their predecessors. Every social scientist who is feeling reasonably honest and able to bear the pain ought to occasionally ask why progress in the social sciences has been so slow in pace and ephemeral in substance.

Many reasons come to mind. Social problems are by nature complex and this complexity leads directly to the difficult and often unsatisfactory nature of research on these problems. It is almost never possible in the social sciences to design critical experiments which might lead to clear insights about social problems. Indeed, the theoretical structures which must exist before critical experiments can be conceptualized often do not exist. Where theory does exist, it is often so simply formulated that it bears no more relationship to the complicated phenomena it seeks to describe than do stick figures to living human beings. It is difficult to think about complicated phenomena clearly; to do so, work must progress in stages. To advance real knowledge it is essential to build on existing work and theory, a condition which implies that as much as possible should be known about the veracity of a theory before it is either discarded or modified. Unfortunately, social scientists often treat the work of their predecessors lightly.

An additional factor which probably contributes to the slow rate at which theoretical models which can predict accurately have been built lies in the fact that it is easier and more exciting to invent new psychological and attitudinal measures than it is to evaluate the characteristics of existing measures. Methodological research is probably

v

dull to most people. Unfortunately, to understand the real world, one must first understand the tools used to develop that understanding.

Such thoughts led us to the present work. When we began, we thought primarily of investigating the validity and reliability of the measures we had used in the 1969 survey. As the work progressed, however, we found it was necessary for us to clarify both our concepts and our theory.

The present work includes a study of 283 respondents selected on the basis of their geographic locations, and 268 respondents selected on the basis of some special characteristics that might relate to their attitudes toward violence. Among the latter were: 67 Jehovah's Witnesses, 36 Quakers and others who attended Quaker meetings, 27 parents of battered children and 32 selected as controls for these parents, 29 students who had probably participated in a street disturbance, 25 young people, mainly Chicano, who had participated in a riot, and 52 prisoners who had been confined to the federal penitentiary in Milan, Michigan.

This work can rightly be regarded as a series of little studies. Such a series is in many ways more complicated than a single major study, and in conducting our series we had much help. Two of our original co-workers, Frank M. Andrews and Robert L. Kahn, contributed much during the intial conceptualization and project planning stages. We are also grateful to Laura Klem for her invaluable consultations with us. Her assistance, encouragement, and guidance served as a major source of support during the data analysis and we are also grateful for her good advice on presenting the results.

Finding and investigating people in criterion groups who could illuminate the validity of the measures which concerned us was a difficult task which we would never have accomplished without substantial help from many. We are indebted to the National Science Foundation, which provided financial support. Dr. Marilyn Heins, Norman Woronoff, and Delores Johnson were of special help to us in our studies of the parents of battered children. Dr. Richard P. Tucker, Hali Giessler, Fran Eliot, and Joanne Lind were especially helpful in assisting us with the study of Quakers and the individuals associated with them. Dr. Henri Enfroy, Clayton Ball, Andrew Blannon, Solomon J. Knight, Sr., and Gordon Pollack helped us in our attempt to understand the philosophy and mores of the Jehovah's Witnesses. We are grateful to Doris Joyner and Lucille Riddle, who interviewed the young people arrested after a small riot we studied in California.

We are greatly indebted to those who served on our staff. Initially, we enjoyed the services of Kendra Head, who served as assistant study director early in the project before graduate school claimed her entirely. Daniel McConochie provided invaluable help while we were planning and carrying out the multiple small studies which were designed to test the validity of our measures. Later, he assisted us with the data analysis. Secretarial and administrative assistance was provided originally by Cynthia Tysinger. Later, during the agonizing process of putting this monograph together, Maureen Compton assumed control of the manuscripts and machines. We are deeply grateful for their help; we would probably not have survived without it. In addition, we are grateful for the secretarial services of Patricia Hawkins. We are also grateful to Doug Truax and his co-workers in the Publishing Division.

We are especially indebted to Robert L. Kahn and Laura Klem for reading this manuscript and making many valuable suggestions. A few of these pages were written entirely by Robert; we are grateful for his contribution.

The four authors of this monograph are scattered now. I cannot ask them how they feel about having arrived at the end of this labor. I, for one, am glad it is done. It was a tedious effort. But the work we have accomplished has opened vistas we had not imagined when we began our work on violence in 1968. Whether we ourselves will ever have the opportunity to explore these new realms seems doubtful in this day of uncertain funding and skyrocketing research costs. Hopefully, someday, someone will build on our labors to carry us one step further toward understanding those forces that lead us to commit violence in the name of virtue.

Monica D. Blumenthal
Ann Arbor, 1975

# TABLE OF CONTENTS

Page

# Chapter 1

# ATTITUDES TOWARD VIOLENCE FOR SOCIAL CHANGE IN CRITERION GROUPS

*Introduction*

Occasionally researchers, like almost everyone else, are overcome by fits of virtue which, although in themselves brief in duration, have consequences more enduring than the original flush of good intent. So, following a 1969 national survey of attitudes toward violence (Blumenthal et al. 1972), it was decided that it would be appropriate and useful to devote some effort to a study of the major measures which had been employed in the original survey. This report summarizes such an endeavor.

The purpose of this new research was to study the measurement characteristics of some of the instruments employed in the 1969 national survey. To what extent could the measures be trusted? What was their reliability, and to what degree did they measure the constructs they were intended to assess? In addition to these traditional problems of reliability and validity, another problem was inherent in the 1969 national study—to what extent were the questions that had been used in 1969 time bound? That is, which of the questions that had seemed so compelling when asked in an era characterized by civil turmoil remained germane at a time when large scale protest was manifestly unpopular?

The extent to which questions in attitude surveys are time bound is not discussed as frequently as are questions of reliability and validity, but it is an important consideration in research assessing attitudes toward contemporary issues, particularly when the issues are in a state of flux. To illustrate, it seems likely that attitudes toward abortion would be expressed differently in the 1970's than they were in the late forties. Since the forties, emphasis in the larger society has moved from concern with slow population growth produced by the Depression to anxiety over the detrimental effects of overpopulation. This shift in emphasis alone would probably have been sufficient to modify popular thinking about abortion. However, it is also true that before the 1970s abortion was criminal in almost all states, while today it is not criminal in any. Formerly, it would have been sensible to assess attitudes toward abortion by inquiring whether or not physicians should be willing to perform acts of civil disobedience by conducting abortions or by refusing to report criminal abortions. Now, it is not. The meaning of questions about civil disobedience in relation to abortion has been radically changed by the decriminalization of abortions. While formerly such questions may have been germane and even thought provoking, currently they would hardly make sense. Thus, the effect of social change on the meaning of attitudinal questions may be profound. It is an issue which affects a number of measures used in the 1969 survey.

One of the major issues in the present research was to establish the validity of the two central dependent variables—a measure of attitudes toward the use of violence to produce social change, and a measure of attitudes toward the use of violence to maintain social control. Validity has been defined as the correlation between a measure and its underlying attribute. Establishing the validity of an attitude measure is not a simple task, not only because it is often difficult to determine what is the attribute underlying an attitude, but also because there are problems in the very conceptualization of an attitude. An attitude has been defined as a psychological representation of societal and cultural influences. As such, an attitude can be thought of as a "relatively enduring organization of beliefs around an object or a situation predisposing one to respond in some preferential manner" (Rokeach 1968, p. 450). Such a statement of what is meant by an attitude implies that the attitude has cognitive and behavioral components. In addition, according to Rokeach (1968), attitudes also contain affective elements, that is, evaluative components which may be directed toward the object of the belief, toward those sharing the belief (or not sharing it), or toward the belief itself.

This conceptualization of the nature of attitudes implies that investigating the validity of a measure of an attitude is a three-part task. The first is to determine how accurately the instrument in question reflects the cognitive component of the individual's attitude, that is, the belief; the second is to measure the extent to which the attitude is associated with a predilection to a specific behavior; and the third is to gauge the accuracy with which the instrument reflects the affective component of the attitude. Each of these three tasks raises separate questions with respect to validity, and each requires a different set of operations to provide an answer.

The first question raised by an inquiry into the reliability and validity of instruments used to measure specific attitudes—that is, how well does the instrument measure the belief which it is intended to measure—raises a number of issues. Among these are whether or not the experimenter and the respondent share the same frame of reference, whether the instrument has characteristics which force the respondent into a format he finds uncomfortable or incongruous with his usual modes of thinking, whether the instrument itself tends to produce a biased response, and whether the characteristics of the interviewer influence the respondent's choice of answers.

One approach to examining how accurately a measure assesses a respondent's beliefs is to evaluate how well the measure relates to measures of other constructs to which it theoretically ought to be related, an approach generally referred to as construct validity. Runkel and McGrath (1972, p. 162) have pointed out that construct validity is a variant of predictive validity and that there are serious problems in the logic of predictive validity. The first difficulty is that construct validation is dependent on the validity of the reference measures. In other words, if one concept is validated in terms of another to which it theoretically ought to be related, the demonstrable validity of the first measure cannot exceed the validity of the second. The second logical difficulty with the idea of construct validity is that the validation of one measure by another is confounded by the problem of ascertaining what the "real link" between the two measures should be. That is, what is the size of the expected relationship?

If two constructs are not identical, it may follow that one, but not the other, can be affected by a third variable; that is, not all the variance in both measures will be explained by the same set of predictors. If such is the case, the first construct, but not the second, may be modified by the presence of some specific independent variables. Consequently, such an independent variable may act to modify the relationship between the two constructs of interest. Furthermore, the validity of the construct used as validation often must be assumed. Sometimes the assumption must be made that there are no variables capable of influencing one of the constructs without equally influencing the other. Neither of these assumptions is necessarily justifiable. Assumptions cannot be avoided in validity studies, and since many such assumptions remain to be tested when the usual kinds of validation studies are complete, validation must remain a slow, piecemeal process.

The second component in validating an attitudinal measure is the study of the relationship between the measure and the behavior it implies. Such studies are confounded by the problem of establishing empirical and theoretical relationships which are separate from the attitude itself. For example, if a predilection toward a behavior is part of the basic nature of an attitude and if establishing such a predilection toward behavior is part of the validation of an attitude, the inquiry is made more difficult by the absence of external information on the strength of the relationship between the attitude in question and the behavior to which it should predispose. The question must be asked, is it a predilection which always implies a behavioral response or does it imply a behavioral response only under certain circumstances? If there is always a behavior implied by a particular attitude, what is the type and magnitude of the behavior which is to occur? If the predilection to a behavior implied by a particular attitude is not invariable, it is also necessary to know under what circumstances the behavior will be elicited. Useful here is Rokeach's (1968, p. 452) notion that attitudes toward the situation as well as attitudes toward the object must be taken into account before behavior can be predicted. Clearly, if an individual holds two conflicting beliefs (for example, that there should be no discrimination in employing blacks and that hiring a black person in the front office is likely to lose business due to customer prejudice) the ensuing behavior (whether or not a black person is hired in the front office) probably results from an interaction of both attitudes (Schuman 1972).

Validating the affective component of an attitude is another separate segment of the investigative task, one rarely attended. Indeed, measuring affects poses problems so complex that the extensive literature on the subject raises more questions than it answers. The studies reported here do not attempt to broach the subject. We shall do no more than to note the omission of this effort.

One additional problem should be considered in attitude studies. Often, in social science it is assumed that an individual can be characterized as possessing an underlying attitude which is *the* attitude epitomizing his position. This thinking may be an extension of conceptualizations in psychological testing where much of the methodology and theory on the validity and reliability has developed. It may be reasonable to think of an individual as having so much intelligence, the main problem being to measure it properly, though even that seems dubious. Some thought about human behavior will convince the observer that performance, presumably based on intelligence, varies widely from moment to moment even when the ostensible nature of the act which is performed is identical. Many characteristics of the subject may affect the results of intelligence testing: fatigue, feelings of well-being, the presence of depression and anxiety, for example. Moreover, characteristics of the subject are not the only factors which influence results. The race of the test administrator (Pettigrew 1964, p. 116) and the expectation of the child's teachers (Rosenthal and Jacobson 1968) all have been shown to affect test results. It might be more sensible to think of an individual's intelligence as having a range rather than an exact value, the extent of the range being determined partly by temporary states of the individual and partly by interactions with the environment. This variability is not only characteristic of intelligence test results, but also of many other kinds of performance. People often work at problem solving tasks in spurts, making great progress on some days and little on others. Other traits or characteristics similarly fluctuate. Indeed, when a trait or characteristic becomes particularly fixed, its immutable persistence is often regarded as an indication of psychopathology.

If variability is characteristic of traits which are presumably life-long in duration, it seems unlikely that there should be *an* attitude which is truly representative of the respondent's belief system on a particular subject. It seems more reasonable to suppose that individuals have sets of attitudes toward specific objects or situations and that those attitudes cover a range of positions. For example, the attitudes of a specific politician on any given issue may vary considerably from one day to the next; but politicians can be differentiated in regard to particular issues, and knowledge that an individual is liberal or conservative about a given problem provides considerable information on the range of attitudes that he may be expected to hold. Presumably, all the statements made by a particular politician regarding a specific issue would fit into a limited range of attitudes. The range of attitudes of two specific politicians might be totally non-overlapping, even though each range encompasses a variety of positions. Thus, an investigation of attitude measures must consider how accurately the instrument in question taps the *range* of the respondent's attitudes with respect to a particular dimension. Indeed, since attitudes, as they have been defined here, have several components, it is probably more reasonable to imagine attitudes as covering a multi-dimensional space rather than just a range. In other words, one approach to the measurement of attitudes might be to ascertain the individual range of attitudes on each of the relevant dimensions. Such an approach would describe the individual's attitude space within which he could always be located. Presumably, the mapping of such a space would give a more stable estimate of the individual's attitudes than is given by a measure of central tendency.

In order to explore the issues outlined above in relation to the measures used in our studies of attitudes toward violence, a variety of projects were undertaken. The largest of these consisted of an initial interview followed by a reinterview conducted in the winter and spring of 1972 with 283 respondents, men and women alike, sixteen years of age and older. One hundred eighty-nine respondents lived in Detroit and the remainder in four southern sampling units: Montgomery, Alabama; East Carroll, Louisiana; Harris, Texas; and Atlanta, Georgia. Most respondents were chosen by a modified probability sample in which the interviewer was allowed to take two interviews at any of six addresses; about half of the Detroit respondents were a standard probability sample. (Details of the procedures by which the respondents were selected are presented in Appendix A.) Specifically, the sample was designed so that it would provide heterogeneity with respect to those demographic characteristics which had been shown to be important in the initial study. Hence, the sample was selected to be approximately half black, race being a crucial variable with respect to the characteristics under investigation. Approximately one-third of the respondents were selected in the South, since previous data had demonstrated that residence in the South modified a number of variables important in research on attitudes toward violence. The reinterviews which repeated the main questions but contained many questions new to the respondents were conducted after approximately seven weeks.

In addition to the study described above, a number of adjunct investigations were conducted, partly in Detroit and partly elsewhere, in which special populations with known characteristics were studied in order to establish the criterion validity of the measures. Data from these groups will not be discussed with data from the respondents selected on a more random basis unless specifically mentioned.

The first measure to be discussed is the Violence for Social Change Index. Basic information about the construction of the measure will be presented and then the relationship of the measure to selected demographic variables will be discussed in order to facilitate understanding of further analysis. In this chapter, the validity of the measure will be considered with respect to data collected from criterion groups. In the second chapter, the reliability of the measure will be described, followed by an examination of some aspects of the construct validity of the index. The third chapter will discuss the Violence for Social Change Index in relation to variables other theorists have considered in relation to this kind of violence.

## Characteristics of the Violence for Social Change Index

The Violence for Social Change Index was originally used in the 1969 national survey as a measure of the extent to which the respondent believed that violence resulting in property damage and personal injury was necessary to bring about change "fast enough." Attitudes concerning the use of violence as a means of producing social change were measured with the following set of statements:

*Changes can be made fast enough without action involving property damage or injury.*

*Protest in which some people are hurt is necessary for changes to come fast enough.*

*Protest in which there is **some** property damage is necessary for changes to be brought about fast enough.*

*Protest in which there is **much** property damage is necessary before changes can be brought about fast enough.*

*Protest in which some people are killed is necessary before changes will take place fast enough.*

The respondent was given a card and asked to check "agree a great deal," "agree somewhat," "disagree somewhat," or "disagree a great deal" in respect to each statement.

The 1972 interview inquired about *two* different situations; the first situation dealt with disturbances caused by blacks, and the second referred to the general necessity for violence in bringing about change. The exact wording of the first question was as follows:

*Many blacks (Negroes/colored people) feel changes are needed in our society. Some people think violence is needed to bring about the changes which would make life better for blacks (Negroes/colored people). We would like to know how much you agree or disagree with each of these opinions about how much violence is necessary for blacks (Negroes/ colored people) to bring about changes.*

The exact wording for the general situation was as follows:

*Some people feel that important changes can be brought about only through violence; others say violence is not necessary. What do **you** think?*

The 1972 percentage distribution of responses to these questions for the general situation is given in Table 1.1. It can be seen from the table that there are marked differences between black and white respondents, with substantially more blacks agreeing that violence is necessary to bring about change fast enough. These data are highly similar to the national data collected in 1969 (Blumenthal et al. 1972), but it should be emphasized that the population investigated in the 1972 study was not comparable to a national sample.

Responses to the question which asked how much violence was necessary to bring about change for blacks were so similar to the percentage responses obtained when the respondents were asked about the general situation that presentation of the exact figures seems

**Table 1.1**

Percentage Responses to Items Measuring the Level of Violence
Necessary to Bring About Change Generally

| | All Respondents | Whites | Blacks |
|---|---|---|---|
| Changes can be made fast enough without action involving property damage or injury. | | | |
| Agree a Great Deal | 50% | 60% | 40% |
| Agree Somewhat | 34 | 31 | 37 |
| Disagree Somewhat | 9 | 4 | 14 |
| Disagree a Great Deal | 7 | 5 | 9 |
| | 100% | 100% | 100% |
| Protest in which some people are hurt is necessary for changes to come fast enough. | | | |
| Agree a Great Deal | 6 | 5 | 7 |
| Agree Somewhat | 22 | 11 | 34 |
| Disagree Somewhat | 28 | 25 | 30 |
| Disagree a Great Deal | 44 | 59 | 29 |
| | 100% | 100% | 100% |
| Protest in which there is *some* property damage is necessary for changes to be brought about fast enough. | | | |
| Agree a Great Deal | 7 | 5 | 9 |
| Agree Somewhat | 20 | 11 | 31 |
| Disagree Somewhat | 30 | 30 | 28 |
| Disagree a Great Deal | 43 | 54 | 32 |
| | 100% | 100% | 100% |
| Protest in which there is *much* property damage is necessary before changes can be brought about fast enough. | | | |
| Agree a Great Deal | 7 | 3 | 12 |
| Agree Somewhat | 9 | 1 | 17 |
| Disagree Somewhat | 24 | 17 | 32 |
| Disagree a Great Deal | 60 | 79 | 39 |
| | 100% | 100% | 100% |
| Protest in which some people are killed is necessary before changes will take place fast enough. | | | |
| Agree a Great Deal | 6 | 6 | 7 |
| Agree Somewhat | 10 | 3 | 18 |
| Disagree Somewhat | 14 | 7 | 22 |
| Disagree a Great Deal | 70 | 84 | 53 |
| | 100% | 100% | 100% |
| N | (283) | (145) | (133) |

Note: In this and all subsequent tables, unless otherwise stated, N's represent the number in the general category. The exact number for each may vary slightly depending on the amount of missing data.

redundant. Responses to these two sets of questions were combined into the Violence for Social Change Index. (For details of the scaling see Blumenthal et al. 1972, Appendix D.) It should be noted that the Violence for Social Change Index used in the 1969 national survey contained responses to a third situation which inquired how much violence was necessary to bring about changes of the type needed by students. This set of questions was not repeated in the 1972 study since it had been demonstrated that an index constructed from two situations had statistical characteristics highly similar to an index consisting of all three (McConochie, Jayaratne and Blumenthal 1973).

Table 1.2 shows the percentage distribution on the Violence for Social Change Index for black and white respondents. The 1969 data are presented mainly for purposes of orientation. In presenting the national survey data no inference is made that the two samples are comparable, and inferences that similarities or differences between the data are due to trends cannot be assumed. Nevertheless, it seems useful

**Table 1.2**

Percentage Responses to the Violence for Social Change Index
in Relation to Race in the 1969 and 1972 Studies

| Violence for Social Change Index | | 1969 Study | | 1972 Study | |
|---|---|---|---|---|---|
| | | Whites | Blacks | Whites | Blacks |
| Low | 1 | 43% | 9% | 40% | 16% |
| | 2-3 | 39 | 34 | 41 | 24 |
| High | 4-7 | 18 | 57 | 19 | 60 |
| | | 100% | 100% | 100% | 100% |
| | N | (1,046) | (303) | (145) | (133) |

Note: The Violence for Social Change Index used in this and subsequent tables of the 1969 data is comparable to that used in the 1972 data (i.e., it is constructed from the same *two*-situation item sets rather than the *three* item sets that were used in the original analysis of the 1969 data). Consequently, the data are not comparable to the data in the monograph, *Justifying Violence: Attitudes of American Men* (Blumenthal et al. 1972).

to present both sets of data to orient the reader as to how the present data relate to those of the earlier study. It can be seen that the Violence for Social Change Index is strongly related to race, black respondents being substantially more likely to score high on the index than white.

*Demographic Correlates of the Violence for Social Change Index*

Table 1.3 gives the associations between selected demographic characteristics and the Violence for Social Change Index. Because of large racial effects in the data, the relationships are presented separately

**Table 1.3**

Relationships between the Violence for Social Change Index and
Selected Demographic Characteristics for White and Black Respondents
in the 1969 and 1972 Studies
(gammas)

| Demographic Characteristic | | 1969 Study | | 1972 Study | |
|---|---|---|---|---|---|
| | | Whites | Blacks | Whites | Blacks |
| Sex | | — | — | -.10 | -.21 |
| Age | | -.11†† | -.06† | -.24‡ | -.18† |
| Education | | -.03†† | .14†† | -.05 | .03 |
| Family Income | | -.07†† | .13†† | -.13 | .03 |
| Town Size | | .05†† | .27†† | -.07 | -.17 |
| Experience in South | | .02 | .07† | .17 | .03 |
| | N | (1,046) | (303) | (145) | (133) |

Notes: In this and all subsequent tables all characteristics where the data have ordinal
or interval properties are scaled so that the higher the score, the larger the characteristic
named. The highest score on town size refers to the most urban category; the highest
score on experience in South is given to those who spent their childhood in the South.
A negative relationship for race indicates whites scored higher than blacks; and for sex
that men scored higher than women.

Level of significance used for gammas in this monograph is based on the Normal Deviation of S (z score) using Table K: Values of z in Blalock, H., *Social Statistics,* McGraw-
Hill, New York, 1970.

†p < .05        ‡p < .01        ††p < .001

for black and white respondents. On the whole, none of the associations
in the 1972 data deviate much from what would have been anticipated
on the basis of the 1969 data. However, there is a slightly larger relationship between age and the index in the 1972 data than was true in the
1969 study. Thus, age is a variable which needs to be considered in the
analysis of the Violence for Social Change Index. Whether the difference between the two studies with respect to age is due to differences
between the two samples or to changes that have occurred over time
cannot be determined from these data.

Table 1.4 presents the percentage distribution on the Violence for
Social Change Index by age for white and black respondents. It can be
seen that among white respondents the association between age and the
index appears to be mainly due to a smaller proportion of younger
people in the lowest category of the index. Among black respondents,
however, those who were 29 or younger not only had less representation
in the lowest category but had substantially more in the three highest
categories (scores 4 through 7).

One other interesting finding in Table 1.3 is that for black respondents there was a tendency toward an association between the Violence

**Table 1.4**

Percentage Responses to the Violence for Social Change Index
in Relation to Age
(whites, N = 145; blacks, N = 133)

| Violence for Social Change Index | 16-29 Years | | 30-49 Years | | 50 Years or Older | |
|---|---|---|---|---|---|---|
| | Whites | Blacks | Whites | Blacks | Whites | Blacks |
| Low      1 | 26% | 11% | 41% | 20% | 57% | 18% |
| 2-3 | 53 | 17 | 41 | 33 | 27 | 25 |
| High   4-7 | 21 | 72 | 18 | 47 | 16 | 57 |
| | 100% | 100% | 100% | 100% | 100% | 100% |
| N* | (47) | (46) | (44) | (40) | (44) | (28) |

Note: In this and all subsequent tables, N*'s represent the exact number under discussion, since they exclude missing data.

for Social Change Index and sex. Among blacks in our population, women were slightly less likely to make high scores on the index than were men (Table 1.5). A trend in this direction existed among whites, but the size of the association was so small as to make the relationship seem doubtful. These data show that in the analysis of the Violence for Social Change Index effects due to race, age, and possibly sex must be considered.

**Table 1.5**

Percentage Responses to the Violence for Social Change Index
for Black Men and Women

| Violence for Social Change Index† | Black Men | Black Women |
|---|---|---|
| Low    1-2 | 21% | 27% |
| 3-4 | 26 | 36 |
| High   5-7 | 53 | 37 |
| | 100% | 100% |
| N | (59) | (74) |

†Because of the small number of respondents, categories are not collapsed in identical fashion across all tables in this monograph.

## The Criterion Validity of the Violence for Social Change Index

Establishing the links between the Violence for Social Change Index and violent behaviors aimed at bringing about social change were of central interest in the present research. There are at least two approaches to studying the relationship between attitudinal measures and behaviors. One is prospective; that is, attitudes are studied and used to predict certain behaviors. The other is retrospective; individuals are selected on the basis of their behaviors and studied to see whether their attitudes are congruent with their behaviors. Of the two approaches the former is greatly preferable. A predictive study is not confounded by the fact that a behavior has already occurred when the attitudes are studied. This precludes the possibility inherent in the retrospective study that the behavior caused the attitude. It is always possible that once an individual has committed an action he will change his attitudes to rationalize his behavior, so that the behavior leads to an attitude rather than the attitude leading to a behavior. Nevertheless, however more desirable they may be theoretically, prospective studies are feasible only under certain circumstances. For example, if the behavior to be observed is relatively frequent, the phenomenon can easily be observed by the experimenter. However, if the behavior is relatively infrequent, a true predictive experimental design is difficult to execute. Under such circumstances the experimenter would be obliged to follow large numbers of individuals for long periods of time before he could discover whether or not the relation between the behavior and the attitude actually exists.

Consider, for a moment, the problem of predicting whether or not an individual would participate in a riot. Rioting is a relatively infrequent behavior. It has been estimated that less than one-fifth of the individuals living in riot areas (Fogelson and Hill 1969, p. 223) actually were involved in riots in any way. In addition, only a tiny part of the geographic area in the country actually became involved in any riots, so that for any particular individual the chances of becoming involved in a riot are very small indeed. This is probably even more true now than it was in the late 1960's since the number of disturbances involving a large number of participants has decreased substantially since that time.

The example of predicting whether or not an individual would participate in a riot illustrates another point which should be considered in any discussion of the relationship between attitudes and behavior— that is, the element played by chance in whether or not a behavior for which the individual has the attitudinal predilection will occur. Riots are relatively infrequent and it is obvious that in order for the potential rioter to become an actual rioter it is necessary for him to have a disturbance in which to riot. It may very well be that personal attributes required to instigate a riot are quite different from those necessary to join one. One can imagine that initiating a riot requires a certain amount of independence, initiative, and creativity as well as a favorable attitude toward the use of violence. One can also imagine joining a riot requires the opportunity to participate in addition to favorable attitudes toward violence. Whether or not a riot occurs, thereby providing the potential rioter the opportunity to join, is dependent on factors that are often unrelated to the individual in question.

In addition to the role chance plays in determining violent behaviors, it is likely that the determinants of violence are multiple. Rokeach (1968) has pointed out that, in the study of attitudes, the attitude toward the situation is as important as the attitude toward the object. So, in examining attitudes toward violence in relation to behavior, it is necessary to know both the individual's attitude toward violence and his attitude toward the specific situation. If the latter were understood as well as the former, prediction would become possible. For example, an individual might have a positive attitude toward the use of a limited amount of violence in the interest of bringing about social change. Such a person might believe that property damage and some personal injury is required to bring about change at a reasonable rate. However, the individual also believes that whatever damage to persons is necessary should be confined to those who are in some way active protagonists in the social conflict. Such a person might participate in rioting by being a bystander, by looting merchandise from a store, or even by throwing rocks at firemen who were trying to extinguish a fire in an empty building. If it should turn out, however, that the building was occupied by three children, our stone-throwing rioter might change his behavior completely and become an active assistant to the firemen. Firemen putting out a fire in a building that houses three children is not the same situation as firemen putting out a fire in an empty building, and the attitude toward the specific situation is more important in determining behavior in this case than is the general attitude toward violence.

In fact, attitudes are always general to some extent, and the situations in which attitudes come into play are always specific. The fire plus children evokes more than one relevant attitude—attitudes toward human life and children as well as attitudes toward social change and rioting. Hence, the resultant force of conflicting attitudes becomes the determinant of the behavior in a concrete situation. The more "real" or concrete the situation, the more likely it is that behavior will be the outcome of such a field of forces and the less likely it is that behavior will be accurately predicted by an abstract instrument such as the Violence for Social Change Index.

Another factor increasing the difficulty in studying the relationship between attitudes toward violence and violent behaviors is the fact that violent behavior is usually not socially acceptable and is sometimes incriminating for the individual. Consequently, it is probably more difficult to obtain accurate reports of such behaviors from individuals than

s of socially acceptable behaviors which are not in-
.ong persons who are ideologically committed to the use
produce social change, one additional factor must be
)unt. Often such individuals are deeply alienated from
ment'' and part of their belief is that the establishment
mu... ....... ;hed before desirable social change can come about. Such individuals are inclined to view research as an establishment practice and are deeply suspicious of scientists. While in theory it might well be desirable to investigate groups with radical ideologies and known predilections to violence, in practice this becomes exceedingly difficult. In fact, at one point in our efforts to validate the Violence for Social Change Index we attempted to interview such a group, but the concerted opposition of our potential respondents made interviewing impossible. Several individuals in this particular group were later jailed for acts of violence, some for acts which they committed after we had initially identified and intended to interview them; but, unfortunately, the interviews never took place.

Because of the difficulties enumerated above, it seemed wise, if theoretically less desirable, to study the relation between the Violence for Social Change Index and behavior by selecting people on the basis of behaviors which had already occurred. Five groups were selected as criterion groups in our validation efforts with respect to the Violence for Social Change Index. These were: a group of college students who had been arrested or had been nominated as participating in a street disturbance near the University of Michigan; a group of individuals, mainly of lower socioeconomic status and Chicano, arrested for participating in a street disturbance in a small town not too far from Los Angeles; a sample of prisoners in a minimum security prison; a group of Jehovah's Witnesses, both black and white; and a group of parents thought to have physically abused their children.

**Ann Arbor Student Arrestees.** The students interviewed were arrested or identified as participating in a disturbance on several consecutive nights in the summer of 1969 near the University of Michigan campus. These students had been part of a larger crowd attracted to the attempt, mostly of ''street people'' and high school youths, to ''liberate'' a street of several blocks adjoining the campus area. The area is heavily populated with student rooming houses and apartments, stores and restaurants, and the effort to take over the area attracted a predictably larger secondary crowd of interested onlookers and fringe participants. The disturbance itself lasted three days. There were attempts at dispersal and control of the crowd by University representatives and city officials; there was also the use of considerable force by the police from the office of the county sheriff. During the disturbance a number of young people were arrested and charged with a variety of offenses including property damage and physical assault (most of these charges were later dropped). Much of the rhetoric used by the crowd leaders was revolutionary in character. Specific demands for change were made. We assumed that "liberating" a street might be regarded as a social change of sorts, and the entire action might be regarded as a form of violence for social change.

Twenty-nine college students were interviewed, 20 of whom had been arrested by the police. The remainder were nominated by the arrestees as having been active participants in the disturbance. For convenience, the entire group will be referred to as the student arrestees. Most of the 29 students attended the University of Michigan, a large midwestern university, while a few attended a smaller state university nearby. A group used for comparison with the student arrestees consisted of those respondents in the 1969 national survey who were college students. The student arrestees are described in considerable detail elsewhere (Blumenthal 1973a).

Table 1.6 shows how the student arrestees scored on the Violence for Social Change Index and compares them with college students in the national sample and college educated men in the sample. It can be seen that the arrestees were far more likely to score high on the Violence for Social Change Index than were other college students. Moreover, college students in the national sample were themselves more apt to agree that violence is necessary to bring about social change fast enough than were men of all ages of similar education who were not in school at the time. The majority of the latter were in the lowest category of the Violence for Social Change Index; only 4 percent of the student arrestees fell in this category.

**Table 1.6**

Percentage Responses to the Violence for Social Change Index
for Student Arrestees, College Students, and
Non-students with Some College Education

| Violence for Social Change Index | | Student Arrestees (Participants in U of M Street Disturbance) | College Students (National Sample) | Non-students with at least Some College (National Sample) |
|---|---|---|---|---|
| Low | 1 | 4% | 35% | 52% |
| | 2-3 | 37 | 38 | 34 |
| High | 4-7 | 59 | 27 | 14 |
| | | 100% | 100% | 100% |
| | N | (29) | (63) | (304) |

Note: p < .001 that the difference between college students and the student arrestees is due to chance (Kolmogorov-Smirnov Test).

These data support the hypotheses that there is a behavioral pre-dilection associated with the Violence for Social Change Index. It is possible, of course, that these positive attitudes toward violence were formed after the disturbance as rationalizations of behavior that had already occurred. But, it is also possible that they existed prior to the disturbance and influenced the behavior of the students.

Interpreting data collected from arrestees who have been re-turned to the community presents many methodological and theoretical problems. Singer, Osborn, and Geschwender (1970, p. 53) point out that respondents may change their opinions in the time lapse which occurs between the disturbance and the interview, so that attitudes investigated after a disturbance are not necessarily identical with attitudes held prior to or during a disturbance. They also point out that arrestees are not necessarily typical of those involved in the dis-turbance, so that it may be erroneous to regard them as representa-tive of the participants. Neither can one assume that those arrested during a disturbance are necessarily those responsible for violence which may have occurred. However, it does seem probable that there would be a larger proportion of individuals who had behaved violently among persons arrested in a disturbance involving violence than there would be in a national sample of respondents, so that there is some justification for using such a comparison to investigate the behavioral correlates of attitudes.

However, the inference that the Violence for Social Change Index is related to violent behavior committed for the sake of social change is not the only explanation of the data. It may be that positive attitudes toward the use of violence for producing social change were charac-teristics of students at the University of Michigan, albeit that seems somewhat unlikely. However, in the absence of data from a random sample of University of Michigan students, the possibility cannot be ruled out. Indeed, Converse and Schuman (1970) have pointed out that attitudes toward one type of violence, namely the Vietnam War, are quite different among those who attended the larger, more prestigious universities than among those who attended other colleges. In a national sample the vast majority of those with some college education are apt to come from smaller, less prestigious schools, including junior colleges. It is possible that University of Michigan students as a whole had more positive attitudes toward violence than those attending other colleges and that the scores of the Ann Arbor arrestees on the Violence for Social Change Index were typical of University of Michigan students. However, it seems unlikely that differences in attitudes toward violence between University of Michigan students and other students would be as large as those shown in this data. Even if University of Michigan students were more oriented toward the necessity of using violence to produce social change than were students at other colleges, one would still have to recognize that this university, like many of the more prestigious institutions, had been more liable to "confrontationist politics" and violent protest than many smaller, less well known universities (Lipset 1969, p. 54). Several episodes involving violence resulting in property damage have occurred at this university, and more radical attitudes toward violence would have been congruent with the more numerous occurrence of violent episodes on this campus than on many others.

**California Arrestees.** A group of young people arrested during a disturbance in a small coastal community in California was selected as a second criterion group. The disturbance, the second occurring within a week, began after an anti-police rally failed to materialize. During a three-hour period, an estimated 150 young people threw rocks and bottles in the Spanish-American district of the community. During the course of the disturbance rioters broke into an elementary school and caused several thousand dollars worth of damage, burning both an American and a state flag in the process. Later, homemade bombs started a fire in the local bank. Firemen were pelted with rocks and bottles and were allegedly hampered by a sniper in their efforts to extinguish the fires. Several firebombs, which failed to ignite, were thrown at the police. A number of police cars suffered from bumps and scratches. Early estimates of the amount of property damage were set at $100,000; however, our interviewers thought that the extent of the damage had been wildly exaggerated.

The respondents interviewed were 23 individuals arrested in the disorder and two others who, while not arrested, were nominated as having been ringleaders in the disturbance by knowledgeable community informants. The respondents were mainly Chicano (84 percent), male (88 percent), and very young (72 percent were under 20, the rest were under 30). The respondents represented 79 percent of all persons arrested in the disorder who were over 16 and who could be physically located. Seven arrestees were never contacted either because they had left town or had no address (or a false one); one potential respondent died suddenly.

The disturbance cannot be considered an organized effort to produce social change, but it can be considered a direct response to social issues requiring change. Much bad feeling existed between the police and the community which was largely Spanish-American. According to the local paper, multiple complaints had been made against the police. The police admitted that there were very few minority officers on the force but complained that policemen were called "pigs" and treated disrespectfully by community residents.

Data collected on the interview showed 84 percent of the arrestees interviewed thought problems with the police were the basic cause of the disturbance; many respondents blamed the disturbance directly on police harrassment. Typical of the responses to the question "What do you think are the basic issues that caused the recent disturbances at _____ ?" was the answer:

> "The police don't show the people any respect. They push people around and treat them any way they want to. Too many policemen are race prejudiced."

A number of respondents felt that future disturbances could best be prevented by simply keeping police out of the area.

In addition to the arrestees' opinion that the disturbance was a response to police abuse, 16 percent mentioned lack of jobs as a basic issue responsible for the outbreak. When asked "What do you think are the most important problems to be solved to prevent such events?" 48 percent of the arrestees mentioned better treatment from the police; also mentioned were better schools (24 percent), more jobs (20 percent), and equality (12 percent.)[1] If the riot was not clearly organized to produce specific political goals, it did have clear political antecedents in the minds of the interviewed arrestees. Certainly, the California arrestees saw social change as the mechanism by which such outbreaks could be prevented. However, the police took a different view. They were inclined to think the disturbance had been generated by "hoodlums" looking for excitement and failed to attribute any political significance to the episode. Nevertheless, since the respondents viewed the episode as a form of violence for social change, it seemed appropriate for us to analyze their behavior in these terms.

The nature of an appropriate control group for the California arrestees is not altogether clear. In retrospect, it would have been desirable to interview a group of young people living in the same districts as the rioters. At the time of the interviewing, however, it was thought that a suitable reference could be selected from the data collected from the national survey two years earlier. This comparison is not ideal because of differences in ethnic composition and socioeconomic status between the California arrestees and the national sample respondents as well as differences in the timing of the interviews. Because of the youth of the California respondents, the comparison group from the national data was weighted so as to simulate the

---

[1] Each respondent was allowed more than one answer so the responses do not sum to 100 percent.

**Table 1.7**

Percentage Responses to the Violence for Social Change Index
for the California Arrestees
and the National Sample Comparison Group

| Violence for Social Change Index | | California Arrestees | National Sample Comparison Group (Weighted)† |
|---|---|---|---|
| Low | 1 | 14% | 30% |
| | 2-3 | 28 | 46 |
| High | 4-7 | 58 | 24 |
| | | 100% | 100% |
| | N | (25) | (424) |

Notes: The Violence for Social Change Index in this table, unlike most data presented in this monograph, consists of the original combination of three rather than two situations.

p < .02 that the difference between the California arrestees and the national sample comparison group is due to chance (Kolmogorov-Smirnov Test).

†Respondents in this group were drawn from the national sample if they were ages 16 to 29 years. A weight was then applied to this group so that its age distribution would approximate the age distribution of the California arrestees.

age distribution of the arrestees. Table 1.7 makes the comparison with respect to the Violence for Social Change Index.

The data indicate that the arrestees agreed more with statements that property damage and personal injury were necessary to bring about social change than did persons of a similar age in the national population. This tends to substantiate the notion that people who are willing to undertake violent action in behalf of social change will have high scores on the Violence for Social Change Index. However, these data leave something to be desired. The national population is almost 90 percent white; the arrestees were 85 percent Chicano. An alternative explanation of the results is that the more positive attitudes toward violence for social change exhibited by the arrestees were characteristic of Chicanos rather than attributable to the arrestees' predilection toward violent behavior. It was true, for example, that black respondents in the 1969 study were far more likely to think violence necessary to bring about social change than were white respondents. Unfortunately, persons of Spanish-American origin are not sufficiently numerous in the national sample data to enable a test of this hypothesis. Even if a large part of the difference in attitudes toward violence for social change could be attributed to ethnic origin, it would not be possible to say that this invalidates the results. There had been a number of disturbances in California at the time of the interviewing which involved Chicano militants, and it seems likely that at that time a higher proportion of Chicanos than whites were likely to be involved in protest, including violent protest. Nevertheless, the percentage of Spanish-Americans who became involved in such protest must have been very small.

An additional factor confounding the comparison between the California arrestees and the national sample comparison group is the fact that the arrestees were far less educated than other Americans their age. Table 1.8 shows 28 percent had less than nine years of schooling compared to 9 percent in the national sample and 76 percent had eleven years of schooling or less compared to 49 percent in the national

**Table 1.8**

Level of Education Attained by the California Arrestees
and the National Sample Comparison Group
(percentage distribution)

| Education | California Arrestees | National Sample Comparison Group (Weighted) |
|---|---|---|
| 9 Years or Less | 28% | 9% |
| 10-11 Years | 48 | 40 |
| High School Graduate | 16 | 31 |
| At Least Some College | 8 | 20 |
| | 100% | 100% |
| N | (25) | (424) |

Note: p < .05 that the difference between the national sample comparison group and the California arrestees is due to chance (Kolmogorov-Smirnov Test).

sample—a significant difference. Moreover, only 24 percent of these young people still were students compared to 64 percent of their age-mates in the national sample. In the 1969 national survey, education accounted for 3 percent of the variance in the Violence for Social Change Index, persons with less education being more inclined to score high on the Violence for Social Change Index. Consequently, the difference high on the Violence for Social Change Index. Consequently, the difference between the California arrestees and the national sample comparison group may have been at least partly due to differences in education.

Table 1.9 examines this question. Since 76 percent of the California arrestees had an eleventh grade education or less, one approach to the problem is to compare the arrestees with national sample respondents their age who had not achieved more than eleven years of schooling. Although this is only an approximate control for the effect of education on attitudes toward violence, it is a conservative one. Increasing

**Table 1.9**

Percentage Responses to the Violence for Social Change Index for the
California Arrestees and the National Sample Comparison
Group with Eleven Years of School or Less, Including and
Excluding Students

| Violence for Social Change Index | | California Arrestees | National Sample Comparison Group with 11 Years of School or Less (Weighted) | National Sample Comparison Group with 11 Years of School or Less (Excluding Students) (Weighted) |
|---|---|---|---|---|
| Low | 1 | 14% | 26% | 35% |
| | 2-3 | 28 | 48 | 38 |
| High | 4-7 | 58 | 26 | 27 |
| | | 100% | 100% | 100% |
| | N | (25) | (149) | (67) |

Notes: The Violence for Social Change Index in this table, unlike most data presented in this monograph, consists of the original combination of three rather than two situations.

$p < .05$ that the difference between the national sample comparison group with 11 years of school or less and the California arrestees is due to chance (Kolmogorov-Smirnov Test).

$p < .02$ that the difference between the non-student national sample comparison group with 11 years of school or less and the California arrestees is due to chance (Kolmogorov-Smirnov Test).

education was associated with less positive attitudes toward violence, and when all those with more than eleven years of school were removed from the national sample, the California arrestees were *more educated* than the respondents remaining in the control group. Table 1.9 shows that even when the effect of education was controlled in this fashion, the California arrestees were still significantly more positively oriented toward the use of violence for social change than were national sample respondents of similar age and education.

One additional factor can be taken into account in the analysis. Far fewer of the California arrestees were students than was true in the national sample group. Since student status might be expected to influence attitudes toward violence, Table 1.9 also presents the percentage responses of national sample respondents of comparable age who did not have more than eleven years of schooling and who were not students at the time of interviewing. It can be seen from the table that nonstudents tended to be slightly more conservative in their responses to the Violence for Social Change Index, and the removal of students from the national sample comparison group increased the apparent deviance of the California arrestees.

All of the difficulties in drawing conclusions from data collected on arrestees which were mentioned with respect to the Ann Arbor students could be cited again here. That would be redundant, but one point does bear amplification. It was mentioned earlier that it is not possible to make inferences about the behavior of persons who have been arrested merely from the fact of their arrest. An arrest indicates *only* that the individual was present at the scene of the disturbance. Our interviewers indicated to us that many community residents felt that the ringleaders in this particular disturbance, including most of those who were most politically conscious and active in fomenting the disturbance, had not been arrested. On the contrary there was some feeling that the rioters who were arrested were actually more likely to be among the innocent and politically naive.

Unfortunately, it is not possible to use the legal disposition of a case to determine the degree of guilt or involvement of an individual. While it seems likely that persons convicted and punished for an offense are guilty, it does not necessarily follow that a person whose case is not brought to trial is not guilty. Many administrative and technical considerations are important in determining whether or not a case reaches trial. Cases may be dropped because of insufficient evidence, because some disposition has been worked out for the defendant (particularly if the defendant is a juvenile), because some general policy has been adopted for a whole set of cases, and so on. Consequently, no effort was made to follow the arrestees to determine whether they were eventually brought to trial and found guilty. One would hope, for the sake of the country if not for the sake of the researcher, that the wheels of justice would grind more exactly. Unfortunately, at the present time such is not the case, and it is unreasonable to rely on the occurrence of a trial and its outcome alone for validation of behavior.

**Jehovah's Witnesses.** The third group chosen as a criterion group was selected on the basis of behaviors characteristically omitted rather than committed. Just as it seems reasonable to suppose that individuals who engage in violent actions to bring about social change should score high on the Violence for Social Change Index, so it seems reasonable to suppose that individuals who eschew violence should score low on the index. This should be particularly true of those who have strong ideological convictions and who demonstrate the strength of those convictions by a willingness to go to jail in lieu of violating their beliefs.

The selection of "nonviolent" groups, however, is not easily accomplished. At first glance, pacifists and conscientious objectors would seem to form logical criterion groups. However, preliminary discussions with such individuals soon demonstrated that many did not hold generalized beliefs that violence is bad; they simply objected to the use of military violence to forward specific national objectives. Indeed, some of the individuals we spoke with were strong social activists who did not object to the violence of property damage as a mechanism for producing social change. It is useful to recall in this connection the paradigm developed early in the study of attitudes toward violence, that those attitudes are differentiated on the basis of the purpose which the violence serves. Hence, it is not unreasonable to find some conscientious objectors with commitments to violence for social change. These observations led to an investigation of established religious sects with explicit ideologies such as the Jehovah's Witnesses.

Since the turn of the century, the Jehovah's Witnesses have consistently maintained their stand of nonviolent "Christian neutrality" through two major world wars and the subsequent military clashes of the "Cold War" period. Their continuing stand against national service of any form, military or civilian, and their refusal to honor symbols of national identity have resulted in periods of prosecution, imprisonment, and mob action in many countries throughout the world, including the United States, Canada, and Germany. The Witnesses, however, have never responded with violence. Instead, they have viewed these periods of adversity as documented proof of the fulfillment of biblical prophecy confirming their role as Jehovah's appointed witnesses to the inevitable destruction of this present "wicked system of things."

The teachings of the Jehovah's Witnesses stem from their conviction that the Bible is the inspired word of God and that biblical passages are accurate in detail. Since the group's formation in the early 1870s, they have continually offered literal interpretation of selected biblical passages in support of their view of man's history as one of continuing decline from the perfect order of the Garden of Eden to the "chaos" of modern society. Wars, and other social stresses of the modern world, are viewed as fulfillments of biblical prophecy signalling the end in the approaching Battle of Armageddon. At that point, Jehovah will settle his 6,000 year dispute with Satan by destroying all the wicked men of Earth and will re-establish a perfect order under the theocratic Heavenly Kingdom to be governed by Jesus Christ. The Witnesses have held sufficient faith in this reading of the Bible to have offered five distinct dates between 1876 and 1925 for the commencement of the great battle. Civilization's continued existence has, at times, been a source of considerable embarrassment to the sect.

The uneventful passage of the predicted days of doom ultimately led to consecutive restatements of each prophecy, altering the significance of the date in question and demonstrating a partial fulfillment of the prophecy in each case (Zygmunt 1970). Of particular interest to this study are the three reinterpretations resulting from the prophetic failures of 1914, 1918, and 1925. The *Watchtower* magazine of November 1, 1914, redefined the significance of that year as marking the "end of the Time of the Gentiles," indicating that God had withdrawn his blessings from the Christian nations of the world. The year 1918 was later viewed as the time when Christ "entered the temple for the purpose of judgment" (Rutherford 1920, as cited in Zygmunt 1970) and in 1925 the *Watchtower* elaborated by pointing to 1918 as the time when God established the heavenly portion of the theocratic Kingdom, cast the Devil down to Earth, and established the "New Nation" (Zygmunt 1970). The Jehovah's Witnesses are presently looking forward to the year 1975 as a turning point in both heavenly and earthly events.

The current teachings of the sect draw heavily from these restatements of prophetic failures and the biblical passages which have been marshalled to support them. The Witnesses believe, therefore, that God has withdrawn all support from the Christian nations and established churches, that the Devil is actively at work causing chaos and wickedness in these final days, and that they are citizens of the "New Nation" under the leadership of Jesus Christ. This view of their citizenship is accompanied by the conviction that they represent a New Society within society; their kingdom is "not of this world" (Stevenson 1967, pp. 160-161). As ambassadors from the Heavenly Kingdom, they willingly render Caesar his just due by paying all taxes and obeying most laws; however, they will not participate in elections, perform jury duty, honor symbols of national identity, or serve in the armed forces of any country (Stevenson 1967). They dislike all forms of human government, including democracy, and argue that social reforms under the present "wicked system of things" are hopeless attempts to forestall the inevitable collapse of present society (Stevenson 1967, pp. 170-171). Their linear view of history leads them to believe that the social problems of this age are unavoidable and, in a sense, welcome in that they signal the approach of the perfect theocratic order of the Heavenly Kingdom which follows the Battle of Armageddon. Until Jehovah acts to end the present order, the forces of social control and social change are mere instruments of Satan's will during his last days of rule over the Earth. This ideology, which includes a strong negative cathexis of temporal social change, led us to hypothesize that the Jehovah's Witnesses would score low on the Violence for Social Change Index.

Jehovah's Witnesses were interviewed at the same time and with the same interview used in interviewing other Detroit respondents. The Witnesses were selected from the membership lists of five congregations. Not more than one member of a married couple was interviewed, the spouses being randomly selected. The Witnesses interviewed cannot be regarded as a sample of Witnesses in Detroit; we knew of at least 22 congregations in the Detroit metropolitan area but were unable to develop access to 17 of these congregations. The Jehovah's Witnesses were a particularly interesting group since they were approximately half black. Attitudes toward the use of violence to produce social change are strongly related to race, and it was considered highly desirable to investigate a group of nonviolent blacks. The Jehovah's Witnesses provided this opportunity.

The Jehovah's Witnesses were essentially like other Detroit respondents with respect to their demographic characteristics (Table 1.10). The whites among them were somewhat more apt to have graduated from high school than were other white Detroit respondents. Black Jehovah's Witnesses had finished just half a year more of school

**Table 1.10**

Selected Demographic Characteristics of White and Black
Detroit Jehovah's Witnesses and Other Detroit Respondents
(percentage distribution)

| | Whites | | Blacks | |
|---|---|---|---|---|
| | Jehovah's Witnesses | Detroit Respondents | Jehovah's Witnesses | Detroit Respondents |
| Education | | | | |
| 9 Years or Less | 17% | 15% | 29% | 30% |
| 10-11 Years | 14 | 29 | 16 | 36 |
| High School Graduate | 41 | 24 | 39 | 25 |
| At Least Some College | 28 | 32 | 16 | 9 |
| | 100% | 100% | 100% | 100% |
| Family Income | | | | |
| $3,999 or Less | 18 | 14 | 18 | 25 |
| $4,000-$7,999 | 11 | 19 | 21 | 33 |
| $8,000-$11,999 | 28 | 15 | 29 | 24 |
| $12,000 or More | 43 | 52 | 32 | 18 |
| | 100% | 100% | 100% | 100% |
| Age | | | | |
| 16-25 Years | 7 | 20 | 18 | 34 |
| 26-40 Years | 24 | 25 | 37 | 24 |
| 41-59 Years | 55 | 31 | 37 | 32 |
| 60 Years or Older | 14 | 24 | 8 | 10 |
| | 100% | 100% | 100% | 100% |
| N | (29) | (104) | (38) | (83) |

Notes: There were no statistically significant differences between white Detroit respondents and white Jehovah's Witnesses (Mann-Whitney U Test).

There were no statistically significant differences between black Detroit respondents and black Jehovah's Witnesses (Mann-Whitney U Test).

than other black Detroit respondents, who had completed ten years of schooling on the average. White Jehovah's Witnesses had family incomes similar to those of other white Detroit respondents, while black Jehovah's Witnesses had somewhat higher incomes (averaging between $8,000 and $9,999) than other Detroit blacks (averaging between $6,000 and $7,999) although the difference was not statistically significant. There were small, nonsignificant, differences in age among the four groups: white Jehovah's Witnesses were four years older on the average than other Detroit whites, and black Jehovah's Witnesses were two years older than Detroit blacks. Thus, the Jehovah's Witnesses did not differ significantly from other Detroit respondents in the demographic characteristics which are known to explain part of the variance in the Violence for Social Change Index.

Table 1.11 shows how Jehovah's Witnesses responded to the Violence for Social Change Index compared to other Detroit respondents of the same race. The data show, as expected, that Jehovah's Witnesses had significantly lower scores on the Violence for Social Change Index than their fellow citizens. Indeed, black Jehovah's Witnesses were

**Table 1.11**

Percentage Responses to the Violence for Social Change Index
for White and Black Detroit Jehovah's Witnesses
and Other Detroit Respondents

| Violence for Social Change Index | | Whites | | Blacks | |
|---|---|---|---|---|---|
| | | Jehovah's Witnesses | Detroit Respondents | Jehovah's Witnesses | Detroit Respondents |
| Low | 1 | 81% | 39% | 73% | 17% |
| | 2-3 | 15 | 40 | 12 | 21 |
| High | 4-7 | 4 | 21 | 15 | 62 |
| | | 100% | 100% | 100% | 100% |
| | N | (29) | (104) | (38) | (83) |

Notes: $p < .001$ that the difference between the white Detroit respondents and the white Jehovah's Witnesses is due to chance (Mann-Whitney U Test).

$p < .001$ that the difference between the black Detroit respondents and the black Jehovah's Witnesses is due to chance (Mann-Whitney U Test).

spectacularly different from other Detroit blacks; 73 percent of the Witnesses fell in the lowest category of the Violence for Social Change Index compared to only 17 percent of other Detroit black respondents. The category to which the individual belonged, that is, whether or not he was white, black, or a Jehovah's Witness, explains 29 percent of the variance in the Violence for Social Change Index. Again, the data support the hypothesis that the index is related to a predilection for behavior.

**Parents of Battered Children.** Two more groups were interviewed to establish the criterion validity of the Violence for Social Change Index; however, the rationale used to select the last two groups differed from the one used in selecting the preceding three. In the national study there was a small negative relationship (gamma = -.2) between attitudes toward the use of violence as a means of social change and as a means of maintaining social control. This finding implies that, on the whole, people's willingness to use instrumental violence for one purpose tells us little about their willingness to use it for another. In other words, many people do not have a generalized attitude toward violence but have different attitudes toward different types of violence. Nevertheless, some American men were prepared to use violence both as a means of producing social change and as a means of maintaining order. These individuals were referred to as "warriors" in the 1969 study (Blumenthal et al. 1972, pp. 179-210), and it seemed reasonable to infer that there might be some persons who would be predisposed to use violence for a variety of purposes. Indeed, the idea that violence is a coping device to which some individuals characteristically resort when they find themselves unable to solve problems by other means is a notion which has been expressed by other workers (Toch 1969).

Two groups were selected on the basis of hypotheses that they might be "warrior" types and, hence, more likely to approve of the use of violence both as a means of producing social change and as a means of maintaining social control. The two groups selected were a group of prisoners in a minimum security federal prison and a group of individuals suspected of child abuse. Clearly, the logic leading to their use as criterion groups for the Violence for Social Change Index is more doubtful than the logic which led to the use of the two groups of arrestees and the Jehovah's Witnesses. The latter three groups were selected on the basis of specific hypotheses concerning the behaviors that should be associated with positive attitudes toward violence for social change. The prisoners and suspected child abusers were not chosen on such specific bases. Rather, they were selected on the basis of the hypothesis that they might have a generalized positive attitude toward violence.

Children who were thought to have been battered by their parents were located through the records of a general hospital which admitted a fair number of such cases. The parents of such a child were included in the sample if their child had been hospitalized as a case of suspected child abuse between April and December of 1971, and if there was an address available for the parent who was suspected of the abuse. In addition, it was stipulated that the case must have had one of the following outcomes: the parent was convicted of child abuse, the child had died, the child had been placed in a foster home, or the child had been made a ward of the court and temporarily removed from its parental home. A control group was selected by choosing parents of

**Table 1.12**

Selected Demographic Characteristics of Black Parents of Battered Children, the Black Control Group, and Other Black Detroit Respondents
(percentage distribution)

| | Black Parents of Battered Children | Black Control Group | Black Detroit Respondents |
|---|---|---|---|
| Sex | | | |
| Men | 11% | 6% | 41% |
| Women | 89 | 94 | 59 |
| | 100% | 100% | 100% |
| Education | | | |
| 9 Years or Less | 22 | 22 | 30 |
| 10-11 Years | 48 | 25 | 36 |
| High School Graduate | 26 | 47 | 25 |
| At Least Some College | 4 | 6 | 9 |
| | 100% | 100% | 100% |
| Family Income | | | |
| $3,999 or Less | 44 | 24 | 25 |
| $4,000-$7,999 | 22 | 40 | 33 |
| $8,000-$11,999 | 17 | 23 | 24 |
| $12,000 or More | 17 | 13 | 18 |
| | 100% | 100% | 100% |
| Age | | | |
| 16-19 Years | 26 | 12 | 16 |
| 20-29 Years | 41 | 63 | 22 |
| 30-39 Years | 15 | 16 | 21 |
| 40-49 Years | 11 | 9 | 14 |
| 50 Years or Older | 7 | 0 | 27 |
| | 100% | 100% | 100% |
| Experience in South | | | |
| Childhood | 46 | 29 | 49 |
| Some Adult | 8 | 26 | 6 |
| No Experience | 46 | 45 | 45 |
| | 100% | 100% | 100% |
| N | (27) | (32) | (83) |

Note: There were no statistically significant differences between the black parents of battered children and the black control group (Mann-Whitney U Test).

children hospitalized with respiratory diseases in the same wards in which the abused children had been housed. The two groups of parents were matched with respect to sex and race whenever possible, but matching for race was difficult since most of the records did not contain the necessary information.

There was considerable difficulty associated with interviewing the parents of the battered children since many had moved, often leaving no forwarding address. In addition, some of the interviews took place under unusual circumstances: one interviewer was obliged to take a respondent to the local methadone clinic; other interviews were conducted in jail. The final response rates were 61 percent for the parents of battered children and 73 percent for the control group.

Because both the criterion and the control groups were predominantly black (87 and 86 percent, respectively), and because there were such very large differences between black and white respondents with respect to the Violence for Social Change Index, the analysis of the two groups was restricted to the black respondents.

Table 1.12 gives the demographic characteristics of the black parents of battered children and their controls. The characteristics of other black Detroit respondents are also shown for comparison. It had been thought that the parents of battered children and their controls would be different from other black Detroit respondents, since the hospital through which the cases were recruited allegedly serves the very poorest segment of the Detroit population, but these differences were not as large as was anticipated. The parents of battered children and their controls were largely women in contrast to the Detroit sample in which the two sexes were evenly distributed. Although none of the differences reach statistical significance, probably because the two groups are so small, it does appear that the parents of battered children were younger, less educated, poorer, and more likely to have immigrated from the South than their controls. The control group, in turn, seems to be younger and somewhat better educated than other black Detroit respondents interviewed.

Table 1.13 shows the employment and marital status of the parents of battered children and their controls. It can be seen that there was a large proportion of single parents in both groups; only about a third were married. However, in this respect they did not differ from other black Detroit respondents. Moreover, a substantial percentage of parents of battered children were unemployed—more than twice as many as among the controls, although the difference is not statistically significant. This is an interesting parallel to the California arrestees, who also had an excessively high unemployment rate in comparison to their control group.

**Table 1.13**

Marital Status and Employment Status of the
Black Parents of Battered Children, the Black Control Group, and
Other Black Detroit Respondents
(percentage distribution)

|  | Black Parents of Battered Children | Black Control Group | Black Detroit Respondents |
|---|---|---|---|
| **Marital Status** | | | |
| Married | 33% | 35% | 37% |
| Single | 45 | 31 | 30 |
| Divorced | 7 | 9 | 11 |
| Widowed | 4 | 3 | 10 |
| Separated | 11 | 22 | 12 |
| | 100% | 100% | 100% |
| **Employment Status** | | | |
| Working | 15 | 22 | 40 |
| Unemployed† | 44 | 19 | 19 |
| Housewife | 30 | 53 | 24 |
| Student | 11 | 6 | 8 |
| Disabled or Retired | 0 | 0 | 9 |
| | 100% | 100% | 100% |
| N | (27) | (32) | (83) |

Note: There were no statistically significant differences between the black parents of battered children and the black control group on marital or employment status (Chi Square Test).

†This category includes 3 percent of the black parents of battered children who were "temporarily laid off" from work.

Table 1.14 shows that parents of battered children scored significantly higher than the control group on the Violence for Social Change

**Table 1.14**

Percentage Responses to The Violence for Social Change Index
for the Black Parents of Battered Children, the Black Control Group,
and Other Black Detroit Respondents

| Violence for Social Change Index | Black Parents of Battered Children | Black Control Group | Black Detroit Respondents |
|---|---|---|---|
| Low   1-2 | 9% | 30% | 25% |
|       3-5 | 60 | 50 | 49 |
| High   6-7 | 31 | 20 | 26 |
| | 100% | 100% | 100% |
| N | (27) | (32) | (83) |

Note: p < .03 that the difference between the black parents of battered children and the black control group is due to chance (Mann-Whitney U Test).

Index. Thus, the criterion group differs from the control in the direction predicted by the hypothesis that violent behaviors will be associated with higher scores on the Violence for Social Change Index. Some of this difference, however, may be due to the demographic differences described earlier.

There is a major difference between this result and the results obtained for the criterion groups described previously: although the behavior for which the parents of battered children were chosen was violence, the violence was not clearly committed in the interest of social change. Thus the difference between the criterion and control groups substantiates a compound hypothesis, the hypothesis being not only that the Violence for Social Change Index is associated with a predilection to violent behaviors, but also that this particular criterion group has a generalized, positive attitude toward violence. This compound hypothesis appears to be confirmed for the case of violence for social change.

It seems reasonable to ask why this particular group should have a more generalized positive attitude toward violence, when such generalizations are not the most common case. Some research workers have postulated that parents who abuse their children are a highly frustrated group of individuals who use violence as a consummatory response. The parents of battered children did in fact have significantly higher scores than the controls on a measure which is probably closely associated with frustration, the Resentment-Suspicion Index (Blumenthal 1973b). (See Table 1.15.) One might speculate that the high level of frustration led both to positive attitudes toward the use of violence as a means of social change and to impulsive assaults on handy children.

**Table 1.15**

Percentage Responses to the Violence for Social Change Index
for the Black Parents of Battered Children
and the Black Control Group

| Resentment-Suspicion Index | | Black Parents of Battered Children | Black Control Group |
|---|---|---|---|
| Low | 1-2 | 4% | 19% |
| | 3 | 7 | 12 |
| | 4 | 15 | 22 |
| High | 5 | 74 | 47 |
| | | 100% | 100% |
| | N | (27) | (32) |

Note: p < .02 that the difference between the black parents of battered children and the black control group is due to chance (Mann-Whitney U Test).

**Prisoners.** The last study carried out in an effort to "anchor" the validity of the Violence for Social Change Index with respect to the behavioral predilection of positive attitudes toward violence was a study of prisoners in a minimum security, federal penitentiary in Milan, Michigan. The Milan Penitentiary houses approximately 550 prisoners, most of whom were convicted of relatively minor crimes (car theft was the most frequent offense) and were serving short-term sentences. The prisoners were generally quite young (the modal age was 21) and there was a high proportion of blacks (about 40 percent) in comparison with the general population.

A random sample of the prison population was selected, every ninth prisoner being included in the sample. The fifty-two members of the sample were interviewed with the same schedule of questions used for the 1969 national study. In addition, the records of the prisoners were systematically coded for mentions of violent behavior. The violent behaviors coded included those in the personal history of the prisoner (for example, whether he had been in fights at home or at school, whether he had been accused of wife-beating or assaults and so on), behaviors for which the prisoner was booked or convicted in the past, and the nature of the offense for which he was presently serving a prison sentence. Finally, the prisoner's record was examined for mentions of violent behavior recorded during his prison stay. The various types of violent behavior were then summarized on the Violent Behaviors Index. (For details of index construction see Appendix C, Blumenthal et al. 1972).

The prisoners' data were compared with those from the national sample respondents; data from the latter were weighted to provide comparability to the prisoners on race and age. This specially weighted

**Table 1.16**

Level of Education Attained by the Prisoners
and the Prisoners' Comparison Group
(percentage distribution)

| Education | Prisoners | Prisoners' Comparison Group† |
|---|---|---|
| 9 Years or Less | 19% | 11% |
| 10-11 Years | 29 | 5 |
| High School Graduate | 40 | 48 |
| At Least Some College | 12 | 36 |
| | 100% | 100% |
| N | (52) | (142) |

†Because of the age and racial composition of the prisoners, a group having comparable characteristics was selected out of the national sample for this analysis.

sample, which will be referred to as the prisoners' comparison group, proved to be somewhat better educated than were the prisoners (Table 1.16).

Table 1.17 shows that the prisoners scored significantly higher than the comparison group on the Violence for Social Change Index. Interestingly enough, those prisoners whose records showed no history

**Table 1.17**

Percentage Responses
to the Violence for Social Change Index
for Prisoners and the Prisoners' Comparison Group

| Violence for Social Change Index | | Prisoners | Prisoners' Comparison Group |
|---|---|---|---|
| Low | 1 | 12% | 32% |
| | 2-3 | 35 | 36 |
| High | 4-7 | 53 | 32 |
| | | 100% | 100% |
| N | | (52) | (142) |

Note: p < .05 that the difference between the prisoners and the prisoners' comparison group is due to chance (Kolmogorov-Smirnov Test).

of violent behavior (about a third of the total) had response distributions on the Violence for Social Change Index somewhat similar to those of the prisoners' comparison group (Table 1.18). The prisoners who did have records of violent behavior had more positive attitudes toward the necessity of using violence to bring about social change. However, since the number of subjects was so small, and since there were educa-

**Table 1.18**

Percentage Responses to the Violence for Social Change Index
in Relation to the Violent Behaviors Index for Prisoners
(prisoners, N = 52)

| Violence for Social Change Index | | Violent Behaviors | | |
|---|---|---|---|---|
| | | None | One | Two-Three |
| Low | 1 | 12% | 19% | 5% |
| | 2-3 | 53 | 31 | 22 |
| High | 4-7 | 35 | 50 | 73 |
| | | 100% | 100% | 100% |
| N* | | (17) | (16) | (18) |

Note: For details of the construction of the Violent Behaviors Index see Blumenthal et al. 1972, Appendix C.

tional differences between the prisoners and the prisoners' comparison group, the data can only be regarded as suggestive.

The analysis in Table 1.19 makes some attempt to compensate for the educational difference between the two groups by comparing only those prisoners and members of the prisoners' comparison group who had a high school education or less. The table shows that the prisoners still scored significantly higher on the Violence for Social Change Index even when the educational differences between the two groups were controlled in this fashion. Thus, data from the prisoners support the hypothesis that the Violence for Social Change Index is associated with a predilection to violent behaviors.

**Table 1.19**

Percentage Responses to the Violence for Social Change Index
for Prisoners and the Prisoners' Comparison Group
with a High School Diploma or Less

| Violence for Social Change Index | | Prisoners with a High School Diploma or Less | Prisoners' Comparison Group with a High School Diploma or Less |
|---|---|---|---|
| Low | 1 | 9% | 36% |
| | 2-3 | 34 | 36 |
| High | 4-7 | 57 | 28 |
| | | 100% | 100% |
| | N | (46) | (92) |

Note: $p < .01$ that the difference between the prisoners and the prisoners' comparison group is due to chance (Kolmogorov-Smirnov Test).

*Summary*

A few summary statements about these validity studies might be in order. These criterion group studies should properly be regarded as attempts to anchor the Violence for Social Change Index in some kind of behavioral reality. They do not, and cannot, give estimates of the extent to which violent or nonviolent behaviors are related to attitudes. Indeed, that may not be a meaningful question since it must immediately be constrained by statements which answer the inquiry as to which violent behaviors are those of concern. Is one predicting "trashing," looting, or rock throwing? Presumably the Violence for Social Change Index would have a different predictive power for each of these.

As has been pointed out, each of these criterion studies is flawed in one way or another. However, some of the defects in experimental design are in opposite directions in different substudies. For example, the Ann Arbor students on the one hand, were largely individuals who attended a large and prestigious university and were presumably better educated than college students in the national sample which served as their comparison group. The California arrestees and the prisoners, on the other hand, were both less educated than their comparison groups. Nevertheless, all three groups deviated from their comparison groups in the direction predicted by the hypothesis that the Violence for Social Change Index has behavioral correlates. Moreover, differences found between the Jehovah's Witnesses and their comparison group cannot be explained on the basis of differences in education.

There are problems associated with the choice of all the groups who were selected on the basis of their violent behaviors. In the case of the Ann Arbor students and the California arrestees it is not certain that any of the people in the groups actually committed the violent behaviors. In regard to the prisoners, the actual commission of the violent acts recorded in the prisoners' records seems likely; however, one must ask whether these men had committed other, non-recorded, violent acts which would have changed our evaluation on the Violent Behaviors Index. One of the serious difficulties in using written records for research purposes is that all the relevant information may not always be included in the record. Sometimes not all the known information is recorded, and it is always possible that relevant information is unknown to the recorder. A similar problem exists with respect to the parents of battered children. It is not certain that all these parents battered their children; it is merely likely that some of them did so.

Nevertheless, in spite of all the reservations which can justifiably be made about each individual study, it is impressive that every group chosen on the basis of criterion behaviors scored in the predicted direction on the Violence for Social Change Index. Such a result could be expected on the basis of chance about 3 percent of the time. These studies do not solve the problem of the validity of the measure, but they do constitute a step in the right direction. Unfortunately, such evidence sheds little light on the capacity of the index to predict violent behaviors in a general population. The most convincing experiment to explore the capacity of such an index to predict violent episodes would be a prospective longitudinal study. Since violence is a relatively rare event, the number of subjects would have to be large and the duration of the observation period might have to be considerable. The practical difficulties with such an experiment are obvious. However, the results obtained in the criterion studies reported here suggest that a true prospective effort may very well be worth the time and expense that would be required.

There is one other point which needs to be taken into account. The studies discussed in this chapter explored the notion that positive attitudes toward violence, as measured by the Violence for Social Change Index, are directly related to violent behaviors. They constitute a series of tests of the hypothesis that attitudes cause behaviors. But, there are at least two forms of that hypothesis as it relates to violence— one direct and one indirect. The direct form states that an individual who has positive beliefs and attitudes toward violence is more likely to engage in certain types of violent behavior. The indirect form says that a group or community or nation of individuals who hold positive attitudes toward violence are likely to show more violent behavior because such positive attitudes and beliefs are transmitted as norms. Such norms give sanction to that minority whose attitudes are so strong, or whose inhibitions are so weak, or whose situations are so oppor- tunity-giving that they commit violence. The indirect hypothesis implies that a cross-cultural study is needed, either between nations or between subgroups within the population. Such a study would be complex; attitudes, inhibitions, opportunity to commit violence, and the need for violence—that is, whether there is a set of conditions that might be ameliorated by violence—all would need to be assessed. But the study would be an interesting one and might produce a realistic, comprehensive picture of the realities which follow from positive attitudes toward violence.

# Chapter 2

# ATTITUDES TOWARD VIOLENCE FOR SOCIAL CHANGE AND PROTEST BEHAVIORS

*Introduction*

In the preceding chapter we endeavored to anchor the Violence for Social Change Index in behavioral reality by considering a number of groups with special behavioral characteristics. That exercise showed that the index was able to differentiate in a predictable fashion a number of groups selected on the basis of their behaviors, violent and nonviolent, from comparison populations. However, such evidence sheds little light on the capacity of the index to predict violent behaviors in a general population. An additional step which can be taken to shed some light on how the index might relate to violent behaviors is to examine the construct validity of the index in relation to measures of the respondent's reported willingness to engage in particular behaviors which are violent or which approach violence.

In order to investigate the construct validity of an attitude measure, it is necessary to understand the nature of the attitude and to specify the theoretical relationships of interest. Using Rokeach's (1968, p. 450) description of an attitude as having components which include beliefs, behavioral predilections, and affects, it follows that the constructs of interest may be any of these three or may be other attitudes which ought to be theoretically related to the attitude being validated. This discussion will focus on the relationship between attitudes toward violence and their implicit predisposition toward violent behaviors. Because the concept of construct validity implies that one is studying the relationship between various constructs, it is useful to know something about the measurement error in the instrument under consideration. So we will begin the discussion by considering some aspects of the reliability of the Violence for Social Change Index, continue by considering the nature of the relationship between attitudes toward violence for social change and violent behaviors, and end by presenting some data which bear on the issue.

## Continuity Correlations of the Violence for Social Change Index

One of the important characteristics of a measure that must be taken into account in discussions of validity is the reliability of the instrument. Every measurement can be thought of in terms of two components, the true value and the measurement error. Measurement error, in turn, has two components, random deviation and systematic bias. The reliability of an instrument reflects the measurement error, since the random portion of that error cannot contribute to the prediction of a second response (Nunnally 1967, p. 172). It is conceivable, however, that response bias could spuriously inflate the reliability of an instrument, although this would not necessarily be true. In any case, the reliability of a measure tells us the relative magnitude of the nonrandom component and hence the maximum possible validity.

Instruments for psychological testing often contain many items which are in some ways repetitive, so that reliability can be tested by considering the relationships between random halves of the instrument and so on. In most survey research the investigator is obliged to collect a relatively large amount of information in a short period of time, so that the use of many repetitive items is often not practical. As a result, many instruments used in survey research are short and do not have the redundancy which is necessary if split-half reliability is to be used. Consequently, repeated use of the instrument in the same population is often the only feasible way to obtain an estimate of reliability. For practical reasons it is usually not possible to retest the respondent within a matter of hours or even days. In the interest of maintaining respondent cooperation, the repeat measurement must often be delayed until the elapse of a considerable period of time. If the time lapse between two measurements is substantial, as it was in this study, any difference which occurs between the first and second measurement may be due either to measurement error or to a real change occurring during the time between measurements. In other words, a correlation over time contains two components, one having to do with the repeatability or repeat reliability of the measure and the other being a function of the stability of the measure. We will refer to the relationship of repeated measures to themselves as continuity correlations. This term refers only to the elapsed time and does not contain implications about reliability or stability. It should be pointed out that while the necessity of using repeat reliability problems due to the elapse of time, split-half reliability engenders other problems which are equally vexing.

The items used in such tests of reliability are not the same, and it is conceivable that reality, so measured, may be a correlation between similar but not identical constructs and, hence, would not be an exact measure of the reliability of the instrument under consideration.

The overall continuity correlation of the Violence for Social Change Index, that is, the correlation between responses to the first and the second interview, was .70 (gamma). The reader will recall that the Violence for Social Change Index consists of two subscales. The first subscale (Violence for Social Change: Blacks) was based on questions inquiring how much violence was necessary to bring about change for blacks, and the second subscale (Violence for Social Change: General) was based on questions inquiring how much violence was necessary to bring about change in general. So, the continuity correlation for the composite index should be compared with continuity correlations for the subscales. In addition, the relationships between indices over time should be compared to the relationships between indices within one interview.

Table 2.1 presents the correlations between the Violence for Social Change subscales between and within the first and second inter-

### Table 2.1
Relationships between the Violence for Social Change
Change Scales between and within the Interview and Reinterview
(all respondents, N = 283)
(gammas, tau_b's, Pearson r's)

| VIOLENCE FOR SOCIAL CHANGE INDEX | | | Gamma | Tau_b | Pearson r |
|---|---|---|---|---|---|
| Interview vs. Reinterview | | | .70 | .60 | .70 |
| **VIOLENCE FOR SOCIAL CHANGE SUBSCALES** | | | | | |
| Interview | | Reinterview | | | |
| Blacks | vs. | Blacks | .63 | .53 | .62 |
| General | vs. | General | .66 | .55 | .65 |
| Blacks | vs. | General | .64 | .54 | .62 |
| General | vs. | Blacks | .63 | .53 | .61 |
| Interview | | | | | |
| Blacks | vs. | General | .80 | .69 | .61 |
| Reinterview | | | | | |
| Blacks | vs. | General | .82 | .72 | .81 |

view. It can be seen that the subscales do not correlate as highly over time as does the complete index. Moreover, the two subscales are more correlated within an interview than they are between the interview and the reinterview. This leads one to suspect that there is some instability with respect to these attitudes over time. Indeed, the two subscales,

Black Change and General Change, refer to somewhat different situations, and one might speculate this factor alone would be sufficient to reduce the correlation between them. However, the correlations between the Violence for Social Change: Blacks and Violence for Social Change: General subscales are so large within both the interview and the reinterview that one is inclined to suspect that attitudes toward the specific situation are not very important in determining responses to the Violence for Social Change Index. Indeed, one might be justified in assuming that much of the difference between the two subscales is due to measurement error.

Table 2.1 also demonstrates that there is remarkably little difference in the size of correlations obtained by calculating gammas and Pearson r's, while tau$_b$'s tend to be somewhat lower than the other statistics. Technically, gamma is a more appropriate statistic for these data than r since the data are ordinal rather than interval. However, since the r's are so similar to the gammas, one might assume that the data did not violate the assumptions underlying the former statistic sufficiently to do it much damage. The next table shows that this is not always the case.

Table 2.2 gives the reliability for the single items in the two Violence for Social Change subscales. It can be seen that, on the whole, the

**Table 2.2**

Test-Retest Reliability for Items in
the Violence for Social Change Subscales
(all respondents, N = 283)
(gammas, tau$_b$'s, Pearson r's)

| Item | Violence for Social Change: Blacks | | | Violence for Social Change: General | | |
|---|---|---|---|---|---|---|
| | Gamma | Tau$_b$ | Pearson r | Gamma | Tau$_b$ | Pearson r |
| Some people hurt | .56 | .41 | .43 | .69 | .50 | .54 |
| Some property damage | .65 | .49 | .50 | .61 | .44 | .49 |
| Much property damage | .72 | .51 | .49 | .67 | .47 | .47 |
| Some people killed | .68 | .45 | .49 | .76 | .51 | .57 |

continuity correlations for single items when measured by gammas are not much different from the correlations for the subscales, although they are somewhat more variable. However, the Pearson r's between items on the first and second interview tend to be somewhat lower. The gamma is, of course, the correct statistic for these data, so that the r seems to provide an underestimate under these circumstances. In any case, the data indicate that it is more reasonable to have confidence in the subscales than in the single items and that there is a gain in the size of the continuity correlation and presumably in the reliability of the Violence for Social Change Index which consists of both subscales.

*Attitudes Toward Violence for Social Change
and the Willingness to Act*

Before examining the relationship between the Violence for Social Change Index and a measure of reported willingness to engage in action, it seems useful to outline the relationships between attitudes toward violence and violent behaviors or behaviors which might lead to violence. To begin with, attitudes toward the use of violence to produce social change may be regarded from three different perspectives. The first is the belief that violence is necessary to produce social change. Such statements imply neither that the individual is willing to engage in violence to produce social change, nor that he approves of such violence when it is utilized by others. Instead, beliefs that violence is a necessary precondition for social change may be nothing more than opinions concerning the facts of social change. It is likely that among those who believe that violence is necessary, there will be some who also approve of the use of such violence as well as some who are willing to engage in it. It is not likely, however, that *all* those who feel violence is necessary to produce social change will be favorably inclined toward violent action.

A second perspective from which attitudes toward violence for social change can be regarded is whether or not people approve of it. It seems probable that almost all people who approve of such violence will also believe that it is necessary; however, it is not likely that all those who approve of the use of violence to bring about social change will be personally prepared to engage in it. Muller (1972) presents data bearing on this point. He hypothesizes that all people who declare the intention of engaging in political violence will approve of political violence, while the reverse will not be true. His data confirm the hypothesis.

Lastly, not all those who are willing to report that they would engage in violence to bring about social change will have actually participated in such activities. Presumably, those who have engaged in violence are only a fraction of those who report themselves willing to do so. Whether or not a person takes violent action must be determined, at least in part, by whether or not the individual has the opportunity to do so. It seems probable that not all individuals who state they would be willing to undertake violent action in behalf of social change will have encountered circumstances appropriate for engaging in such behaviors. It is probably also true that among those who say they would be prepared to commit violence for the sake of social change, there will be some who would change their minds when faced with the occasion. There is always a gap between fantasy and reality, and its breadth is not often realized until the two collide. It may also be that there will be some among those who report themselves unwilling to use violence, who will do so if the occasion arises; but such actions would be inconsistent and, consequently, are likely to be infrequent.

Implicit in the statements above is a kind of Guttman Scale in which specific attitudes toward violence for social change and violent behaviors may be arranged. The most inclusive step on this scale is the belief that violence is necessary to produce social change. It is on this level that the Violence for Social Change Index is cast. The next level is approval of violence; not all persons who believe violence is necessary to bring about social change will approve of its use. Next, among those who approve, some will profess willingness to engage in violence. Last, among those who are willing to engage in violence, some will actually do so given the occasion, and even fewer will have done so.

It is important to understand this relative scale in assessing questions about attitudes toward violence and violent behaviors because it is erroneous to make inferences concerning a greater degree of behavioral predilection from questions that actually concern a lower level of involvement. Questions concerning the necessity of violence probably cast too broad a net, including many who are not personally committed to violence among the positive respondents. Questions inquiring about past violent behaviors will elicit too few positive replies from respondents to provide an accurate estimate of the potential for violence.

In assessing the relationship between attitudes toward violence for social change and the willingness to engage in violent behaviors, it is necessary to consider seriously the possibility that there may be important variables modifying such relationships. For example, one might speculate that an individual who believed strongly that violence was necessary to bring about social change would be more likely to undertake such actions if he also believed that there was a high likelihood of success. If, in contrast, the individual thought that the likelihood of success for any particular action was apt to be small, it seems reasonable to suppose that he would be less likely to act in accordance with his beliefs. In this example, the probability of success acts as a variable which might modify the relationship between the belief in the necessity of violence and violent behaviors. One sensible hypothesis would be that the relationship between positive attitudes toward violence and violent behaviors would be stronger among those who believe the action has a high probability of success than among those who think the probability is low. Similarly, one might hypothesize that the expectation that actions will lead to personal difficulty or the imposition of sanctions might also play a moderating role. One might expect that those who show a high concern with avoiding personal difficulty would be less likely to show consistent relationships between their attitudes and their behaviors than those who are not preoccupied with avoiding the unpleasant consequences of their actions.

In order to understand the meaning of the Violence for Social Change Index, it is important to know how attitudes toward the necessity of violence in bringing about social change are related to violent behaviors. A beginning of such understanding is implicit in the study of the criterion groups discussed previously. However, the criterion groups only serve as anchor points at the behavioral extremes. It is not possible from such studies alone to make inferences about the extent to which the Violence for Social Change Index is likely to be related to behavior in the population at large. In attempting such assessments it is crucial to consider that only a very small percentage of the population has actually been involved in any action which might be interpreted as a form of violence for social change and that the absolute number of such persons which would be located by any random sample survey would be small indeed. Consequently, it is not practical to inquire about behaviors that have already occurred; one might better inquire what the respondent declares himself willing to do.

It can be argued that correlating an attitude toward the necessity of using violence with a report of what the respondent is willing to do in the way of protesting is only correlating one attitude (the attitude toward the necessity of using violence) with another (the attitude toward protest). Consequently, the argument might go, one is no closer than before to discovering the behavioral validity of the Violence for Social Change Index. But this is not quite the case. In the preceding discussion it was pointed out that the attitude toward the necessity of using violence is not the same as approval of such violence, and approval of violence is not the same as the willingness to use it. Indeed, the first attitude includes the second and the second the third, but it is likely that among those that adhere to the first, there are many who do not adhere to the third. Each successive attitude is one step closer to behavior. The statement that one is willing to behave in a certain way must be considered as being as close to actual behaviors as one can get by asking questions. Surely it is closer to behavior than the general attitude that some behavior is necessary to reach a specific goal. People are expected to behave the way they say they will, and they generally do, although, there are always exceptions. A self-report about willingness to behave is not a piece of behavior but only a self-report, in spite of the fact that some researchers seem to imply just that notion. Nevertheless such self-reports are likely to be approximations of behavior and may reasonably be regarded as such. There is some evidence which supports this approach. For example, Weinstein (1972) has demonstrated that behaviors can be predicted far more accurately when both attitudes toward issues and actions are known than when predictions are made from attitudes toward issues alone.

### Protest and Violent Behaviors

In order to investigate the extent to which the Violence for Social Change Index is related to violent behaviors, it is useful to consider the entire array of protest behaviors. These can be regarded as occurring on a continuum which ranges from peaceful to violent. On the one end are protest behaviors which are clearly not destructive of persons or property and which contain no threat of destruction either explicit or implicit. Prayer meetings and vigils are clearly of this type. Such activities are legal and protected by law. In the middle of the violent-nonviolent continuum of protest behaviors are actions which are not destructive of persons or property but which are disruptive of other people's routines and which may convey implicit threats of destruction. Picket lines and sit-ins may be of this character. Picketing and similar activities may or may not be legal depending on the specific situation and the kind of court involvement which has occurred. Injunctions against picketing or sit-ins may be obtained, and it is reasonable to assume that such activities may be viewed as socially less acceptable than the activities mentioned earlier and so may be subject to more reporting bias.

It is useful to remember, however, that while activities such as sit-ins and picketing are not violent in themselves, they may be disruptive and they may engender violence from others. Indeed, peaceful demonstrations have sometimes been used deliberately to provoke violence on the part of others as a means of gathering sympathy for the cause of the putative victims. The issues raised by the provocative use of nonviolent techniques are complicated and will not be considered here; nevertheless, it should be remembered that nonviolent behaviors can, and often do, escalate the behavior of others into violence.

On the violent end of the protest behaviors continuum are actions such as "trashing," arson, bombing, assassination, and so on. These activities are not only violent but also criminal and, consequently, likely to be seen as dangerous and socially unacceptable by respondents. It seems reasonable to think that activities or even willingness to engage in such activities are likely to be substantially underreported. Consequently, in the 1972 interview, questions about what behaviors the respondent would be willing to undertake in the name of social change were phrased largely in terms of nonviolent and disruptive behaviors rather than violent ones. This strategy assumes that those who are not willing to engage in disruptive behaviors would also be unwilling to engage in violent ones. The exact wording of the questions was as follows:

> *Which of the following things would you be willing to do to bring about a change you felt was very important? Would you sign a petition?*
>
> *Hold a protest meeting with a permit?*
>
> *Be in a sit-in?*
>
> *Block traffic?*
>
> *Interfere with work in an office building?*

The percentage distribution to the protest behaviors items for black and white respondents is given in Table 2.3. It can be seen that many of the items are highly skewed. Almost everybody is willing to "sign a petition," and hardly anybody is willing to "block traffic" or "interfere with work in an office building." The table suggests that people may be overstating what they would do at the nonviolent end of the continuum since a number of studies have shown that many people are reluctant to sign petitions, even when these are innocuous documents such as copies of the Declaration of Independence or Bill of Rights. Of course, the phrasing of the question stem may have something to do with the overwhelming willingness of the respondents to state that they would be willing to "sign a petition"; the stem asks the respondent what he would be willing to do to bring about a change he felt was *very important*. It is also quite possible that the respondents were underrepresenting their willingness to participate in more disruptive behaviors. Judging from the alacrity with which the truckers were willing to block the nation's traffic in response to what they regarded as unfair gasoline prices, it seems likely that there is a great deal more potential for disruptive behavior in the United States than might be inferred from the modest responses of our respondents to these items. Table 2.3 also shows differences between black and white respondents on almost every item. In each case, except "sign a petition," blacks were more willing to participate in the protest activity mentioned than were whites. This is hardly surprising in view of the fact that blacks have been far more oriented toward protest than whites in the recent past.

### The Protest Behaviors Index

In order to facilitate analysis, as many of the items as possible were combined into an index. In general, our philosophy of index con-

**Table 2.3**

Percentage Responses to Items Measuring Protest Behaviors

| | All Respondents | Whites | Blacks |
|---|---|---|---|
| Sign a petition | | | |
| No | 3% | 2% | 4% |
| Not Sure | 3 | 1 | 4 |
| Yes | 94 | 97 | 92 |
| | 100% | 100% | 100% |
| Hold a protest meeting with a permit | | | |
| No | 27 | 36 | 19 |
| Not Sure | 6 | 5 | 5 |
| Yes | 67 | 59 | 76 |
| | 100% | 100% | 100% |
| Be in a sit-in | | | |
| No | 47 | 59 | 33 |
| Not Sure | 12 | 13 | 12 |
| Yes | 41 | 28 | 55 |
| | 100% | 100% | 100% |
| Block traffic | | | |
| No | 87 | 94 | 79 |
| Not Sure | 5 | 1 | 9 |
| Yes | 8 | 5 | 12 |
| | 100% | 100% | 100% |
| Interfere with work in an office building | | | |
| No | 86 | 92 | 79 |
| Not Sure | 6 | 3 | 10 |
| Yes | 8 | 5 | 11 |
| | 100% | 100% | 100% |
| N | (283) | (145) | (133) |

struction is that items should relate to one another at moderate levels and that relationships between items in an index should be stable across a variety of subgroups in the population. This strategy is detailed in Appendix E.

Table 2.4 gives the relationships between the protest behaviors items and shows that all items are highly interrelated. Inspection of the bivariate tables (not represented here) on which these gammas are based shows that the respondents appear to have scaled the items on a violent-nonviolent continuum. For example, 96 percent of those who said they were willing to participate in a sit-in also said they would be willing to "hold a protest meeting with a permit," while only 58 percent of those who said they would be willing to participate in a protest

**Table 2.4**

Relationships between Items Measuring Protest Behaviors
(all respondents, N = 283)
(gammas)

|  | Protest with permit | Be in a sit-in | Block traffic | Interfere with work |
|---|---|---|---|---|
| Sign a petition | .65 | .69 | 1.00 | .43 |
| Protest with permit |  | .82 | .83 | .50 |
| Be in a sit-in |  |  | .96 | .79 |
| Block traffic |  |  |  | .89 |

meeting were also willing to participate in a sit-in. Similarly, all those who said they would be willing to "block traffic" to bring about a change they believed to be very important were also willing to participate in a protest meeting with a permit, while only 12 percent of those willing to participate in a protest meeting were also willing to "block traffic."

These data demonstrate that the respondents did indeed regard the continuum of protest and disruptive behaviors as though they formed a kind of Guttman Scale. Those who were willing to engage in more disruptive behaviors were very likely to be willing to also utilize less forceful tactics, while the converse was not true. Presumably, the same phenomenon will be true of more violent behaviors. People who are willing to use violence will also be willing to use disruption, while the reverse proposition will not hold.

Of the original five items, three were combined additively to form the Protest Behaviors Index: "hold a protest meeting with a permit," "be in a sit-in," and "block traffic." The higher the score on the index, the more protest behaviors the respondent was willing to undertake. (Details of index construction are given in Appendix E.)

*Demographic Correlates of the Protest Behaviors Index*

Table 2.5 shows the relationships between the Protest Behaviors Index and selected demographic characteristics. The index appears to be related to a variety of demographic characteristics, with race showing the strongest relationship, followed by sex, town size, and age.

Table 2.6 shows that there is a substantial difference on the Protest Behaviors Index between white and black respondents; blacks were more likely to score high on this index than whites. This difference reflects the differences cited earlier with respect to the individual items. Moreover, these data are similar to those of Muller (1972) who found blacks in Waterloo, Iowa, more willing than whites to disobey unjust

**Table 2.5**

Relationships between the Protest Behaviors Index
and Selected Demographic Characteristics
(all respondents, N = 283)
(gammas)

| Demographic Characteristic | Gamma |
|---|---|
| Race | .44‡ |
| Sex | -.26† |
| Age | -.23‡ |
| Education | .03 |
| Town Size | .24† |
| Experience in South | -.02 |

†p < .005      ‡p < .001

laws and to participate in sit-ins, demonstrations, and even violent demonstrations.

**Table 2.6**

Percentage Responses to the Protest Behaviors Index
in Relation to Race

| Protest Behaviors Index | | Whites | Blacks |
|---|---|---|---|
| Low | 1 | 39% | 19% |
| | 2 | 34 | 27 |
| | 3 | 21 | 34 |
| High | 4 | 6 | 20 |
| | | 100% | 100% |
| | N | (145) | (133) |

Table 2.7 gives the percentage distribution for men and women on the Protest Behaviors Index. As one might have expected, women

**Table 2.7**

Percentage Responses to the Protest Behaviors Index
in Relation to Sex

| Protest Behaviors Index | | Men | Women |
|---|---|---|---|
| Low | 1 | 22% | 36% |
| | 2 | 32 | 30 |
| | 3 | 29 | 25 |
| High | 4 | 17 | 9 |
| | | 100% | 100% |
| | N | (131) | (152) |

tended to score lower on this index than men. This is in keeping with the notion of many social scientists that men are more politically oriented and more likely to engage in political behaviors than women (Campbell et al. 1960, p. 489). It is also commensurate with the often repeated observation that women are proportionately less likely to be participants in protests involving violence (Fogelson and Hill 1968, p. 234).

Table 2.8 shows the distribution of the Protest Behaviors Index when both sex and race are taken into account. One can see that in this population white women are most apt to score low on this index followed by white men; black women score somewhat higher on the index than white men; and black men are likely to score highest of all. In fact, there seems to be a marked effect of both race and sex, although analysis of variance indicates it is only an additive one (eta = .36). Within sex, women score lower than men; within race, whites score lower than blacks. White women appear to be substantially more like white men than like black women. Similarly, the distributions for black men are more like those of black women than of white men. Consequently, one interpretation of Table 2.8 is that norms in respect to

**Table 2.8**

Percentage Responses to the Protest Behaviors Index
for White Men, White Women, Black Men, and Black Women

| Protest Behaviors Index | | White Men | White Women | Black Men | Black Women |
|---|---|---|---|---|---|
| Low | 1 | 31% | 47% | 9% | 24% |
| | 2 | 37 | 30 | 27 | 29 |
| | 3 | 24 | 19 | 35 | 33 |
| High | 4 | 8 | 4 | 29 | 14 |
| | | 100% | 100% | 100% | 100% |
| | N | (71) | (74) | (59) | (74) |

protest behaviors are primarily determined by race and secondarily by sex. In this context it is revealing that black women appear more willing to participate in protest behaviors than white men. Intuitively, this arrangement by race and sex reflects what seems to have been occurring in the United States, although, we do not know from this sample if similar data would be obtained nationally. If the predilection to political and aggressive behavior among men is partially determined by the biology of gender, as some have contended, the high level of willingness to take action by black women makes it clear that biology can be overcome by culture.

Table 2.9 shows the Protest Behaviors Index in relation to whether the respondent's dwelling place was located in a more rural or a more urban area. It can be seen that the more urban the respondent, the more likely he is to score high on the index. This is particularly true for those who live in large cities (defined as having a population of 100,000 or more). Part of this relationship may be due to the fact that in the population investigated more black than white respondents lived in urban areas; however, there was still a relationship between the Protest Behaviors Index and town size among white respondents

**Table 2.9**

Percentage Responses to the Protest Behaviors Index
in Relation to Town Size
(all respondents, N = 283)

| Protest Behaviors Index | Rural-Town | Small City | Large City |
|---|---|---|---|
| Low    1 | 38% | 40% | 23% |
| 2 | 29 | 27 | 33 |
| 3 | 29 | 25 | 27 |
| High   4 | 4 | 8 | 17 |
| | 100% | 100% | 100% |
| N* | (52) | (52) | (176) |

Note: Rural-town (population under 20,000); small city (population 20,000-99,999) and large city (population 100,000 or more).

**Table 2.10**

Percentage Responses to the Protest Behaviors Index
in Relation to Age
(all respondents, N = 283)

| Protest Behaviors Index | 16-19 Years | 20-29 Years | 30-39 Years | 40-49 Years | 50-59 Years | 60 Years or Older |
|---|---|---|---|---|---|---|
| Low    1 | 28% | 19% | 22% | 36% | 37% | 41% |
| 2 | 19 | 30 | 39 | 28 | 32 | 36 |
| 3 | 39 | 30 | 18 | 31 | 21 | 23 |
| High   4 | 14 | 21 | 21 | 5 | 10 | 0 |
| | 100% | 100% | 100% | 100% | 100% | 100% |
| N* | (36) | (67) | (49) | (42) | (38) | (47) |

considered separately.[1] Thus, among the respondents in this study the index reflects the apparent pattern of protest in the United States, with

[1] The distribution of black respondents is so concentrated in urban areas that it is not very helpful to calculate the relationship between town size and other variables among blacks separately.

urban dwellers more likely to say they would engage in such behaviors than rural respondents.

Table 2.10 shows the relationship between the Protest Behaviors Index and age. There was a distinct tendency for respondents who were in their fourth decade or older to score lower on the Protest Behaviors Index than did younger respondents. However, these data do not allow us to distinguish whether the differences observed are differences due to age or characteristics of the cohort.

### The Protest Behaviors Index and Violence for Social Change

Table 2.11 shows the relationships between the Protest Behaviors and the Violence for Social Change Index for different subpopulations. The relationships are all positive but disappointingly small. The

**Table 2.11**

Relationships between the Protest Behaviors Index
and the Violence for Social Change Index for Selected Subgroups
(gammas)

|  | N | Gamma |
|---|---|---|
| All Respondents | (283) | .26§ |
| Whites | (145) | .14 |
| Blacks | (133) | .16 |
| Men | (131) | .29‡ |
| Women | (152) | .24† |
| White Men | (71) | .14 |
| Black Men | (59) | .10 |
| White Women | (74) | .14 |
| Black Women | (74) | .18 |

†p < .05        ‡p < .005        §p < .001

association for all respondents is a gamma of .26; this relationship becomes smaller within race, suggesting that the overall effect is at least partially due to the difference between the races. However, the relationships within race and sex become very small indeed. Thus, it appears that much of the association between the Protest Behaviors and the Violence for Social Change Index can be attributed to the differences between the races and the sexes. Still, the relationship is a meaningful one since there are real social implications resulting from the fact that persons in one group of respondents, namely blacks, were more likely than other respondents both to report themselves willing to engage in protest behaviors and to agree that violence is necessary to bring about change. Nevertheless, the relationships are small and cast some doubt on the construct validity of the Violence for Social Change Index.

The size of the relationships between the Protest Behaviors Index and the Violence for Social Change Index (Table 2.11) raises the question whether the theoretical relationship of these two constructs is correctly postulated when it is formulated as a simple first order association. To answer this question it is necessary to digress and consider the properties of another construct which we will show to have a modifying effect on the association between the Violence for Social Change Index and the Protest Behaviors Index.

## Avoiding Problems as a Motif in Violent Behaviors

Preliminary conversations with informants who were Jehovah's Witnesses suggested that one of the values which might be important in explaining their attitudes toward violence was the norm of uninvolvement or neutrality. An important tenet of the Jehovah's Witnesses' belief seemed to be that it is inappropriate and undesirable for individuals to be "involved" in secular affairs. The Witnesses were very clear on this point, and they frequently explained that although one should render unto Caesar the things that are Caesar's, Jehovah's Witnesses should attend to the Lord's business leaving "carnal" affairs to others. It seems clear that if an individual were truly disengaged from the affairs of this world he would be highly unlikely to become involved in violent efforts to produce social change. A value of neutrality, strongly held, might very well serve as an effective deterrent from the passions and commitments which lead individuals to believe and act forcefully in the interest of change.

The Jehovah's Witnesses' belief, as we understood it, implied a valuation of disengagement. One might think that such uninvolvement would be a part of a continuum ranging from strong beliefs in neutrality or uninvolvement to beliefs in participation, the ethic of "doing it yourself" and personal mastery. The following items were designed to measure this dimension:

*It is best to stay neutral on things others have strong feelings about.*

*People should stand up for themselves even if it leads to trouble.*

*Nothing will ever get done if people just wait for the government to act.*

*People who make speeches stirring people up should be put in prison before they cause serious trouble.*

*It is better to avoid a fight than take a chance on getting hurt.*

*There is no point in individual citizens trying to do anything about social problems such as poverty.*

*Sometimes a person has to take the law into his own hands to see that justice gets done.*

*When police don't stop crime in a neighborhood people should set up their own patrols.*

**Table 2.12**

Percentage Responses to Items Measuring the
Neutrality-Involvement Continuum
(whites, N = 145; blacks, N = 133; all respondents, N = 283)

|  |  | Agree a Great Deal | Agree Some-what | Disagree Some-what | Disagree a Great Deal |
|---|---|---|---|---|---|
| It is best to stay | All Respondents | 22% | 43 | 23 | 12 |
| neutral on things | Whites | 16% | 37 | 28 | 19 |
| others have strong | Blacks | 30% | 50 | 17 | 3 |
| feelings about. |  |  |  |  |  |
| People should stand up | All Respondents | 37% | 43 | 17 | 3 |
| for themselves even if | Whites | 33% | 45 | 19 | 3 |
| it leads to trouble. | Blacks | 42% | 39 | 16 | 3 |
| Nothing will ever get | All Respondents | 29% | 37 | 26 | 8 |
| done if people just | Whites | 30% | 32 | 28 | 10 |
| wait for the | Blacks | 30% | 42 | 23 | 5 |
| government to act. |  |  |  |  |  |
| People who make speeches | All Respondents | 13% | 25 | 40 | 22 |
| stirring people up | Whites | 13% | 25 | 35 | 27 |
| should be put in prison | Blacks | 12% | 26 | 45 | 17 |
| before they cause |  |  |  |  |  |
| serious trouble. |  |  |  |  |  |
| It is better to avoid a | All Respondents | 45% | 41 | 11 | 3 |
| fight than to take a | Whites | 41% | 41 | 15 | 3 |
| chance on getting hurt | Blacks | 50% | 42 | 5 | 3 |
| There is no point in | All Respondents | 37% | 38 | 16 | 9 |
| individual citizens | Whites | 7% | 12 | 36 | 45 |
| trying to do anything | Blacks | 12% | 20 | 41 | 27 |
| about social problems, |  |  |  |  |  |
| such as poverty. |  |  |  |  |  |
| Sometimes a person | All Respondents | 10% | 26 | 30 | 34 |
| has to take the law | Whites | 7% | 27 | 28 | 38 |
| into his own hands to see | Blacks | 12% | 24 | 34 | 30 |
| that justice gets done. |  |  |  |  |  |
| When police don't stop | All Respondents | 17% | 39 | 23 | 21 |
| crime in a neighbor- | Whites | 17% | 45 | 20 | 18 |
| hood, people should set | Blacks | 17% | 32 | 26 | 25 |
| up their own patrols. |  |  |  |  |  |

Note: Percentages across each row total 100%.

The percentage distribution to these items for black and white respondents is given in Table 2.12. It can be seen that on the whole there are relatively small differences between the two races. However, black respondents tended to agree more strongly with the item about staying neutral than did whites.

The items which had been designed to measure the uninvolvement-involvement continuum proved to be a heterogeneous lot which did not occupy the same psychological space. In part this appeared to be a function of the fact that some of the items were oriented toward determining what the citizen should do in lieu of government action, while others were oriented toward more general statements of neutrality. Three of the items, "It is best to stay neutral on things others have strong feelings about," "It is better to avoid a fight than to take a chance on getting hurt," and "People who make speeches stirring people up should be put in prison before they cause serious trouble," did show characteristics which made them suitable for combination into an index. These items were summed to form the Avoid Problems Index; the higher the score on the index, the more the respondent agreed that it was best to maintain neutrality. (Details of index construction are given in Appendix E.)

## Demographic Correlates of the Avoid Problems Index

Table 2.13 shows the relationships between the Avoid Problems Index and selected demographic characteristics. It can be seen that the largest relationship is between the index and education, followed by smaller relationships with age and race.

**Table 2.13**

Relationships between the Avoid Problems Index and
Selected Demographic Characteristics
(all respondents, N = 283)
(gammas)

| Demographic Characteristic | Gamma |
|---|---|
| Race | .28‡ |
| Sex | .04 |
| Age | .28‡ |
| Education | -.37‡ |
| Town Size | .10 |
| Experience in South | -.15† |

†p < .05        ‡p < .001

Table 2.14 shows the relationship between the Avoid Problems Index and education. Apparently the better educated set less value on avoiding difficulty and involvement, for they were more likely than those with less education to score low on the index. This is particularly true of those who had at least some college education. One interpretation of this result is that education leads to an increased willingness of

**Table 2.14**

Percentage Responses to the Avoid Problems Index
in Relation to Education
(all respondents, N = 283)

| Avoid Problems Index | | 9 Years or Less | 10-11 Years | High School Graduate | At Least Some College |
|---|---|---|---|---|---|
| Low | 1-2 | 10% | 29% | 36% | 51% |
| | 3-4 | 42 | 40 | 45 | 31 |
| High | 5-6 | 48 | 31 | 19 | 18 |
| | | 100% | 100% | 100% | 100% |
| | N* | (67) | (80) | (71) | (62) |

the individual to commit himself. Why this should be so is problematical. It is true that research on student activism has repeatedly found that student activists come from highly educated families (Lipset 1969, p. 52; Blumenthal 1973a). Consequently, some relationships between an index measuring "involvment" and education might well have been anticipated. It is also true that at least one of the items (agitators should be imprisoned) could be construed as relating to tolerance for dissent, and it is known that such tolerance is higher among those with some college education (Zellman and Sears 1971). However, this single item is not sufficient to explain the size of the relationship. Perhaps the less educated are more fearful of the consequences of becoming entrapped in difficulty if they do not remain neutral. After all, those with less education usually have fewer resources to assist them, and it may be that involvement is more costly for the poor. An alternative view is that it is not education itself which leads to an increased willingness to encounter difficulty but simply that those who are likely to become educated are those who are already willing to face problems.

Table 2.15 shows the relationship between the Avoid Problems Index and age. It can be seen that older people are more likely to have high scores on this index than are younger people. Part of this difference may be due to the fact that younger people are apt to be somewhat better educated than older individuals in our population (Table 2.16), or it may be that the index simply reflects the willingness of youth to make a commitment, a willingness that tends to disappear with increasing years.

**Table 2.15**

Percentage Responses to the Avoid Problems Index
in Relation to Age
(all respondents, N = 283)

| Avoid Problems Index | | 16-19 Years | 20-29 Years | 30-39 Years | 40-49 Years | 50-59 Years | 60 Years or Older |
|---|---|---|---|---|---|---|---|
| Low | 1-2 | 41% | 46% | 35% | 25% | 16% | 18% |
| | 3-4 | 34 | 39 | 45 | 40 | 39 | 38 |
| High | 5-6 | 25 | 15 | 20 | 35 | 45 | 44 |
| | | 100% | 100% | 100% | 100% | 100% | 100% |
| | N* | (36) | (67) | (49) | (44) | (38) | (45) |

**Table 2.16**

Respondent's Level of Education
in Relation to Age
(percentage distribution)
(all respondents, N = 283)

| Education | 16-19 Years | 20-29 Years | 30-39 Years | 40-49 Years | 50-59 Years | 60 Years or Older |
|---|---|---|---|---|---|---|
| 9 Years or Less | 8% | 9% | 10% | 34% | 37% | 53% |
| 10-11 Years | 64 | 21 | 37 | 21 | 21 | 17 |
| High School Graduate | 20 | 34 | 26 | 27 | 21 | 15 |
| At Least Some College | 8 | 36 | 27 | 18 | 21 | 15 |
| | 100% | 100% | 100% | 100% | 100% | 100% |
| N* | (36) | (67) | (49) | (44) | (38) | (47) |

Note: Gamma for all respondents is .20 (p < .001).

Table 2.17 gives the percentage distribution on the Avoid Problems Index by the race of the respondent. It can be seen that white respondents were more likely to have low scores on this index than were their black counterparts. In part, the differences between the two

**Table 2.17**

Percentage Responses to the Avoid Problems Index
in Relation to Race

| Avoid Problems Index | | Whites | Blacks |
|---|---|---|---|
| Low | 1-2 | 39% | 22% |
| | 3-4 | 38 | 42 |
| High | 5-6 | 23 | 36 |
| | | 100% | 100% |
| | N | (145) | (133) |

races may be a reflection of their differential education. Table 2.18 indicates that among respondents in this study, as is true nationally, blacks were not as well educated as whites. However, Tables 2.19 and 2.20 show that for both black and white respondents there is an inverse relationship between education and the Avoid Problems Index

**Table 2.18**

Level of Education Attained by White and Black Respondents
(percentage distribution)

| Education | | Whites | Blacks |
|---|---|---|---|
| 9 Years or Less | | 15% | 33% |
| 10-11 Years | | 27 | 31 |
| High School Graduate | | 24 | 27 |
| At Least Some College | | 34 | 9 |
| | | 100% | 100% |
| | N | (145) | (133) |

**Table 2.19**

Percentage Responses to the Avoid Problems Index
in Relation to Education for White Respondents
(white respondents, N = 145)

| Avoid Problems Index | | 9 Years or Less | 10-11 Years | High School Graduate | At Least Some College |
|---|---|---|---|---|---|
| Low  1-2 | | 9% | 36% | 47% | 51% |
| 3-4 | | 43 | 46 | 35 | 31 |
| High  5-6 | | 48 | 18 | 18 | 18 |
| | | 100% | 100% | 100% | 100% |
| | N* | (21) | (39) | (34) | (49) |

Note: Gamma for white respondents is -.29 (p < .001).

**Table 2.20**

Percentage Responses to the Avoid Problems Index
in Relation to Education for Black Respondents
(black respondents, N = 133)

| Avoid Problems Index | | 9 Years or Less | 10-11 Years | High School Graduate/ At Least Some College |
|---|---|---|---|---|
| Low  1-2 | | 11% | 22% | 31% |
| 3-4 | | 44 | 33 | 50 |
| High  5-6 | | 45 | 45 | 19 |
| | | 100% | 100% | 100% |
| | N | (44) | (40) | (48) |

Note: Gamma for black respondents is -.34 (p<.001).

such that those with less education are likely to score higher on this index. So, it is not race alone that is responsible for the association between the index and education.

This evidence suggests that the proportionately lower education of black respondents may account for some of the difference between whites and blacks on this index. However, it can be seen by comparing Tables 2.19 and 2.20 that black respondents with more than nine years of education still scored somewhat higher on the index than did white respondents with an equivalent education. Thus, there is an association between race and the Avoid Problems Index which cannot be accounted for by differences in education.

One additional factor which needs to be taken into account in examining the Avoid Problems Index in relation to race is that black respondents answered differently on the index depending on the region of the interview. Table 2.21 demonstrates that black respondents inter-

**Table 2.21**

Percentage Responses to the Avoid Problems Index
for Black Detroit and Black Southern Respondents

| Avoid Problems Index | | Black Detroit Respondents | Black Southern Respondents |
|---|---|---|---|
| Low | 1-2 | 29% | 10% |
| | 3-4 | 42 | 44 |
| High | 5-6 | 29 | 46 |
| | | 100% | 100% |
| | N | (83) | (50) |

**Table 2.22**

Percentage Responses to the Avoid Problems Index
for Jehovah's Witnesses, Quakers,
and Other Detroit Respondents

| Avoid Problems Index | | Jehovah's Witnesses | | Quakers | Detroit Respondents | |
|---|---|---|---|---|---|---|
| | | Whites | Blacks | Whites | Whites | Blacks |
| Low | 1-2 | 26% | 24% | 91% | 36% | 29% |
| | 3-4 | 33 | 30 | 6 | 40 | 52 |
| High | 5-6 | 41 | 46 | 3 | 24 | 29 |
| | | 100% | 100% | 100% | 100% | 100% |
| | N | (104) | (83) | (29) | (38) | (36) |

Notes: p < .01 that the difference between the white Jehovah's Witnesses and the Detroit whites is due to chance (Mann-Whitney U Test).

p < .05 that the difference between the black Jehovah's Witnesses and the Detroit blacks is due to chance (Mann-Whitney U Test).

viewed in the South scored higher on the Avoid Problems Index than those interviewed in the Detroit area. So, what appears to be a difference due to race may be an effect produced by an interaction between being black and living in the South. That black respondents living in the South scored higher on the Avoid Problems Index is not surprising in view of attitudes toward blacks which have been common in the South in the past. Passivity and avoidance of difficulty has been one of the major coping devices of black Southerners until very recently, although one might speculate that such attitudes are probably changing.

Table 2.22 shows the percentage distribution of Detroit Jehovah's Witnesses, Quakers,[2] and black and white Detroit respondents on the Avoid Problems Index. It can be seen that the Jehovah's Witnesses did tend to score somewhat higher on this index than other Detroit respondents, although they did not deviate as much as we had anticipated they would. More interesting than the responses of the Jehovah's Witnesses on this index are the responses of the Detroit Quakers. The Quakers, who were studied because of their pacifist behaviors, differ substantially from the Jehovah's Witnesses in that they are strong believers in social action. Thus, one might have expected on the basis of their social activism that Quakers would score low on this index, and indeed, they did. Ninety-one percent of them fell in the two lowest categories.

### Avoiding Problems and Attitudes Toward Violence for Social Change

The hypothesis explored in the following analysis is that the Avoid Problems Index serves to moderate relationships between the respondent's attitudes and the behaviors he is willing to undertake. It is possible that among people who placed a high value on avoiding difficulty, associations between attitudes and behavior will be substantially diminished. For example, one might believe that it is a good thing to tell the truth but avoid doing so because of negative consequences that might result from an honest statement. So, a supervisor might not give an honest evaluation of an employee's effort if the supervisor thought the employee would dislike him for doing so. One can imagine that similar reasoning might influence the relationships between attitudes toward the use of violence to produce social change and a person's willingness to behave violently on behalf of such a change. Indeed, there is some experimental evidence that suggests that such might be the case. Frideres, Warner, and Albrecht (1971) have shown that persons who are favorable to the use of marijuana are more likely to vote for the legalization of marijuana in an experimental situation if they can cast their votes

---

[2] A more complete description of the Quakers is given in Chapter 4.

anonymously, or, in a public vote, if they know that others are favorably inclined to marijuana use. When subjects are obligated to cast their votes publicly, while knowing that others in the voting situation are opposed to marijuana use, they are likely to vote in opposition to their convictions. One might speculate that the moderating variable in this experiment is the expectation of sanctions (in the form of mild interpersonal difficulty) by subjects obliged to vote on an issue where their own convictions are in conflict with those of others. One might anticipate that the expectation of sanctions or personal difficulty would play a very general role in the relationships between attitudes and behavior.

As a first step in the analysis, the first order relationships between the Avoid Problems Index and the Violence for Social Change Index will be considered. Table 2.23 shows that there are no significant zero order relationships between the two indices. As a second step the reader should recall that there were only small relationships between the

**Table 2.23**

Relationships between the Avoid Problems Index
and the Violence for Social Change Index for Selected Subgroups
(gammas)

|  | N | Gamma |
|---|---|---|
| All Respondents | (283) | -.02 |
| Whites | (145) | -.17 |
| Blacks | (133) | -.10 |
| Younger than 40 Years of Age | (152) | .08 |
| 40 Years of Age or Older | (129) | -.04 |
| 11 Years of School or Less | (148) | -.14 |
| At Least Some College | (63) | -.07 |

Violence for Social Change Index and the Protest Behaviors Index (Table 2.11). One possible explanation of this result is that there are some who, although they believe that violence is necessary to produce change at a reasonable rate, do not wish to become involved personally at least partly because they wish to remain neutral and avoid problems. Such people should score high on the Avoid Problems Index, and one would expect that they would show only low relationships between the Violence for Social Change Index and the Protest Behaviors Index. However, among those who do not place a high priority on remaining neutral and avoiding problems one would expect a substantial relationship between the Violence for Social Change and the Protest Behaviors Indices. Table 2.24 shows this is the case. Individuals who scored in

**Table 2.24**

Relationships between the Violence for Social Change Index
and the Protest Behaviors Index for Respondents with
Low or High Scores on the Avoid Problems Index
(gammas)

|  | N | Low Avoid Problems (Score 1-3) | N | High Avoid Problems (Score 4-6) |
|---|---|---|---|---|
| All Respondents | (144) | .41§ | (137) | .12 |
| Whites | (86) | .31† | (58) | -.18 |
| Blacks | (56) | .42‡ | (76) | -.02 |

†p < .05    ‡p < .005    §p < .001

the upper half of the Avoid Problems Index showed virtually no association between the Violence for Social Change and the Protest Behaviors Indices. Indeed, among white respondents there was a tendency
for the relationship to reverse, suggesting that perhaps these respondents may have been biasing their answers in what they believed to be a
socially acceptable direction. Table 2.24 also shows that those who had
low scores on the Avoid Problems Index showed the anticipated relationship between Protest Behaviors and Violence for Social Change.
The relationship is maintained within race, as it ought to be. Thus,
the relationship between the Protest Behaviors Index and the Violence
for Social Change Index cannot be attributed simply to racial differences. Attitudes toward violence for social change are related to
willingness to engage in protest behaviors, both disruptive and nondisruptive, provided the respondent's predilection for avoiding difficulty has been taken into account.

**Table 2.25**

Percentage Responses to the Violence for Social Change Index
in Relation to the Protest Behaviors Index for Respondents
with Low Scores on the Avoid Problems Index

| | Protest Behaviors Index | | | | | | | |
|---|---|---|---|---|---|---|---|---|
| | All Respondents Low on Avoid Problems | | | Whites Low on Avoid Problems | | | Blacks Low on Avoid Problems | |
| Violence for Social Change Index | Low 1 | 2 | High 3-4 | Low 1 | 2 | High 3-4 | Low 1-2 | High 3-4 |
| Low       1 | 40% | 37% | 10% | 44% | 50% | 14% | 18% | 4% |
|           2-3 | 40 | 35 | 38 | 44 | 33 | 59 | 32 | 17 |
| High    4-7 | 20 | 28 | 52 | 12 | 17 | 27 | 50 | 79 |
| | 100% | 100% | 100% | 100% | 100% | 100% | 100% | 100% |
| N* | (35) | (43) | (58) | (25) | (30) | (29) | (22) | (28) |

Table 2.25 shows convincingly the increase in reported willingness to participate in protest of increasing force (and illegality—the sequence of action in the index is "hold a protest meeting with a permit," "be in a sit-in," "block traffic") with an increasingly positive attitude toward violence for social change among those who do not emphasize avoiding problems. These data indicate that the motif of wishing to stay out of trouble or valuing neutrality may be an important mediating variable in the relationship between attitudes and behaviors.

These data illustrate two important points. One is that the Violence for Social Change Index shows a reasonable relationship to the respondent's reported willingness to participate in protest actions. The second is that relationships between attitudinal and behavioral constructs may be complicated and not necessarily easily predicted on an a priori basis. The profound effect that the Avoid Problems Index has on the relationship between attitudes toward violence for social change and what the respondent states he is willing to do to bring about such change illustrates this point nicely. One can imagine other variables which might have such strong moderating effects. For example, whether or not the individual believes that violence will actually be effective in bringing about a desired change might play an equally important moderating role on the relationship between attitudes toward violence and violent behavior. The finding that there are major moderating effects which influence the relationship between attitudes and behaviors underlines the point made earlier that it is important to understand the nature of the theoretical relationships between attitudes and behavior before studies of construct validity can be designed and executed. It emphasizes the importance of understanding the assumptions which underlie validation efforts and focuses attention on the complexity of the task.

The Avoid Problems Index was helpful in solving a second puzzle which had been presented by our data. There is much documentation in the literature of social psychology on the relationship between frustration and aggression. The frustration-aggression hypothesis which was originally proposed by Dollard et al. (1939) has been elaborated by many workers, most notably Berkowitz (1962). In the 1969 national survey it had been anticipated that there would be a substantial relationship between a measure of frustration, the Resentment-Suspicion Index, and the Violence for Social Change Index. This expectation was not strongly supported by the data (Blumenthal 1973b). There was a small correlation (gamma = .3) between the Resentment-Suspicion Index and the Violence for Social Change Index, but this correlation was not found among black men; indeed, when the analysis was conducted for white men only, the correlation became quite small (gamma = .2).

Geller and Howard (1972) have suggested that black activism tends to be instrumental while white activism is more expressive, and these findings could be taken as support for this notion. However, as we shall show, there are alternative explanations for the phenomenon.

The Resentment-Suspicion Index was repeated in the present study with results very similar to those found in the national data. The demographic associations of this index (shown in Table 2.26) provide some support for the notion that the index is a measure of frustration. The table shows that among the respondents of the 1972 interview, the most important demographic correlate was race, with black respondents being substantially more likely to score high on the index than whites.

**Table 2.26**

Relationships between the Resentment-Suspicion Index
and Selected Demographic Characteristics
(all respondents, N = 283)
(gammas)

| Demographic Characteristic | Gamma |
|---|---|
| Race | .56‡ |
| Sex | .00 |
| Age | -.08 |
| Education | -.28‡ |
| Family Income | -.33‡ |
| Town Size | .20† |
| Experience in South | -.26‡ |

†p < .01       ‡p < .001

Table 2.27 shows the extent of this difference. Thirty-eight percent of the black respondents fell in the highest category of the Resent-

**Table 2.27**

Percentage Responses to the Resentment-Suspicion Index
in Relation to Race

| Resentment-Suspicion Index | | | Whites | Blacks |
|---|---|---|---|---|
| Low | 1 | | 24% | 5% |
| | 2 | | 28 | 14 |
| | 3 | | 22 | 23 |
| | 4 | | 15 | 20 |
| High | 5 | | 11 | 38 |
| | | | 100% | 100% |
| | | N | (145) | (133) |

ment-Suspicion Index in contrast to only 11 percent of the white. We have previously shown in the national data that this difference cannot be attributed solely to differences in socioeconomic status between the two races since black men still scored higher on the index than did white men in the same social class (Blumenthal 1973b). That blacks scored higher than whites on an index which presumably measures frustration seems reasonable in view of longstanding discriminatory practices in the United States. Table 2.26 also shows that the Resentment-Suspicion Index relates negatively to income, one of the few measures investigated in this study which shows such an association. Table 2.28 shows the distribution of responses of the Resentment-Suspicion Index by income. Over 40 percent of those with incomes

**Table 2.28**

Percentage Responses to the Resentment-Suspicion Index
in Relation to Family Income
(all respondents, N = 283)

| Resentment-Suspicion Index | | Under $2,000 | $2,000-3,999 | $4,000-5,999 | $6,000-7,999 | $8,000-11,999 | $12,000-15,999 | $16,000 or More |
|---|---|---|---|---|---|---|---|---|
| Low | 1 | 12% | 2% | 15% | 0% | 13% | 21% | 33% |
| | 2 | 16 | 14 | 17 | 19 | 27 | 35 | 21 |
| | 3 | 12 | 15 | 24 | 37 | 28 | 14 | 22 |
| | 4 | 12 | 26 | 20 | 22 | 15 | 16 | 14 |
| High | 5 | 48 | 43 | 24 | 22 | 17 | 14 | 10 |
| | | 100% | 100% | 100% | 100% | 100% | 100% | 100% |
| | N* | (25) | (42) | (42) | (27) | (47) | (43) | (42) |

under $4,000 fell in the highest category of the index in contrast to only 10 percent of those with incomes of $16,000 or more. Indeed, this association between the Resentment-Suspicion Index and income is maintained within race as it should be if the measure is truly a measure of frustration. Among white respondents the index relates to income with a gamma of -.22 (p < .01); among black respondents, with a gamma of -.26 (p < .005).

Table 2.26 also shows the expected association between the Resentment-Suspicion Index and education; the more educated the respondent the less likely he was to score high on the index. Table 2.29 shows that among those who had at least some college education only 6 percent scored in the highest category of the index in contrast with more than a third of those who had a ninth grade education or less. Part of this association is probably due to racial differences in the amount of education received. Black respondents in our population

**Table 2.29**

Percentage Responses to the Resentment-Suspicion Index
in Relation to Education
(all respondents, N = 283)

| Resentment-Suspicion Index | | 9 Years or Less | 10-11 Years | High School Graduate | At Least Some College |
|---|---|---|---|---|---|
| Low | 1 | 9% | 13% | 14% | 24% |
| | 2 | 13 | 21 | 30 | 23 |
| | 3 | 19 | 18 | 25 | 26 |
| | 4 | 21 | 19 | 10 | 21 |
| High | 5 | 38 | 29 | 21 | 6 |
| | | 100% | 100% | 100% | 100% |
| | N* | (68) | (80) | (71) | (62) |

had substantially less education than did their white counterparts (only 11 black respondents had any college education). However, the association between the index and education is maintained within race, albeit at minimal levels (among white respondents, gamma = -.17; among black, gamma = -.19; $p < .05$ for both), so the effect of education cannot be attributed solely to racial differences. It is not clear whether the association with education is due to education per se, or whether the effect is more dependent on the differences in income or the living standard which are associated with education of varying levels. Indeed, no causal inference can reasonably be made on the basis of these data, although it seems reasonable that there should be a causal relationship between a lack of education with its attendant deprivations and a sense of frustration.

Table 2.30 shows the relationship between the Resentment-Suspicion Index and the Violence for Social Change Index. The association between the two indices is modest in the population as a whole, but this association appears to be due mainly to a relationship which

**Table 2.30**

Relationships between the Resentment-Suspicion Index
and the Violence for Social Change Index
(gammas)

| | N | Gamma |
|---|---|---|
| All Respondents | (283) | .34‡ |
| Whites | (145) | .26† |
| Blacks | (133) | .17 |

†$p < .01$    ‡$p < .001$

is true for white (gamma = .26) but not for black respondents. The findings are very similar to those from the 1969 study. The first order relationships given here provide only very modest support for the theory that aggression is caused by frustration. In view of the long standing nature of that theory and the massive accumulation of evidence which relates to it, this result is disappointing.

However, it is conceivable that frustration only becomes translated into positive attitudes toward violence among those who are not afraid to take risks and who do not have a predilection for wishing to avoid problems. Table 2.31 sheds some light on this issue. The table shows that among those who scored low on the Avoid Problems Index the anticipated relationship between the Resentment-Suspicion Index and the Violence for Social Change Index exists. Moreover, the rela-

**Table 2.31**

Relationships between the Resentment-Suspicion Index
and the Violence for Social Change Index
for Respondents with Low or High Scores on the Avoid Problems Index
(gammas)

|  | N | Low Avoid Problems (Score 1-3) | N | High Avoid Problems (Score 4-6) |
|---|---|---|---|---|
| All Respondents | (144) | .46‡ | (134) | .24† |
| Whites | (86) | .45‡ | (58) | .00 |
| Blacks | (56) | .36† | (76) | .09 |

†p < .05     ‡p < .001

tionship is true among both black and white respondents so that it cannot be attributed to differences between the races. This finding is an interesting one. It demonstrates that the relationship between a specific attitude, which one might think to be a response to frustration, and the antecedent frustration can be profoundly modified by attitudes which have little direct relationship to either the frustration or attitudes toward violence. The data suggest that when theorizing about relationships between attitudes and behaviors one must consider the possibility of modifying factors and that careful exploration of such variables is necessary in investigating relationships between affects and attitudes as well as between attitudes and behaviors.

*Summary*

The relationship between attitudes toward the use of violence for social change and violent behaviors has been reviewed. It has been pointed out that the belief that violence is necessary to bring about change does not imply that the believer approves of such violence; that approval of such violence does not imply that the approver is himself prepared to engage in it; and that those who are psychologically prepared to engage in such violence will not necessarily have the opportunity to engage in it. Consequently, the belief that violence is necessary to bring about social change will be held by more people than are prepared to engage in violence in pursuit of such change.

It was also pointed out that protest behaviors can be ranged on a continuum from those which are clearly nonviolent through those which are clearly violent. Within the range of protest behaviors it seems likely that those who will use the most violent forms of protest will avail themselves of all less violent forms, while those who are willing to engage in some nonviolent protest behaviors will not necessarily be willing to use disruptive or violent ones. The data examined support these propositions.

In the population investigated it was found that there was a small relationship between the Violence for Social Change Index, which measures the extent to which the respondent believes that violence is necessary to bring about social change, and his reported willingness to engage in protest behaviors. The zero order correlation appeared to be based largely on differences between the two races on both indices, black respondents being more likely to believe that violence is necessary to bring about social change and more willing to engage in a variety of protest behaviors to produce it.

The data also indicate that whether or not the respondent wished to remain neutral or avoid problems exerts a strong moderating effect on the relationship between attitudes toward violence for social change and reported willingness to undertake protest actions. Among those who had a strong wish to avoid difficulty, there appears to be no relationship between the Violence for Social Change Index and the Protest Behaviors Index, while among those who set little value on avoiding difficulty, the relationship between the two indices reaches moderate size, even when the two races are considered separately. It seems sensible that avoiding sanctions or other difficulties should modify the relationship between an attitude and the predilection to behavior it implies. In addition, the wish to avoid problems also appears to modify the relationship between a measure of frustration and attitudes toward the use of violence for social change. Among those with little concern about avoiding difficulty, a measure of frustration (the Resentment-Suspicion Index) relates at moderate levels to the Violence for Social Change Index, while among those who value avoidance of problems, it does not.

These data illustrate the complexity of the relationships between attitudes toward violence and violent behaviors. It is suggested that there may be other variables which have major effects in moderating such relationships. For example, one might suspect that the respondent's estimate of the likelihood of a particular action resulting in the desired end would serve to moderate relationships between attitudes and behaviors. An increase in knowledge of such moderating factors is essential in coming to a better understanding of the relationship between attitudes toward violence and violent behaviors.

# Chapter 3

# CAUSAL MEASURES AND ATTITUDES TOWARD VIOLENCE FOR SOCIAL CHANGE

*Introduction*

The main objective of the present set of studies was to expand our knowledge of the quality and methodological properties of the central measures in our theoretical model of attitudes toward violence. At the same time, the 1972 interviews presented an excellent opportunity to study the relationship between the variables of interest to our model and those which are focal points in the research of others.

The data in our previous work demonstrated that attitudes toward different types of violence were not necessarily related. It is important to underscore here that we are not studying generalized attitudes toward violence but attitudes toward the use of violence as a means of producing social change and as a means of maintaining social control. Violence for social change has to do with protest, rebellion, and revolution. Violence for social control usually has to do with the force used by the state to maintain order within the society. Clearly, these two types of violence have political ramifications, and it is not surprising that much of the theorizing about them has been carried out by political scientists. It is their work to which we now propose to join our own.

The 1969 national study, which centered mainly on attitudes toward violence, was undertaken on the assumption that attitudes are related to behaviors and that they imply predilections to specific types of behavior. So, it was supposed that understanding the factors which contribute to the formation of positive attitudes toward violence would lead quite directly to a better understanding of the factors that lead to violent behaviors. Indeed, our current data show that attitudes are related to behaviors, although there is not yet proof concerning the direction of causality. Political scientists have theorized mainly about the origin of politically violent behaviors. However, it seems reasonable

to assume that the variables which have been cited by political scientists as causal in civil strife should relate to our measures of attitudes
toward political violence, that is, violence directed at producing social
change.

In this chapter the relationship between attitudes toward violence
for social change and some of the variables which have been thought to
play a causal role in politically oriented civil violence will be examined.
These variables are political trust or political cynicism, political alienation, and relative deprivation. In addition, a personality variable will
be considered in relation to attitudes toward violence for social change,
namely, the extent to which the individual believes that he has control over his own fate, that is, the beliefs generally summarized under
the rubric of internal-external control. None of these variables turns
out to be as powerful a predictor of attitudes toward violence for
social change as those cited in our original model (Blumenthal et al.
1972, p. 17), but the data suggest some modifications in theory, underscore some of the complexities which need to be taken into account
in constructing theories about civil violence, and raise some interesting
questions which hopefully will be answered by future research.

One might ask, why bother the reader with data about hypotheses
which are only weakly supported and sometimes not supported at all?
But the theories we consider here are plausible and have won a considerable place for themselves in the social science literature. Our
measures have now been given substantial validity and we understand
their defects. If we cannot find support for these theories within the
framework of our instrumentation, serious doubt is cast on the validity
of the theories tested. This alone would excuse the presentation of
many negative results; but more than this, the data do suggest modification and improvement which may well lead to theories which will be
substantiated by a variety of data. It is precisely such change and modification which allows understanding to move forward, however slow and
painful the process.

## POLITICAL CYNICISM AND ATTITUDES TOWARD
## VIOLENCE FOR SOCIAL CHANGE

There is a body of political theory which states that the potential
for political violence is related to the extent to which the public views
the political authority structure with confidence and trust. The notion of
trust in government was developed by Easton (1965, pp. 267-340) under
the rubric of "diffuse support" for the regime and was developed
further by Gamson (1968, pp. 39-52) who refers to such support as
"political trust." Gamson (1968, p. 48) states that low political trust

combined with high political efficacy (that is, the belief that influence is both possible and necessary) is an optimal combination for mobilization. Conversely, he states that alienated groups, when these are defined as those who have little trust in government and perceive themselves as having little influence on governmental processes, are more likely than others to rely on constraints or force in dealing with the political structure. Aberbach and Walker (1970a) comment similarly that the rise and fall of political trust is an important barometer of social conflicts and tensions. They state that if a political system is sufficiently flexible to make the adjustments required by those who are distrustful, outbursts of violence which might otherwise be generated can be avoided. Moreover, they contend that if distrustful groups are denied access to decision makers or if the institutions are too rigid to change, destructive conflict and breakdown in the social order become more likely.

Muller (1972) divides political trust into three components: (1) endorsement of the legitimating ideology of the regime, that is, the values and norms that constitute its rationale; (2) conviction that regime structure consists of worthy institutions; and (3) trust in the public officials who wield the power in the regime. He finds that there is a moderate relationship between a measure which he labels "Trust in the Political Authorities" and a measure of "Potential for Political Violence" (Muller 1972). Unfortunately, eight of Muller's eighteen items measuring "Trust in the Political Authorities" are items which probably measure identification with the police which we regard as a variable distinct from trust in government. It is already known that identification with the police is correlated with attitudes toward the use of violence for social change (Blumenthal et al. 1972, p. 165). In addition, six of Muller's eighteen items inquire about fairness in the courts, a factor which has been shown to influence attitudes toward violence (Blumenthal et al. 1972, p. 61). Thus, it is not clear that Muller actually tested the specific hypothesis that trust in government is related to the potential for political violence, since the positive relationship between "Trust in the Political Authorities" and "Potential for Political Violence" which he finds might be due either to identification with police or fairness in the courts. Whether diffuse support for the regime is related to "Potential for Political Violence" remains to be tested. Other researchers also report some evidence that trust in government is related to attitudes toward violence. Aberbach and Walker (1970a) find that political trust is related to positive responses to the question "Can you imagine a situation in which you would riot?" Unfortunately, this question which asks the respondent about his proclivities toward violence is not clearly worded. One does not know whether the respondent is replying that he can imagine a situation (perhaps, a wildly bizarre one which is unlikely to happen) or whether he is saying ''yes,'' there are circumstances (not too different from those current) in which he would riot.

In the 1972 interview the hypothesis that political trust is related to political violence was tested by examining the relationships between the Survey Research Center's (SRC) Political Cynicism Scale (Robinson, Rusk, and Head 1972) and the Violence for Social Change and Protest Behaviors Indices. The theory suggested in the literature implies that there should be correlations between political cynicism and positive attitudes toward violence and protest behaviors.

The Political Cynicism Scale, which has been used extensively in national surveys, consists of the following items:

*Do you think people in the government waste **a lot** of the money we pay in taxes, waste **some** of it, or **don't waste very much of it?***

*How much of the time do you think you can trust the government in Washington to do what is right—**just about always**, **most of the time**, or only **some of the time?***

*Would you say the government is pretty much run by a **few big interests** looking out for themselves, or that it is run for the **benefit of all** the people?*

*Do you feel that almost all of the people running the government are smart people who usually **know what they are doing**, or do you think that quite a few of them **don't seem to know what they're doing?***

*Do you think **quite a few** of the people running the government are a little crooked, **not very many are**, or do you think **hardly any** of them are crooked at all?*

The percentage distribution for white, black, and all respondents is given in Table 3.1. It can be seen that there were substantial black-white differences with respect to some but not all of the items. Similar proportions of black and white respondents agreed that the government wastes a lot of the taxpayers' money. The same is true for the item inquiring whether the government is run by a few big interests or for the benefit of all, although blacks were slightly more cynical than whites. However, black respondents were substantially more cynical than

**Table 3.1**

Percentage Responses to Items Measuring Political Cynicism

|  | All Respondents | Whites | Blacks |
|---|---|---|---|
| **Government wastes taxes** | | | |
| Not Very Much | 7% | 4% | 9% |
| Some | 32 | 35 | 28 |
| A Lot | 61 | 61 | 63 |
|  | 100% | 100% | 100% |
| **Government can be trusted** | | | |
| Just about Always | 9 | 12 | 6 |
| Most of the Time | 30 | 44 | 15 |
| Some of the Time | 61 | 44 | 79 |
|  | 100% | 100% | 100% |
| **Government is run by few big interests** | | | |
| Benefit of All | 45 | 51 | 38 |
| Few Big Interests | 55 | 49 | 62 |
|  | 100% | 100% | 100% |
| **Government people know what they're doing** | | | |
| Know What They're Doing | 41 | 53 | 29 |
| Don't Know What They're Doing | 59 | 47 | 71 |
|  | 100% | 100% | 100% |
| **People in government are crooked** | | | |
| Hardly Any | 16 | 22 | 9 |
| Not Very Many | 41 | 49 | 32 |
| Quite a Few | 43 | 29 | 59 |
|  | 100% | 100% | 100% |
| N | (283) | (145) | (133) |

whites on the remaining items. These differences between black and white respondents were similar to responses obtained in surveys of national samples. Indeed, the percentage responses of white respondents in our study population were within a few percentage points of the distributions found among respondents in the 1970 and 1972 pre-election study (Miller, Brown, and Raine 1973).[1] The one exception to this observation is that in the 1972 pre-election study substantially more respondents in the national sample thought that "quite a few" of the people running the government were crooked than was true for our population. Nevertheless, it is interesting to know that the respondents in our population showed response distributions very similar to those found in a representative national population.

    [1] The percentage of blacks in the United States population is approximately 11 percent; consequently, the percentage distributions in national surveys reflect mainly white opinion. Since blacks and whites differ substantially in their scores on the political cynicism items, white respondents would be the most appropriate comparison group in our data for a national sample where the data are not given separately for the two races.

Four of the five items in the SRC Political Cynicism Scale were combined into an index, the Political Cynicism Index. The fifth item, "Do you feel that almost all of the people running the government are smart people who usually know what they are doing, or do you think that quite a few of them don't seem to know what they're doing," did not relate consistently to the others and was omitted from the index (see Appendix E for details of index construction).[2] The higher the score on the index, the more the respondent expressed cynical beliefs about government.

Table 3.2 shows the relationship between the Political Cynicism Index and selected demographic characteristics. It can be seen that there is a moderate relationship between the index and race. Black

**Table 3.2**

Relationships between the Political Cynicism Index
and Selected Demographic Characteristics
(all respondents, N = 283)
(gammas)

| Demographic Characteristic | Gamma |
|---|---|
| Race | .38§ |
| Sex | -.06 |
| Age | .11 |
| Education | -.04 |
| Family Income | -.14† |
| Town Size | .21‡ |
| Experience in South | -.10 |

†p < .05      ‡p < .01      §p < .001

respondents were substantially more likely to score high on the Political Cynicism Index than were whites (Table 3.3). Otherwise, relationships between the index and demographic variables are small. Moreover, the relationship between the Political Cynicism Index and town size is not maintained within race (among white respondents political cynicism relates to town size with a gamma of .09; among blacks -.01). Consequently, it may be concluded that the apparent association is largely a reflection of the fact that black respondents tended to score higher than whites on the index and were more likely to be found in urban locations. That trivial associations were found between political cynicism and

[2] The fact that this item does not fit with the others is interesting since the item probably has a double frame of reference. One interpretation is that the cynical response would be, "quite a few people in the government don't know what they're doing." Another interpretation is that the most cynical response would be, "of course they know what they're doing—(the bastards)." One would not expect an item with such a double frame of reference to correlate with items that have a clear cut meaning because of the statistical "noise" created by the response heterogeneity.

Table 3.3

Percentage Responses to the Political Cynicism Index
in Relation to Race

| Political Cynicism Index | | Whites | Blacks |
|---|---|---|---|
| Low | 1 | 32% | 12% |
| | 2 | 24 | 20 |
| | 3 | 26 | 35 |
| High | 4 | 18 | 33 |
| | | 100% | 100% |
| | N | (145) | (133) |

demographic characteristics such as education and family income is similar to findings reported by Aberbach and Walker (1970a) in a study of black and white Detroiters.

Table 3.4 shows the relationship between the Political Cynicism Index and the Violence for Social Change and Protest Behaviors Indices for white, black, and all respondents. The relationships are small and there is no association between the two measures among white respondents. There is, however, a small association found among black respondents.

Table 3.4

Relationships between the Political Cynicism Index
and the Violence for Social Change and Protest Behaviors Indices
(gammas)

| | N | Violence for Social Change Index | Protest Behaviors Index |
|---|---|---|---|
| All Respondents | (283) | .19‡ | .20‡ |
| Whites | (145) | -.02 | .01 |
| Blacks | (133) | -.21† | .30‡ |

†p < .05      ‡p < .005

Table 3.5 shows the distribution of responses on the Violence for Social Change Index in relation to political cynicism among black respondents. It can be seen that only 32 percent of those who were low on the Political Cynicism Index scored in the high category of the Violence for Social Change Index, while 52 percent of those who scored high on the Political Cynicism Index fell in the high category of the Violence for Social Change Index. Thus, for black respondents there is a definite association between political cynicism and positive attitudes toward the use of violence to produce change.

**Table 3.5**

Percentage Responses to the Violence for Social Change Index
in Relation to the Political Cynicism Index
(black respondents, N = 133)

|  | Political Cynicism Index | | |
|---|---|---|---|
| | Low | | High |
| Violence for Social Change Index | 1-2 | 3 | 4 |
| Low    1-2 | 35% | 20% | 20% |
|       3-4 | 33 | 32 | 28 |
| High   5-7 | 32 | 48 | 52 |
| | 100% | 100% | 100% |
| N * | (34) | (44) | (36) |

Table 3.6 shows the relationship between the Protest Behaviors Index and the Political Cynicism Index among black respondents. Among those who fell in the highest category on the Political Cynicism Index, 68 percent fell in the two highest categories of the Protest Behaviors Index in contrast to only 38 percent of blacks in the lowest categories of the Political Cynicism Index. So, for blacks in this population there appears to be a high degree of political distrust among those who reported themselves willing to undertake protest activities. Whether there is also a relationship among blacks between political cynicism and actual protest behaviors, violent and nonviolent, remains to be seen. But, one might reasonably speculate that such a relationship probably exists. While what people say they will do and what they actually do in the end are not necessarily the same. statements indicating willingness to behave do represent the individual's assessment of the

**Table 3.6**

Percentage Responses to the Protest Behaviors Index
in Relation to the Political Cynicism Index
(black respondents, N = 133)

|  | Political Cynicism Index | | |
|---|---|---|---|
| | Low | | High |
| Protest Behaviors Index | 1-2 | 3 | 4 |
| Low    1 | 29% | 11% | 16% |
|       2 | 33 | 31 | 16 |
|       3 | 31 | 34 | 40 |
| High   4 | 7 | 24 | 28 |
| | 100% | 100% | 100% |
| N * | (42) | (45) | (43) |

probability that he will behave in a given way, and such statements of willingness to behave can be taken as statements of intent or approximations of behavior. This analysis indicates some support for the hypothesis that political cynicism is associated with a predilection for political violence, although the hypothesis is supported mainly by data from the black segment of the population in this study, since the level of association among all respondents was rather small.

## Political Orientation and Political Cynicism

It is interesting that the associations between the Violence for Social Change and Protest Behaviors Indices and the Political Cynicism Index are true for black but not white respondents. Since it seems unreasonable that a political theory should be applicable to only one race, alternative explanations for the phenomenon must be sought. Miller et al. (1973) have pointed out that those who are politically cynical can be divided into two categories. Some are dissatisfied because the government is moving too slowly to solve social problems such as racial discrimination and income distribution; others are dissatisfied because they believe that too much is being done to solve these problems while not enough is being done to solve problems related to social control. Some people in the United States are greatly in favor of and preoccupied with social control; one such group, those who voted for Wallace, made clear both their desire for law and order and their distrust of the existing order. Thus, among those who are very similar in the extent of their political cynicism, there are people who have totally different policy preferences. This heterogeneity of political preferences among the politically cynical may provide some explanation for the findings among white respondents in this study. The Violence for Social Change Index is probably an instrument which is more oriented toward the political left than the right. It is true that a right-oriented individual might score high on the scenario in the index which inquires how much violence is necessary to bring about change in general; it is unlikely that such an individual would score high on the scenario which asks how much violence is necessary to bring about changes needed by blacks. Social change ameliorating the disadvantages endured by blacks in our culture is an issue more likely to be endorsed by the liberally oriented than by others. Such considerations make it reasonable to suppose that politically right-wing individuals would score low on the Violence for Social Change Index, while they might very well score high on the Political Cynicism Index. It seems reasonable to speculate that many black respondents are liberally oriented politically and that there would be relatively few blacks who are oriented toward the political right. If this were correct, it would follow that blacks who are cynical about government are more likely to be cynics of the left than cynics of the right. Consequently, it may be that the associations between the Political Cynicism Index and the Violence for Social Change and Protest Behaviors Indices among blacks are true not so much because the population is black but because the population is more oriented to the political left than the right. It is also probably true that there are more individuals with right-wing political beliefs among whites than among blacks. However, not all whites are oriented to the right by any means; many are of liberal or moderate persuasion. Consequently, among white respondents one would expect a mixture of cynics of the right and of the left. If one had knowledge of the individual's beliefs about political issues, one might find that the Violence for Social Change Index is positively associated with political cynicism among those who are oriented toward the left and negatively associated with political cynicism among those who are oriented toward the right. If such were the case, one would expect the associations to disappear when the two populations are viewed together.

While not ideal for the purpose, there are data in the interview which lend themselves to a test of this hypothesis. Included in the interview were a series of items which asked the respondent how much political power he thought was held by various groups. The exact question was as follows:

> Now we would like to ask your opinion about how much political power different groups or people have in the United States. I mean how much power they have to get laws passed in their favor. Do you think that labor unions have **too much power, about the right amount of power,** or have **too little power** in this country?

The respondent was then asked his opinion about poor people, the military, young people, blacks, women, black militants, senior citizens, and big business. The percentage responses to these questions are given in Table 3.7. It can be seen that most black and white respondents believed that poor people and senior citizens have too little political power and that big business has too much. About a third of each group believed that the military have too much political power, while very few believe they have too little. Opinions of black and white respondents did not differ sharply with respect to the political power of women and young people, although black respondents were slightly more inclined than white to believe that these groups need more political power. However, there was a substantial difference between black and white respondents' views regarding labor unions. Interestingly enough,

**Table 3.7**

Percentage Responses to Items Inquiring about
the Political Power of Specific Groups
(all respondents, N = 283; whites, N = 145; blacks, N = 133)

|  | Too Much | About Right | Too Little |
|---|---|---|---|
| **Labor Unions** | | | |
| All Respondents | 39% | 45 | 16 |
| Whites | 57% | 39 | 4 |
| Blacks | 20% | 51 | 29 |
| **Poor People** | | | |
| All Respondents | 1% | 9 | 90 |
| Whites | 1% | 14 | 85 |
| Blacks | 0% | 5 | 95 |
| **The Military** | | | |
| All Respondents | 35% | 56 | 9 |
| Whites | 36% | 57 | 7 |
| Blacks | 34% | 56 | 10 |
| **Young People** | | | |
| All Respondents | 16% | 51 | 33 |
| Whites | 21% | 51 | 28 |
| Blacks | 12% | 51 | 37 |
| **Blacks** | | | |
| All Respondents | 8% | 37 | 55 |
| Whites | 12% | 59 | 29 |
| Blacks | 4% | 14 | 82 |
| **Women** | | | |
| All Respondents | 5% | 51 | 44 |
| Whites | 3% | 59 | 38 |
| Blacks | 7% | 44 | 49 |
| **Black Militants** | | | |
| All Respondents | 47% | 37 | 16 |
| Whites | 67% | 29 | 4 |
| Blacks | 26% | 46 | 28 |
| **Senior Citizens** | | | |
| All Respondents | 3% | 37 | 60 |
| Whites | 2% | 37 | 61 |
| Blacks | 4% | 38 | 58 |
| **Big Business** | | | |
| All Respondents | 77% | 22 | 1 |
| Whites | 80% | 20 | 0 |
| Blacks | 73% | 26 | 1 |

Note: Percentages across each row total 100%.

blacks were more inclined to believe unions have too little political power, while the majority of white respondents believed unions have too much. This difference in belief may be related to the fact that blacks have yet to establish themselves in large numbers in those positions where the union influence for better pay and working conditions has been strong. There were also marked racial differences on the question which asked how much power is held by blacks and black militants, black respondents being far more likely than whites to think these two groups have too little power.

One might have expected that respondents would have similar opinions about a number of these groups. For example, one might have thought respondents would hold similar attitudes toward the political power of poor people, blacks, women, and young people since these groups have been the objects of considerable concern to individuals with liberal orientations toward social problems. One might also have thought that big business and the military would be linked in people's assessments since these groups constitute the much discussed military-industrial complex. In fact, analysis demonstrated that opinions about the political power of the groups mentioned did not form such clusters. Rather, there appear to be diverse viewpoints which considered the claims to political power for each group separately. Nevertheless, it is possible to identify among the respondents a group of people who believed that poor people, blacks, and women have too little political power. Such individuals might well be oriented to the left on political issues, and we will define them as having a left political orientation. In addition, a group of individuals can be identified who believe that either poor people, or blacks, or women, or young people have too much political power. One could imagine that respondents making such responses would tend to be oriented to the right politically. This group will be our operational definition of right orientation. These definitions are, of course, operational and therefore arbitrary. Their arbitrariness should be kept in mind in the following discussion.

### Political Cynicism and Attitudes Toward Violence
### Among Cynics of the Left and Right

Our previous speculation suggests that among those who are oriented toward the left, as defined above, increased political cynicism should be associated with more positive attitudes toward violence and with a higher degree of willingness to engage in protest behaviors, while this will not be so among those who are oriented to the right. Table 3.8 shows that such appears to the case. The table shows that the expected association between political cynicism and positive attitudes toward violence for social change appears among those who stated that blacks, the poor, and women have too little political power, and there is also a trend in that direction on the Protest Behaviors Index. Table 3.9 shows that, among those who were oriented toward the left on political issues, 66 percent of those who were high on the Political Cynicism Index were also high on the Violence for Social Change Index. Only 20 percent of those low on the Political Cynicism Index fell in the four highest Violence for Social Change categories. Among those who were oriented toward the right, no relationship between either the Violence for Social Change or the Protest Behavior Indices and Political Cynicism appears. Indeed, there are small negative relationships. So, it appears that political orientation is a factor which moderates the relationship between political cynicism and positive attitudes toward violence and protest.

**Table 3.8**

Relationships between the Political Cynicism Index and
the Violence for Social Change and Protest Behaviors Indices
for Respondents with either Left or Right Political Orientation

| | | Left Political Orientation † | Right Political Orientation‡ |
|---|---|---|---|
| Violence for Social Change Index | | .36§ | -.12 |
| Protest Behaviors Index | | .20 | -.09 |
| | N | (69) | (50) |

†This group consists of all respondents stating that poor people, blacks, and women had too little power.

‡This group consists of all respondents stating that either poor people, young people, blacks, or women had too much political power.

§p < .01

**Table 3.9**

Percentage Responses to the Violence for Social Change Index
in Relation to the Political Cynicism Index
for Respondents with Left Political Orientation
(respondents with left political orientation, N = 69)

| | | Political Cynicism Index | |
|---|---|---|---|
| | | Low | High |
| Violence for Social Change Index | | 1-2 | 3-4 |
| Low    1-3 | | 80% | 34% |
| High    4-7 | | 20 | 66 |
| | | 100% | 100% |
| | N * | (25) | (38) |

Our exploration of this hypothesis is meager and limited by the data available in the interview; nevertheless, the hypothesis is important and deserves more thorough exploration in future research. One might speculate that if the analysis could be conducted among those who scored low on the Avoid Problems Index and were also politically oriented toward the left, the relations might be even higher. It seems intuitively appealing that cynicism about what the government will do should be directly related to attitudes that violent protest is necessary to bring about change and to the willingness to undertake such protest among those who are both oriented toward the left and willing to engender difficulty on behalf of a cause. Unfortunately, the number of cases in these data is not large enough to allow a test of this hypothesis.

It seems reasonable to inquire whether there were any substantial demographic differences between the left-oriented and right-oriented respondents which might account for the differences in the relationships of their scores on the Political Cynicism and the Violence for Social Change Indices. Table 3.10 shows that there were proportionately more black than white respondents among those with a left political orientation and fewer among those with a right orientation. Only 31 percent of the former are white in contrast to 63 percent of the latter. Since the data show that political cynicism is associated with positive attitudes toward violence for social change among black but not white respondents, it would be desirable to conduct an analysis among left- and right-oriented individuals separately for the two races. Unfortunately, the size of the population investigated was too small to allow it. Nevertheless, since there were members of both races in both

**Table 3.10**

Race in Relation to Political Orientation
(percentage distribution)

|  |  | Left Political Orientation | Other | Right Political Orientation |
|---|---|---|---|---|
| Whites |  | 31% | 58% | 63% |
| Blacks |  | 69 | 42 | 37 |
|  |  | 100% | 100% | 100% |
|  | N | (69) | (164) | (50) |

groups, it seems unlikely that race is the only determinant of the results.

Table 3.11 shows that women were slightly overrepresented among both those with left and right political orientation, so the association between the Political Cynicism Index and the Violence for Social

Change Index cannot be due to differences in the distribution of the two sexes on the political spectrum.

**Table 3.11**

Sex in Relation to Political Orientation
(percentage distribution)

|  |  | Left Political Orientation | Other | Right Political Orientation |
|---|---|---|---|---|
| Men |  | 36% | 53% | 38% |
| Women |  | 64 | 47 | 62 |
|  |  | 100% | 100% | 100% |
|  | N | (69) | (164) | (50) |

As Table 3.12 shows, respondents with a right political orientation were somewhat less educated than both those who were oriented toward the left and those who fell in neither category. It would be helpful to control the effects of education in a more definitive analysis; however, education has only a small relationship to the Violence for Social

**Table 3.12**

Respondent's Level of Education
in Relation to Political Orientation

| Education |  | Left Political Orientation | Other | Right Political Orientation |
|---|---|---|---|---|
| 9 Years or Less |  | 18% | 25% | 32% |
| 10-11 Years |  | 30 | 25 | 36 |
| High School Graduate |  | 30 | 26 | 16 |
| At Least Some College |  | 22 | 24 | 16 |
|  |  | 100% | 100% | 100% |
|  | N | (69) | (164) | (50) |

Change Index and virtually none to either the Protest Behaviors or the Political Cynicism Indices. Consequently, it is unlikely that the profound differences in the relation of political cynicism to positive attitudes toward violence and willingness to undertake protest could be accounted for by educational differences between the right- and left-oriented groups. In addition to the apparent differences in education, those with a left orientation were proportionately younger than those with a right-wing political orientation (Table 3.13).

In summary, it appears that there were differences in age, race, and education associated with the political orientations described. This

**Table 3.13**

Age Distribution of Respondents
with Left, Right, or Other Political Orientation

| Age | Left Political Orientation | Other | Right Political Orientation |
|---|---|---|---|
| 29 Years or Younger | 45% | 39% | 18% |
| 30-39 Years | 21 | 17 | 14 |
| 40-49 Years | 12 | 17 | 18 |
| 50-59 Years | 13 | 9 | 28 |
| 60 Years or Older | 9 | 18 | 22 |
| | 100% | 100% | 100% |
| N | (69) | (164) | (50) |

is hardly surprising; one would expect a more liberal orientation among a younger population which contained a higher proportion of blacks and that a right orientation would be more prominent among older, less educated individuals. However, it is unlikely that these variables alone determine the differences in a relationship between the Political Cynicism Index and the Violence for Social Change Index in the two extreme groups. Nevertheless, it would be comforting if the observation could be repeated in a dataset which is large enough to allow for the analyses which would control for these demographic differences.

The data cited above do not supply unequivocal support for the hypothesis that political trust is directly related to the potential for political violence. The results obtained here show support for the hypothesis only among black respondents and those who were politically oriented toward the left. The data do underscore how complex any adequate theory will have to be before it will be possible to accurately predict behavior from attitudes. Clearly no simple minded notions will have predictive power. The relationships, like life itself, are too complicated. Nevertheless, even if further work were to show that political cynicism increases the tendency toward violent protest only among blacks and those who are politically oriented toward the left, the association would be an important one. Revolts and revolutions do not require majorities. Indeed, political violence is often perpetrated by very small groups. The sample used in this study was small and not representative, so the findings can only be generalized very cautiously; in spite of this they are intriguing. Much collective violence in the United States in recent years has been related to racial problems and other social issues which are primarily of concern to those with liberal orientations. If cynicism toward government moves blacks and their

liberal supporters closer to violence, it is a matter for serious consideration. Recently, a great deal of evidence has indicated a substantial
decline in the degree of trust with which Americans view their government (Miller 1972). Clearly, such trends are not likely to reduce the
propensity for violence in this country. If lack of trust in the government
breeds violence, then it behooves the government to make itself more
trustworthy. At the present moment in history, major efforts would
have to be made by the federal government to bring about such trust.

The data presented bear on one type of violence that might be
used to further a specific set of goals. But, the paradigm may be far
more general than the specifics laid out here. Stated in general terms,
the paradigm would be as follows: cynicism about government will be
related to a belief that violence is necessary to bring about a specific
result among those who perceive that result as essential. In this form the
paradigm has many applications; for example, one might consider the
1973 disruptions and violence caused by truckers whose goal was a
reduction in gasoline prices. One might guess that the truckers felt
profoundly cynical about the government's willingness to act in their
behalf. The result—serious disruption and violence used as a bargaining chip.

There are many situations in the United States which contain the
same elements: a much desired goal and cynicism about the government's good intentions or willingness to act. It should be possible to
identify these situations with appropriate questions and, one would
hope, to ameliorate the problems before violence erupts.

## Political Cynicism and the Avoid Problems Index

Since the major hypothesis suggested by the work of Easton
(1965), Gamson (1968), Muller (1972), and others that a lack of diffuse
support for the regime is related to the potential for political violence
is only partially supported by these data, it seems reasonable to test
some alternative hypotheses. It is possible to view political cynicism as
a specific form of frustration, that is frustration with government. Presumably, if one thinks that the people in the government are crooked,
are likely to do less than their best, are not to be trusted, and are wasting
the taxpayers' money, one is likely to feel some frustration about it.
Interestingly enough, the Political Cynicism Index does not show much
relationship to the Resentment-Suspicion Index, which is the measure
of frustration used in this study. (Among all respondents the gamma is
only .17, while it is .09 among whites and -.02 among blacks.) Consequently, although political cynicism may be a specific frustration, it
apparently does not increase general frustration. However, previous

experience with frustration as measured by the Resentment-Suspicion Index demonstrated that the relationship between the Resentment-Suspicion Index and the Violence for Social Change Index can be substantially modified by the Avoid Problems Index (cf. Chapter 2). Consequently, reasoning that the Political Cynicism Index might be vulnerable to a similar effect since it is also a kind of frustration, a parallel analysis was conducted. The hypothesis tested was that among those who have a vested interest in avoiding difficulty there will be no relationship between political cynicism and positive attitudes toward violence, while among those who have no compunctions about staying out of trouble a positive relationship will exist. However, Table 3.14 shows that the Avoid Problems Index does not moderate the relationship between the Political Cynicism Index and either the Violence for Social Change or Protest Behaviors Indices. None of the differences between the size of the gammas reach significant levels.[3]

**Table 3.14**

Relationships between the Political Cynicism Index and
the Violence for Social Change and Protest Behaviors Indices
for Respondents with Low and High Scores
on the Avoid Problems Index
(gammas)

| Violence for Social Change Index | N | Low Avoid Problems (Score 1-3) | N | High Avoid Problems (Score 4-6) |
|---|---|---|---|---|
| All Respondents | (144) | .23‡ | (137) | .15 |
| Whites | ( 86) | .01 | ( 58) | -.08 |
| Blacks | ( 56) | .22 | ( 76) | .17 |
| Protest Behaviors Index | | | | |
| All Respondents | (144) | .15 | (137) | .24† |
| Whites | ( 86) | -.09 | ( 58) | .13 |
| Blacks | ( 56) | .41‡ | ( 76) | .22 |

†p < .05        ‡p < .01

## Political Cynicism as a Moderator Variable

One additional possibility remains: political cynicism might have a moderating action rather than a direct effect. It is conceivable, for example, that feelings of resentment and frustration are more likely to

---

[3] The significance of the differences between the gamma pairs was tested according to the method of Goodman and Kruskal (1963).

be positively related to positive attitudes toward violence among those who are cynical about the government than among those who trust the government. Presumably, those who trust the government believe that it will act beneficially to reduce frustration. Indeed, the idea that political cynicism acts as a moderating variable rather than having a direct effect on violence is appealing. One can imagine that there might be people who are quite cynical about the government but who are not personally frustrated or needy. One would think that such people would be unlikely to act violently to produce social change unless they are strongly identified with others and were to do so for purely ideological or altruistic reasons. One might also think that persons who were both politically cynical and suffering from frustration would be likely to believe that violence is necessary to bring about social change and to act violently to bring about that change.

Table 3.15 shows that this hypothesis is not clearly substantiated. When all respondents are considered, the relationship between the Resentment-Suspicion Index and Violence for Social Change is not different among those who were low on cynicism and those who were high. When white respondents are considered alone, a difference of the type postulated appears. Among those who were cynical about the government, feelings of frustration were related to the attitude that violent protest is necessary to bring about change. Among whites who were not cynical about government, such a relationship did not exist. However, this shift in relationships was not to be found among black respondents. Indeed, there was a trend in the opposite direction;

**Table 3.15**

Relationships between the Violence for Social Change Index and
the Resentment-Suspicion Index for Respondents
with Low and High Scores on the Political Cynicism Index
(gammas)

|  | N | Low Political Cynicism (Score 1-2) | N | High Political Cynicism (Score 3-4) |
|---|---|---|---|---|
| All Respondents | (124) | .27† | (153) | .34§ |
| Whites | ( 81) | .10 | ( 64) | .45‡ |
| Blacks | ( 43) | .31 | ( 89) | .09 |

†p < .01        ‡p < .005        §p < .001

however, the number of black respondents who scored low on the Political Cynicism Index was so small that the finding among this group must be regarded with skepticism.

*Summary*

The hypothesis that political cynicism is related to the potential for political violence has been examined by investigating the relationship of the Political Cynicism Index to the Violence for Social Change Index and the Protest Behaviors Index. The hypothesis was only weakly supported when all respondents were considered together. Among black respondents political cynicism appeared to be related both to attitudes toward violence for social change and to the behaviors that the respondent was willing to undertake in behalf of change. Among white respondents no relationship appeared between political cynicism and either attitudes toward violence for social change or the level of protest behavior the respondent was willing to undertake. However, when respondents were divided into those who were politically oriented toward the left and those oriented toward the right, the association between the Political Cynicism Index and the Violence for Social Change Index appeared to hold for those with a left orientation. This finding suggests that the political orientation of the individual must be taken into account in understanding the relationship between political cynicism and potential for political violence. This paradigm may very well have considerable generality and might best be stated as follows: political cynicism will lead to an increased potential for political violence in any group which strongly desires specific goals and which believes these goals will not come about in the ordinary course of events. Unfortunately, these data are suggestive rather than conclusive because the small number of cases makes it impossible to explore all the possible alternative explanations of the results. Nevertheless, the data suggest that the basic hypothesis that political cynicism or trust in government is related to the potential for political violence does deserve further investigation in future research which has a sufficiently large data base to make the indicated analyses possible.

## POLITICAL ALIENATION
## AND ATTITUDES TOWARD VIOLENCE FOR SOCIAL CHANGE

An important variant of the hypothesis that political trust or cynicism is related to political violence is that those who are politically alienated will be more likely to resort to violence than those who are not. According to Gamson (1968, p. 42) alienation contains two dimensions: political trust (or cynicism) and political efficacy. The concept of political efficacy was originally developed by Campbell, Gurin, and Miller (1954, p. 187) who define it as the "feeling that individual political action does have, or can have, an impact upon the political process." It has been studied in relation to political participation in a variety of surveys (Campbell et al. 1960, pp. 103-105; Converse 1972, pp. 325-357).

According to Gamson (1968), the alienated are those who are distrustful of government and feel they have little or no influence in the conventional political system. Gamson suggests that such groups are likely to rely on constraints as a means of bringing about change. He points out that the alienated have little to lose by resorting to violence since they cannot fear further loss of influence in a political process in which they have no influence and which is unlikely to act in their behalf. Gamson's hypothesis suggests that those who are high on political cynicism and low in their perceived political efficacy should be likely to have favorable attitudes toward the use of violence and greater willingness to use forceful protest behaviors.

Four items were included in the reinterview of the 1972 survey which bear on the question of political efficacy. These were:

> *How much political power do you think people like you have? (A great deal, Some, Not very much, None)*

> *Do you think that people like you have **too little** political power, or **just about the right amount?***

> *If you made an effort to change this (unjust or harmful) law, how likely is it that you would succeed: **very likely, somewhat likely, not very likely, not likely at all?***[4]

> *Have you ever done anything to try to influence a national decision? (Yes, No)*

The percentage distribution for white, black, and all respondents is given in Table 3.16. Black respondents were more apt to give responses indicating feelings of low political efficacy than were whites. For example, more black than white respondents felt they had no political power or not very much. It is interesting that in relation to changing an unjust law black and white respondents saw themselves as having a similar level of political influence; two-thirds of both groups thought it unlikely that they could have any effect in changing a harmful law. However, black respondents were more apt to regard themselves as politically powerless than were whites. Thus, one might speculate that while the two groups assessed themselves similarly with respect to the actual amount of political power that they possessed, blacks saw a greater need for such power than did whites. It is interesting in this respect that more black than white respondents had attempted to in-

---

[4] This question was preceded by an open-ended one which read "Suppose a law was being considered by the Congress in Washington, and you thought the law was very unjust or harmful. What do you think you could do about it?"

fluence national decisions (Table 3.16). This finding suggests that black respondents perceived a greater need for influence than did whites and were more likely to act to exert such influence.

Of the four items in the interview which inquired about the respondent's sense of political efficacy, only two related to each other with sufficient consistency to allow index construction. These two, the first two items in Table 3.16, were combined into the Respondent's Political Power Index. The higher the score on the index, the more the

### Table 3.16

Percentage Responses to Items Inquiring about the
Political Power of the Respondent
(1972 reinterview)

| | All Respondents | Whites | Blacks |
|---|---|---|---|
| How much political power do you think people like you have? | | | |
| A Great Deal | 2% | 3% | 1% |
| Some | 30 | 38 | 22 |
| Not Very Much | 49 | 42 | 55 |
| None | 19 | 17 | 22 |
| | 100% | 100% | 100% |
| Do you think that people like you have too little political power, or just about the right amount? | | | |
| Too Little | 59 | 46 | 72 |
| About the Right Amount | 41 | 54 | 28 |
| | 100% | 100% | 100% |
| If you made an effort to change this (unjust or harmful) law, how likely is it that you would succeed? | | | |
| Very Likely | 6 | 5 | 8 |
| Somewhat Likely | 27 | 27 | 26 |
| Not Very Likely | 36 | 42 | 30 |
| Not Likely at All | 31 | 26 | 36 |
| | 100% | 100% | 100% |
| Have you ever done anything to try to influence a national decision? | | | |
| Yes | 77 | 66 | 89 |
| No | 23 | 34 | 11 |
| | 100% | 100% | 100% |
| N | (240) | (120) | (116) |

Note: In this and all subsequent tables using the reinterview data, the total sample size is decreased since 15 percent of respondents did not complete the reinterview.

respondent perceived himself as having political efficacy. (See Appendix E for details of index construction.)

Table 3.17 shows the demographic correlates of the Respondent's Political Power Index. As might have been expected, black respondents scored lower on the index than did white. The percentage distribution for this relationship is given in Table 3.18, which shows that 60

**Table 3.17**

Relationships between the Respondent's Political Power Index
and Selected Demographic Characteristics
(1972 reinterview respondents, N = 240)
(gammas)

| Demographic Characteristic | Gamma |
|---|---|
| Race | -.37§ |
| Sex | .04 |
| Age | .09 |
| Education | .18‡ |
| Family Income | .16† |
| Town Size | -.05 |
| Experience in South | .15 |

†p < .05        ‡p < .01        §p < .001

percent of black respondents fell in the two lowest categories of the index in contrast to only 33 percent of white. Clearly, blacks in this population perceived themselves as having less political efficacy than

**Table 3.18**

Percentage Responses to the Respondent's Political Power Index
in Relation to Race
(1972 reinterview)

| Respondent's Political Power Index | | | Whites | Blacks |
|---|---|---|---|---|
| Low | 1-2 | | 33% | 60% |
| | 3-4 | | 39 | 28 |
| High | 5 | | 28 | 12 |
| | | | 100% | 100% |
| | | N | (120) | (116) |

whites. Table 3.17 also shows small relationships to income and education in the expected direction. Those with lower incomes or less education were likely to view themselves as having less political efficacy; however, these relationships are not large enough to exert much influence on the analysis which follows.

Table 3.19 shows the relationship between the Respondent's Political Power Index and the Violence for Social Change and Protest Behaviors Indices. There are no significant relationships

**Table 3.19**

Relationships between the Respondent's Political Power Index and the Violence for Social Change and Protest Behaviors Indices
(1972 reinterview)
(gammas)

|  | N | Violence for Social Change Index | Protest Behaviors Index† |
|---|---|---|---|
| All Respondents | (240) | -.12 | -.09 |
| Whites | (120) | .11 | .11 |
| Blacks | (116) | -.17 | -.10 |

†The Protest Behaviors Index appears in the 1972 interview; the Respondent's Political Power Index in the 1972 reinterview. Thus, the relationships are probably influenced by changes occurring over time and probably represent an underestimate of the "true" relationship.

between the Respondent's Political Power Index and either the Violence for Social Change or Protest Behaviors Index. Gamson's (1968) hypothesis, however, does not predict such a zero order relationship. Instead, the hypothesis implies that it is those who are both politically distrustful and have a low sense of political efficacy who are likely to resort to the use of force.

Table 3.20 shows the results of an analysis of variance testing Gamson's hypothesis among all respondents. It can be seen that the hypothesis is supported, albeit at a low level of significance. While there is no main effect for either the Political Cynicism or Respondent's Political Power Index, there is a significant interaction between them. Those respondents who were high on Political Cynicism and low on Political Power had the highest mean score on the Violence for Social Change Index. However, when data are analysed for white and black respondents separately, differences do not reach significant levels although this is probably a function of the very small number of cases in each cell. It is not surprising that Gamson's (1968) hypothesis cannot be supported within race as well as among all respondents. Black respondents did feel more politically powerless than whites and showed substantially more political cynicism. Since these characteristics were not evenly distributed in the population studied, it is not remarkable

**Table 3.20**

Analysis of Variance of the Violence for Social Change Index
by the Political Cynicism and Respondent's Political Power Indices
(1972 reinterview respondents, N = 240)

| Respondent's Political Power Index | Political Cynicism Index | | | |
|---|---|---|---|---|
| | | Low | | High |
| | N | 1-2 | N | 3-4 |
| | | $\overline{X}$ | | $\overline{X}$ |
| Low 1-2 | (31) | 2.23 | (70) | 3.56 |
| Medium 3 | (21) | 3.14 | (20) | 2.30 |
| High 4-5 | (43) | 2.51 | (37) | 2.62 |

| | df | Sum of Squares | Mean Squares | F Ratio |
|---|---|---|---|---|
| Political Cynicism Index | 1 | 9.51 | 9.51 | 3.03 |
| Respondent's Political Power Index | 2 | 16.16 | 8.08 | 2.57 |
| Interaction A × B | 2 | 36.09 | 18.04 | 5.74† |
| Anova Error | 216 | 678.91 | 3.14 | — |

†p < .05

that the effect disappears when the two races are examined separately. The social significance of the relationship is still real. It should also be pointed out that the measures of political efficacy used here are not those which are usually employed (Converse 1972, p. 325). Perhaps those might have given a better account of themselves. However, Gamson is not specific about what kind of efficacy he means. It is not clear whether personal efficacy, generalized political efficacy, or efficacy relating to specific political issues is indicated by his hypothesis. This makes it difficult to decide how adequately the hypothesis has been tested.

It would be interesting to examine Gamson's (1968) hypothesis in a group of respondents who were known to be oriented to the left on political issues. It might very well be that stronger support for the hypothesis could be found in such a group. Similarly, one might expect more support for the hypothesis among those who are low on the Avoid Problems Index. Unfortunately, the number of cases available in these data is too small to allow the analysis.

Gamson's (1968) hypothesis also suggests that those who are low on political efficacy and high on political cynicism should score high on the Protest Behaviors Index. This hypothesis was not upheld when the analysis was conducted either among all respondents or when white and black respondents were examined separately. This suggests that political alienation, like frustration, is more important in forming attitudes than in leading to behavior.

*Summary*

Political alienation, defined as a combination of high political distrust and low perceived political efficacy, related to attitudes toward violence for social change, although only at low levels of significance. Moreover, there is no evidence in these data that political alienation influences the respondent's willingness to take protest action. It has been suggested that a better test of the hypothesis could be made among a group of respondents whose orientation on political issues was known, but these data do not allow such an analysis. In any case, there is only weak support in these data for the hypothesis that political alienation is related to the predilection for political violence.

## RELATIVE DEPRIVATION AND ATTITUDES TOWARD VIOLENCE FOR SOCIAL CHANGE

One widely held explanation for civil strife and political violence is the hypothesis of relative deprivation which has focused on the gap between what people desire to achieve or possess and what they have actually attained. The theory has appeal, partly because it incorporates an older and highly respectable psychological theory for which there is considerable experimental support, namely, the frustration-aggression hypothesis (Berkowitz 1961). According to the relative deprivation hypothesis, an individual who feels deprived, either in relation to some reference group or in relation to some privately held expectation becomes frustrated, and the frustration leads to aggression. However, this study demonstrates—and Berkowitz himself concedes—that the relation between frustration and aggression must be regarded as a bit tenuous and subject to a considerable array of inhibitory and countervailing forces (Berkowitz 1972).

An early variant of the relative deprivation hypothesis was proposed by Davies (1972, p. 67), who suggests that an intolerable gap between "what the people want and what they get" is a necessary prerequisite to revolution. Davies argues that revolution is most likely to take place when a prolonged period of economic growth is followed by a sharp reversal. During the time of economic growth, the capacity of the system to satisfy wants ("actual need satisfaction") increases, but at the same time societal aspirations ("expected need satisfactions") rise, perhaps slightly faster than the economic capacity to fulfill them. When economic decline leads to a decrease in the capacity of the system to provide actual need satisfaction, expected need satisfactions continue to increase at their previous rate, leading to intolerable discrepancies between the actual and the expected. (This conceptualization is referred to as the J-curve hypothesis.)

Feierabend, Feierabend, and Nesvold (1972) extended the J-curve hypothesis by specifically incorporating the frustration-aggression theory of Dollard et al. (1939) and Berkowitz (1961, 1962, 1972).

> On the basis of frustration-aggression theory, it is postulated that frustration induced by the social system creates the social strain and discontent that in turn are the indispensable preconditions of violence. The common sense assertion that revolutionary behavior has its roots in discontent, and the more technical postulate that frustration precedes aggression, are parallel statements indicating a common insight (Feierabend, Feierabend, and Nesvold 1972, p. 108).

Feierabend, Feierabend, and Nesvold (1972) refer to their conceptualization of the gap between social expectations and social achievement as "systemic frustration." They postulate that systemic frustration is a function of the discrepancy between present social aspirations and expectations, on the one hand, and social achievements, on the other. In addition, present expectations of future frustrations contribute to the level of present frustration. Like Davies (1972), Feierabend, et al., are primarily concerned with system-level analyses and consider their notion of systemic frustration appropriate for use with aggregate data.

In a cross-national analysis of political stability, Feierabend and Feierabend (1972, p. 136) operationalized systemic frustration as the ratio between social want satisfaction and social want formation. Their indicators of social satisfaction include gross national product and caloric intake per capita as well as the numbers of physicians, newspapers, radios, and telephones per unit of population. Their indicator of social want formation is based on the degree of literacy and urbanization of each country in question. In general, their data support the hypothesis that higher levels of systemic frustration are associated with higher levels of political instability.

Gurr (1968) has put forth a causal model of civil strife which postulates that "a psychological variable, relative deprivation, is the basic precondition for civil strife of any kind and that the more widespread and intense deprivation is among members of a population, the greater is the magnitude of strife in one or another form." The term "relative deprivation" has been used frequently in sociological research and typically describes the situation in which an individual feels deprived with respect to the status or accomplishments of a specific reference group. Gurr, however, adopts a more generalized definition based on the belief that individuals can feel deprived with respect to their own expectations as well as in relation to the accomplishments of a reference group. Therefore, he defines relative deprivation as the perception of discrepancy between value expectations (the goods and conditions of the life to which actors believe they are justifiably entitled) and value capabilities (the amount of goods and conditions they think they are able to get and keep). Gurr argues that relative deprivation is a form of frustration which naturally gives rise to anger. Anger, in turn, is a motivating state "for which aggression is an inherently satisfying response" (Gurr 1968). Using aggregate data to test his hypothesis, Gurr finds high correlations between macro measures and the total magnitude of civil strife. He believes that feelings of relative deprivation can be inferred from macro measures on aggregate data. It is not clear, however, that feelings of relative deprivation can be accurately measured by such approximate tools.

Muller (1972) points out that "developing an operational system based on macro indicators is not the most felicitous way to begin testing a theory conceptualized largely in terms of psychological characteristics of individuals." Indeed, Gurr (1970, p. 29) himself suggests the use of micro measures to test his theoretical conceptualizations. Muller (1972) tested several specific variants of the relative deprivation hypothesis in survey data collected from 503 respondents in Waterloo, Iowa. He found only a small correlation between his measure of "Potential for Political Violence" and "Short Term Welfare Gratification," a measure of relative deprivation based on a modification of Cantril's Ladder. Moreover, the relationship disappears when the respondent's trust in the political authority and beliefs in the efficacy of past violence are used as controls in the analysis.

Grofman and Muller (1973) have elaborated on the relative deprivation hypotheses and examined the relationship between a variety of relative deprivation scales derived from Muller's adaptation of Cantril's Self-Anchoring Scale and potential for political violence. In addition to examining the relationship between "Potential for Political Violence" and the respondent's present, past, and anticipated (future) feelings of relative deprivation, Grofman and Muller examined measures which include changes in the individual's feeling of deprivation over time. Thus, they studied whether feelings of deprivation have increased or decreased from the past to the present, whether increasing or decreasing deprivation is anticipated, and the pattern of the change. The varying patterns in perceived relative deprivation were related to potential for political violence. However, most of the associations found in the data were trivial, so Grofman and Muller found very little support for any of the variants of the relative deprivation hypothesis. One exception to these results is the finding that any change in the level of relative deprivation, irrespective of whether the change is for the better or the worse, is associated with an increase in the potential for political violence. These findings are similar to those of Bowen et al. (1968) who studied a sample of respondents living in Cleveland's poverty areas and found that expectation of change in the respondent's feeling of relative deprivation was associated with a greater orientation toward protest irrespective of whether the anticipated change was for the better or the worse.

In spite of the relatively weak support for the relative deprivation hypothesis in the data of other researchers, a measure of relative deprivation—Cantril's Ladder (Cantril and Roll 1971, p. 17)—was included in the reinterview schedule of the 1972 study. Cantril's Ladder is a self-anchoring scale which has been used to measure aspirations and concerns in an eighteen-nation cross-national study (Cantril 1965); national data from the United States are also available. The device has been used in a number of studies by political scientists to measure relative deprivation and is recommended by Gurr (1970, p. 29) as an appropriate tool for studying the construct. During the reinterview, the respondent was asked the following questions:

> *All of us want certain things out of life. When you think about what really matters in your own life, what are your wishes and hopes for the future? In other words, if you imagine your future in the best possible light, what would your life be like then, if you are to be happy? Take your time in answering; such things aren't easy to put into words.*
>
> *Now, taking the other side of the picture, what are your fears and worries about the future? In other words, if you imagine your future in the worst possible light, what would your life be like then? Again, take your time in answering.*

These questions were designed to create a frame of reference from which the respondent could more judiciously consider the three questions which follow. After the respondent had been given a chance to answer the open-ended questions cited above, he was handed a card picturing the ladder and was given the following instructions:

> *Here is a picture of a ladder. Suppose we say that the top of the ladder represents the best possible life for you and the bottom represents the worst possible life for you.*
>
> *Where on the ladder do you feel you personally stand at the present time? Step Number _____ .*

*Where on the ladder would you say you stood five years ago?*
*Step Number _____ .*

*And where do you think you will be on the ladder five years*
*from now? Step Number _____.*

Table 3.21 shows how respondents located themselves on the
ladder steps. It can be seen that black respondents saw themselves as
being considerably more distant from their "best possible" life than did
whites. Fifty-three percent of black respondents indicated the fifth step
or below when asked about their present standing on the ladder (Present
Deprivation). Only 27 percent of the white respondents indicated similar positions. Thus, blacks viewed their present life as more deprived
than did whites in the population studied.

Similar black-white differences appeared when the respondents

### Table 3.21

Percentage Responses to Present, Past,
and Future Standing on Cantril's Ladder
(all respondents, N = 240; whites, N = 120; blacks, N = 116)
(1972 reinterview)

| | Present Standing on Cantril's Ladder | | | |
|---|---|---|---|---|
| | Worst Possible Life 0-4 | 5 | 6-7 | Best Possible Life 8-10 |
| All Respondents | 19% | 21 | 35 | 25 |
| Whites | 8% | 19 | 42 | 31 |
| Blacks | 29% | 24 | 28 | 19 |

| | Past Standing on Cantril's Ladder | | | | |
|---|---|---|---|---|---|
| | Worst Possible Life 0-1 | 2-3 | 4-5 | 6-7 | Best Possible Life 8-10 |
| All Respondents | 11% | 19 | 29 | 21 | 20 |
| Whites | 3% | 12 | 33 | 26 | 26 |
| Blacks | 18% | 27 | 24 | 16 | 15 |

| | Future Standing on Cantril's Ladder | | | |
|---|---|---|---|---|
| | Worst Possible Life 0-6 | 7 | 8 | 9 | Best Possible Life 10 |
| All Respondents | 16% | 17 | 21 | 19 | 27 |
| Whites | 18% | 21 | 21 | 22 | 18 |
| Blacks | 13% | 13 | 21 | 17 | 36 |

Note: Percentages across each row total 100%.

were asked their relative position on the ladder five years earlier (Past Deprivation). Sixty-nine percent of black respondents located themselves on the fifth step or below, compared to only 48 percent of white respondents. Interestingly enough, the black-white differences were reversed when respondents were asked where they expected to find themselves five years later (Future Deprivation). Thirty-six percent of black respondents thought they would be living the best possible life for them, an opinion which only 18 percent of white respondents shared. So, the data indicate that blacks in the study population expected to progress much more rapidly than did whites.

Two additional measures are derived from Present, Past, and Future Deprivations. The first is the difference between the respondent's present standing and past standing on the ladder (Present Deprivation minus Past Deprivation). This measure, called Past Progress, indicates how rapidly and in what direction the respondent has progressed along the ladder. The second, called Expected Progress, is the difference between the respondent's present and future standings on the ladder (Future Deprivation minus Present Deprivation).

Tables 3.22 and 3.23 show the distribution of responses on the Past Progress and Expected Progress measures. It can be seen that

**Table 3.22**

Percentage Responses to the Past Progress Scale
(1972 reinterview)

| Past Progress Scale | | All Respondents | Whites | Blacks |
|---|---|---|---|---|
| Past better than present | | 20% | 23% | 17% |
| No change from past | | 20 | 25 | 15 |
| Past one step worse | | 13 | 11 | 13 |
| Past two steps worse | | 20 | 19 | 23 |
| Past three or more steps worse | | 27 | 22 | 32 |
| | | 100% | 100% | 100% |
| | N | (240) | (120) | (116) |

slightly more black than white respondents felt that changes between the past and present had been beneficial. Only 32 percent of the black respondents felt that their lives had neither changed nor become worse over the previous five years in contrast to 48 percent of the white respondents. Moreover, Table 3.23 shows that black respondents were far more optimistic about what the future held for them than were whites. Forty-one percent of white respondents felt that either their lives would not improve or things would get worse. In contrast, only

20 percent of black respondents held such a dim view of the future. Fifty-one percent of black respondents believed that the future would be at least three steps better than the present. Only 15 percent of the whites in the study anticipated such progress.

**Table 3.23**

Percentage Responses to the Expected Progress Scale
(1972 reinterview)

| Expected Progress Scale | All Respondents | Whites | Blacks |
|---|---|---|---|
| Present better than future | 6% | 9% | 5% |
| No change from present | 24 | 32 | 15 |
| Future one step better | 15 | 20 | 7 |
| Future two steps better | 23 | 24 | 22 |
| Future at least three steps better | 32 | 15 | 51 |
| | 100% | 100% | 100% |
| N | (240) | (120) | (116) |

Table 3.24 shows the demographic correlates of the three primary relative deprivation measures. As might have been anticipated from results already discussed, the associations between the three primary

**Table 3.24**

Relationships between the Present Deprivation, Past Deprivation, and Future Deprivation Scales and Selected Demographic Characteristics
(1972 reinterview respondents, N = 240)
(gammas)

| Demographic Characteristic | Present Deprivation | Past Deprivation | Future Deprivation |
|---|---|---|---|
| Race | .42†† | .46†† | -.26‡ |
| Sex | -.06 | -.08 | .02 |
| Age | -.24†† | -.18‡ | .10 |
| Education | -.19§ | -.12 | -.05 |
| Family Income | -.19§ | -.15† | .02 |
| Town Size | .23‡ | .01 | .14 |
| Experience in South | .00 | -.12 | .20† |

†p < .05     ‡p < .01     §p < .005     ††p < .001

relative deprivation measures and race are substantial. There are small relationships between Present Deprivation and age, education, family income, and whether the respondent lived in a more rural or uban area.

When the relationship between Present Deprivation and family income is calculated separately within race, a significant association is found among white (gamma = -.25, p < .05) but not black respondents (gamma = .08). This is disappointing. Although it is clear that the perception of deprivation is not the same as the reality of deprivation, one would have expected that there would be some relationship between feelings of deprivation and the reality of deprivation. Indeed, the relative deprivation hypothesis of civil disorder is rooted in the idea that such relationships between reality and feelings of deprivation exist. Surely income is the best measure of access to material goods in our society, and one would expect income to be related to measures that purport to assess feelings of deprivation.

Similarly, education should be associated with these measures. However, there is only a small association between education and Present Deprivation which is not maintained within race (among whites the gamma is -.18; among blacks the gamma is .04). Thus, it seems probable that much of the apparent relationship between education and Present Deprivation when all respondents are considered together is due to differences between the races. One would have thought that persons with less education would feel more deprived in relation to others since they have, in fact, achieved less. Education is often regarded as the keystone to success, and it is disconcerting that a measure which presumably measures attributes engendered by frustration does not reflect the frustrations which a lack of education causes in this society. Altogether, the key demographic correlates of the measures are considerably smaller than might have been expected if the instrument were a valid measure of feelings of relative deprivation. These low correlations suggest that Cantril's Ladder may not be measuring such feelings accurately.

Table 3.24 also shows a small relationship between Present Deprivation and town size, which does not reach significance when the races are considered separately (among white respondents the gamma is .06; among black it is .23). Thus, it appears that much of the association between Present Deprivation and town size is due to the fact that more black than white respondents lived in urban areas.

The small relationship between Present Deprivation and age is shown in Table 3.25. Respondents under thirty were considerably less likely to locate themselves on steps near their best possible life than were those who were older. This raises some interesting questions: do older people locate themselves close to their best possible life because they have achieved all that they wished or because they have given up wishing for things that they no longer believe they can achieve? Conversely, do young people see themselves as being more distant from

**Table 3.25**

Percentage Responses to the Present Deprivation Scale
in Relation to Age
(1972 reinterview respondents, N = 240)

| Present Deprivation Scale | | 16-19 Years | 20-29 Years | 30-39 Years | 40-49 Years | 50-59 Years | 60 Years or Older |
|---|---|---|---|---|---|---|---|
| Best Possible Life | 1 | 6% | 18% | 36% | 28% | 25% | 40% |
| | 2 | 28 | 18 | 20 | 23 | 16 | 32 |
| | 3 | 19 | 9 | 13 | 10 | 9 | 15 |
| | 4 | 16 | 32 | 13 | 18 | 34 | 10 |
| Worst Possible Life | 5 | 31 | 23 | 18 | 21 | 16 | 3 |
| | | 100% | 100% | 100% | 100% | 100% | 100% |
| | N * | (32) | (56) | (39) | (39) | (32) | (38) |

their best possible life because they have great hopes for the future or because they feel themselves deprived?

Such questions raise some problematic issues about the concept underlying Cantril's measuring device. A person may locate himself on the ladder far below his best possible life either because he is very optimistic about his opportunity to achieve *or* because he feels deprived in relation to what he believes to be his entitlement. The nature of the perceived deprivation seems to be quite different in these two cases. One would think that feelings of relative deprivation engendered by optimism about the future would be associated with feelings of personal control over one's fate, hopefulness, and a general enthusiasm about life. One might also think that feelings of relative deprivation which grow out of the perception that one is not receiving his due would be accompanied by feelings of resentment, hopelessness, and perhaps apathy. If the two types of relative deprivation that Cantril's Ladder is apparently measuring do have such very different correlates, the heterogeneity implied ought to preclude the ladder from having very strong correlates with any particular variable; questions with multiple frames of reference rarely do.

Table 3.26 shows the demographic correlates of the derived measures. The data suggest that part of the reason young people are more likely to place themselves low on the present ladder in relation to their best possible life lies in their hopes for the future. There is a moderate correlation between Expected Progress, which measures the difference between Present and Future Deprivation, and age, suggesting that the younger respondents saw themselves as more likely to do well in the future than did those who were older. Neither Past Deprivation nor Future Deprivation have demographic correlates large enough to be taken seriously, with the single exception of race. As might have

**Table 3.26**

Relationships between the Past Progress and Expected Progress Scales
and Selected Demographic Characteristics
(1972 reinterview respondents, N = 240)
(gammas)

| Demographic Characteristic | Past Progress Scale | Expected Progress Scale |
|---|---|---|
| Race | -.24† | -.55‡ |
| Sex | .04 | -.02 |
| Age | .02 | .41‡ |
| Education | -.01 | .06 |
| Family Income | .05 | .12 |
| Town Size | .17 | .04 |
| Experience in South | .15 | .11 |

†p < .05    ‡p < .001

been expected, black respondents were likely to consider themselves as having been more deprived in the past than were white. The reverse, however, is true with respect to Future Deprivation; here blacks expected to be relatively closer to their "best possible life" five years later than did whites. These data suggest that there was a sense of increased expectation among blacks which was probably not commensurate with reality. While conditions such as income have improved for blacks over the years, they have not improved at the same rate as for whites, and it seems unlikely that the gap will be closed in the near future (Flax 1971, p. 25). The relationship detailed in Table 3.27 suggests that the reason younger respondents showed more Present Deprivation lies more in their anticipations of future achievements than in disappointments with their present circumstances. Over 30 percent of those under thirty saw themselves as being three steps closer to their best possible life five years in the future. This reflected a degree of optimism not shared by any other age category.

With the exception of the relationship to race and age, neither Past Progress nor Expected Progress shows any notable demographic correlates. While it is conceivable that beliefs about future well-being are based mainly on fantasy, Past Progress, like Present Deprivation, should show at least modest relationships to income and education since these factors probably serve as crucial determinants of access to material goods. If Cantril's Ladder is measuring only concepts based on fantasy, it is not serving the function it was intended to serve by theorists on relative deprivation. Theorizing about relative deprivation as a source of civil disturbance implies that feelings of relative deprivation are related to the availability of material resources. Indeed, the

**Table 3.27**

Percentage Responses to the Expected Progress Scale
in Relation to Age
(1972 reinterview respondents, N = 240)

| Expected Progress Scale | 16-19 Years | 20-29 Years | 30-39 Years | 40-49 Years | 50-59 Years | 60 Years or Older |
|---|---|---|---|---|---|---|
| Present better than future | 0% | 4% | 0% | 3% | 10% | 26% |
| No change from present | 6 | 9 | 28 | 23 | 44 | 40 |
| Future one step better | 19 | 14 | 23 | 24 | 3 | 3 |
| Future two steps better | 38 | 43 | 36 | 29 | 23 | 31 |
| Future at least three steps better | 37 | 30 | 13 | 21 | 20 | 0 |
| | 100% | 100% | 100% | 100% | 100% | 100% |
| N * | (32) | (56) | (39) | (38) | (30) | (35) |

core of the theory implies that it is changes in the availability of resources that gives rise to increasing aspirations, and it is the failure of the system to fulfill these increased aspirations that leads to revolutionary discontent.

## Relative Deprivation in Relation to Frustration

The first substantive question to be answered is whether or not feelings of relative deprivation are indeed related to feelings of frustration. Table 3.28 shows that the relationships between the Resentment-Suspicion Index and the relative deprivation measures are relatively small. Only Present Deprivation correlates with the Resentment-

**Table 3.28**

Relationships between the Resentment-Suspicion Index and
the Present Deprivation, Past Deprivation, Future Deprivation, Past Progress,
and Expected Progress Scales
(1972 reinterview)
(gammas)

| | All Respondents | Whites | Blacks |
|---|---|---|---|
| Present Deprivation | .34§ | .34§ | .19 |
| Past Deprivation | .19† | .14 | .03 |
| Future Deprivation | .05 | .16 | .12 |
| Past Progress | .01 | .02 | .11 |
| Expected Progress | -.21‡ | -.06 | -.10 |
| N | (240) | (120) | (116) |

†p < .01        ‡p < .005        §p < .001

Suspicion Index, and the correlation does not hold among black respondents. In addition, multiple regression analyses show that Future Deprivation and Past Deprivation are not able to increase the proportion of the variance in the Resentment-Suspicion Index over what is explained by feelings of Present Deprivation. So, the expected relationships between relative deprivation and one measure of frustration are small and do not reach significance among black respondents.

There are three possible explanations for the failure to find at least moderate associations between the relative deprivation measures and the Resentment-Suspicion Index. One is that the underlying theory is incorrect, in other words, that feelings of deprivation do not lead to frustration. This seems unlikely; it is contrary to human experience, in which feelings of deprivation and frustration go hand in hand. The other two explanations lie in the domain of measurement error and seem more probable. Either the Resentment-Suspicion Index is not a good measure of frustration or Cantril's Ladder is not a good measure of relative deprivation. The available evidence indicates that the former explanation is less likely than the latter. The Resentment-Suspicion Index has been demonstrated in two separate studies to relate to those demographic characteristics which theoretically ought to be related to feelings of frustration in our society (Blumenthal 1973b; see Chapter 2). The measures derived from Cantril's Ladder are notably lacking in those demographic correlates which are to be expected. Moreover, the Ladder has been severely criticized on the grounds that its questions are too abstract for respondents to comprehend. In a methodological study of survey questions, Cantril's Ladder was found to be more complicated and less likely to be understood by the respondent than any of the other measures investigated (Cannell and Robison 1971, p. 289). Consequently, if one of the two measures is deficient, it seems more likely that it is Cantril's Ladder than the Resentment-Suspicion Index.

## *Relative Deprivation and Violence for Social Change*

Table 3.29 shows the relationship between the Violence for Social Change Index and the Present Deprivation, Past Deprivation, Future Deprivation, Past Progress, and Expected Progress Scales. The relationships are small and they are not sustained within race. Furthermore, in the case of the dynamic measure, Expected Progress, the relationship to the Violence for Social Change Index is in the wrong direction. The more the respondent believed that his life would improve relative to the present, the higher he was apt to score on the Violence for Social Change Index. This may be due to racial differences. Black

**Table 3.29**

Relationships between the Violence for Social Change Index and
the Present Deprivation, Past Deprivation, Future Deprivation, Past Progress,
and Expected Progress Scales
(1972 reinterview)
(gammas)

|  | All Respondents | Whites | Blacks |
|---|---|---|---|
| Present Deprivation | .18‡ | .08 | .06 |
| Past Deprivation | .14† | .02 | -.03 |
| Future Deprivation | -.07 | -.02 | .03 |
| Past Progress | -.04 | .01 | .05 |
| Expected Progress | -.24§ | -.15 | -.06 |
| N | (240) | (120) | (116) |

†p < .05        ‡p < .01        §p < .001

respondents anticipated greater improvements in their lives than did
whites and black respondents also scored higher on the Violence for
Social Change Index, but it is still true that the results contradict what
theory predicts should be the case.

Table 3.30 shows that the relative deprivation measures fare no
better in relation to the Protest Behaviors Index than they do in respect
to the Violence for Social Change Index. Only Present and Past

**Table 3.30**

Relationships between the Protest Behaviors Index and the
Present Deprivation, Past Deprivation, Future Deprivation, Past Progress,
and Expected Progress Scales
(1972 reinterview)
(gammas)

|  | All Respondents | Whites | Blacks |
|---|---|---|---|
| Present Deprivation | .18† | .06 | .14 |
| Past Deprivation | .16† | -.02 | .14 |
| Future Deprivation | -.04 | .04 | -.01 |
| Past Progress | -.04 | .05 | .01 |
| Expected Progress | -.23‡ | -.10 | -.15 |
| N | (240) | (120) | (116) |

†p < .05        ‡p < .005

Deprivation and Expected Progress show significant associations with
the level of protest in which the individual was willing to participate;

these associations are small, and one is in the wrong direction. More-over, the relationships become smaller and nonsignificant within race, indicating that racial differences account for most of what little association there is.

## Summary

The failure to find a relationship between relative deprivation and attitudes toward the use of violence to bring about social change is puzzling. The theory is attractive and not easy to abandon. One possible explanation lies in the method of measuring relative deprivation. One can quarrel with the wording of Cantril's question. The respondent is asked to imagine his future in "the best possible light." It is not clear from the question whether it is legitimate for the respondent to imagine that he will win a lottery ticket and spend the rest of his life as a millionaire. Presumably, such a contingency is not ruled out by the manner in which the question is phrased. But, it is unlikely that such an imaginative approach on the part of the respondent would contribute to the information that the investigator wishes to ascertain. Implicit in the concept of relative deprivation is the notion that the individual will have some idea of the best life that a person like himself deserves or is entitled to. The fact of social stratification is old, and many societies in which social stratification is severe, rigid, and immutable have survived successfully for centuries. In such societies, people in various levels of stratification must accept the stratum in which they exist without questioning its legitimacy. Presumably, they aspire to what can be achieved within their level of stratification. Similar stratifications exist within our society, and in considering relative deprivation the relevant issue is probably the extent to which the respondent feels deprived in relation to what he believes to be his entitlement.

Grofman and Muller (1973) point out that the relative deprivation hypothesis has been variously defined. Some have considered discrepancies from what the individual believes to be his "just desserts"; some, discrepancies from the achievements to which the individual aspires; and some, discrepancies between the person and the individuals with whom he identifies. These various statements of the relative deprivation hypothesis are not mutually exclusive, and unfortunately the wording of Cantril's Ladder does not speak exactly to any of them. It may be that a clearer statement of the question in terms of one of the definitions cited above, together with a simpler and less abstract measuring device, would provide more support for the theory, but it is not found in these data.

In his review of social evaluation theory in relation to some racial issues Pettigrew (1967) points out that feelings of relative deprivation imply judgments about whether or not specific conditions are unfair, and such concepts are closely related to notions of distributive justice. Judging from our work, it seems reasonable to speculate that the idea of justice or fairness may be more centrally related to attitudes toward violence than are feelings of deprivation. It is the perceived injustice underlying the deprivation that gives rise to anger or frustration. During the Second World War many people were deprived of things to which they had become accustomed. For example, gasoline was rationed; moreover, it was not distributed equally. Nevertheless, on the whole there was a general atmosphere of acceptance and even cooperation, perhaps because the distribution was viewed as fair, just, and necessary. Perhaps a measure which assessed feelings of deprivation and the respondent's perception of the extent to which the deprivation is fair would make a better case for the relative deprivation theory than do these data.

## INTERNAL-EXTERNAL CONTROL AND ATTITUDES TOWARD VIOLENCE FOR SOCIAL CHANGE

A psychological orientation toward issues of power and powerlessness in relation to militancy and violence has developed parallel to and almost completely independently of the political scientists' preoccupation with the same issues. Studies of militants have shown that those who approve of or take part in action to effect change are persons who feel they have the power to do so (they have competence, personal control). Nonmilitants are likely to be those who have little confidence in their ability to control events; in this sense, the nonmilitant feels powerless (Caplan 1971, p. 145). On the other hand, despite feelings of self-efficacy, militants blame the system for preventing them from exercising their capabilities; in this sense, the militant feels powerless.

The concept of internal-external control was originally developed by Rotter (1966) within his theory of social learning and was subsequently applied to a variety of human behaviors. As originally defined by Rotter, internal control refers to the belief that rewards in life are contingent on one's own actions. External control refers to the belief that reinforcements occur independently of one's own actions and that life is determined more by chance and fate than by one's own efficacy. Gurin et al. (1969) have differentiated three components within the internal-external control concept. They distinguish between internal-external control as a cultural norm and internal-external control as a personal characteristic. The former is named "control ideology" and the latter "personal control." The control ideology dimension seems to measure "the respondent's ideology or general beliefs about the role of internal and external forces in determining success and failure in the culture at large'' (Gurin et al. 1969). It is a sort of ''Protestant Ethic'' dimension, and the items used by Gurin et al. are usually worded in the third person. Personal control measures the internal-external dimension in reference to an individual's *own* life, that is, the person's feelings about his *own* power to control outcomes. All of these items which are in the forced choice format are worded in the first person. In an analysis of data obtained from white undergraduates, Mirels (1970) also found that the first person items fell on a separate factor. While both personal control and control ideology deal with external control as an unspecified force, a third set of items developed by Gurin et al. (1969) ascertains feelings toward ''the system'' as a specific external force responsible for social and economic failure or success of individuals. This dimension may be particularly important among those who are the victims of economic and social forces that disadvantage them. Gurin et al., point out that low income groups may experience many external obstacles that are due to the characteristics of the socioeconomic system. For example, the operation of the labor market may lead to layoffs. A blue collar worker subject to such vagaries of employment may correctly perceive that his well-being is controlled by forces which he cannot direct or manage. Similarly, blacks may correctly perceive that racial discrimination acts to deprive them of opportunity. Such are the perceptions which are measured by the items classified under ''system blame.''

Internal-external control has been investigated in various studies of militancy and rioters. For example, in a study of black high school seniors using data collected during the 1967 Detroit riot, Forward and Williams (1970) found that those reacting positively to the riot had a high sense of personal control and also a belief that it was the system and not individual ability which prevented blacks from achieving their goals. These findings can be generalized as meaning that black militants have a sense of personal efficacy and see themselves as capable individuals, while they blame the system for preventing them from actualizing their capabilities.

Caplan (1971, pp. 151-152) supports this view of the black militant in a reanalysis of data from several studies comparing militants and nonmilitants.

It seems clear from the findings in these studies that while the militant feels a strong sense of personal power, he also feels unable to manipulate these external forces, i.e., he is high on personal efficacy but low on political efficacy.

Finally, Crawford and Naditch (1970) have used the internal-

external dimension in conjunction with a measure of relative deprivation to help explain attitudes toward militancy:

> It is our hypothesis that, while knowing the individual's
> level of relative deprivation will be of some use for predicting
> his feelings of discontent and political disaffection, precise
> behavioral predictions can only be made when the individ-
> ual's level of relative deprivation is considered in conjunc-
> tion with the behavioral means for reducing relative depriva-
> tion which he perceives as available to him.

Whether an individual believes that the behavioral means for reducing
his level of relative deprivation are available to him or are governed
by some force outside his control indicates his position on an internal-
external dimension. According to Crawford and Naditch (1970), who
used the Rotter I-E Scale as a measure of internal-external control,
respondents who are internally oriented and who also have high levels
of relative deprivation will be most likely to engage in or approve
of social and political protest.

In the current study the three internal-external control dimensions investigated by Gurin et al. (1969) were distinguished. Nine items
were selected to represent the dimensions of personal control, control
ideology, and system blame.[5] The items and the percentage distribution
of responses among white, black, and all respondents are given in
Table 3.31. As might have been expected, black respondents were

**Table 3.31**

Percentage Responses to Items Measuring Internal-External Control
(1972 reinterview)

|  | All Respondents | Whites | Blacks |
|---|---|---|---|
| **Personal Control Items** |  |  |  |
| When I make plans I am almost certain I can make them work. | 41% | 52% | 30% |
| It is not always wise to plan too far ahead because many things turn out to be a matter of good or bad luck anyhow. | 59 | 48 | 70 |
|  | 100% | 100% | 100% |
| What happens to me is my own doing. | 65 | 70 | 59 |
| Sometimes I feel that I don't have enough control over the direction my life is taking. | 35 | 30 | 41 |
|  | 100% | 100% | 100% |

---

[5] Personal communication from Gerald Gurin in 1972.

**Table 3.31** (continued)
Percentage Responses to Items Measuring Internal-External Control
(1972 reinterview)

| | All Respondents | Whites | Blacks |
|---|---|---|---|
| I've usually felt pretty sure my life would work out the way I wanted it to. | 30 | 35 | 25 |
| There are times when I haven't been very sure that my life would work out the way I wanted it to. | 70 | 65 | 75 |
| | 100% | 100% | 100% |

Control Ideology Items

| | All Respondents | Whites | Blacks |
|---|---|---|---|
| Becoming a success is a matter of hard work; luck has little or nothing to do with it. | 64 | 67 | 60 |
| Getting a good job depends mainly on being in the right place at the right time. | 36 | 33 | 40 |
| | 100% | 100% | 100% |
| Knowing the right people is important in deciding whether a person will get ahead. | 43 | 45 | 40 |
| People will get ahead in life if they have the skills and do a good job; knowing the right people has nothing to do with it. | 57 | 55 | 60 |
| | 100% | 100% | 100% |
| People who don't do well in life often work hard, but the breaks just don't come their way. | 44 | 52 | 36 |
| Some people just don't use the breaks that come their way; if they don't do well, it's their own fault. | 56 | 48 | 64 |
| | 100% | 100% | 100% |

System Blame Items

| | All Respondents | Whites | Blacks |
|---|---|---|---|
| People who are born poor have less chance to get ahead than other people. | 23 | 30 | 15 |
| People who have the ability and work hard have the same chance as anyone else, even if their parents were poor. | 77 | 70 | 85 |
| | 100% | 100% | 100% |
| It's the lack of skills and abilities that keep most unemployed people from getting a job; if they had the skills, most of them could get a job. | 56 | 56 | 56 |
| Many people with skills can't get a job; there just aren't any jobs for them. | 44 | 44 | 44 |
| | 100% | 100% | 100% |
| Most people who are unemployed just haven't had the breaks in life. | 30 | 30 | 30 ° |
| Most people who are unemployed have had the opportunities; they haven't made use of the opportunities that came their way. | 70 | 70 | 70 |
| | 100% | 100% | 100% |
| N | (240) | (120) | (116) |

more externally oriented than white respondents, that is, they scored lower on all three personal control items. On two of the three control ideology items, black respondents showed greater agreement with the internal control responses than white. Blacks in our population seemed to endorse a cultural ethic of internal control more strongly than whites; yet blacks felt they had less control over their own lives. There is little difference between white and black respondents on two of the three items measuring system blame. For one item, blacks were slightly less likely than whites to endorse the ethic of system blame, an interesting paradox since one might think blacks would be more sensitive than whites to the strictures imposed by system constraints.

We had hoped that dimensional analysis of the internal-external control items would replicate the findings of Gurin et al. (1969). Unfortunately, it did not do so. In the control ideology set, the item about becoming a success did not relate well to the item which states "people who don't do well in life often work hard, but the breaks don't come their way" (gamma = -.13). In the system blame set, the item which begins "people who are born poor have less of a chance to get ahead than other people" did not relate well to the item which begins "it's the lack of skills and abilities that keep most people from getting a job" (gamma = .08). Moreover, the relationships which did exist for the study population as a whole were not maintained consistently in the demographic subgroups.

The reasons for the failure to replicate the analysis by Gurin et al. (1969) are not entirely clear, although two deserve mention. First, the method of analysis used here differs from that used by Gurin et al., ours being based on cluster techniques rather than factor analysis. However, we have duplicated many analyses using cluster techniques and factor analysis on the same data, and the outcome of the two methods are rarely substantially different. Second, the population which was investigated in this study was strikingly different from that used by Gurin et al. Their factor analysis was based on samples of college students from ten southern universities. The respondents in this study are far more heterogeneous with respect to age, education, and race and are more typical of those found in a general population.

In spite of the fact that the items did not meet our usual criteria for index construction, the nine items were combined into three indices along the lines suggested by the analysis of Gurin et al., so that their original construction and operationalization could be investigated in relation to our concepts of violence. The Personal Control Index is an additive index based on the three items listed under that label in Table 3.31; the higher the score on the index, the more the respondent believed in his own ability to control his fate. Similarly, the three items under control ideology in Table 3.31 were combined additively to form the Control Ideology Index. The higher the score on the Control Ideology Index, the more the respondent subscribed to the generalized belief that life is controlled by the individual rather than by fate. Lastly, the three items under the heading "system blame" in Table 3.31 were combined into the System Blame Index. The higher the score on the index, the more the individual attributed the responsibility for failure to the system. (Details of index construction are given in Appendix E.)

### Demographic Correlates of the Internal-External Control Indices

Table 3.32 shows the demographic correlates of the Internal-External Control Indices. It can be seen that the Personal Control Index is the only one of the three indices to show significant demographic correlates; these are race, education, and family income.

**Table 3.32**

Relationships between the Internal-External Control Indices
and Selected Demographic Characteristics
(1972 reinterview respondents, N = 240)
(gammas)

| Demographic Characteristic | Personal Control Index | Control Ideology Index | System Blame Index |
|---|---|---|---|
| Race | -.29† | .06 | -.01 |
| Sex | -.18 | .05 | .13 |
| Age | .00 | .09 | -.08 |
| Education | .23‡ | -.06 | .09 |
| Family Income | .23‡ | .03 | -.01 |
| Town Size | -.06 | -.03 | .04 |
| Experience in South | .09 | -.17 | -.17 |

†p < .005    ‡p < .001

Table 3.33 shows that among black respondents only 34 percent scored in the two highest personal control categories, in contrast to 53 percent of white respondents. Discrimination in the United States undoubtedly results in many arbitrary junctures for blacks, which sharply curtail their ability to manage their own lives. No wonder they are less likely than whites to see themselves in control of their own lives.

Those with lower incomes also scored lower on the Personal Control Index than those with higher incomes. Table 3.34 shows that this association is almost a step function; only about one-third of those respondents who had incomes of less than $10,000 a year scored in the

**Table 3.33**

Percentage Responses to the Personal Control Index
in Relation to Race
(1972 reinterview)

| Personal Control Index | | | Whites | Blacks |
|---|---|---|---|---|
| Low | 1 | | 18% | 29% |
| | 2 | | 29 | 37 |
| | 3 | | 30 | 26 |
| High | 4 | | 23 | 8 |
| | | | 100% | 100% |
| | | N | (120) | (116) |

**Table 3.34**

Percentage Responses to the Personal Control Index
in Relation to Family Income
(1972 reinterview respondents, N = 240)

| Personal Control Index | | $3,999 or Less | $4,000-$5,999 | $6,000-$9,999 | $10,000-$15,999 | $16,000 or More |
|---|---|---|---|---|---|---|
| Low | 1 | 19% | 38% | 27% | 17% | 15% |
| | 2 | 46 | 31 | 38 | 17 | 24 |
| | 3 | 28 | 25 | 27 | 37 | 27 |
| High | 4 | 7 | 6 | 8 | 29 | 34 |
| | | 100% | 100% | 100% | 100% | 100% |
| | N * | (57) | (32) | (52) | (52) | (33) |

two highest categories on the Personal Control Index, in contrast to almost two-thirds of those with higher incomes. The relationship between the Personal Control Index and income is true for white (gamma = .23, p< .05) but not for black respondents (gamma = -.04) when the two races are considered separately. Perhaps being black is such an overriding limitation with respect to personal control that income can have no further influence.

Table 3.35 gives the percentage distribution of the Personal Control Index in relation to education. The table shows that among those who had not finished high school less than 10 percent fell in the highest category of the index, in contrast to about one-quarter of those who had completed high school. Such a relationship between education and personal control is to be expected. Education is the acquired personal attribute which is most likely to be a key to personal success and security. It is the uneducated who are likely to be underemployed, unemployed, and unemployable. Moreover, the uneducated have fewer

**Table 3.35**

Percentage Responses to the Personal Control Index
in Relation to Education
(1972 reinterview respondents, N = 240)

| Personal Control Index | | 9 Years or Less | 10-11 Years | High School Graduate | At Least Some College |
|---|---|---|---|---|---|
| Low | 1 | 28% | 30% | 17% | 20% |
| | 2 | 38 | 36 | 31 | 26 |
| | 3 | 26 | 28 | 29 | 28 |
| High | 4 | 8 | 6 | 23 | 26 |
| | | 100% | 100% | 100% | 100% |
| | N * | (53) | (64) | (65) | (54) |

choices in the type of employment open to them. The type of work that one does determines not only one's access to resources which allow one to control the environment but also determines how much control one has over one's time. The relationship between the Personal Control Index and education is significant among black (gamma = .23, $p < .05$) but not among white respondents (gamma = .11) when the two races are considered separately.

### Internal-External Control and Violence for Social Change

The literature suggests that the internal-external orientation should be related both to the Violence for Social Change Index and the Protest Behaviors Index. Of the three internal-external indices, one would expect that the System Blame Index would relate most strongly to the Violence for Social Change Index. Neither the Control Ideology Index nor the Personal Control Index should show first order relationships, although the literature does imply that militants are individuals who both feel efficacious and locate the source of many of life's problems in the "system." Consequently, one would expect individuals who are high on both the Personal Control Index and System Blame Index to score high on the Violence for Social Change Index and the Protest Behaviors Index.

Table 3.36 gives the first order correlations for the three indices. It can be seen that only Personal Control shows significant levels of associations, although these are not maintained within race. So, our data provide no support for the notion that blaming the system is associated with perceptions that violence is necessary to produce social change. One possibility is that the hypothesis has failed because of a measurement problem. Furthermore, the forced choice format may be confusing to respondents. The statements are rather long and may be

hard to keep in mind, although respondents were given a written copy
to which they could refer during the interviewing procedure.

**Table 3.36**

Relationships between the Violence for Social Change Index
and the Internal-External Control Indices
(1972 reinterview)
(gammas)

|  | N | Personal Control Index | Control Ideology Index | System Blame Index |
|---|---|---|---|---|
| All Respondents | (240) | -.14† | .00 | .11 |
| Whites | (120) | -.04 | -.05 | .18 |
| Blacks | (116) | -.02 | -.04 | .15 |

†p < .05

A test of the second hypothesis, which states that there will be a
significant interaction between the Personal Control and the System
Blame Indices in relation to the Violence for Social Change Index,
also fails. The interaction fails to reach significance in an analysis
of variance. Indeed, the mean values of the Violence for Social
Change Index in relation to the Personal Control and System Blame
Indices show not the slightest trend in the hypothesized direction
(Table 3.37). Similar analyses conducted in relation to the Protest
Behaviors Index also fail to show significant interactions. Although
evidence for an association between the internal-external control
indices and attitudes toward the necessity of using violence as a means
of producing social change was not found, the internal-external control indices could be related more to a predilection for action than to
ideology. Consequently, it seems reasonable to investigate the internal-

**Table 3.37**

Analysis of Variance of the Violence for Social Change Index
by the Personal Control and System Blame Indices
(1972 reinterview respondents, N = 240)

|  | | Personal Control Index | | |
|---|---|---|---|---|
| System Blame Index | N | Low 1-2 | N | High 3-4 |
|  |  | X̄ |  | X̄ |
| Low    1 | (40) | 2.95 | (42) | 2.19 |
| Medium  2 | (42) | 3.17 | (32) | 3.46 |
| High    3 | (41) | 3.07 | (21) | 2.47 |

external control indices in relation to the Protest Behaviors Index.

Table 3.38 shows the relationship between the three internal-external control indices and the Protest Behaviors Index. There is a small relationship between the Protest Behaviors Index and the System

**Table 3.38**

Relationships between the Protest Behaviors Index and
the Internal-External Control Indices
(1972 reinterview)
(gammas)

|  | N | Personal Control Index | Control Ideology Index | System Blame Index |
|---|---|---|---|---|
| All Respondents | (240) | -.04 | -.08 | .20† |
| Whites | (120) | .09 | -.07 | .36‡ |
| Blacks | (116) | -.04 | -.18 | .11 |

†p < .05    ‡p < .005

Blame Index among all respondents. This association appears to be largely due to a correlation of the two measures among white but not black respondents. This finding is interesting since most of the work on internal-external control in relation to militancy has been done among blacks rather than whites. Since this is the case, it is disappointing that the relationship does not hold among black respondents.

One additional hypothesis suggested by the work of Crawford and Naditch (1970) was tested. This hypothesis states that those who are externally oriented and who have strong feelings of relative deprivation will show predilections for political violence. The hypothesis was tested by conducting an analysis of variance of the Violence for Social Change Index in relation to Cantril's Ladder and the System Blame Index. A parallel analysis was conducted with the Protest Behaviors Index. Neither analysis shows significant interactions. Because we had considerable doubt about the measurement characteristics of Cantril's Ladder, we tested the hypothesis again using the Resentment-Suspicion Index as a measure of frustration, since, presumably, those who have strong feelings of relative deprivation will feel frustrated. One translation of the Crawford and Naditch hypothesis might be that those who are high on frustration as measured by the Resentment-Suspicion Index and high on System Blame will have a predilection for political action including political violence as measured by the Violence for Social Change Index or the Protest Behaviors Index. None of the analyses of variance conducted showed significant interactions, and the mean values in the matrices generated did not suggest any strong additive effect for any pair of independent variables.

The literature suggests rather strongly that a belief in one's personal efficacy coupled with a belief that the system is to blame are characteristics of black militants. Our data do not provide support for this speculation. However, even if there is not a strong, direct, or interactive relationship between the Personal Control and System Blame Indices, it is still possible that these indices relate indirectly to attitudes toward violence, perhaps by increasing frustration. Consequently, the relationships between the Resentment-Suspicion Index and the Internal-External Control Indices were examined (Table 3.39). It can be seen that Personal Control is related to Resentment-Suspicion among black, white, and all respondents. This is as expected. The inability

**Table 3.39**

Relationships between the Resentment-Suspicion Index and
the Internal-External Control Indices
(1972 reinterview)
(gammas)

|  | N | Personal Control Index | Control Ideology Index | System Blame Index |
|---|---|---|---|---|
| All Respondents | (240) | -.34†† | -.01 | .16† |
| Whites | (120) | -.23† | .07 | .16 |
| Blacks | (116) | -.31§ | .00 | .32‡ |

†p < .05    ‡p < .01    §p < .005    ††p < .001

to control the outcome of one's life should lead to resentment and the data show that this is indeed the case. Table 3.40 shows that among

**Table 3.40**

Percentage Responses to the Resentment-Suspicion Index
in Relation to the Personal Control Index
(1972 reinterview respondents, N = 240)

| Resentment-Suspicion Index | Personal Control Index | | | |
|---|---|---|---|---|
|  | Low 1 | 2 | 3 | High 4 |
| Low    1 | 11% | 4% | 16% | 30% |
| 2 | 14 | 18 | 25 | 39 |
| 3 | 18 | 29 | 24 | 11 |
| 4 | 25 | 17 | 15 | 17 |
| High   5 | 32 | 32 | 20 | 3 |
|  | 100% | 100% | 100% | 100% |
| N * | (56) | (76) | (67) | (36) |

those who fell into the highest category on Personal Control only 3 percent fell into the highest category of the Resentment-Suspicion Index, in contrast to 32 percent of those in the lowest category of the Personal Control Index. The System Blame Index also related to the Resentment-Suspicion Index among blacks and all respondents considered together.

Most of the studies which have been done on internal-external control in relation to militancy have been conducted on groups of activists or groups which had given some indication of their involvement. These data have shown that among those who are low on the Avoid Problems Index frustration is related to positive attitudes toward violence. One might speculate that activists are likely to be people who are low on avoiding problems. This suggests that feelings of lack of personal control and the perception that the system is to blame for problems may be directly related to protest orientation among those whose personality characteristics make them prone to action.

*Summary*

Gurin et al. (1969) have conceptualized internal-external control as consisting of three major dimensions: personal control, control ideology, and system blame. The existing literature which is concerned mainly with black militants suggests that of the three dimensions, system blame should be most closely related to activism and militancy. Thus, it was anticipated that there would be a relationship between the System Blame Index and the Violence for Social Change and Protest Behaviors Indices. However, no such relationship was found. There was a small relationship between the System Blame Index and the Protest Behaviors Index when all respondents were considered together, but the relationship was true for white but not black respondents. This finding is somewhat puzzling since most of the relevant literature is concerned with findings for black militants. There was some relationship between the system blame dimension and a measure of frustration among blacks. Thus, the perception that the system is to blame for difficulty may lead to frustration among blacks which in turn, among those who are not oriented toward avoiding problems, leads to the perception that violence is necessary to bring about social change. Interestingly enough, Personal Control, or the individual's conception of how much control he has over his own life, is more consistently related to frustration than is the measure of System Blame. The differences between what the data show and what was anticipated on the basis of previous work may be partly due to the fact that most of the previous work had been carried out with people who were known to have some commitment to action, a condition which is not likely to be true of a more general population.

## OVERVIEW

Political cynicism, political alienation, relative deprivation, and internal-external control—these are the variables which have been promulgated as important in relation to political violence and these are the variables which have been investigated in relation to attitudes toward violence and protest behaviors. The data described in this chapter provide only very weak support for the hypotheses conceived by other researchers—and, in some cases, no support at all—and yet the hypotheses explored here are central to the ideas about political violence developed by political scientists. How can we explain our failure to provide substantial support for these crucial concepts? It is easy to resort to methodological arguments. Indeed, we have presented data which make serious consideration of the quality of the instruments used for measuring the constructs compelling. This is particularly true for the measures of relative deprivation and of internal-external control. Nevertheless, it seems probable that more profound reasons underlie the failure of the hypotheses, and these are issues related to the lack of complexity of the hypotheses tested. Our study of political cynicism provides an example of the kind of change which will probably have to be made in all hypotheses relating to political violence. The variable political cynicism was included in the study because of existing hypotheses which stated that political cynicism is a causal factor in civil violence. Our data did not show strong support for this hypothesis when only the zero order relationships were considered. Only among black respondents did the anticipated relationship appear. However, when the population studied was partitioned on the basis of political orientation, it was found that political cynicism relates to positive attitudes toward violence, just as theory says it should, but only among those who are politically oriented to the left. So the hypothesis is true, but not in the simple form in which it was originally stated. We suspect that similar reasons explain the failure to confirm other hypotheses investigated here. Their formulations are too simplistic to conform to the real world. Future work in this field should amplify existing theory and cast it on a more complex level. Such complexity may not be as satisfying as simple statements, but it is more likely to reflect reality and to serve as an accurate predictor of behaviors occurring in real life.

# Chapter 4

# VIOLENCE FOR SOCIAL CONTROL: MEASUREMENT CHARACTERISTICS AND CRITERION VALIDITY

*Introduction*

The use of violence as a means of maintaining social control was the second major focus of interest in our 1969 study of attitudes toward violence. At the time the instrument for measuring attitudes toward the use of violence in maintaining social control was first created, there was very little question about what the thrust of the measuring instrument ought to be. It seemed clear that the focus of attention should be directed at measuring how much force the respondent was willing to advocate.

In considering the Violence for Social Control Index it is helpful to remember the era in which it was created. The year was 1968, a time which followed major riots in the urban centers of the nation by about a year. Whether or not there were to be more such upheavals was uncertain. In the preceding years the use of force in controlling civil disturbances had often been badly managed. The Report of the National Advisory Commission on Civil Disorder (1968, p. 301) emphasized that the police had on occasion responded to threats of disorder with excessive, poorly planned force and an inappropriate choice of weapons. Such over-response of government to civil disturbance was vividly depicted and widely televised during the 1968 Democratic convention. The encounters between the police and demonstrators left liberal television viewers thoroughly outraged. The study team assigned to investigate the convention in Chicago referred to the encounter as a "police riot" (Walker 1968, p. xxii). However, the average citizen did not share the horror of the country's liberals and was more likely than not to have approved of the events (Robinson 1970).

It is undeniable that the authors shared a strong liberal bias which influenced not only our view of the events but also our choice of measures. To us the issue of the day appeared to be whether force as a means of social control should be used at all, rather than under what circumstances and in what situations its use was appropriate. At the time we were not familiar with the technology and logistics of crowd control and, indeed, were only dimly aware that there might be orderly procedures involving sequential patterns of force for controlling crowds in riots. Like many liberally oriented academicians, we were inclined to view force with distaste and to regard it as unnecessary and immoral.

In the ensuing years it became clear that the issues were more complex than we had earlier envisioned. The emergence of a true radical terrorism on the left, broadly advertised with strident rhetoric, forced many liberals into serious reflection on the proper uses of force by the state. This reconsideration resulted from the realization that ideologies which include resort to bombs and arson create situations which are not easily managed. Moreover, some radical ideologies explicitly stated that the old must be destroyed before meaningful social change could come about. Such verbal expressions of destruction, punctuated by occasional acts of terrorism such as bombings, were often associated with an explicit unwillingness to negotiate, compromise, or work toward mutual settlements. Developments of this nature made it difficult to avoid considering the proper use of force by the society to protect itself from outrageous infringement. And, many who had found such considerations distasteful were obliged to consider the proper use of force for the first time.

At the same time that radical movements made themselves felt, repeated pronouncements from three presidential commissions, the National Advisory Commission on Civil Disorders (1968), the National Commission on the Causes and Prevention of Violence (1969), and the President's Commission on Campus Unrest (1970), forced the public to reconsider the weaponry used by the police in the cause of maintaining order. All these developments influenced how people think about the use of violence as a means of social control and what might be the best way of measuring such attitudes. On the whole, the events served to emphasize the complexity of the issues and to blur the meaning of the dimension originally thought to be most important, that is, the level of force to be used in maintaining social control. The events implied that a more appropriate way of measuring attitudes toward violence for social control might be to explore in detail the circumstances under which force was thought to be necessary. Such considerations imply that the respondent should be presented with a large number of highly specific scenarios, carefully graded to range from peaceful protest through disruption to actual violence. The point in the continuum of disturbances where the respondent felt that specific levels of force should be used to contain the disturbance could then be ascertained. Unfortunately, at the time the original measures of attitudes toward the use of violence as a means of social control were constructed, such considerations lay in the future; and the major dimension measured was the level of police force the respondent felt was appropriate, although it should be pointed out that the original study did measure the level of force felt to be appropriate in three different situations.

The change in the tenor of the times was reflected in the respondent's reaction to the questions in the Violence for Social Control Index during the actual interviewing process in 1972. There had been little problem in getting respondents to answer the questions in the index in 1969. However, during pretests for the 1972 round of interviewing, the interviewers reported that some respondents were inclined to balk at the questions and to qualify their answers with statements such as "It depends." Such comments indicated the unease the respondents felt at the direction of the questioning, an unease which the researchers came to share.

The issues raised in the preceding discussion imply that in measuring attitudes toward violence for social control other lines of questioning, in addition to the level of police force advocated, need to be considered seriously. A supplement to the level of force required might come in the form of a set of questions about the kinds of situations in which respondents felt force to be appropriate. A series of scenarios might be developed in which the respondent is given far more detail concerning not only the nature of the situation requiring control, but also the methods of control which have already been used in the situation. This series of scenarios would assess which situations were seen as requiring specific levels of police force. Presumably, respondents more oriented toward the use of violence for social control would be willing to apply it to a larger variety of situations and to apply it earlier than would be those who are less oriented toward the use of force in social control.

Alternative methods of measuring attitudes toward violence for social control also need consideration. It is conceivable that these attitudes could be measured by considering how respondents feel about the number and the nature of nonviolent behaviors which might be used by the authorities to avert violence. For example, one might ask whether or not the police should try to negotiate with the leaders of a disturbance or whether community leaders should be used to try to "cool" potential disturbances. One might ask if the respondent approves of tactics which involve isolation and containment of the trouble spot or if the police should be slow to act. For example, when the Indians seized Wounded Knee, the Federal government seemed to respond with a foot dragging strategy; it seems likely that that unhappy episode could have become a major catastrophe if the agents of social control had moved more vigorously and with more force. But, do Americans recognize and approve of such tactics and, if they do, under what circumstances do they do so? Such questions require further thought.

A rough beginning to an investigation of the acceptability of non-violent alternative methods of social control, such as negotiation, was made in the 1972 interviews. Two sets of questions, one about the prison riot in Attica and the other about the respondent's attitudes toward the control of school disturbances explored such issues. Data collected from these questions, which will be discussed in detail subsequently, indicated that the approaches suggested above may be useful. However, the data also suggest that such questions are not easily written and that it will take considerable thought and effort to develop meaningful items and item sequences. In addition, the data suggest that responses to questions about alternative methods of social control will not correlate highly with questions that deal with the amount of force that should be used. Instead, it seems likely that such questions will add new and necessary dimensions to the measurement of attitudes toward violence for social control.

### Measuring Attitudes Toward Violence for Social Control

Attitudes toward violence for social control were measured in the 1972 study by asking the respondent how the police should handle two types of disturbances, one involving "hoodlum gangs" and the other involving blacks. For each situation the respondent was read a brief scenario describing the disturbance and was then handed a card on which he was asked to indicate how the police should handle the situation described. The exact format of these questions is shown on the right. The first disturbance about which the respondent was asked in the 1972 study was a set of questions requesting opinions about how the

|  | Almost Always | Sometimes | Hardly Ever | Never |
|---|---|---|---|---|
| A. The police should let it go, not do anything. | ☐ | ☐ | ☐ | ☐ |
| B. Police should make arrests without using clubs or guns. | ☐ | ☐ | ☐ | ☐ |
| C. Police should use clubs, but not guns. | ☐ | ☐ | ☐ | ☐ |
| D. The police should shoot, but not to kill. | ☐ | ☐ | ☐ | ☐ |
| E. The police should shoot to kill. | ☐ | ☐ | ☐ | ☐ |

police should handle situations involving hoodlum gangs. The question was as follows:

> *There have been times when gangs of hoodlums have gone into a town, terrified people, and caused a lot of property damage. How do you think the police should handle this situation?*

The respondent was then handed a printed card which contained the questions asking how the police should handle the situation and was allowed to fill it out without further interference from the interviewer. The second situation about which the respondent was asked reads as follows:

> *When you think about big city riots (ghetto disturbances/ inner city disturbances) involving Negroes (black people/ colored people) and police, how do you think the police should handle the situation?*

The percentage distribution of responses to the questions in the Violence for Social Control Index in the ghetto disturbance situation is given in Table 4.1. It can be seen that white respondents thought that making arrests without the use of clubs or guns, using clubs but not guns, and shooting though not to kill were all actions which ought to be used with approximately equal frequency. Black respondents thought the less forceful methods should be used more often than the more lethal ones, although the level of force advocated was still quite high.

**Table 4.1**

Percentage Responses to Items Measuring the Level of Control
Advocated for Use by Police in the Ghetto Disturbance Situation

| | All Respondents | Whites | Blacks |
|---|---|---|---|
| The police should let it go, not do anything.† | | | |
| Almost Always | 6% | 0% | 14% |
| Sometimes | 14 | 8 | 21 |
| Hardly Ever | 14 | 11 | 16 |
| Never | 66 | 81 | 49 |
| | 100% | 100% | 100% |
| Police should make arrests without using clubs or guns. | | | |
| Almost Always | 24 | 26 | 21 |
| Sometimes | 55 | 46 | 64 |
| Hardly Ever | 12 | 14 | 11 |
| Never | 9 | 14 | 4 |
| | 100% | 100% | 100% |
| Police should use clubs, but not guns. | | | |
| Almost Always | 10 | 12 | 8 |
| Sometimes | 63 | 65 | 61 |
| Hardly Ever | 19 | 16 | 20 |
| Never | 8 | 7 | 11 |
| | 100% | 100% | 100% |
| The police should shoot, but not to kill. | | | |
| Almost Always | 19 | 23 | 12 |
| Sometimes | 49 | 51 | 47 |
| Hardly Ever | 17 | 16 | 19 |
| Never | 15 | 10 | 22 |
| | 100% | 100% | 100% |
| The police should shoot to kill. | | | |
| Almost Always | 1 | 1 | 0 |
| Sometimes | 26 | 33 | 19 |
| Hardly Ever | 22 | 25 | 18 |
| Never | 51 | 41 | 63 |
| | 100% | 100% | 100% |
| N | (283) | (145) | (133) |

†Only respondents with interview forms A and C (N = 146; See Appendix B) were asked this question.

**Table 4.2**

Percentage Responses to Items Measuring the Level of Control
Advocated for Use by Police in the Hoodlum Gangs Situation

| | All Respondents | Whites | Blacks |
|---|---|---|---|
| **The police should let it go, not do anything.†** | | | |
| Almost Always | 8% | 5% | 10% |
| Sometimes | 11 | 4 | 19 |
| Hardly Ever | 9 | 8 | 10 |
| Never | 72 | 83 | 61 |
| | 100% | 100% | 100% |
| **Police should make arrests without using clubs or guns.** | | | |
| Almost Always | 21 | 19 | 22 |
| Sometimes | 60 | 52 | 68 |
| Hardly Ever | 6 | 10 | 3 |
| Never | 13 | 19 | 7 |
| | 100% | 100% | 100% |
| **Police should use clubs, but not guns.** | | | |
| Almost Always | 14 | 20 | 8 |
| Sometimes | 59 | 62 | 53 |
| Hardly Ever | 14 | 8 | 22 |
| Never | 13 | 10 | 17 |
| | 100% | 100% | 100% |
| **The police should shoot, but not to kill.** | | | |
| Almost Always | 31 | 36 | 24 |
| Sometimes | 41 | 40 | 43 |
| Hardly Ever | 15 | 18 | 13 |
| Never | 13 | 6 | 20 |
| | 100% | 100% | 100% |
| **The police should shoot to kill.** | | | |
| Almost Always | 2 | 4 | 0 |
| Sometimes | 28 | 29 | 26 |
| Hardly Ever | 24 | 27 | 21 |
| Never | 46 | 40 | 53 |
| | 100% | 100% | 100% |
| N | (283) | (145) | (133) |

†Only respondents with interview forms A and C (N = 146; See Appendix B) were
asked this question.

Table 4.2 gives the percentage distribution of responses for the hoodlum gangs situation. In general the distribution of responses appears to be highly similar to those obtained in the ghetto disturbance situation; however, black respondents showed a small tendency to advocate more force in the hoodlum gangs situation than they did in the ghetto disturbance questions.

The responses to the questions for each situation were combined into a scale which took into account the pattern of responses in the entire question set. The scaling has been described in detail elsewhere (Blumenthal et al. 1972, Appendix D). Scale scores for the two situations, the one referring to hoodlum gangs (Violence for Social Control: Hoodlum Gangs) and the other referring to ghetto disturbances by blacks (Violence for Social Control: Blacks), were averaged to form the Violence for Social Control Index. The higher the score on the index, the more violent the pattern of force advocated by the respondent.

The 1969 Violence for Social Control Index differed from that used in the 1972 study by averaging responses to three rather than two situations describing disturbances. The national study had asked a series of questions not included in the 1972 interviews inquiring how the police should handle disorders on campuses. Reanalysis of the national data indicated that a Violence for Social Control Index averaged from only the hoodlum gangs and black disturbances had many of the same statistical characteristics as the original Violence for Social Control Index which had included a third subscale (McConochie,

**Table 4.3**

Percentage Responses to the Violence for Social Control Index
in the 1969 and 1972 Studies

|  |  | 1969 Study | | 1972 Study | |
|---|---|---|---|---|---|
|  |  | Whites | Blacks | Whites | Blacks |
| Violence for Social Control Index |  |  |  |  |  |
| Low | 0-2 | 18% | 33% | 13% | 27% |
|  | 3-6 | 47 | 44 | 40 | 44 |
| High | 7-9 | 35 | 23 | 47 | 29 |
|  |  | 100% | 100% | 100% | 100% |
|  | N | (1,046) | (303) | (145) | (133) |

Note: The Violence for Social Control Index used in this and subsequent tables on the 1969 data is comparable to that used in the 1972 data (i.e., it is constructed from *two* situation item sets, hoodlum gangs and black rioters, rather than the *three* item sets that were used in the original analysis of the 1969 data). Consequently, the data are not comparable to the data in the monograph *Justifying Violence: Attitudes of American Men* (Blumenthal et al. 1972).

Jayaratne, and Blumenthal 1973). Consequently, to conserve interviewing time, the set of questions about campus disturbances was omitted from the 1972 series of interviews.

Table 4.3 shows the percentage distribution of responses to the Violence for Social Control Index in the 1972 interview and for the 1969 national sample for black and white respondents. In both studies blacks scored lower on the index than did whites. In the 1972 data white respondents appeared to score slightly higher on the index than was true for the 1969 national data. Whether this was due to the profound difference between the two populations interviewed, to a change in national attitudes between the time of the first and second interview, or merely to a random fluctuation cannot be ascertained from these data.

## Demographic Correlates of the Violence for Social Control Index

Table 4.4 shows the Violence for Social Control Index in relation to selected demographic characteristics. On the whole the associations are approximately what one would have predicted from the earlier national study, with the one exception that age appears to have a stronger relationship to the index in the 1972 data than it did in the 1969 data. However, in the 1969 study, when the index was based on all

**Table 4.4**

Relationships between the Violence for Social Control Index
and Selected Demographic Characteristics for White and Black Respondents
in the 1969 and 1972 Studies
(gammas)

| Demographic Characteristics | 1969 Study | | 1972 Study | |
|---|---|---|---|---|
| | Whites | Blacks | Whites | Blacks |
| Sex | — | — | -.09 | .01 |
| Age | .08†† | .00 | .17† | .18† |
| Education | -.16†† | -.02 | -.18† | -.11 |
| Family Income | -.05†† | .03 | -.05 | .00 |
| Town Size | -.10†† | .00 | -.03 | .01 |
| Experience in South | -.16†† | .02 | -.13 | -.14 |
| N | (1,046) | (303) | (145) | (133) |

†p < .05     ††p < .001

three question sets the association was larger (Blumenthal et al. 1972, p. 213). In any case, the size of the association is small, with older respondents more likely to show high scores on the index than those who were younger.

*Continuity Correlations of the Violence for Social Control Index*

**Continuity Correlations of the Index, the Subscales, and the Items.**
In discussing the continuity correlation of the Violence for Social
Control Index, the relationships of the overall index between the 1972
interview and the 1972 reinterview will be compared with the continuity
correlations of the separate subscales and the individual items. The
possibility that learning affects the size of the correlation will be
explored; the relationships between the continuity correlation and some
demographic characteristics will be discussed, and some thought will
be given to the dual components of all continuity correlations,
reliability, and stability.

The complexity of the Violence for Social Control Index is reflected in continuity correlations which are considerably lower than
those obtained for the Violence for Social Change Index. The gamma
between scores on the first and second interview for the overall index
was .54 (Pearson $r = .63$). The continuity correlations for the two subscales were lower. The gamma was .42 for the subscale which inquired
about the hoodlum gangs situation (Violence for Social Control:
Hoodlum Gangs) (Pearson $r = .49$) and was .50 for the subscale which
inquired about the ghetto disturbances (Violence for Social Control:
Blacks) (Pearson $r = .57$). These relationships are given in Table
4.5. The table shows that for the subscales correlations obtained
by calculating gammas are very similar to, albeit somewhat lower, than

**Table 4.5**

Relationships between the Violence for Social Control Scales
within and between the Interview and Reinterview
(all respondents, $N = 283$)
(gammas, $tau_b$'s, Pearson $r$'s)

| VIOLENCE FOR SOCIAL CONTROL INDEX | | Gamma | $Tau_b$ | Pearson $r$ | Variation Explained ($R^2$) |
|---|---|---|---|---|---|
| Interview vs. Reinterview | | .54 | .49 | .63 | 40% |
| **VIOLENCE FOR SOCIAL CONTROL SUBSCALES** | | | | | |
| Interview | Reinterview | | | | |
| Hoodlum Gangs | Hoodlum Gangs | .42 | .38 | .49 | 24% |
| Blacks | Blacks | .50 | .45 | .57 | 32% |
| Hoodlum Gangs | Blacks | .42 | .37 | .49 | 24% |
| Blacks | Hoodlum Gangs | .51 | .46 | .58 | 34% |
| Interview | | | | | |
| Hoodlum Gangs vs. Blacks | | .54 | .48 | .62 | 40% |
| Reinterview | | | | | |
| Hoodlum Gangs vs. Blacks | | .59 | .54 | .66 | 44% |

correlations obtained by computing Pearson r's. Tau$_b$'s tend to be slightly lower than gammas. The data for these measures are ordinal rather than interval and thus do not meet all the assumptions of the r. However, the magnitudes of the three statistics (gammas, tau$_b$'s, and r's) are very much alike, suggesting that it is reasonable to use Pearson r's with these measures in spite of their ordinal character. These considerations will be of some importance in subsequent analyses where, because of the relatively small number of cases in the current study, it becomes more convenient to use r's in multiple regression analyses rather than eta's in the more appropriate multiple classification analyses. The data fulfill the requirements of multiple classification analyses more exactly, but multiple classification analyses require a far larger number of cases than multiple regression techniques. (For further discussion see Appendix C.)

Table 4.5 shows that there is considerable gain in reliability when two subscales are combined into a single index. Thus, the Violence for Social Control Index on the interview accounts for 40 percent of the variance in that index on the reinterview, while Violence for Social Control: Blacks accounts for only 32 percent of its variance on the reinterview, and Violence for Social Control: Hoodlum Gangs can predict only 24 percent of its variance on the reinterview.

Since the continuity correlation for the overall index is relatively low, and since it is clear that using two subscales in combination has some advantage over using one, it might be asked whether using three subscales in combination (as in the 1969 national study) would be more reliable than using two. One guess about this can be made by computing the Spearman Brown Coefficient (Guilford 1954, p. 354) for the three subscales in the 1969 data and comparing this with the coefficient for the two subscales used in the 1972 data. This calculation shows that the three subscales have a Spearman Brown Coefficient of .77, while the two subscales have a coefficient of .70. These data suggest that a Violence for Social Control Index comprised of three subscales would show slightly higher continuity correlations than would the two-item index. Whether the gain in reliability is high enough to offset the increased bulk of the instrument is problematical.

The correlations between subscales within an interview are slightly higher than the correlations between the interview and reinterview. Since the subscales within an interview inquire about different situations, it is reasonable to suppose that these correlations should be smaller than would be correlations between identical question sets. One might speculate that since the correlations within an interview are actually higher than the correlations between the first and the second interview, that real changes over time may contribute to the

low continuity correlations. However, the data available are not sufficient to differentiate between the error measurement and true change
occurring over time.

The relatively low continuity correlations of the Violence for
Social Control Index may be partly a reflection of the respondent's
ambivalence about how much violence is appropriate as a means of
social control. Ambivalence is a natural part of the human condition.
Many of us are of two minds about the same issue, and the phenomenon
of a person vacillating between two quite different positions is sufficiently common in everyday life that it is more likely to arouse
sympathy than wonder in the observer. If adherence to two quite different beliefs about the use of violence for social control plays a part
in producing the low continuity correlations, one would expect that
more ambivalent respondents would have lower continuity correlations
than those who are more single minded.

To a limited extent this hypothesis can be tested in the present
data. To do so, one can consider respondents who had the same or
highly similar responses to the two Violence for Social Control situations within an interview in relation to those who had widely different
responses. One interpretation of a large difference in responses is that
the respondent held quite different attitudes toward the two situations
and that it is the interaction between the attitude toward the use of
violence for social control and the attitude toward the situation which
produces differences in the scores. It is also possible that it is ambivalence about how much force ought to be used for social control
which produces the varying responses rather than a difference in the
attitudes toward the two situations. Using the variation in scores
within interviews as an operational definition of ambivalence, the data
show that those who gave very similar answers within one interview
had higher continuity correlations (gamma = .64) than those who
responded to the two Violence for Social Control situations quite
differently within an interview (gamma = .43). These statistics cannot
be demonstrated to be significantly different, but they are
in the anticipated direction, suggesting that ambivalence about violence
for social control may play a role in determining the size of the continuity correlations.

Table 4.6 shows the continuity correlations of the individual items
in the Violence for Social Control Index. The correlations for three of
the four items contained in the index are substantially lower than the
continuity correlation of the overall index. Only the item "the police
should shoot to kill" has continuity correlations which are higher than
those of the index. Not only are the continuity correlations of the
items lower than those of the indices when they are measured as

gammas, but the correlations are proportionately lower still when the statistic used is a tau$_b$ or a Pearson r.

**Table 4.6**

Test-Retest Reliability for Items
in the Violence for Social Control Subscales
(all respondents, N = 283)
(gammas, tau$_b$'s, Pearson r's)

| | Violence for Social Control: Hoodlum Gangs | | | Violence for Social Control: Blacks | | |
|---|---|---|---|---|---|---|
| | Gamma | Tau$_b$ | Pearson r | Gamma | Tau$_b$ | Pearson r |
| Police should make arrests without using clubs or guns. | .47 | .32 | .36 | .49 | .33 | .40 |
| Police should use clubs, but not guns. | .25 | .15 | .15 | .33 | .20 | .19 |
| The police should shoot, but not to kill. | .29 | .21 | .27 | .55 | .40 | .47 |
| The police should shoot to kill. | .71 | .52 | .57 | .69 | .49 | .54 |

The variation in the reliability of these items raises serious issues. One reason for the low reliability may be that the item is "bad" from a methodological point of view. One must ask whether the item is ambiguous, has multiple frames of reference, or is too "difficult" for the respondent. By "difficult" we mean that the question contains uncommon words, requires a high degree of skill to answer, or involves a level of abstraction which cannot be expected from the average respondent. It seems unlikely that the item about the police using clubs but not guns, which has the lowest reliability, is ambiguous. It is true that the sketches describing the situation in which police control is required are somewhat vague, but the situation is equally vague for all four of the items in the index, so that this is not a satisfactory explanation of why the "clubs but not guns" item is less reliable than the others in the set. It is unlikely that the item has multiple frames of reference. No alternative interpretation of the item has ever been proposed by the interviewers or the respondents. The item does not contain uncommon words, but the situation detailed in the sketch which precedes the Violence for Social Control items may require the respondent to abstract more than he is able to. The level of abstraction required to decide whether the police should use clubs but not guns may be large if the respondent approaches the issue from a pragmatic rather than an ideological point of view. It is easy to say what the police should do if one has a definite ideology about the use of force. It is difficult if one has no such ideology and if one is trying to decide what is practically useful.

When the questions included in the Violence for Social Control Index are considered in detail, the complex nature of this set of questions becomes evident. A response almost seems to require either that the respondent imagine a situation far more concrete and specific than that described in the brief scenarios read by the interviewer, or that he have a definite philosophy regarding the use of force. In addition, the questions in the Violence for Social Control Index implicitly require that the respondent have some knowledge of appropriate tactics for the control of civil disturbances. All this is a great deal to ask of respondents, perhaps more than is realistic.

There is another issue in the assessment of a particular item which borders on the methodological but is not methodological in nature. It may be a matter of interest to know public opinion on a particular issue because an issue exists. For example, it might be important to understand public opinion on the negative income tax. It may be, however, that the concept of a negative income tax has been too little explained or is too complicated for some people to grasp so that opinions about it are not well formulated in the respondent's mind. Vague and poorly formulated beliefs are likely to show variable responses on repeated measurement. Such variability has several implications in addition to its contribution to the "unreliability" of the item. One might suppose, for example, that opinions which are not held in a fixed manner could be made more stable or could be more easily changed through education and information than beliefs which are fixed in nature. One could speculate that responses to the item about the police using clubs but not guns may be subject to such change through education. The item asks about a definite level of force which is part of the continuum of physical violence which can be used as a means of social control. Many respondents may feel they do not have sufficient information to answer the question; they might think the question deals with a technical problem which should be decided on the basis of the immediate factors in the specific situation where control is required. If such were the case, it seems reasonable to suppose that the respondent would have no set opinion about the matter and that he might easily change his mind from one moment to the next.

It is interesting in this respect that respondents who were rated by the interviewer as having a "good" understanding of the interview responded somewhat less reliably on the Violence for Social Control Index (gamma = .49) than respondents who were thought to have only "fair" or "poor" understanding of the interview (gamma = .68). This could be interpreted as evidence against the preceding argument. But, it could also imply that individuals who were thoughtful about the questions were more inclined to think that they did not have enough information to answer the questions decisively. One interpretation of the low reliability of the item on the use of clubs rather than guns is that respondents are not sufficiently informed about appropriate measures for crowd control.[1] If such were the case, one could expect that a widespread effort to educate the public might result in respondents having more definite ideas about the appropriate means of force by the police and in an increase in the reliability of the item in future studies.

Another interpretation of the current data is that the "clubs but not guns" item might be a good candidate for deletion from the index. However, since the Violence for Social Control Index involves a complicated scaling based on the analysis of the pattern of responses rather than on a straightforward additive model, a complex reanalysis of the data would be required to determine if rescaling were feasible.

As might have been expected from the continuity correlations for the Violence for Social Control subscales (Table 4.5), the continuity correlation for the items in the ghetto disturbance situation are slightly higher than those for the hoodlum gangs situation (Table 4.6). In any case it seems clear that there is a substantial gain in reliability by combining items into indices.

**Learning and Continuity Correlations.** The lowest correlations among the Violence for Social Control subscales are those involving the Violence for Social Control: Hoodlum Gangs as it appears in the first interview. This subscale is based on the first set of questions on attitudes toward violence to appear in the interview, so one might suspect that learning is influencing the size of the continuity correlations.

There are several changes in the interviewing procedure at this juncture. Until the question about hoodlum gangs is asked, the interviewer dutifully records all the responses made by the respondent. However, with the Violence for Social Control: Hoodlum Gangs questions, the procedure changes. The respondent is handed a card and

---

[1] Both the President's Commission on Campus Unrest (1970) and the National Advisory Commission on Civil Disorders (1968) made strong statements about the use of force in the control of civil disturbances. The National Advisory Commission pointed out that there is a definite catalogue of procedures which can be used to disperse such disturbances and that there is an order in which weapons of increasing force ought to be employed: nonlethal, noninjurious methods such as tear gas should be fully used before higher levels of force are employed. Moreover, the National Advisory Commission cited the use of batons as an effective weapon of crowd control which should be fully utilized before the police resort to more destructive weapons (Report of the National Advisory Commission on Civil Disorders 1968, p. 491).

instructed to check off the responses he finds most appropriate; for the first time the respondent must grapple with filling out a form. In addition to the change in the respondent's behavioral task, there is also a change in the frame of reference within which the respondent is asked to answer. While previously he had been asked to respond mainly in terms of whether or not he agreed with particular statements, he must now respond in terms of how often certain actions should be undertaken.

These changes in procedure, occurring at the time the first set of Violence for Social Control questions are asked, make it necessary for the respondent to readapt himself to the interviewing situation by learning how to use the new interview instrument. If learning is required, one would expect a higher rate of error until the learning process is completed and, consequently, lower continuity correlations for relationships with indices.

Several specific hypotheses can be derived from the general hypothesis that learning occurs during the first Violence for Social Control item sequence (Violence for Social Control: Hoodlum Gangs). If one supposes that a new task is apt to be performed less accurately than a task where learning has been completed, it follows that a larger proportion of the responses to the new task is attributable to error than is true for tasks where learning is not necessary. If the error component of the Violence for Social Control: Hoodlum Gangs subscale on the first interview is larger than in any of the subsequent subscales, one would expect that correlations involving this first subscale would be lower than comparable correlations involving other subscales.

Specifically, correlations between the two Violence for Social Control subscales should be higher within the 1972 reinterview than within the 1972 interview. In addition, the continuity correlation between the first (interview) and second (reinterview) Violence for Social Control: Hoodlum Gangs subscales should be smaller than the continuity correlations for the Violence for Social Control: Blacks subscales. The correlation between the first Hoodlum Gangs subscale and the second Blacks subscale should be somewhat smaller than the relationship between the second Hoodlum Gangs subscale and the first Blacks subscale. These hypotheses are depicted schematically in Figure 4.1. (Table 4.5 gives the relationships shown in Figure 4.1 in more detail.) The figure demonstrates that the differences between the correlations are in the predicted direction for all three cases. There is of course a one-eighth probability that such relative relationships would have occurred by chance; nevertheless, this evidence indicates that serious consideration should be given to the possibility that learning affects responses to items in the Violence for Social Control Index.

**Figure 1**

Hypothesized and Actual Size of Correlations between
Violence for Social Control Subscales If Learning is a Factor in the
Response to Violence for Social Control
(gammas)

Violence for Social Control Subscales

Interview

(A)   Violence for Social Control: Hoodlum Gangs
(B)   Violence for Social Control: Blacks

Reinterview

(A')   Violence for Social Control: Hoodlum Gangs
(B')   Violence for Social Control: Blacks

Hypothesized and Actual Size of Correlations

| Within Interview | | | Between Interviews | | |
|---|---|---|---|---|---|
| AB | < | A'B' | AA' | < | BB' |
| .54 | | .59 | .42 | | .50 |
| | | | AB' | < | A'B |
| | | | .42 | | .51 |

There would be no perfect remedies to this problem unless the index were substantially altered and simplified. The effect could be controlled if alternate forms of the interview were used which varied the order of appearance of the indices. It might be possible to reduce the amount of learning required for the Violence for Social Control Index somewhat if the respondent were obliged to check answers on some other set of questions prior to the introduction of the index. It might also be possible to allow the respondent to answer an extra set of Violence for Social Control questions so that the first set could be discarded as a "learning" trial. One suspects, however, that the real solution lies in altering the measure.

**Continuity Correlations in Selected Demographic Subgroups.** If learning is an important ingredient in determining the continuity correlations of the Violence for Social Control Index, differences in the continuity correlations among different subgroups are to be expected. Specifically, one would think that such correlations would be higher among the better educated, and one might speculate that they would be higher among white respondents than among black, since blacks are likely to have attended schools of lesser quality than whites and in our population are likely to have completed less schooling. Table 4.7 shows some of these relationships. It can be seen that the anticipated differences in continuity correlations are not present. In fact, there is remarkably little difference shown in the size of the correlations for different subgroups. These findings suggest that learning plays only a small part in accounting for the relatively low continuity correlations and that other factors such as measurement error, stability, and ambivalence must be more important.

Table 4.7

Test-Retest Reliability for the Violence for
Social Control Index for Selected Subgroups
(gammas)

|  | N | Gamma |
|---|---|---|
| All Respondents | (283) | .54 |
| Whites | (145) | .53 |
| Blacks | (133) | .50 |
| Men | (131) | .51 |
| Women | (152) | .54 |
| 10 Years of School or Less | (104) | .56 |
| At Least Some College | ( 63) | .57 |
| Southern Respondents | ( 94) | .45 |
| Detroit Respondents | (189) | .60 |
| 25 Years of Age or Younger | ( 84) | .50 |
| 40 Years of Age or Older | (129) | .56 |

In summary, the continuity correlations for the Violence for Social Control Index are somewhat lower than what one would like, suggesting that the measure is in need of improvement or at least supplementation. The data clearly show that the index provides a more reliable measure than do the items and that an index incorporating two subscales performs more reliably than does a single subscale. The data suggest that there may be some learning required from the respondent when the first set of Violence for Social Control questions are presented and that this learning effect contributes to the low continuity correlations. The low continuity correlations do not appear to be associated strongly with any particular demographic characteristic.

## The Criterion Validity of the Violence for Social Control Index

Determining the criterion validity of the Violence for Social Control Index is a more difficult task than establishing the criterion validity of the Violence for Social Change Index, because the nature of the criterion behavior is less clear. The questions combined in the index are measures of attitudes toward what the *police* should do. There is no implication in this measure that the individual himself would engage in violence to maintain social control; instead, the questions inquire what the respondent deems proper, or at least necessary, in the way of police behaviors. The Violence for Social Control Index cannot be construed as an indication of personal willingness to act—that is, it is not a measure of vigilantism.

These considerations suggest that the most appropriate group for studying the criterion validity and the behavioral implications of the Violence for Social Control Index would be the police. However, it would not be adequate simply to interview policemen under the supposition that as a group they should score high on the Violence for Social Control Index. Policemen are trained professionals and part of their training consists of instruction in the proper use of force. It may well be that a thoroughly trained policeman would be much less likely to think the use of physical force appropriate than the average citizen who has had no such instruction. For example, it is known that during the Detroit riots the U.S. Army, whose forces had had specialized training in riot control, was responsible for far fewer injuries and deaths than were the national guard and the police, who had not had specialized training at that time (Report of the National Advisory Commission on Civil Disorders 1968, p. 107).

Considerable emphasis has been placed on increasing the education of police and guardsmen in relation to the appropriate use of force in civilian disturbances (Report of the President's Commission on Campus Unrest 1970, pp. 11-12), and it may be that such training has now had the desired effect on police attitudes. The professional training of police implies that validity studies of the Violence for Social Control Index using policemen as criterion groups must be conducted in relation to actual behaviors of specific policemen. For example, one could study policemen who had shot or physically injured someone in the course of their work and compare them to policemen who had not engaged in such behaviors; the former should have higher scores on the index than the latter. Indeed, the feasibility of such a study was explored with the Detroit police; however, it was not possible to convince the police of the value of such an investigation, undoubtedly because of the sensitivity of the information required.

Since it was not possible to perform the most appropriate criterion validity study, namely, a study involving violent and nonviolent policemen, it became necessary to search for substitute studies. Three types of criterion groups were considered. The first were groups who are opposed to violence for social control on the basis of ideological reasons; the second were groups who, on the basis of some personal unpleasant experience with the forces of violence for social control, might be expected to have formed negative attitudes toward them; and the third are those who, for one reason or another, might be expected to have a generalized positive attitude toward violence. These groups will be referred to as the ideological, experiential, and warrior-like, respectively. Representatives of each will be discussed in turn.

Since none of the three types of groups which have been mentioned represent an ideal criterion group for assessing the validity of the Violence for Social Control Index, it is useful to explore what claims to criterion validity can be made for each of the three types. The strongest case for the appropriateness of such groups can be made for those who oppose violence for social control for ideological reasons. Since the ideology of such groups is known a priori, no hypotheses are necessary other than the one which states that those persons who are opposed to violence for social control for ideological reasons should score low on the Violence for Social Control Index.

This is not true for the other two types of groups for whom subsidiary hypotheses must be substantiated if the hypothesis that the Violence for Social Control Index has validity is to be confirmed. In order for experiential groups to perform as expected on the Violence for Social Control Index, it is necessary not only that the index be a valid measure, but also that the experiences with the forces of social control have the postulated effects of causing the people to develop negative attitudes toward the use of violence for social control. In the case of the groups dubbed "warriors" it is necessary not only for the index to have validity, but also for the groups to possess the generalized positive attitude toward violence that is thought to characterize them. Since the argument for the use of the experiential group and the warrior types seems more tenuous, criterion groups selected on the basis of their ideologies will be discussed first.

Two nonviolent criterion groups whose attitudes were thought to be directly germane to the issue of the validity of the Violence for Social Control Index on an ideological basis were the Quakers and the Jehovah's Witnesses. Both groups were selected on the basis of their values concerning participation in one form of violence—war. There are many ways of looking at war in addition to ideological ones; for example, it may be seen as economically or imperialistically motivated. Whatever the viewpoint, war is instrumental and, like police actions, it is a form of violence exercised by the state. It is often described by the state in defensive and reactionary terms so that it may be seen as a form of violence for social control in which the target population is usually outside the national boundary. Both the Quakers and the Jehovah's Witnesses were selected because the conscientious objector status of many of their members demonstrates the extent of their belief that at least one form of violence for social control—war—is undesirable.

**Jehovah's Witnesses.** The Jehovah's Witnesses, who were also discussed in Chapter 1, believe that it is not appropriate for members of their sect to serve in the armed forces of any country; indeed, they prefer going to jail to registering with the selective service board. In addition, the Witnesses will neither serve as policemen nor as private security guards. On the basis of their ideology, which is substantiated by their willingness to suffer incarceration for their beliefs, it was hypothesized that the Witnesses would score lower on the Violence for Social Control Index than do other Detroit respondents. Table 4.8 shows that this was the case. Both white and black Jehovah's Witnesses scored significantly lower on the index than did other white and black Detroit respondents. So the attitudes of the Witnesses which are implicit in their ideology appear to be accurately reflected by their

**Table 4.8**

Percentage Responses to the Violence for Social Control Index
for White and Black Detroit Jehovah's Witnesses
and Other Detroit Respondents

| Violence for Social Control Index | Whites | | Blacks | |
|---|---|---|---|---|
| | Jehovah's Witnesses | Detroit Respondents | Jehovah's Witnesses | Detroit Respondents |
| Low    0-2 | 26% | 16% | 33% | 24% |
| 3-6 | 63 | 35 | 49 | 41 |
| High   7-9 | 11 | 49 | 18 | 35 |
| | 100% | 100% | 100% | 100% |
| N | (29) | (104) | (38) | (83) |

Notes: p < .001 that the difference between white Jehovah's Witnesses and white Detroit respondents is due to chance (Mann-Whitney U Test).
p < .001 that the difference between the black Jehovah's Witnesses and black Detroit respondents is due to chance (Mann-Whitney U Test).

scores on the Violence for Social Control Index, a finding which speaks to the validity of the instrument.

**Quakers.** In many ways the Quakers are quite different from the Jehovah's Witnesses. The Witnesses believe strongly that one should keep both eyes firmly glued on the Lord's affairs; the Quakers, or at least some of them, are strong proponents of service to mankind. The Witnesses believe that all the members of a congregation need to be guided and they exert considerable social pressure to make members adhere to multiple norms regarding behavior. The Quakers believe strongly that an individual should follow the dictates of his own conscience. Consequently, they expend great effort to help their members turn inward to reach their own best moral conclusions, and they exert themselves to provide social support to enable individuals to follow the dictates of their own conscience.

The Jehovah's Witnesses are highly organized in their structural and organizational arrangements. Members are obliged to spend a great deal of time in meetings learning the tenets of their belief. They are also required to spend time actively proselytizing. Thus, the organization of the Witnesses is highly formalized. This is not true of Quakers, at least not Quakers in the immediate vicinity of Detroit. Locally, the membership is loosely organized, so that many people who are functionally active in the meetings are not formally Quakers, while some people who are formal members of the group are not active. Since the emphasis is on the individual's commitment to the dictates of his own conscience, it is difficult to state explicitly the ideology of the sect. However, Quakers are strong proponents of peace and brotherhood and have often acted as "honest brokers" to bring about conciliation between warring groups. Many Quakers have been conscientious objectors, and this particular sect is one of the few which was recognized as a pacifist religion by the selective service in the past. On the basis of this information about the group, it was hypothesized that Quakers and other individuals closely associated with the movement should be low on the Violence for Social Control Index.

The Quakers interviewed were selected from congregation lists of two Detroit congregations. One member of each household on the list was selected randomly. This group of respondents was not a systematic sample of all Detroit Quakers; we know of at least one congregation which would not consent to be interviewed, and there may be smaller fellowships in the area about which we were not informed. Since there is no strong central organization, it was difficult to locate systematically groups which might be identified as formal assemblies of Quakers. Not all persons who were considered to be members of the congregation formally considered themselves Quakers. Of the thirty-six individuals selected from the lists of congregation participants and interviewed, ten stated that they were not officially Quakers. However, our informants were so definite in stating that nonmembers were likely to be as active as members, that it seemed reasonable to include the nonmembers in the criterion group. Both the official members and the attenders will be referred to as Quakers. The response rate of the group initially selected for participation was 71 percent.

No truly appropriate group is available for comparison with the Quakers. All those interviewed from the Quaker congregation lists were white and had at least some college education; 47 percent of them had graduate degrees (Table 4.9). It was decided that they could probably best be compared to other college-educated Detroit respondents. Table 4.9 shows that the Detroit Quakers were still over-educated relative to the college-educated whites in Detroit. Moreover, the Quaker group was considerably wealthier than its Detroit comparison group; over three-fourths of the former had incomes over $16,000 a year in contrast to slightly less than half of the latter.

**Table 4.9**

Selected Demographic Characteristics of Detroit Quakers and
Other White Detroit Respondents with at Least Some College Education
(percentage distribution)

|  | Detroit Quakers | Detroit Whites with at Least Some College |
|---|---|---|
| Sex† | | |
| Men | 58% | 58% |
| Women | 42 | 42 |
| | 100% | 100% |
| Education‡ | | |
| Some College | 14 | 52 |
| B.A. or Equivalent | 39 | 33 |
| Graduate Degree | 47 | 15 |
| | 100% | 100% |
| Income§ | | |
| $3,999 or Less | 0 | 3 |
| $4,000-$7,999 | 3 | 15 |
| $8,000-$11,999 | 14 | 13 |
| $12,000-$15,999 | 5 | 22 |
| $16,000 or More | 78 | 47 |
| | 100% | 100% |
| Age† | | |
| 16-19 Years | 3 | 6 |
| 20-29 Years | 11 | 31 |
| 30-39 Years | 36 | 21 |
| 40-49 Years | 17 | 12 |
| 50-59 Years | 28 | 15 |
| 60 Years or Older | 5 | 15 |
| | 100% | 100% |
| N | (36) | (33) |

†No statistically significant differences between Detroit Quakers and Detroit whites with some college or more (Mann-Whitney U Test).

‡$p < .01$ that the difference between Detroit Quakers and Detroit whites with some college or more is due to chance (Mann-Whitney U Test).

§$p < .003$ that the difference between Detroit Quakers and Detroit whites with some college or more is due to chance (Mann-Whitney U Test).

It was hypothesized that the Quakers would have lower scores on the Violence for Social Control Index than their comparison group because of their pacifist stance. Table 4.10 shows that this is the case; thus supporting the criterion validity of the Violence for Social Control Index. However, the differences in education and income between the Quakers and comparison group would tend to accentuate the difference on the Violence for Social Control Index between the two groups. Because of the small number in both groups, it is not possible to manipulate the data further to explore this possibility. Some sense of proportion can be gained, however, by examining the data from the 1969 national survey. Table 4.11 gives the scores on the Violence for Social

### Table 4.10

Percentage Responses to the Violence for Social Control Index for Detroit Quakers and Other White Detroit Respondents with at Least Some College Education

| Violence for Social Control Index | | Detroit Quakers | Detroit Whites with at Least Some College |
|---|---|---|---|
| Low | 0-2 | 75% | 16% |
| | 3-6 | 22 | 48 |
| High | 7-9 | 3 | 36 |
| | | 100% | 100% |
| | N | (36) | (33) |

Note: p < .001 that the difference between the Detroit Quakers and Detroit whites with some college or more is due to chance (Mann-Whitney U Test).

Control Index for white respondents in the 1969 study with some college education, with Bachelor's degrees or equivalent, and with graduate degrees. By comparing Tables 4.10 and 4.11, it can be seen in the 1969 national data that the Detroit Quakers were substantially lower on

### Table 4.11

Percentage Responses to the Violence for Social Control Index for White College-Educated Respondents
(1969 study)

| Violence for Social Control Index | | Some College: No Bachelor's Degree | Bachelor's or Equivalent | Graduate Degree |
|---|---|---|---|---|
| Low | 0-2 | 23% | 29% | 23% |
| | 3-6 | 40 | 42 | 63 |
| High | 7-9 | 37 | 29 | 14 |
| | | 100% | 100% | 100% |
| | N | (162) | (105) | (51) |

the Violence for Social Control Index than were white respondents with graduate degrees. It seems likely that the differences between the Detroit Quakers and other Detroit respondents were more a product of their ideology than their differences in education. These data support the validity of the Violence for Social Control Index.

**Student and California Arrestees.** A second set of criterion groups was available in the form of the student protesters and the California arrestees. Both these groups had had direct encounters with the police. In both groups most of the respondents had been arrested and it is clear that all these respondents were present while an active confrontation with the police was occurring. In the case of the Ann Arbor students, there was considerable application of force by the sheriff's department, which occasioned complaints by students and faculty alike after the disturbance. It can be surmised that there was also considerable police force used in the case of the California disturbance. Many charges of police brutality were made prior to that outbreak; indeed, the reader may recall that the disturbance occurred when an anti-police rally failed to materialize as scheduled. Thus, it is likely that both groups consisted of people who had been exposed firsthand to unpleasant experiences with the police and the use of police force.

One might speculate that personal experience on the receiving end of police force, or observing such force applied to one's friends and other people with whom one identifies, might lead people to adopt negative attitudes toward such force. Such speculation leads to the hypothesis then that both the student and the California arrestees should favor the use of minimal amounts of force by the police. Tables 4.12 and 4.13 show this hypothesis was supported. Both groups

**Table 4.12**

Percentage Responses to the Violence for Social Control Index
for the Student Arrestees and College Students

| Violence for Social Control Index | | Student Arrestees (Participants in U of M Street Disturbance) | College Students (National Sample) |
|---|---|---|---|
| Low | 0-2 | 72% | 24% |
| | 3-6 | 25 | 54 |
| High | 7-9 | 3 | 22 |
| | | 100% | 100% |
| | N | (29) | (63) |

Note: p < .001 that the difference between the student arrestees and college students in the national sample is due to chance (Kolmogorov-Smirnov Test).

scored substantially lower on the Violence for Social Control Index than did their comparison groups. In both cases the differences were spectacular. In the case of the Ann Arbor student arrestees, 72 percent fell in the two lowest categories of the Violence for Social Control Index in comparison with 24 percent of college students in the

Table 4.13

Percentage Responses to the Violence for Social Control Index
for the California Arrestees and
the National Sample Comparison Group

| Violence for Social Control Index | | California Arrestees | National Sample Comparison Group |
|---|---|---|---|
| Low   0-2 | | 88% | 30% |
|       3-6 | | 12 | 50 |
| High  7-9 | | 0 | 20 |
| | | 100% | 100% |
| | N | (25) | (424) |

Note: p < .001 that the difference between the California arrestees and the national sample comparison group is due to chance (Kolmogorov-Smirnov Test).

national sample. In the case of the California arrestees, 88 percent fell in the two lowest categories of the Violence for Social Control Index in comparison with 30 percent of their age-matched comparison group in the national sample.

It is not possible to say whether these two criterion groups held negative attitudes toward the use of police force before their encounters with the police, or whether they developed these attitudes as a result of the confrontation as was hypothesized they might. Indeed, there is a very real possibility that some of the very large differences between the student and California arrestees and their respective comparison groups is due to ideological principles held by members of these two groups prior to their arrest. Nevertheless, the results are in the predicted direction, and the differences are large enough to be astonishing. It would be helpful if we had had a measure of what these attitudes were prior to the disturbance and if there had been an opportunity to measure a change in attitude as a result of the encounter. However, these data are not available, and we will have to take the results for what they are, a small piece of evidence suggesting that the Violence for Social Control Index has some criterion validity.

**Prisoners and Parents of Battered Children.** In discussing the validity of the Violence for Social Control Index, it was proposed that some people might have a generalized positive attitude toward violence.

Such people were presumed to use violence as a generalized coping response and were nicknamed "warriors." Two groups of individuals were proposed as possibly falling into this category: first, the parents of battered children, and second, a group of prisoners in a minimum security prison. In the discussion of the Violence for Social Change Index, it was pointed out that the reasoning which led to the utilization of these two groups for criterion validity was considerably more tenuous than was true for the other examples.

The reservations cited previously are also germane here. There is no specific reason for thinking that parents of battered children or prisoners should be more favorably inclined toward violence as a means of social control. The only link between these groups and that type of violence is the hypothesis that they had a generalized positive attitude toward all types of violence. Indeed, there is some reason to think that prisoners and parents of battered children should be less favorably inclined toward violence as a means of social control than are others. It is known that the prisoners have had extensive contact with the police, and it may be suspected that some of them at least will have been the object of some physical force by the police during the course of their arrest. Such experiences should act in the opposite direction from the one predicted above, that is, the physical contact with the police should make the prisoners feel less favorably inclined toward violence for social control. There is a small amount of evidence that the prisoners may have had such an unfavorable view of police acts; 40 percent of the prisoners stated that police frisking people was an act of violence in contrast to only 21 percent of the comparison group.

A similar argument can be raised in the case of the parents of battered children. All of them had experienced extensive contacts with social workers whose job it was to investigate the child abuse problem and to make a recommendation to the courts about the disposition of the child and the parents. Some of the parents suspected of child abuse were eventually arrested and convicted. We surmised this because some of the respondents were in jail. What percentage of the parents of battered children actually came in contact with the police or were arrested is not known since the records were inaccessible to us. In any case, an argument can be made that the parents of battered children might be expected to be less favorably inclined toward the use of violence for social control on the basis of the likelihood that some of them have probably had unhappy personal experiences at the hands of the police. It seems clear that we are treading on doubtful territory in utilizing the prisoners and parents of battered children as criterion validity groups.

Table 4.14 gives the distribution of responses to the Violence for Social Control Index among the prisoners and their comparison group (the national sample respondents whose data were weighted to approximate the age and racial characteristics of the prisoners; see Chapter 1 for more detail). It can be seen that there is a significant difference between the prisoners and their comparison group in the direction opposite to that predicted on the basis of the criterion validity of the Violence for Social Control Index.

**Table 4.14**

Percentage Responses to the Violence for Social Control Index
for the Prisoners and the Prisoners' Comparison Group

| Violence for Social Control Index | | Prisoners | Prisoners' Comparison Group |
|---|---|---|---|
| Low | 0-2 | 42% | 26% |
| | 3-6 | 54 | 55 |
| High | 7-9 | 4 | 19 |
| | | 100% | 100% |
| | N | (52) | (142) |

Note: $p < .001$ that the difference between the prisoners and the prisoners' comparison group is due to chance (Kolmogorov-Smirnov Test).

It had previously been shown that within the prisoner group there was a correlation of .3 (gamma) between the Violent Behaviors Index and the prisoners' scores on the Violence for Social Control Index (Blumenthal et al. 1972, p. 66). Thus, there was an association between violent behaviors which are not politically motivated and the Violence for Social Control Index. However, there was also a definite tendency for the prisoners to score lower on the index than did national sample respondents who were similar in race and age. One possible explanation of this finding, which goes contrary to the hypothesis predicting that the prisoners should be higher on the Violence for Social Control Index than others, is that through their contact with the police the prisoners have come to think that social control ought to be obtained with a minimum of violence. In some respects the prisoners are like the California arrestees and the Ann Arbor students. All have had direct contact with the police, and one can assume that some of the prisoners have been objects of police force and that most friends or acquaintances who have been the object of such force. One might guess that such attentions might have decreased the level of violence thought appropriate for social control. Thus, the positive relationship between violent behaviors and attitudes toward this kind of violence starts from a lower baseline.

Table 4.15 lends some credence to this line of thinking. The table subdivides the prisoners according to the number of violent behaviors

**Table 4.15**

Percentage Responses to the Violence for Social Control Index
in Relation to the Violent Behaviors Index for Prisoners
(prisoners, N = 52)

| Violence for Social Control Index | | | Violent Behaviors | | |
|---|---|---|---|---|---|
| | | | None | One | Two-Three |
| Low | 0-1 | | 47% | 35% | 5% |
| | 2-4 | | 30 | 47 | 61 |
| High | 5-9 | | 23 | 18 | 34 |
| | | | 100% | 100% | 100% |
| | | N* | (17) | (16) | (18) |

cited in their records. It can be seen that those for whom no violent behaviors were recorded scored considerably lower on the Violence for Social Control Index than did their comparison group in Table 4.14. Conversely, prisoners for whom two or more violent behaviors were recorded were less likely to score in the lowest category of the index than either prisoners with no violent mentions or the comparison group in Table 4.14, albeit these differences are probably not significant. The more violent among the prisoner group were more likely to score high on the Violence for Social Control Index.

It is interesting that the prisoners were far more favorably inclined toward violence for social control than were either the student arrestees or the California arrestees (compare Table 4.14 with Tables 4.12 and 4.13). Whether this is because the student and California arrestees held their attitudes on the basis of ideology, or whether arrest during a civil disturbance is an experience which is more effective in producing negative attitudes toward the use of violence as a means of social control is not clear. Certainly the prisoners' scores were very different from the two groups with which one might expect them to compare. It is also interesting that the difference between the prisoners and their comparison group on the Violence for Social Control Index was relatively small compared to the difference between the arrestees and their comparison groups. One reason for this might be that among the more violent prisoners an increasingly positive attitude toward violence for social control offsets the negative effects of the experiential factor. Direct contact with the police (and presumably police force) may act as a more powerful variable in determining attitudes toward the use of social control than do personality characteristics which predispose the individual to hold positive attitudes toward violence.

The second group of individuals for whom it was postulated that there might be a relationship between a specific kind of violent behavior and the Violence for Social Control Index was the parents of the battered children (see Chapter 1 on the selection and composition of this group). Table 4.16 shows that, as was true of the prisoners, the parents of battered children did not score high on the index. Arguments similar to those made for the prisoners can be used to explain the nega-

**Table 4.16**

Percentage Responses to the Violence for Social Control Index
for the Black Parents of Battered Children and the Black Control Group

| Violence for Social Control Index | | Black Parents of Battered Children | Black Control Group |
|---|---|---|---|
| Low | 0-2 | 23% | 13% |
| | 3-6 | 42 | 50 |
| High | 7-9 | 35 | 37 |
| | | 100% | 100% |
| | N | (27) | (32) |

tive findings for the parents of battered children, at least some of whom had had contact with the police. Such experiences might act to mitigate positive attitudes toward violence for social control. In any case, neither the data from the prisoners nor from the parents of battered children substantiate the validity of the Violence for Social Control Index.

*Summary*

Among the groups investigated for their criterion validity, the two groups chosen on the basis of their ideology, Quakers and Jehovah's Witnesses, scored in the expected direction on the Violence for Social Control Index. It should be pointed out that both these groups were chosen because of their negative view of violence for social control, so that only one end of the scale has been anchored in this kind of behavioral validity. It would be helpful if it were possible to locate individuals (for example, assaultive police or guards) who should be high on the Violence for Social Control Index, however, this proved a difficult feat and those data are yet missing. Nevertheless, the fact that groups committed to pacifist positions did score in the expected direction on the Violence for Social Control Index does contribute to establishing the validity of this scale.

The second two groups, the student and California arrestees, were expected to score low on the Violence for Social Control Index, not because of their ideologies, but because members of the two groups very likely had had unpleasant personal experiences on the receiving end of violence used to restore social order in disturbances. In fact, both groups substantiated the hypotheses, even though members of the two groups differed enormously with respect to major demographic characteristics. The Ann Arbor student arrestees were undoubtedly the children of the affluent and privileged, while the California arrestees were the progeny of poor aliens. Nevertheless, both apparently had identical responses to their experiences; both groups scored low on the Violence for Social Control Index.

The last two groups, prisoners and parents of battered children, were selected on the basis of violent behaviors, or at least antisocial behavior. It was hypothesized that nonpolitical violent behaviors might show themselves through a generalized tendency to form positive attitudes toward violence. Both groups did in fact show more positive attitudes toward the use of violence as a means of producing social change than did their comparison groups. However, neither showed the anticipated positive attitudes toward the use of violence for social control. The reasons underlying this failure to substantiate the hypothesis may be multiple. In the first place, the assumption that predilections toward specific kinds of nonpolitical violent behaviors result in generalized tendencies to hold positive attitudes toward violence simply may not be correct. However, the fact that the Violence for Social Control Index related to the Violent Behaviors Index among the prisoners indicates that such generalized tendencies probably do exist. The most likely explanation of the data is that extensive contacts with the police and other social agencies by the prisoners and parents of battered children have resulted in negative attitudes toward the use of violence for social control, and that the effect of these contacts over-rides other influences.

Generally, the data seem to indicate that the Violence for Social Control Index does have some criterion validity, although this is not as well documented as is true for the Violence for Social Change Index. A major defect in this documentation is the absence of a criterion group which should and does score high on this measure. Nevertheless, the data are promising and suggest that further effort in providing criterion validity for this measure should be undertaken.

# Chapter 5

# ATTITUDES TOWARD VIOLENCE FOR SOCIAL CONTROL AND PRISON RIOTS, SCHOOL DISTURBANCES, AND CORPORAL PUNISHMENT

*Introduction*

Investigating the construct validity of the Violence for Social Control Index is a simpler proposition than establishing its criterion validity. Violence as a means of maintaining, restoring, or ensuring social control covers a broad category of behaviors. Wars, for example, can be interpreted as a form of social control, that is, the attempt of one nation to exert control over another. Certain aspects of child rearing can also be construed in these terms. Physical punishments such as slapping or spanking can be regarded as a form of violence, and the disciplinary context in which they are administered can be viewed as a form of social control. Corporal punishment in the schools can also be viewed as a form of violence for social control. It is true that the degree of actual violence—the amount of force and the extent of injury—varies widely in the three examples. Moreover, it could be argued that the amount of actual violence or physical force inherent in an activity will influence how people think about it and that for this reason we should be careful about combining three such widely different behaviors under one rubric. However, our previous work indicates that people are likely to define an action as "violence" or "not violence" on bases other than the actual amount of physical force involved (Blumenthal et al. 1972, pp. 71-95). Their other responses, then, tend to be consistent with their definitions. Consequently, there is some justification for viewing such widely disparate behaviors as hitting children and waging wars as members of the same category.

In studying the construct validity of the Violence for Social Control Index we should recognize that there are at least two components to the beliefs underlying the attitudes which the index measures. The first is the extent to which there is a perceived need for social control. Presumably, some people will have strong beliefs that social control is necessary and desirable, while others will not. The second component involved in the Violence for Social Control Index concerns the amount of force the individual believes necessary to produce such control. Not all those who believe that social control is necessary will believe that it should be achieved violently. Among those who believe in the desirability of social control, there is likely to be a full spectrum of belief about the amount of force necessary to implement it. Among those who do not believe in the necessity of social control, there should be only few who believe in the use of force to maintain it.

### Violence for Social Control and the Punitive Law Enforcement Index

There were among the 1972 interview items two which related to the issue of whether or not the respondent thought social control desirable. These were:

*There would be less violence if our present laws were always enforced.*

*One cause of violence is that the punishments for breaking the law are not tough enough.*

Both items were answered on a four-point agree-disagree scale. Presumably people who agree that violence is caused by inadequate enforcement of the law and who think that the punishments for breaking the law ought to be increased in severity are likely to believe in the necessity of social control.

Table 5.1 presents the percentage responses to these two items for white, black, and all respondents. The majority of people, black and white alike, agree with both statements. The black respondents are somewhat less likely than the white to agree strongly with the proposition that more vigorous law enforcement will reduce the amount of violence or that increasing the punitive aspect of law enforcement will reduce violence. Nevertheless, the differences between the races are not as large as might have been anticipated.

The two items were combined into the Punitive Law Enforcement Index. The higher the score on this index, the more the respondent agreed with the proposition that the law ought to be enforced vigorously. (Details of index construction are given in Appendix E.) The demographic correlates of the Punitive Law Enforcement Index are given in Table 5.2. There is a substantial association between this index and

Table 5.1

Percentage Responses to Items Measuring
the Desirability of Social Control

| | All Respondents | Whites | Blacks |
|---|---|---|---|
| There would be less violence if our present laws were always enforced. | | | |
| Agree a Great Deal | 47% | 54% | 40% |
| Agree Somewhat | 30 | 21 | 38 |
| Disagree Somewhat | 16 | 19 | 15 |
| Disagree a Great Deal | 7 | 6 | 7 |
| | 100% | 100% | 100% |
| One cause of violence is that punishments for breaking the law are not tough enough. | | | |
| Agree a Great Deal | 44 | 55 | 34 |
| Agree Somewhat | 28 | 24 | 32 |
| Disagree Somewhat | 20 | 16 | 22 |
| Disagree a Great Deal | 8 | 5 | 12 |
| | 100% | 100% | 100% |
| N | (283) | (145) | (133) |

age, as well as smaller associations with race, education, and town size. Table 5.3 shows the percentage distribution of responses to the Punitive Law Enforcement Index according to age. While only 8 percent of the respondents under twenty scored in the highest category of the index, 60 percent of those over sixty did so. Interestingly enough, there appears to be something of a dividing line at age thirty. Those over thirty were considerably more likely to have scored in the highest cate-

Table 5.2

Relationships between the Punitive Law Enforcement Index
and Selected Demographic Characteristics
(all respondents, N = 283)
(gammas)

| Demographic Characteristic | Gamma |
|---|---|
| Race | -.26‡ |
| Sex | .10 |
| Age | .44‡ |
| Education | -.20‡ |
| Family Income | .01 |
| Town Size | -.16† |
| Experience in South | .01 |

†p < .05      ‡p < .001

**Table 5.3**

Percentage Responses to the Punitive Law Enforcement Index
in Relation to Age
(all respondents, N = 283)

| Punitive Law Enforcement Index | | | 16-19 Years | 20-29 Years | 30-39 Years | 40-49 Years | 50-59 Years | 60 Years or Older |
|---|---|---|---|---|---|---|---|---|
| Low | 1 | | 39% | 29% | 10% | 9% | 7% | 2% |
| | 2-4 | | 53 | 58 | 55 | 48 | 51 | 38 |
| High | 5 | | 8 | 13 | 35 | 43 | 42 | 60 |
| | | | 100% | 100% | 100% | 100% | 100% | 100% |
| | | N* | (36) | (67) | (49) | (44) | (38) | (47) |

gory, while respondents under thirty appeared to have been considerably more likely to score in the lowest category of the Punitive Law Enforcement Index. We do not know, of course, whether such findings would be similar for a national population, but the age difference is interesting and very much what might have been expected from observation of the contemporary social scene. Young people have been in the vanguard of movements for social change, and they have often voiced objections to social control and law enforcement, particularly law enforcement which they regard as oppressive.

The Punitive Law Enforcement Index is also related to race. Table 5.4 shows that 43 percent of the white respondents fell in the

**Table 5.4**

Percentage Responses to the Punitive Law Enforcement Index
in Relation to Race

| Punitive Law Enforcement Index | | | Whites | Blacks |
|---|---|---|---|---|
| Low | 1 | | 14% | 19% |
| | 2-4 | | 43 | 60 |
| High | 5 | | 43 | 21 |
| | | | 100% | 100% |
| | | N | (145) | (133) |

highest category of this index, while only 21 percent of black respondents did so. Nevertheless, there was considerable variation of opinion among both races.

The relationship between the Punitive Law Enforcement Index and education is not as strong as might have been expected. Table 5.5 shows that there was a tendency for a larger percentage of respondents with some college education to score in the lowest category of the index, although 30 percent of them also scored in the highest category.

Table 5.2 also indicates that there was a very small relationship between the Punitive Law Enforcement Index and whether or not the respondent lived in a more urban or rural area. This relationship is probably largely due to the previously discussed relationship between

**Table 5.5**

Percentage Responses to the Punitive Law Enforcement Index
in Relation to Education
(all respondents, N = 283)

| Punitive Law Enforcement Index | | 9 Years or Less | 10-11 Years | High School Graduate | At Least Some College |
|---|---|---|---|---|---|
| Low | 1 | 4% | 15% | 17% | 30% |
| | 2-4 | 52 | 53 | 59 | 40 |
| High | 5 | 44 | 32 | 24 | 30 |
| | | 100% | 100% | 100% | 100% |
| | N* | (68) | (80) | (71) | (63) |

the index and race, since the gammas within race become even smaller and lose significance.

Table 5.6 shows that the Punitive Law Enforcement Index is associated with attitudes toward violence for social control among the respondents taken as a whole. This relationship, however, seems to

**Table 5.6**

Relationships between the Punitive Law Enforcement Index
and the Violence for Social Control Index for Selected Subgroups
(gammas)

| | N | Gamma |
|---|---|---|
| All Respondents | (283) | .31‡ |
| Whites | (145) | .41‡ |
| Blacks | (133) | .17† |
| Younger than 30 Years of Age | (103) | .11 |
| 30 Years of Age or Older | (178) | .40‡ |

†p < .05      ‡p < .001

exist largely because of a moderate association among respondents who are white or at least 30 years old. The association was small among blacks and insignificant among those under thirty. The data seem to show some relationship between attitudes toward the need for social control and attitudes toward the use of violence as a means of social control, although the relationship was larger for some groups than others. The relationship which was present among older respondents is reminiscent of the fire and brimstone approach to moral training. Reliance on such methods to bring the erring to salvation have been common in human history. One can easily imagine that some people believe that the deterrence of evil depends on the severity of punishment. That young people subscribe less to this view is encouraging since there is very little evidence that the amount of force determines its deterrent effect.

There has been a strong movement recently to emphasize rehabilitation rather than punishment for criminals and to stress the development of skills and talents in the treatment of potential offenders. Such policies have often been labeled as mindless permissiveness, and it seems likely that such policies would find more favor among the young than the old. It is not surprising that among the young, attitudes toward violence as a means of maintaining social control are not related to a perceived need for social control. There are nonviolent methods of ensuring control, and perhaps those young people who see the need for social control favor such alternatives to physical force.

To the extent that these data indicate that there is a relationship between the belief that social control is necessary and the Violence for Social Control Index, they provide some modest support for the construct validity of the index. One might speculate that since the relationship did not hold true for all subgroups in the population some may have had social philosophies which were not based on ideas of control but on other notions—perhaps ideas of mutual cooperation and contribution. Young people in the study population scored decidedly lower on the Punitive Law Enforcement Index; they were also apt to score low on the Violence for Social Control Index. It might be that their low scores were based on alternative views of what societal relations ought to be—a hopeful sign if true, and one that ought to be explored in the future. Just what kind of an ideology underlies the rejection of punitive law enforcement? Is it an idealized view of mankind, a new concept of social order, or a decriminalization of what we view as crime? Answers to these questions would be interesting and might supply some useful alternatives to the use of violence for social control.

## The Construct Validity of the Violence for Social Control Index

Three additional sets of questions included in the interview relate to the construct validity of the Violence for Social Control Index. All three sets were questions asking about behaviors which might be classified as forms of violence for social control. The first set of questions solicited opinions about the Attica Prison riot which can be regarded as a concrete example of a situation in which a disorder occurred which was quelled by a considerable amount of violence. As such, it is a real example of the kind of imaginary episode about which our measure of Violence for Social Control inquired. Moreover, the riot at Attica Prison was also an episode of violence for social change—the outbreak occurred only after the prisoners had attempted to negotiate with prison officials for a variety of improvements in prison life. At the time, the riot generated a great deal of press coverage and considerable public interest. During the course of the upheaval serious consideration was given to the possibility of New York's Governor Rockefeller entering into negotiations with the prison inmates. Some thought at the time that such negotiations might bring an end to the upheaval and allow a relatively peaceful settlement. However, the negotiations did not occur, and the prison disturbance was not ended until after troops had been sent to quell the uprising.

The introduction of the troops resulted in a considerable amount of bloodshed; and while the inmates were originally held responsible for the deaths of the prison guards during the outbreak, later evidence indicated that the hostages originally thought to have been killed by the prisoners had actually been killed by bullets from the riot-control troops. The Attica incident had occurred several months before the interview, but we thought that many respondents would still recall it clearly and have opinions about it. As an example of violence used for social control, the episode allowed us to make inquiries about attitudes and opinions which we expected to have direct correlations with the Violence for Social Control Index.

The second set of items postulated to relate to the Violence for Social Control Index inquired about the respondents' attitudes toward the control and management of disturbances in the secondary schools. This set of questions was hypothesized as being less directly related to the index than were the Attica questions, since school disturbances involve children and younger adolescents rather than older adolescents and young adults. It is conceivable that attitudes toward children involved in disturbances might be quite different from attitudes toward adults involved in disturbances. Moreover, disturbances in the secondary schools are rarely viewed as being very serious.

The last set of items which were hypothesized to be a form of violence for social control concerned the use of physical punishment in disciplining small children. This set of items was thought to be least directly related to the Violence for Social Control Index because of the very different nature of the object of violence and the type of physical force administered.

*The Attica Prison Riot and Violence for Social Control*

The questions which inquired about attitudes toward the prison riot at Attica were as follows:

*Did you happen to hear about the prison riot at Attica?*

*(If yes) Were you **very interested** in what happened at Attica at the time, or were you not too interested?*

*(If very interested) You may remember, the authorities called in troops to put down the riot. On the whole do you think the authorities handled the riot **well** or **not**?*

*Do you think that the troops should have been called in **sooner** than they were, later—were they called **just about the right time**, or should they **not have been called at all**?*

*Some think Governor Rockefeller should have talked to the prisoners to try to end the riot; others think not. What do you think?*

*If the prisoners at Attica got what they demanded, like better food, medical care, and vocational training, do you think the prison system would **improve** or **get worse**?*

*Do you think that the death of the hostages and prisoners could have been prevented or not?*

Of the respondents interviewed, 92 percent of the whites and 75 percent of the blacks indicated that they had heard about the prison riots. Of those who had heard about the riot, 80 percent of the whites and 78 percent of the blacks indicated that they had been very interested at the time. Only those who indicated they were very interested were asked the additional five questions about the riot.

Table 5.7 shows percentage distributions of responses for black and white respondents who indicated that they had been very interested at the time. There were substantial differences between the blacks and whites interviewed. Forty-one percent more black than white respondents thought that the riot had been badly managed. Forty-three percent of black respondents, in contrast to 15 percent of white, thought that troops should not have been called into the prison riot, and 90 percent of the blacks compared to 51 percent of the whites thought that the deaths of the hostages could have been prevented. Thus, substantially more black than white respondents thought that excessive and unnecessary violence had been used in controlling the disturbance. Moreover, more black than white respondents thought it would have been appropriate to use one of the alternatives to violence that were available at the time. The overwhelming majority of black respondents felt that Governor Rockefeller should have talked to the prisoners. These very substantial differences between white and black respondents imply that, in the subsequent analyses, relationships within race must be considered as well as the data for respondents as a whole.

Of the five substantive questions which were asked about the Attica Prison riot, two seem very directly related to attitudes toward violence for social control. The first of these is the question asking whether the deaths of hostages and prisoners could have been prevented. Presumably, those people who thought that the deaths of the

**Table 5.7**

Percentage Responses to Items Inquiring about the Attica Prison Riot for Respondents Who Were Very Interested

|  | Whites | Blacks |
|---|---|---|
| **Did authorities handle riot well?** | | |
| Well | 58% | 12% |
| Don't Know | 11 | 16 |
| Not Well | 31 | 72 |
|  | 100% | 100% |
| **Should troops have been called sooner?** | | |
| Sooner | 45 | 38 |
| Just Right | 36 | 15 |
| Later | 4 | 4 |
| Shouldn't Have Been Called | 15 | 43 |
|  | 100% | 100% |
| **Governor should have talked?** | | |
| Should Not Have Talked | 39 | 9 |
| Don't Know | 7 | 1 |
| Should Have Talked | 54 | 90 |
|  | 100% | 100% |
| **Would prison system improve?** | | |
| Improve | 80 | 96 |
| Won't Change | 11 | 4 |
| Get Worse | 9 | 0 |
|  | 100% | 100% |
| **Were hostage deaths preventable?** | | |
| Not Preventable | 35 | 5 |
| Don't Know | 14 | 5 |
| Preventable | 51 | 90 |
|  | 100% | 100% |
| N | (106) | (77) |

prisoners could not have been prevented were people who had great faith in the use of violence to restore social control. It might be inferred that those who thought the deaths of the hostages and prisoners could have been prevented probably had reservations about the amount of force which should be utilized to restore order.

Table 5.8 shows that, of those respondents who believed that the deaths could not have been prevented or who said they were not sure, 53 percent fell in the three highest categories of the Violence for Social Control Index in contrast to only 36 percent of those who thought the deaths preventable. The relationship found among all respondents was also found among those who were white. Among black respondents, such an overwhelming majority believed that the deaths could have been prevented that the gamma must be regarded with some caution.

**Table 5.8**

Percentage Responses to the Violence for Social Control Index
in Relation to Attitudes toward Avoidability of Attica Deaths
(all respondents, N = 185; whites, N = 106; blacks, N = 77)

| Violence for Social Control Index | | Not Avoidable/Don't Know | | | Avoidable | | |
|---|---|---|---|---|---|---|---|
| | | All Respondents | Whites | Blacks | All Respondents | Whites | Blacks |
| Low | 0-2 | 9% | 6% | 25% | 26% | 26% | 26% |
| | 3-6 | 38 | 39 | 38 | 38 | 36 | 40 |
| High | 7-9 | 53 | 55 | 37 | 36 | 38 | 34 |
| | | 100% | 100% | 100% | 100% | 100% | 100% |
| | N* | (58) | (49) | (8) | (117) | (50) | (62) |

Note: Gamma for all respondents is -.30 (p < .005).
Gamma for whites is -.26 (p < .05).
Gamma for blacks is -.08.

The second question which appears to relate quite directly to the issue of violence for social control is the one which asks whether the riot was handled well or not. Presumably, those who thought that the Attica Prison riot was handled "well" would fall in that category of people who approve of substantial amounts of police violence since substantial violence was used to quell that disorder. As Table 5.9 shows, those respondents who thought that the Attica riot had been handled well (or were not sure) were more likely to score high on the Violence for Social Control Index than those who thought the riot had not been handled well. Fifty-four percent of those who believed the riot had been handled well fell in the three highest Violence for Social Control categories, in contrast to only 27 percent of those who felt the riot had

**Table 5.9**

Percentage Responses to the Violence for Social Control Index
in Relation to the Item Asking How Well Attica Riot Was Handled
(all respondents, N = 185; whites, N = 106; blacks, N = 77)

| Violence for Social Control Index | Well/Don't Know | | | Not Well | | |
|---|---|---|---|---|---|---|
| | All Respondents | Whites | Blacks | All Respondents | Whites | Blacks |
| Low   0-2 | 10% | 10% | 11% | 30% | 28% | 31% |
| 3-6 | 36 | 35 | 39 | 43 | 46 | 42 |
| High  7-9 | 54 | 55 | 50 | 27 | 26 | 27 |
| | 100% | 100% | 100% | 100% | 100% | 100% |
| N* | (89) | (69) | (18) | (84) | (31) | (49) |

Note: Gamma for all respondents is -.40 (p < .001).
Gamma for whites is -.38 (p < .005).
Gamma for blacks is -.36 (p < .05).

been handled poorly. This relationship is true for white and black respondents considered separately, as well as for all respondents considered together.

A third question, which seems less directly related to the use of violence, inquired whether or not Governor Rockefeller should have talked with the prisoners. This was an inquiry into whether or not the respondent believed that a particular nonviolent strategy should have been used as an attempt to regain social control. It seems reasonable to suppose that people who answered this question affirmatively would be less likely to favor violence for social control than those who answered negatively. At least, it may be presumed that those who thought the governor should have talked with the prisoners would be willing to postpone the use of violence while other modes of coping were being tried.

Table 5.10 shows the expected relationship between the Violence for Social Control Index and the item inquiring whether Governor Rockefeller should have negotiated with the prisoners. One-quarter of those who believed that he should have talked to the rioters fell in the three lowest categories of the Violence for Social Control Index in contrast to only 7 percent of those who thought he should not have. The relationship between the Violence for Social Control Index and whether or not the respondent thought the governor should have negotiated is upheld when white respondents are considered separately. Among black respondents, such a high proportion believed that the governor should have talked with the prisoners that the gamma must be considered with some caution.

**Table 5.10**

Percentage Responses to the Violence for Social Control Index
in Relation to the Item Asking Whether Governor Rockefeller
Should Have Talked to Prison Rioters
(all respondents, N = 185; whites, N = 106; blacks, N = 77)

| Violence for Social Control Index | Should Not Have Talked/ Don't Know | | | Should Have Talked | | |
|---|---|---|---|---|---|---|
| | All Respondents | Whites | Blacks | All Respondents | Whites | Blacks |
| Low    0-2 | 7% | 4% | 14% | 25% | 27% | 26% |
| 3-6 | 36 | 32 | 72 | 40 | 41 | 38 |
| High   7-9 | 57 | 64 | 14 | 35 | 32 | 36 |
| | 100% | 100% | 100% | 100% | 100% | 100% |
| N* | (55) | (47) | (7) | (119) | (52) | (62) |

Note: Gamma for all respondents is -.34 (p < .001).
Gamma for whites is -.45 (p < .001).
Gamma for blacks is .19

The relationship between the Violence for Social Control Index
and the respondents' opinions about the decision to bring troops in to
quell the disturbance is shown in Table 5.11. It can be seen that there

**Table 5.11**

Percentage Responses to the Violence for Social Control Index
in Relation to When the Troops Should Have Been Called
(all respondents, N = 185)

| Violence for Social Control Index | | Sooner | Just Right | Later or Shouldn't Have Been Called |
|---|---|---|---|---|
| Low    0-2 | | 17% | 12% | 29% |
| 3-6 | | 33 | 40 | 43 |
| High   7-9 | | 50 | 48 | 28 |
| | | 100% | 100% | 100% |
| | N* | (64) | (42) | (51) |

Note: Gamma is -.26 (p < .005).

is a small relationship among all respondents which is maintained among
white (gamma = -.31) but is not significant for black respondents
(gamma = -.12). The relationships, though small, are in the predicted
direction: those who thought the troops should have been called in
sooner were more likely to score high on the Violence for Social Control
Index than those who thought the troops should have been called later
or not at all.

Further thought about the item suggests that the question may have been confusing since it contained two dimensions: whether or not the troops should have been called, and when they should have been called (if they should have been called at all). The two dimensions lead to a double frame of reference which may account for the small size of the relationship between the item and the Violence for Social Control Index and for the failure of the relationship to reach significant levels among blacks.

To summarize, it was postulated that the Attica riot represented a specific instance of violence for social control and that, as such, opinions about the disorder ought to be correlated with the Violence for Social Control Index. The hypothesized relationships exist, although they are small and often not upheld among blacks, among whom the distributions of responses tend to be skewed and are not easily subject to analysis. Nevertheless, these relationships provide some modest support for the construct validity of the Violence for Social Control Index.

## School Disturbances and Violence for Social Control

In a related effort to develop understanding of the construct validity of the Violence for Social Control Index, attitudes toward disturbances in the school were investigated by means of the following question:

> *Some high schools and even junior high schools have been having trouble with violence. Some schools have had disturbances and have had to shut down. Have you heard about this kind of trouble in any school that you know about?*

Seventy-four percent of whites and 63 percent of blacks interviewed answered that they had heard of such disturbances. Those who responded positively were then asked:

> *Were you interested in the disturbance at the school or didn't you pay too much attention to it?*

Fifty-nine percent of the white and 47 percent of the black respondents who had heard of such disturbances indicated interest. Those indicating interest were asked:

> *What was the disturbance you heard about?*
>
> *What do you think causes disturbances like the one you were talking about?*
>
> *Some people tell us that the reason schools have disturbances is because school authorities refuse to listen to the*

*students and the community. Others say that has nothing to do with it. Do you think disturbances are caused by the school authorities not listening, or do you think that has nothing to do with it?*

*Some schools have set up councils where school officials, community members, parents, students, and teachers can all talk about school problems together. Some say such councils might reduce violence. Others say not. Do you think such councils will reduce violence or not?*

*Some people tell us that the way to handle school problems is to have a much stricter discipline code. Others say the discipline codes are unfair and cause more trouble than they cure. Do you think stricter discipline codes will reduce violence, or do you think they will cause more trouble?*

*Some people have told us that having policemen in the schools will help reduce violence. Others say having policemen in the schools helps cause the trouble. What do you say?*

The distribution of responses to the items inquiring about school disturbances are shown in Table 5.12. There are substantial differences between black and white respondents. More blacks than whites in our sample felt that disturbances are caused by communication problems. About three-quarters of both black and white respondents agreed that councils oriented toward increasing communication would reduce the amount of violence occurring in the schools. When the questions were directly related to disciplinary practices, differences between black and white respondents became striking. A smaller percentage of black than white respondents believed that policemen in the schools would cause trouble, while a slightly larger percentage of black respondents believed that the police's presence in the school would reduce violence. In addition, more black than white respondents believed that strict discipline codes would reduce violence.

One might have guessed from the previous data—which show blacks less likely than whites to believe in the use of violence for social control and less likely to have high scores on the Punitive Law Enforcement Index—that blacks would be less apt to favor strict discipline policies and police in the schools than whites. However, these data go in precisely the opposite direction from what might have been anticipated. These opinions of black respondents are sufficiently interesting to warrant some explanation.

One reason why proportionately more blacks than whites favored

**Table 5.12**

Percentage Responses to Items Inquiring about School Disturbances
for Respondents Who Indicated Interest

|  | Whites | Blacks |
|---|---|---|
| School authorities not listening | | |
| Authorities Refuse to Listen | 39% | 69% |
| Not Sure | 18– | 11 |
| Nothing to Do With It | 43 | 20 |
|  | 100% | 100% |
| Councils reduce violence | | |
| Will Reduce Violence | 76 | 75 |
| Not Sure | 10 | 12 |
| Will Not Reduce Violence | 14 | 13 |
|  | 100% | 100% |
| Strict discipline code | | |
| Stricter Codes Reduce Violence | 33 | 57 |
| Not Sure | 12 | 7 |
| Stricter Codes Cause Trouble | 55 | 36 |
|  | 100% | 100% |
| Policemen in schools | | |
| Policemen Will Reduce Violence | 48 | 58 |
| Not Sure | 11 | 13 |
| Policemen Will Cause Trouble | 41 | 29 |
|  | 100% | 100% |
| N | (86) | (62) |

strict discipline codes and police in the schools may be that questions
about school disturbances are oriented toward prevention rather than
toward action and punishment. In such cases, black respondents may
have felt that a strong stance should be taken in prevention, while a
more relaxed hand should be used in the execution of punishment.
Perhaps people feel differently about displaying force as a preventive
measure and about using force to achieve a goal. An alternative
explanation might be that black respondents simply regarded the school
situation as unique and different from other situations in which violence
or a show of violence might be used for social control. Or, it may be
that attitudes toward what should be done in the school are related to
those concerning the use of physical force in child rearing. As we shall
see, there are substantial differences between black and white respondents with respect to such practices, with blacks more inclined than
whites to favor physical methods.

The relationship between the Violence for Social Control Index
and attitudes toward school discipline codes is given in Table 5.13. Here
we see that among white respondents who thought that stricter disci-

**Table 5.13**

Percentage Responses to the Violence for Social Control Index
in Relation to the Item Asking Whether Stricter Codes Cause Trouble
or Reduce Violence
(whites, N = 86; blacks, N = 62)

| Violence for Social Control Index | Stricter Codes Cause Trouble | | Stricter Codes Reduce Violence | |
|---|---|---|---|---|
| | Whites | Blacks | Whites | Blacks |
| Low    0-2 | 20% | 28% | 9% | 22% |
| 3-6 | 44 | 36 | 29 | 42 |
| High   7-9 | 36 | 36 | 62 | 36 |
| | 100% | 100% | 100% | 100% |
| N* | (36) | (36) | (45) | (22) |

Note:  Gamma for whites is .31 (p < .05).
      Gamma for blacks is -.02.

pline codes would reduce violence, 62 percent were high on the Violence for Social Control Index, in contrast to only 36 percent of those
who thought such codes would cause trouble. Similarly, those who
thought strict discipline codes would cause trouble were likely to score
low on the Violence for Social Control Index. This relationship was
not sustained among black respondents.

Table 5.14 shows the relationships between the Violence for
Social Control Index and the questions about whether or not there

**Table 5.14**

Percentage Responses to the Violence for Social Control Index
in Relation to the Item Asking Whether
Police in Schools Reduce Violence or Cause Trouble
(whites, N = 86; blacks, N = 62)

| Violence for Social Control Index | Policemen Will Cause Trouble | | Policemen Will Reduce Violence/Not Sure | |
|---|---|---|---|---|
| | Whites | Blacks | Whites | Blacks |
| Low    0-2 | 18% | 22% | 9% | 32% |
| 3-6 | 40 | 48 | 32 | 24 |
| High   7-9 | 42 | 30 | 59 | 44 |
| | 100% | 100% | 100% | 100% |
| N* | (38) | (34) | (44) | (25) |

Note:  Gamma for whites is .21
      Gamma for blacks is .03

ought to be police in the schools. The pattern of relationships was similar to that found with the question about discipline codes. Among white respondents, those who favored the use of police in the schools or who were not certain whether or not police should be used showed a tendency to score high on the Violence for Social Control Index. Among black respondents, there was not even a tendency in this direction. Perhaps it is a difference in attitudes toward prevention and toward the use of force as a means of control that accounts for the lack of the anticipated relationships. In any case, this item does not contribute to the construct validity of the Violence for Social Control Index.

It is interesting that the anticipated relationships between the Violence for Social Control Index and questions about school disturbances generally hold for white but not black respondents. It may be that blacks have a different attitude toward education than do whites. While it is true that there are barriers to opportunity based on race per se, it is also true that blacks are relatively less educated than whites (Flax 1971, p. 21) and so are doubly disadvantaged. This circumstance may cause black parents to emphasize education and to have firm ideas about ensuring that the education will take place. It is also true that many black children attend ghetto schools where the incidence of crime, including theft and assault, is high. It may be that the respondent's endorsement of a severe discipline policy and the presence of the police in schools is more a reflection of the need to prevent school crime than of any ideological or political consideration.

The remaining two questions in the series, whether disturbances in the schools are caused by the authorities not listening and whether formalized communication would reduce violence, are not related to the Violence for Social Control Index either for white or black respondents. Indeed, there is no a priori reason why they should be. As might have been anticipated, blacks in the sample were far more likely to think that violence is a reaction to an unresponsive authority than were whites (Table 5.12). It is interesting and hopeful that about three-quarters of both black and white respondents felt that school councils and other formal devices for ensuring communications would reduce violence.

## Corporal Punishment and Violence for Social Control

The last set of items that we thought might be related to the Violence for Social Control Index concerned child-rearing practices. Child rearing may be regarded as a form of social control and the use of physical punishments in child-rearing practices might be regarded as a form of violence. During the interview the respondent was asked the following set of questions:

*Here is a situation that sometimes occurs with young children. Think about how you would handle this situation if you had a child about **five or six years old.***

*You have something **very** important that you want your child to do for you **right away**. He is watching television. You tell him what you want done and ask him to do it **right away**. He says he'll do it when the program is over, in about an hour.*

*What would you do if something like that happened?*

The respondent was given an opportunity to answer this question and was then given a closed-ended question asking how often he would engage in a specific set of behaviors under the circumstances described. The stem for the closed-ended questions was as follows:

*This is a list of things that some parents we've talked with say they do when such things happen. When he says he will do something later and you want it done **right away**, how often would you do each of the following?*

Of the ten items that followed, four involved use of physical punishment or the threat of such punishment: "hit or spank him," "spank him until he can't sit down," "hit him with a belt or paddle," and "tell him you will hit or spank him if he doesn't do it right away." The frequency distributions for these items for white, black, and all respondents are given in Table 5.15.

It can be seen that there was a substantial difference between white and black respondents on these questions, blacks having been more likely to respond "usually" or "sometimes" to the physical punishment items than were whites. In fact, the differences between whites and blacks were so large on three of the four items that it appears that black and white respondents had entirely different norms with respect to the use of physical punishment in child rearing.

Three of these items—"hit or spank him," "spank him until he can't sit down," and "hit him with a belt"—were combined to form the Physical Punishment Index. The higher the respondent's score on the index, the more frequently he said he would use physical punishments (details of index construction are given in Appendix E).

Table 5.16 shows the relationship between the Physical Punishment Index and selected demographic characteristics. It can be seen that there is a large relationship between race and the index; black respondents reported that they would use physical punishment more

**Table 5.15**

Percentage Responses to Items Inquiring about Child-Rearing Practices

|  | All Respondents | Whites | Blacks |
|---|---|---|---|
| Tell him you will hit or spank him if he doesn't do it right away. | | | |
| Usually | 21% | 14% | 28% |
| Sometimes | 38 | 27 | 49 |
| Rarely | 22 | 31 | 13 |
| Never | 19 | 28 | 10 |
|  | 100% | 100% | 100% |
| Hit or spank him | | | |
| Usually | 16 | 10 | 23 |
| Sometimes | 51 | 44 | 58 |
| Rarely | 25 | 32 | 17 |
| Never | 8 | 14 | 2 |
|  | 100% | 100% | 100% |
| Spank him until he can't sit down | | | |
| Usually | 3 | 1 | 5 |
| Sometimes | 10 | 6 | 14 |
| Rarely | 16 | 18 | 15 |
| Never | 71 | 75 | 66 |
|  | 100% | 100% | 100% |
| Hit him with a belt or paddle | | | |
| Usually | 19 | 1 | 17 |
| Sometimes | 29 | 11 | 49 |
| Rarely | 17 | 17 | 17 |
| Never | 45 | 71 | 17 |
|  | 100% | 100% | 100% |
| N | (283) | (145) | (133) |

**Table 5.16**

Relationships between the Physical Punishment Index
and Selected Demographic Characteristics
(gammas)

| Demographic Characteristic | All Respondents | Whites | Blacks |
|---|---|---|---|
| Race | .61§ | — | — |
| Sex | -.09 | — | — |
| Age | -.08 | — | — |
| Education | -.29§ | -.18† | -.15 |
| Family Income | -.27§ | -.13 | -.19† |
| Town Size | .16† | -.09 | -.03 |
| Experience in South | -.36§ | -.33‡ | -.11 |
| N | (283) | (145) | (133) |

†p < .05    ‡p < .005    §p < .001

often than did white. Indeed, Table 5.17 shows that 67 percent of black respondents fell in the two highest categories of the index in comparison with 20 percent of white respondents.

Table 5.16 also shows a number of other relationships between the demographic characteristics and the Physical Punishment Index, however, most of these relationships are small and often not significant when blacks and whites are considered separately, so that many of these associations are probably due to racial differences. For example, there is a small relationship between the Physical Punishment Index and education; the lower the level of education the more likely the

**Table 5.17**

Percentage Responses to the Physical Punishment Index
in Relation to Race

| Physical Punishment Index | | | Whites | Blacks |
|---|---|---|---|---|
| Low | 1 | | 38% | 7% |
| | 2 | | 23 | 11 |
| | 3 | | 19 | 15 |
| | 4 | | 10 | 26 |
| High | 5 | | 10 | 41 |
| | | | 100% | 100% |
| | | N | (145) | (133) |

respondent was to recommend physical punishment. However, this relationship diminishes when blacks and whites are considered separately, although it remains significant among white respondents. Similarly, there is a small relationship between the Physical Punishment Index and family income, lower income being associated with increasing scores on the index. Again, the relationship diminishes when the two races are considered separately, and it remains significant only among black respondents. Nevertheless, these relationships are in the direction which indicates that heavier reliance on corporal punishment is associated with lower socioeconomic status.

There is also a relationship between the Physical Punishment Index and experience in the South. This association cannot be attributed solely to racial differences since it is still true when white respondents are considered separately. Table 5.18 shows that respondents who spent their childhood in the South were more likely to think physical punishment appropriate than were those who had no southern experience.

Table 5.19 shows the relationship between the Physical Punishment Index and the Violence for Social Control Index. It can be seen

**Table 5.18**

Percentage Responses to the Physical Punishment Index
in Relation to the Respondent's Experience in the South
(all respondents, N = 283)

| Physical Punishment Index | | | Experience in the South | | |
|---|---|---|---|---|---|
| | | | Childhood Experience | Adult Experience | No Experience |
| Low | 1 | | 11% | 39% | 32% |
| | 2 | | 11 | 14 | 25 |
| | 3 | | 20 | 22 | 12 |
| | 4 | | 26 | 11 | 10 |
| High | 5 | | 32 | 14 | 21 |
| | | | 100% | 100% | 100% |
| | | N* | (132) | (28) | (120) |

that, when all respondents are considered together, there is no relationship between the two indices; however, there is a modest relationship among white but not black respondents. Table 5.20 gives the distribution of responses on the Physical Punishment Index in relation to the Violence for Social Control Index among white respondents. The lack of an association when all respondents are considered together is probably due to the fact that, in relation to whites, blacks tended to be higher on the Physical Punishment Index and lower on the Violence for Social Control Index. So, the combination of the two races may have cancelled out an association which is true for white respondents.

**Table 5.19**

Relationships between the Physical Punishment Index
and the Violence for Social Control Index for Selected Subgroups
(gammas)

| | N | Gamma |
|---|---|---|
| All Respondents | (283) | .01 |
| Whites | (145) | .28† |
| Blacks | (133) | .02 |
| Whites with No Experience in the South | ( 82) | .20 |
| Whites with Childhood Experience in the South | ( 41) | .62† |

†p < .001

**Table 5.20**

Percentage Responses to the Physical Punishment Index
in Relation to the Violence for Social Control Index
(white respondents, N = 145)

| Physical Punishment Index | | Violence for Social Control Index | | |
|---|---|---|---|---|
| | | Low 0-3 | 4-6 | High 7-9 |
| Low | 1 | 55% | 39% | 30% |
| | 2 | 26 | 29 | 17 |
| | 3 | 10 | 22 | 20 |
| High | 4-5 | 9 | 10 | 33 |
| | | 100% | 100% | 100% |
| | N* | (31) | (41) | (66) |

Note: Gamma for white respondents is .28.

The high association between the Physical Punishment Index and the Violence for Social Control Index among white respondents who had spent their childhood in the South is interesting. Cash (1941, p. 43) has alleged that a tendency toward violence developed in the South on the basis of a frontier tradition which created a strong sense of individuality and autonomy. Moreover, he contends, this individualism demanded that crime be punished directly and immediately. It is conceivable that the same type of reasoning may be applied to childrearing practices in this region. It is known that 24 percent of the variance in the national homicide rate can be explained in terms of southerness after the effects of urbanization, education, income, unemployment, age, and wealth have been partialled out (Hackney 1969, p. 394). Thus, it would appear that there are unique characteristics of the region in relation to violence, perhaps those on which Cash speculates. In any case, the number of cases in our analysis is very small and the finding should be replicated before too much emphasis is placed on it.

That there is a relationship between attitudes toward violence for social control and the Physical Punishment Indices among white but not black respondents requires some discussion. It is clear from the data that black respondents have very different norms about the use of physical punishment than do whites in the sample. There are several possible explanations of these findings. Blacks may view the roles and rights of children differently from whites. Or, they may have a more structured concept of the relation between parents and children. For example, blacks may have more fixed notions that children ought to obey and respect their parents and elders than do whites whose ideas may center more on assisting the child in developing his own personality. Such differences in values have been suggested as distinguishing between middle class and working class parents (Kohn 1963). It may be that the differences between black and white respondents are partly due to differences in class. Another possible explanation of the difference between the two races may be that blacks view physical punishment as being totally different from violence for social control, that is, the two concepts may be compartmentalized in the minds of black respondents. Physical punishment and violence used as a means of social control are after all very different phenomena. It is only one type of abstract thinking that draws analogies between them. To the extent that this abstract thinking is correct, notions about physical punishment are relevant to the construct validity of the Violence for Social Control Index. However, it is not necessarily true that all people will share the same abstractions. (One of our colleagues recently pointed out that physical punishment in child rearing could also be viewed as a form of violence for social change.) It is clear that black respondents did not regard violence for social control and physical punishment of children as being similar. Their perception of the relationship between these two concepts is as likely to be valid as ours. The data among blacks does not support the construct validity of the Violence for Social Control Index. The relationship between the Violence for Social Control Index and the Physical Punishment Index for whites does lend some modest support to the construct validity.

## Other Issues on Violence for Social Control

There are other issues which are raised by these data. In our initial study of attitudes toward violence, we had investigated the possibility that there might be a generalized set toward violence. If such had been the case, there should have been a large correlation between attitudes toward the use of violence for social control and attitudes toward the use of violence for social change. In fact, a small negative correlation was demonstrated between these two indices for American men generally, indicating that a generalized set toward violence was not an important factor in explaining attitudes toward violence. To a limited extent, the present work is based on the idea that there may be a generalized set toward violence as a means of maintaining social control, irrespective of the specific context in which it is applied. The data for white respondents indicate that this is the case to a limited extent, but the data for black respondents imply that blacks hold quite different kinds of attitudes toward violence when it is used to control different types of situations and different types of people. It is interesting and significant that when questions are asked of black respondents which relate directly to the use of violence by government forces to control a specific situation, the Attica riot, their attitudes toward that situation could be predicted by the more generalized Violence for Social Control Index. When, however, the arena of control is moved to child-rearing practices and practices relating to school discipline policies, the Violence for Social Control Index loses its predictive capacity for blacks but not for whites.

There are two possible explanations for this phenomenon. One is the explanation given above that there may be subcategories of attitudes toward violence for social control which are held relatively independently, just as attitudes toward the use of violence to maintain social control appear to be quite independent of attitudes toward the use of violence to produce social change. The other is that some of the factors known to be important determinants of violence may influence differently the two types of violence for social control: (1) the type specified by our index, and (2) physical punishment as a means of controlling children. For example, we have shown previously that identification with the actors in the violence is one of the important variables modifying attitudes toward violence for social control. The most important identifications relating to the Violence for Social Control Index are identification with black protesters and the police, while in the violence for social control of child rearing the most important identifications are those that relate to the child and to the adult whose role it is to rear that child. It has been a relatively recent trend to regard children as human beings in their own right, with personalities and wishes that need to be considered. Previously, it was often thought that children required incessant instruction and exposure to the superior standards of adults in order to turn out properly. One might think that proponents of the latter point of view would be less inclined to identify with a child than proponents of the former. Moreover, one might think that persons who are inclined to regard children as primarily in need of instruction rather than self-development might also feel more identified with the authoritarian aspects of the parental role than are others. There is some indication that this may be true (Kamii and Radin 1967). It has also been true in the past that individuals of low socioeconomic status tended to lag behind the fashions of the middle class with respect to child-rearing practices. These speculations suggest that there may be substantial differences between blacks and whites in their identifications that relate to the use of physical punishment in child rearing. In any case, these are speculations—we have no evidence to substantiate them.

*Summary*

The construct validity of the Violence for Social Control Index was explored in relation to the respondents' beliefs in the necessity for social control in the Attica Prison riot, in relation to opinions about how disturbances in the schools ought to be managed, and in relation to the use of corporal punishment as a discipline practice. In general, the index showed construct validity for white but not for black respondents. Thus, the index behaves for whites as though it were part of some generalized schema about the use of force as a means of maintaining control, while among blacks it does not. It is true that with respect to the questions about the Attica Prison riot the responses of black respondents were so skewed that they cannot be regarded as a fair test of the hypothesis, but this disclaimer cannot be made for the questions about the necessity of social control nor for the questions about school disturbances or child-rearing practices. For black respondents these issues clearly did not relate to the Violence for Social Control Index.

These findings lead to an interesting question. The construct validity of the Violence for Social Control Index is not based on knowledge of the real correlates of violence for social control but on abstract speculations about what such correlates ought to be, the speculations emanating mainly from white, academic, middle class individuals. It must be asked, as minority groups have often done, how reasonable is it for social scientists to impose their own conceptualizations on the real world and to judge success or failure on the basis of the extent to which the real world obeys their precepts? This question does not have clear and immediate answers, but these data show that the question itself deserves our serious consideration.

# Chapter 6

# NEW MEASURES FOR OLD:
# THE RHETORIC OF VIOLENCE

*Introduction*

In fairy tales and nursery rhymes, kindly godmothers, magicians, and good witches constantly convert old, worn out, and nonfunctional items into new and immeasurably better objects for the benefit of heroes and heroines. So, pumpkins become carriages, mice become footmen, and tattered rags are transformed into resplendent finery. In survey research, the investigator is frequently faced with the question of how to trade in old measures for new. Such exchanges invariably cause a dilemma. The characteristics of the old measure are known and important assessments using the instrument have been made, but the measure may be outdated or found wanting in some essential characteristic. The new measure is unknown and comparative data are lacking but it seems more in keeping with the times and may possess some essential characteristic lacking in the old instrument. Moreover, there are no infallible guidelines for evaluating in advance whether the new measure is better than the old. Trades may be made, but it is often not immediately clear whether the new measure is, indeed, more splendid than the old.

A variety of circumstances may lead the researcher to seek new measures. The search may be for an instrument which can be more readily understood, which is more reliable, or which has other, more desirable statistical characteristics. Or the researcher may wish to replace a measure which has become superannuated by changes in manners or morals with one that is more in keeping with the mood of the time. Conceptual clarification of the underlying construct may make the revision of measures compelling. Such clarification may lead the researcher to conclude that the original measures were not sufficiently inclusive, discriminating, or clearly enough ordered to provide truly meaningful data. In the current project there were two sets of variables for which it became desirable to generate new items measuring the same domains. This chapter deals with the items involving the rhetoric

of violence. The new and old measures of the second and more important set of items—those concerning identification with various groups—
will be discussed in Chapters 7 and 8.

Ideally, any effort to compare new measures with old instruments
should include both instruments in their entirety. If both sets of
measures are available, as was the case with the effort to improve the
measurement of rhetoric, parallel analysis can provide optimal opportunities for comparison. Unfortunately, the length and redundancy of
the old and new measures of identification made it impossible to include
both in a single interview. The rhetoric measures therefore illustrate a
more complete comparison of old and new instruments and consequently will be considered first.

### The Rhetoric of Violence

The search for a different way of measuring the rhetoric associated with violence was instigated more by problems of popular
usage than by technical considerations. At the time of the 1969 survey,
draft card burning was a relevant issue which, according to national
data, incensed many people. By 1972 the nation had turned to an all-
volunteer army and the war in Vietnam, which had been the major
cause of the furor over the draft, was drawing to a close; the draft
card issue no longer seemed germane. Certainly, it seemed unreasonable to inquire about draft card burning in the all-or-none terms that
had been used in the original survey—"Do you think of *draft card
burning* as violence?"—a question which essentially limited the
answers to "yes" or "no."

The original questions which had been used to investigate the
respondent's use of rhetoric were as follows:

*Here are six questions about things that have been in the
news. Tell me if you think of these as violence. I don't mean
if they lead to violence, but if you think about them **as
violence in themselves.***

The respondent was then asked nine questions which included the
following:

*Do you think of student protest as violence?*

*Do you think of sit-ins as violence?*

*Do you think of draft card burning as violence?*

By 1972 it was clear that more militant actions had been added to the
repertory of protest behaviors in the four years since the first interview
schedule was written. It seemed appropriate in 1972 to inquire how the

respondent viewed protest behaviors such as blocking traffic or interfering with work in office buildings which had become popular more recently.

Issues of conceptualization as well as salience influenced the decision to revise the measures dealing with rhetoric. The President's Commission on Campus Unrest (1970) served an important function for our research by clarifying the difference between protest, disruption, and violence. The Commission asserted that most protest is orderly and peaceful, and that activities such as holding meetings, picketing, and conducting vigils, demonstrations, and marches are all protected by the First Amendment. The Commission defined disruptive protest as that which interfered with the normal activities and the rights of others to carry on their affairs. The Commission distinguished between disruption and violence by defining violence as physical injury to people and willful destruction of property (President's Commission on Campus Unrest 1970, p. x). These distinctions served to clarify issues which should have been conceptualized more clearly in our research. Consequently, in the 1972 effort to understand the rhetoric of violence, efforts were made to distinguish between disruptive and nondisruptive activities.

## The Correlates of Rhetoric

The 1969 study demonstrated that the respondent's definition of violence is one of the important correlates of attitudes toward the use of violence as a means of social control. The data showed clearly that the individual's rhetoric influenced the course of action recommended. The study thus provided concrete information supporting the widely held notion that rhetoric can inflame, that is, the words which are used to label certain actions as "violence" are not only pejorative but may also be used to rationalize retaliatory physical violence. The 1969 national study showed that if the respondent thought that protest activities such as student protests, sit-ins, or draft card burning were violent in themselves, he was more likely to advocate high levels of police force in controlling disturbances. If he thought that police actions such as beating students, shooting looters, or frisking people were *not* violent, he was more likely to advocate high levels of force as a means of social control. These two sets of definitions form the basis of the Is Protest Violence? Index and the Are Police Acts Violence? Index. (For details of index construction see Blumenthal et al. 1972, Appendix C.) These indices, jointly, accounted for 16 percent of the variance in attitudes toward violence for social control in the 1969 study.

The rhetoric measured by the Are Police Acts Violence? Index also correlated with whether or not people thought violence would be necessary to produce social change. The more violent police acts were thought to be, the more likely the respondent was to believe that violence would be necessary to bring about needed social change. Altogether, this index accounted for 6 percent of the variance in the Violence for Social Change Index in the national survey (Blumenthal et al. 1972, p. 233). In some ways this finding is the converse of what was true for the Is Protest Violence? Index. Shooting people (even looters) and beating people (even students) are violent in the literal sense of "a force which injures and abuses" (Webster 1969, p. 933). Whether frisking involves violence is a more doubtful matter, depending on the actual practice; frisking should not involve physical violence, but sometimes it does as has been documented by social scientists (Reiss 1968). Thus, the relationship of the Are Police Acts Violence? Index to the Violence for Social Control Index implies that those who saw the violent behaviors of the police for what they are—physically forceful or injurious acts—were more inclined to believe that violence is necessary to produce social change. In the case of the Is Protest Violence? Index, the respondent was asked whether he thought student protest, sit-ins, and draft card burning were or were not violence and was given the option of replying "yes," "no," or "both." This index showed that it was those who viewed peaceful protest behaviors as being violent who were more in favor of violence as a means of social control. Violence, in the one case, is seen as an appropriate response to real violence, in the other to imagined violence. In both instances, however, the stronger the perceptions of an act as violence, the more violence is thought to be an appropriate response.

It would have seemed reasonable to think that people who believe protest is violence would be less likely to engage in it, particularly since the 1969 study showed that American men are inclined to think that violence is bad, unnecessary, and worthless. However, the 1969 data failed to show that those who labeled protest as violent (as measured on the Is Protest Violence? Index) were any less likely to think that violence is necessary to produce social change. One possible explanation for the absence of the anticipated relationship lies in the measurement of the respondent's definition of violence in the 1969 study.

Two major problems exist in the interview questions used to measure rhetoric. The first lies with the trichotomized response scale. The respondent was not allowed to answer on a graduated continuum and, hence, may have been forced into a frame of reference which did not accurately reflect his beliefs. The second problem is that the three items in the index vary with respect to the amount of violence they imply. One is clearly nonviolent in nature (draft card burning); two may or may not be disruptive or violent (sit-ins and student protest). Consequently, multiple frames of reference may have unintentionally been built into the index; some of those interviewed may have been responding more to the disruptive aspects implicit in the items, others to the peaceable protest. Such considerations prompted us to present the 1972 respondents with a larger list of protest activities, which could be more clearly designated as disruptive or nondisruptive. In addition, opportunity for varying responses was increased. Respondents in the 1972 interview were asked the following questions:

> *Here are some political actions people have taken to bring about change. We would like to know how violent you think each of these is, **in and of itself.** Do you think being in a sit-in is at the **violent end** or at the **not violent** end or **in between?** Using the line at the top of the card please point to where you think it belongs.*

The respondent was then asked to locate the following activities on a seven-point scale ranging from "violent" to "not violent":

> *Being in a sit-in.*
>
> *Signing a petition.*
>
> *Holding a protest meeting.*
>
> *Holding a march without a permit from city officials.*
>
> *Filing a Federal lawsuit in court.*
>
> *Interfering with work in an office building.*
>
> *Holding a march with a permit from city officials.*
>
> *Blocking traffic as a protest.*
>
> *Holding a protest meeting without a permit.*

The percentage distribution of responses for white, black, and all respondents is given in Table 6.1.

Most black and white respondents agreed that "signing a petition" and "filing a federal lawsuit in court" are not violent activities. There was some difference of opinion between black and white respondents as to whether "holding a march with a permit from city officials" was violent or not. A large majority of black respondents (80 percent) thought not, but only 43 percent of white respondents placed this activity at the extreme "not violent" end of the continuum. "Being in a sit-in" shows a similar pattern. It was considered mainly "not violent" by both white and black respondents, but the response pattern is more extreme for blacks.

"Holding a march without a permit from city officials," "interfering with work in an office building," "blocking traffic as a protest," and "holding a protest meeting without a permit" were all considered to be toward the violent end of the continuum, although there was some diversity of opinion as to whether or not such activities constitute violence. It is interesting that so many respondents thought "holding a protest meeting without a permit" violent. Although the right to assemble is protected under the First Amendment and the right of any authority to require a permit for such activities has been contested, most respondents nevertheless labeled a protest meeting violent if it were conducted without a permit. These data are similar to the 1969 findings which indicated that American men had a tendency to consider violent any activities which were regarded as illegitimate, irrespective of whether or not they involved physical force.

Two indices were constructed from the items listed in Table 6.1. The Is Dissent Violence? Index contains the items "being in a sit-in," "signing a petition," and "holding a protest meeting." The Is Disrup-

**Table 6.1**

Percentage Responses to Items Inquiring
Whether Protest and Disruption are Violence
(whites, N = 145; blacks, N = 133; all respondents, N = 283)

| | Not Violent 1 | 2 | 3 | 4 | 5 | 6 | Violent 7 |
|---|---|---|---|---|---|---|---|
| **Being in a sit-in** | | | | | | | |
| All Respondents | 46% | 15 | 6 | 24 | 4 | 1 | 4 |
| Whites | 33% | 25 | 10 | 20 | 6 | 2 | 4 |
| Blacks | 59% | 5 | 2 | 28 | 2 | 1 | 3 |
| **Signing a petition** | | | | | | | |
| All Respondents | 85% | 6 | 3 | 3 | 1 | 1 | 1 |
| Whites | 86% | 6 | 2 | 4 | 0 | 1 | 1 |
| Blacks | 84% | 6 | 3 | 3 | 2 | 0 | 2 |
| **Holding a protest meeting** | | | | | | | |
| All Respondents | 45% | 13 | 12 | 18 | 5 | 3 | 4 |
| Whites | 37% | 19 | 13 | 17 | 8 | 4 | 2 |
| Blacks | 54% | 6 | 10 | 20 | 2 | 1 | 7 |
| **Holding a march without a permit from city officials** | | | | | | | |
| All Respondents | 9% | 3 | 5 | 19 | 20 | 12 | 32 |
| Whites | 7% | 4 | 4 | 19 | 24 | 15 | 27 |
| Blacks | 12% | 3 | 5 | 18 | 18 | 7 | 37 |
| **Filing a Federal lawsuit in court** | | | | | | | |
| All Respondents | 75% | 8 | 4 | 9 | 1 | 2 | 1 |
| Whites | 71% | 11 | 4 | 8 | 1 | 3 | 2 |
| Blacks | 79% | 4 | 3 | 9 | 2 | 1 | 2 |

**Table 6.1** (continued)

Percentage Responses to Items Inquiring
Whether Protest and Disruption are Violence
(whites, N = 145; blacks, N = 133; all respondents, N = 283)

| | Not Violent | | | | | | Violent |
|---|---|---|---|---|---|---|---|
| | 1 | 2 | 3 | 4 | 5 | 6 | 7 |
| **Interfering with work in an office building** | | | | | | | |
| All Respondents | 8% | 5 | 7 | 19 | 16 | 19 | 26 |
| Whites | 6% | 6 | 8 | 14 | 19 | 26 | 21 |
| Blacks | 9% | 3 | 6 | 25 | 12 | 12 | 33 |
| **Holding a march with a permit from city officials** | | | | | | | |
| All Respondents | 60% | 13 | 8 | 11 | 3 | 2 | 3 |
| Whites | 43% | 24 | 11 | 14 | 3 | 3 | 2 |
| Blacks | 80% | 2 | 3 | 9 | 1 | 1 | 4 |
| **Blocking traffic as a protest** | | | | | | | |
| All Respondents | 4% | 3 | 4 | 14 | 13 | 21 | 41 |
| Whites | 3% | 1 | 4 | 8 | 19 | 27 | 38 |
| Blacks | 6% | 5 | 4 | 21 | 6 | 14 | 44 |
| **Holding a protest meeting without a permit** | | | | | | | |
| All Respondents | 9% | 7 | 5 | 19 | 13 | 15 | 32 |
| Whites | 5% | 10 | 8 | 15 | 16 | 18 | 28 |
| Blacks | 15% | 4 | 1 | 24 | 9 | 10 | 37 |

Note: Percentages across each row total 100%.

tion Violence? Index contains the items "interfering with work in an office building," "holding a march without a permit from city officials," and "blocking traffic as a protest." Both indices are simple additive measures; and for both, the higher the score the more violent the respondent thought the activities mentioned. (For a more detailed description of the index construction, see Appendix E.)

*Demographic Characteristics and the Is Dissent Violence?, Is Disruption Violence?, and Is Protest Violence? Indices*

Table 6.2 shows that the two new indices (Is Dissent Violence? and Is Disruption Violence?) are less correlated with demographic characteristics than is the Is Protest Violence? Index which was originally used in the 1969 study. The latter shows a negative relationship to education, a positive relationship to age, and a tendency to relate to sex and the respondent's experience in the South.

Table 6.3 shows that the less educated respondents were more likely to score high on the Is Protest Violence? Index. This is similar

**Table 6.2**

Relationships between the Is Protest Violence?,
the Is Dissent Violence?, and the Is Disruption Violence? Indices,
and Selected Demographic Characteristics
(all respondents, N = 283)
(gammas)

| Demographic Characteristic | Is Protest Violence? Index | Is Dissent Violence? Index | Is Disruption Violence? Index |
|---|---|---|---|
| Race | -.16 | -.17† | -.05 |
| Sex | .20† | .16 | .11 |
| Age | .30‡ | .08 | .20‡ |
| Education | -.31‡ | -.15† | -.12† |
| Family Income | -.07 | -.13† | -.10 |
| Town Size | -.04 | -.18† | -.11 |
| Experience in South | -.18† | -.02 | -.12 |

†p < .05        ‡p < .001

**Table 6.3**

Percentage Responses to the Is Protest Violence? Index
in Relation to Education
(all respondents, N = 283)

| Is Protest Violence? Index | | 9 Years or Less | 10-11 Years | High School Graduate | At Least Some College |
|---|---|---|---|---|---|
| Low | 1 | 12% | 29% | 40% | 51% |
|  | 2-3 | 67 | 56 | 52 | 44 |
| High | 4 | 21 | 15 | 8 | 5 |
|  |  | 100% | 100% | 100% | 100% |
|  | N* | (67) | (80) | (71) | (63) |

to the findings in the 1969 data where education was also negatively correlated with the Is Protest Violence? Index (in 1969, the gamma was -.32 for white men and -.21 for black men; in 1972, the gamma was -.30 for whites and -.46 for blacks). Table 6.3 shows that 51 percent of those who had at least some college education fell in the lowest category of this index, in contrast to only 12 percent of those who had less than ten years of schooling. These data are similar to those of other researchers who have shown that the well educated are likely to show a higher tolerance for dissent than those who are less educated (Zellman and Sears 1971). According to Zellman and Sears, there is some evidence that tolerance for dissent is influenced more by the education of the parents than the schooling of the individual. Since level of education tends to be stable within families, the apparent relationship between tolerance for protest and education may actually be an association due to the education of the individual's parents, but these data cannot shed light on that issue.

The distribution on the Is Protest Violence? Index by the age of the respondent, given in Table 6.4, shows that respondents who had passed their fourth decade are more likely to score high on this index

### Table 6.4

Percentage Responses to the Is Protest Violence? Index
in Relation to Age
(all respondents, N = 283)

| Is Protest Violence? Index | | 16-19 Years | 20-29 Years | 30-39 Years | 40-49 Years | 50-59 Years | 60 Years or Older |
|---|---|---|---|---|---|---|---|
| Low | 1 | 45% | 42% | 41% | 29% | 13% | 17% |
| | 2 | 33 | 37 | 33 | 32 | 32 | 37 |
| | 3 | 14 | 19 | 20 | 23 | 21 | 28 |
| High | 4 | 8 | 2 | 6 | 16 | 34 | 18 |
| | | 100% | 100% | 100% | 100% | 100% | 100% |
| | N* | (36) | (67) | (49) | (44) | (38) | (46) |

those than who were younger. This effect may be partly due to the fact that older respondents tended to be slightly less educated than younger respondents, but it is unlikely that education accounts for the entire relationship. Whether the relationship between age and the Is Protest Violence? Index is due to age per se, or whether it is a function of a difference between cohorts, is not clear from the present data. It is interesting that black respondents in the 1972 data showed response distributions which are very similar to those of black men in the 1969 data. White respondents in 1972, however, showed response distributions in relation to age which are more like those of black than was true in 1969. In the 1972 study, young people of both races were apt to believe that protest is not violence, and this tendency among whites is more marked than it was four years earlier. Whether these data suggest that whites have moved toward a greater acceptance of protest during the last four years or whether the differences are due to a profound difference in the two samples is not clear.

In findings parallel to those for the Is Protest Violence? Index, younger respondents were less likely to think of disruption as violent than were older individuals (Table 6.5). Again, the question of whether or not this is a difference between cohorts is an interesting one. Within the last decade the use of violence as a political tactic has received much publicity. Such tactics were widely promulgated by the Students for a Democratic Society during the period of student turbulence in the 1960's. It may be that those who were young at the time were most affected by the rhetoric. If such were the case, one might expect in a few years to see young people less apt to label disruption violent than those a few years older who were young when the rhetoric of violence and disruption was at its peak. It may also be that young people generally, irrespective of the character of the time, tend to view disruption as less violent than do their older fellows. It is not altogether clear that young people outgrow radical politics, although the life histories of some prominent student radicals suggest that such may be the case. In either case, data collected at varying points in time would be required to decide whether the association between youth and the tendency to regard disruption as nonviolent is a characteristic mainly of age, or of the cohort, or an interaction of the two factors. In any case, it is clear that among our respondents the young were less likely to regard disruptive activities as violence than were those who were older.

**Table 6.5**

Percentage Responses to the Is Disruption Violence? Index
in Relation to Age
(all respondents, N = 283)

| Is Disruption Violence? Index | | 16-19 Years | 20-29 Years | 30-39 Years | 40-49 Years | 50-59 Years | 60 Years or Older |
|---|---|---|---|---|---|---|---|
| No | 1 | 28% | 20% | 18% | 14% | 13% | 9% |
| | 2-4 | 61 | 70 | 51 | 60 | 60 | 56 |
| Yes | 5 | 11 | 10 | 31 | 26 | 27 | 35 |
| | | 100% | 100% | 100% | 100% | 100% | 100% |
| | N* | (36) | (66) | (49) | (43) | (37) | (46) |

Table 6.6 shows that women were somewhat more likely to score high on the Is Protest Violence? Index than were men, although the differences are not impressive. This finding seems consistent with the stereotyped notions of sex role differences between men and women. In our society it is often thought that men are more accepting of aggressive behaviors while women view such actions negatively, in this case as violence.

The two new indices measuring the respondent's perception of dissent and disruption as violence generate only one association with demographic characteristics, that is, the relationship between the Is Disruption Violence? Index and age, with younger people being less likely to consider disruption as being violent. While five other gammas

**Table 6.6**

Percentage Responses to the Is Protest Violence? Index
in Relation to Sex

| Is Protest Violence? Index | | | Men | Women |
|---|---|---|---|---|
| Low | 1 | | 37% | 28% |
| | 2 | | 35 | 34 |
| | 3 | | 19 | 22 |
| High | 4 | | 9 | 16 |
| | | | 100% | 100% |
| | | N | (131) | (152) |

(for the Is Dissent Violence? and Is Disruption Violence? Indices) in Table 6.2 reach significance, they are so small as to be trivial.

*Relationships between the New Measures and the Old*

One crucial piece of information in understanding the relationships between new measures and the ones they are designed to replace is the extent of the association between them. Since the Is Dissent Violence? and Is Disruption Violence? Indices were each meant to replace a different aspect of the Is Protest Violence? Index, it is their combined association which is of interest. Table 6.7 shows the correlation between the Is Dissent Violence? Index and the Is Protest Violence? Index in the first column, and the correlation between the Is Disruption Violence? Index and the Is Protest Violence? Index in the second. The third column gives the multiple correlation predicting the Is Protest Violence? Index from the Is Dissent Violence? and Is Disruption Violence? Indices, and the fourth column shows the multiple correlation corrected for shrinkage.[1] Because the three indices do show some association with demographic characteristics, the correlations are presented for a variety of subgroups within our population.

It can be seen in Table 6.7 that the association between the two new measures and the old are disappointingly small. Is Dissent Violence? and Is Disruption Violence? show a moderate relationship to the Is Protest Violence? Index among those who are white, those who

---

[1] This is the first time in this analysis that a multiple correlation is used. Because most of the analysis has been conducted using gammas, a statistic particularly suited to the use of ordinal data, one might question the use of multiple regression rather than Multiple Classification Analysis here. From a pragmatic point of view, MCA requires a rather large number of cases in comparison with multiple regression. This problem is discussed in some detail in Appendix C which deals with the problem of corrections for shrinkage.

**Table 6.7**

Relationships between the Is Protest Violence? Index
and the Is Dissent Violence?, and Is Disruption Violence? Indices
for Selected Subgroups
(stepwise multiple regression)

| | N | Is Dissent Violence? (Pearson r) | Is Disruption Violence? (Pearson r) | Is Dissent Violence? and Is Disruption Violence? Predicting Is Protest Violence? | |
| --- | --- | --- | --- | --- | --- |
| | | | | Multiple R | Multiple R (Corrected) |
| All Respondents | (283) | .35‡ | .27‡ | .38 | .37 |
| Whites | (145) | .55‡ | .21‡ | .55 | .55 |
| Blacks | (133) | .11 | .35‡ | .35 | .35 |
| Men | (131) | .31‡ | .28‡ | .37 | .36 |
| Women | (152) | .36‡ | .25‡ | .37 | .37 |
| Younger than 40 Years of Age | (152) | .23‡ | .20† | .27 | .26 |
| 40 Years of Age or Older | (129) | .44‡ | .27‡ | .45 | .44 |
| 11 Years of School or Less | (148) | .33‡ | .25‡ | .36 | .35 |
| At Least Some College | ( 63) | .51‡ | .35‡ | .53 | .52 |

†p < .05          ‡p < .01

have had some college education, and those who are over 40 years old.
The table also shows that in the remaining subgroups the multiple
correlations are all below .4, a level of association which is so small as
to cast serious doubt on the proposition that the Is Dissent Violence?
and Is Disruption Violence? Indices measure the same concept as the
Is Protest Violence? Index.

There is an interesting difference between black and white
respondents. Among whites, the Is Protest Violence? Index relates
most closely to the Is Dissent Violence? Index (Pearson r = .55). Indeed, the Is Disruption Violence? Index has a considerably lower
correlation with the Is Protest Violence? Index (Pearson r = .21), and
it does not explain any of the variance in that index over and above what
can be explained by the Is Dissent Violence? Index. Thus, it appears
that among white respondents the Is Protest Violence? Index is determined more by whether dissent is defined as violence than by whether
disruption is defined as violence. Among black respondents exactly
the opposite is true. The Is Disruption Violence? Index has some
correlation with the Is Protest Violence? Index (Pearson r = .35), while

the Is Dissent Violence? Index is not significantly related to the Is Protest Violence? Index (Pearson r = .11) and makes no contribution to the explanation of the variance in the Is Protest Violence? Index over and above what is already explained by the Is Disruption Violence? Index. So, it appears that among black respondents scores on the Is Protest Violence? Index are related more to the perception of disruption as violence than by perceptions of the violence or non-violence of dissent. Why this should be so is not clear, but the difference does suggest that whites and blacks may be speaking from quite different frames of reference when they discuss the violence or nonviolence of protest.

Why the associations between the Is Protest Violence? Index and the two new measures should be so small is somewhat puzzling. One possibility is that the differences in measurement technique used in the three indices are responsible for the small size of the association. The Is Protest Violence? Index is based primarily on a "yes/no" response, while the other two indices are based on seven-point scales borrowed from semantic differential techniques. The seven-point scale is undoubtedly the more abstract of the two measuring devices and may be somewhat confusing and difficult for respondents to understand and use. The fact that those who had had some college education showed a higher degree of association between the Is Protest Violence? Index and the other two indices than did those who had had less than a high school education suggests that there may be some truth in this speculation.

*Relationships between the Is Protest Violence?, the*
*Is Dissent Violence?, and the Is Disruption Violence? Indices*
*and the Violence for Social Control and Social Change Indices*

In spite of the relatively low association between the Is Protest Violence? Index and the Is Dissent and Is Disruption Violence? Indices, it is possible that there might be sufficient overlap between the measures that the two new indices could do as well as the old in explaining the variance in the Violence for Social Change Index and the Violence for Social Control Index. Table 6.8 shows the correlations between the Is Protest Violence? Index and the Violence for Social Control Index and the multiple correlations of Is Dissent Violence? and Is Disruption Violence? predicting Violence for Social Control for selected subgroups in our population. It can be seen that the Is Protest Violence? Index almost always shows a larger association with the Violence for Social Control Index than do the Is Dissent Violence? and Is Disruption Violence? measures in combination. Moreover, the last two indices have almost no association with attitudes

**Table 6.8**

Relationships between the Violence for Social Control Index
and the Is Protest Violence?, Is Dissent Violence?,
and Is Disruption Violence? Indices for Selected Subgroups
(stepwise multiple regression)

| | N | Is Protest Violence? (Pearson r) | Is Dissent Violence? (Pearson r) | Is Disruption Violence? (Pearson r) | Is Dissent Violence? and Is Disruption Violence? Predicting Violence for Social Control | |
| --- | --- | --- | --- | --- | --- | --- |
| | | | | | Multiple R | Multiple R (Corrected) |
| All Respondents | (283) | .28§ | -.08 | .14‡ | .14 | .14 |
| Whites | (145) | .28§ | .22‡ | .22‡ | .27 | .26 |
| Blacks | (133) | .24‡ | -.07 | .07 | —† | —† |
| Men | (131) | .45§ | .14 | .25‡ | .25 | .25 |
| Women | (152) | .17 | .05 | .07 | —† | —† |
| Younger Than 40 Years of Age | (152) | .20 | .07 | .15 | .15 | .15 |
| 40 Years of Age or Older | (129) | .24‡ | .05 | .06 | —† | —† |
| 11 Years of School or Less | (148) | .30§ | .12 | .14 | .14 | .14 |
| At Least Some College | ( 63) | .27 | -.04 | .07 | —† | —† |

†The first predictor entered with an F-ratio of less than 1.
‡p < .05    §p < .01

## Table 6.9

Relationships between the Violence for Social Change Index and
the Is Protest Violence?, Is Dissent Violence?
and Is Disruption Violence? Indices
(stepwise multiple regression)

| | N | Is Protest Violence? (Pearson r) | Is Dissent Violence? (Pearson r) | Is Disruption Violence? (Pearson r) | Is Dissent Violence? and Is Disruption Violence? Predicting Violence for Social Change | |
| --- | --- | --- | --- | --- | --- | --- |
| | | | | | Multiple R | Multiple R (Corrected) |
| All Respondents | (283) | -.12 | -.12 | -.15† | .16 | .15 |
| Whites | (145) | -.08 | .03 | -.22† | .25 | .24 |
| Blacks | (133) | -.08 | -.20† | .10 | .20 | .20 |
| Men | (131) | -.05 | -.18 | -.19 | .23 | .21 |
| Women | (152) | -.15 | -.05 | -.10 | .10 | .10 |
| Younger Than 40 Years of Age | (152) | -.11 | -.15 | -.13 | .17 | .15 |
| 40 Years of Age or Older | (129) | -.04 | -.06 | -.13 | .13 | .13 |
| 11 Years of School or Less | (148) | -.15 | -.10 | -.05 | .10 | .10 |
| At Least Some College | ( 63) | -.29 | -.05 | -.33† | .36 | .34 |

†p < .05

toward violence for social control among women, blacks, those with at least some college education, or those 40 years of age or older. Thus, it appears that the new measures can in no way be considered comparable to the old with respect to attitudes toward violence for social control.

Table 6.9 examines the parallel question in relation to the Violence for Social Change Index. Here, it can be seen that the Is Dissent Violence? Index together with the Is Disruption Violence? Index almost always shows a somewhat higher relationship to the Violence for Social Change Index than is true of the Is Protest Violence? Index. However, the two indices together rarely account for more than a small percentage of the variance, and the gain in explanatory power hardly seems worth the additional interviewing time required to ask the new set of questions. Thus, it would appear that the attempt to replace the Is Protest Violence? Index with a more up to date and discriminating measure has not resulted in an improvement; on the contrary the new measures do not explain as large a fraction of the variance in the criterion measures as did the old.

## Summary

A variety of reasons made it desirable to revise the measure which had been used to assess what actions respondents labeled as violent in 1969. Some of the items of the Is Protest Violence? Index had become superannuated with the end of the Vietnam War and by changes and clarification of our concepts of how violence is defined. Two new indices were constructed from an item pool which included items based on advances in conceptualization. The two new indices correlated poorly with the original Is Protest Violence? Index. Furthermore, the new indices correlated less well with the Violence for Social Control Index than did the original Is Protest Violence? Index. The two new indices were able to explain slightly more of the variance in the Violence for Social Change Index than did the original Is Protest Violence? Index. However, the marginal utility of the new indices appears to be quite low and it was concluded that the new measures were not a good substitute for the old. The reason for the apparent failure of the new measures to substitute well for the old instrument is not clear, although it may lie in the more abstract response scale which was utilized in the new measures.

# Chapter 7

# MEASURING IDENTIFICATION

*Introduction*

One of the important predictors of attitudes toward violence is identification with the persons or groups involved in the violence. The model of attitudes toward violence developed in our previous work (Blumenthal et al. 1972) proposed that the extent to which an individual identifies with the victim of violence acts as a force which diminishes the amount of violence justified for use against that group. In addition, the model proposed that the extent to which an individual identifies with the aggressor in an act of violence serves to increase the perception of that particular act of violence as justifiable. If an individual thinks of an aggressor in negative terms, the aggressor's violent behavior is less likely to be justified than if the aggressor is viewed neutrally or as an ally. This hypothesis was supported by the data collected in the 1969 national study, both in relation to attitudes toward violence for social change and violence for social control. It was concluded that identification was a major variable in explaining attitudes toward violence.

In the 1969 survey, attitudes toward violence involving police, blacks, and students were all studied so that it was necessary to measure identification with police, black protesters, and white student demonstrators. In the 1972 study, attitudes toward violence involving students were not investigated so that identification with white student demonstrators was not included in the interview; only identification with police and black protesters were investigated.

There were a number of technical difficulties with the items originally used to measure identification in the 1969 national study. Their characteristics were such as to preclude their combination into indices. This undesirable statistical characteristic caused considerable awkwardness in the data analysis because of the large number of items which had to be included in each analysis. Consequently, it was decided to generate a new set of items to measure the same constructs measured by the earlier identification items. Hopefully, the new items would have characteristics which would allow their combination into indices and thus simplify the analysis. The procedures by which the new items were chosen were elaborate and have been outlined in Appendix D.

Table 7.1 shows the percentage distribution of responses to those identification items included in the 1972 interview which were also included in the identification indices. It can be seen that, when all respondents are considered together, there is a tendency for responses to identification items concerning the police to be skewed toward the positive end of the scale, while responses to the identification items for the black protesters are skewed more toward the negative side. Moreover, white and black respondents tended to answer these questions differently, so that black respondents sometimes disagreed with items

**Table 7.1**

Percentage Responses to Items Measuring Police and
Black Protesters Identification

| | Police Items | | | Black Protesters Items | | |
|---|---|---|---|---|---|---|
| | All Respondents | Whites | Blacks | All Respondents | Whites | Blacks |
| **Most (policemen/black protesters) are trying to be helpful.** | | | | | | |
| Agree a Great Deal | 56% | 77% | 34% | 21% | 6% | 38% |
| Agree Somewhat | 35 | 19 | 52 | 42 | 33 | 49 |
| Disagree Somewhat | 7 | 3 | 11 | 20 | 31 | 9 |
| Disagree a Great Deal | 2 | 1 | 3 | 17 | 30 | 4 |
| | 100% | 100% | 100% | 100% | 100% | 100% |
| **The (police/black protesters) are getting more than their share of the tax dollar.** | | | | | | |
| Agree a Great Deal | 8 | 3 | 14 | 15 | 28 | 1 |
| Agree Somewhat | 16 | 9 | 26 | 22 | 29 | 13 |
| Disagree Somewhat | 47 | 48 | 45 | 34 | 32 | 38 |
| Disagree a Great Deal | 29 | 40 | 15 | 29 | 11 | 48 |
| | 100% | 100% | 100% | 100% | 100% | 100% |
| **Most (policemen/black protesters) are trustworthy.** | | | | | | |
| Agree a Great Deal | 40 | 60 | 19 | 10 | 4 | 18 |
| Agree Somewhat | 38 | 34 | 42 | 41 | 27 | 54 |
| Disagree Somewhat | 15 | 5 | 26 | 31 | 35 | 27 |
| Disagree A Great Deal | 7 | 1 | 13 | 18 | 34 | 1 |
| | 100% | 100% | 100% | 100% | 100% | 100% |

**Table 7.1** (continued)

Percentage Responses to Items Measuring Police and
Black Protesters Identification

| | Police Items | | | Black Protesters Items | | |
|---|---|---|---|---|---|---|
| | All Respondents | Whites | Blacks | All Respondents | Whites | Blacks |
| **In general, there would be fewer problems if (police/ black protesters) had more power.** | | | | | | |
| Agree a Great Deal | 29 | 37 | 21 | 11 | 3 | 20 |
| Agree Somewhat | 24 | 27 | 20 | 21 | 8 | 36 |
| Disagree Somewhat | 26 | 21 | 32 | 33 | 31 | 35 |
| Disagree a Great Deal | 21 | 15 | 27 | 35 | 58 | 9 |
| | 100% | 100% | 100% | 100% | 100% | 100% |
| **Most (policemen/black protesters) are interested in making the world a better place for all of us.** | | | | | | |
| Agree a Great Deal | 41 | 56 | 25 | 23 | 5 | 43 |
| Agree Somewhat | 40 | 35 | 45 | 35 | 24 | 46 |
| Disagree Somewhat | 14 | 7 | 22 | 24 | 37 | 9 |
| Disagree a Great Deal | 5 | 2 | 8 | 18 | 34 | 2 |
| | 100% | 100% | 100% | 100% | 100% | 100% |
| **Most (policemen/black protesters) are people who use bad language and are disrespectful.** | | | | | | |
| Agree a Great Deal | 4 | 0 | 9 | 11 | 17 | 4 |
| Agree Somewhat | 16 | 11 | 22 | 21 | 26 | 16 |
| Disagree Somewhat | 36 | 27 | 46 | 42 | 41 | 43 |
| Disagree a Great Deal | 44 | 62 | 23 | 26 | 16 | 37 |
| | 100% | 100% | 100% | 100% | 100% | 100% |
| **The police/black protesters) are getting so much power that the average citizen has to worry.** | | | | | | |
| Agree a Great Deal | 8 | 4 | 13 | 19 | 31 | 5 |
| Agree Somewhat | 11 | 3 | 19 | 22 | 26 | 18 |
| Disagree Somewhat | 39 | 31 | 47 | 32 | 33 | 32 |
| Disagree a Great Deal | 42 | 62 | 21 | 27 | 10 | 45 |
| | 100% | 100% | 100% | 100% | 100% | 100% |
| N | (283) | (145) | (133) | (283) | (145) | (133) |

that evoked a positive response from white respondents, and vice
versa. The skew of the items is probably closely related to their essential

validity; for example, one would expect black respondents to be positively identified with black protesters and so would expect responses from blacks to be skewed on such items. Nevertheless, the skew creates some difficulties in separate analyses for the two races. Fortunately the distribution of responses is generally less skewed when all respondents are considered together.

Seven of the item stems were combined into two indices: four items were combined into the Positive Identification Index, and three of the negative items form the Anti-Identification Index. Each index exists in two forms, one for black protesters and one for the police, so that there are four identification indices in all. The specific items included in the indices are as follows:

### Positive Identification Index Items

*Most (policemen/black protesters) are trying to be helpful.*

*Most (policemen/black protesters) are trustworthy.*

*In general, there would be fewer problems if (the police/black protesters) had more power.*

*Most (policemen/black protesters) are interested in making the world a better place for all of us.*

### Anti-Identification Index Items

*The (police/black protesters) are getting more than their share of the tax dollar.*

*Most (policemen/black protesters) are people who use bad language and are disrespectful.*

*(The police/black protesters) are getting so much power that the average citizen has to worry.*

Table 7.2 shows the distribution of responses to the four identification indices among black, white, and all respondents. White and black respondents showed quite different response patterns to the identification indices. Larger percentages of white than black respondents showed positive attitudes toward the police and negative attitudes toward black protesters. It is interesting that the attitudes of white respondents fell in more skewed distributions than those of black respondents. All the identification indices are considerably more skewed when considered for white or black respondents separately than for the population as a whole, a characteristic which should be remembered in the subsequent analysis.

**Table 7.2**
Percentage Responses to the Identification Indices

| Anti-Police Identification Index | | All Respondents | Whites | Blacks |
|---|---|---|---|---|
| Low | 1 | 17% | 28% | 4% |
| | 2 | 29 | 39 | 20 |
| | 3 | 23 | 19 | 26 |
| | 4 | 21 | 13 | 30 |
| High | 5 | 10 | 1 | 20 |
| | | 100% | 100% | 100% |
| **Positive Police Identification Index** | | | | |
| Low | 1 | 5 | 2 | 8 |
| | 2 | 10 | 3 | 21 |
| | 3 | 21 | 13 | 30 |
| | 4 | 23 | 23 | 20 |
| | 5 | 23 | 32 | 13 |
| High | 6 | 18 | 27 | 8 |
| | | 100% | 100% | 100% |
| **Anti-Black Protesters Identification Index** | | | | |
| Low | 1 | 11 | 4 | 17 |
| | 2 | 23 | 9 | 40 |
| | 3 | 16 | 16 | 16 |
| | 4 | 26 | 31 | 21 |
| High | 5 | 24 | 40 | 6 |
| | | 100% | 100% | 100% |
| **Positive Black Protesters Identification Index** | | | | |
| Low | 1 | 25 | 45 | 3 |
| | 2 | 20 | 31 | 8 |
| | 3 | 22 | 15 | 27 |
| | 4 | 21 | 7 | 36 |
| | 5 | 9 | 2 | 18 |
| High | 6 | 3 | 0 | 8 |
| | | 100% | 100% | 100% |
| | N | (283) | (145) | (133) |

## Demographic Correlates of the Identification Indices

**Race.** Table 7.3 shows the association between the four identification indices and selected demographic characteristics. It can be seen that by far the strongest association is with race. Black respondents tended to be high on the Anti-Police Identification Index and low on the Positive Police Identification Index. The converse relationships were true among white respondents. In addition, black respondents tended to score low on the Anti-Black Protesters Index and high on the Positive Black Protesters Index. Whites, again, tended to respond in the opposite pattern. These relationships to race are plausible. A measure of identification with black protesters to which black people did not respond substantially more positively than white would be suspect indeed. Aberbach and Walker (1970b) have pointed out that there is a growing sense of community among blacks, irrespective of

Table 7.3

Relationships between the Identification Indices and<br>Selected Demographic Characteristics<br>(all respondents, N = 283)<br>(gammas)

| Demographic Characteristic | Identification Index | | | |
|---|---|---|---|---|
| | Anti-Police | Positive Police | Anti-Black Protesters | Positive Black Protesters |
| Race | .61†† | -.55†† | -.67†† | .82†† |
| Sex | -.11 | .01 | .03 | -.08 |
| Age | -.15† | .32†† | .29†† | -.13† |
| Education | -.18§ | -.05 | .01 | -.25†† |
| Family Income | -.23†† | .16‡ | .09 | -.24†† |
| Town Size | .29†† | -.32†† | -.41†† | .38†† |
| Experience in South | -.03 | .13 | .15† | -.26†† |

†p < .05     ‡p < .01     §p < .005     ††p < .001

class. Black protest is viewed by many blacks as a movement conducted for the benefit of all black people rather than just the poor among them. Consequently, one would expect that blacks would be more identified with black protesters than are whites. The large association with race is one measure of the validity of the items.

The finding that black respondents were far less identified with police than were whites is in keeping with the findings of past research on black attitudes toward the police. Our 1969 national survey (Blumenthal et al. 1970, p. 145) showed that black men were less identified with police than were whites, and many other studies show similar results. For example, in one small study, Brooks and Friedrich (1970) found blacks described the police significantly more negatively than did whites on ten bipolar semantic differentials. Moreover, negative attitudes on the part of blacks toward police seem to have some basis in reality. Campbell and Schuman (1968, p. 43) found 22 percent of black men, in contrast to 6 percent of whites, report having been frisked for "no good reason" while 7 percent of black men, in contrast to 2 percent of white, report having endured unnecessary roughness during arrests. Moreover, Rossi and Berk (1972, p. 203) have shown that respondents' beliefs in police roughness are correlated with police reports of abrasive practices. Thus beliefs about roughness shared by blacks are very likely based on reality. It is also probable that blacks suffer disproportionately from other unpleasant experiences at the hands of the police. For example, Ferdinand and Luchterhand (1970) find that police are apt to give harsher dispositions to black than white juvenile delinquents, irrespective of the type of offense. Moreover, these differences cannot be attributed to differences in age or sex. Thus, there is good reason to believe blacks would be less identified with police than whites, and the size of the associations between the Police Identification Indices and race (Table 7.3) indicate this is the case, at least among these respondents.

**Town Size.** The size of the association between the identification indices and race is such that the effect of race on the relationship between these indices and other variables will have to be taken into account in subsequent analyses. A case in point is the relationship between the identification indices and town size (Table 7.4). Town size is related to each of the four indices in the direction that would be anticipated if the relationship were mainly due to the fact that proportionately more black than white respondents live in large cities. So, those living in large cities score higher on the Anti-Police Identification Index and lower on the Positive Police Identification Index. Similarly, those living in large cities score lower on the Anti-Black Protesters Identification Index and higher on the Positive Black Protesters Identification Index than those living in smaller communities. Consequently, one might ask whether the association between the identification indices and town size is maintained when black and white respondents are considered separately. Table 7.4 shows the results of this analysis. It can be seen that the size of the association between the identification indices and the town size of the respondent's dwelling

**Table 7.4**

Relationships between the Identification Indices and
Town Size for White, Black, and All Respondents
(gammas)

| Identification Index | | All Respondents | Whites | Blacks |
|---|---|---|---|---|
| Anti-Police | | .29‡ | .12 | -.06 |
| Positive Police | | -.32‡ | -.10 | -.20 |
| Anti-Black Protesters | | -.41‡ | -.17 | .35† |
| Positive Black Protesters | | .38‡ | .13 | .13 |
| | N | (283) | (145) | (133) |

†p < .05      ‡p < .001

is considerably reduced and tends to disappear when the data are examined for white and black respondents separately. It appears then that much of the apparent relationship between the identification indices and town size is due to the disproportionate number of black respondents living in the more urban dwelling places in the study population.

**Age.** The third demographic variable considered in relation to the identification indices is age. Age shows consistently significant relationships to the identification indices, although the size of the relationships varies considerably (Table 7.5). Young people are apt to score somewhat higher on the Anti-Police Identification Index and likely to score lower on the Positive Police Identification Index. Conversely, young people are less likely to score high on the Anti-Black Protesters Identification Index and show a tendency to score higher on the Positive Black Protesters Identification Index. These characteristics of our population are what might have been expected. Young people, rightly or wrongly, often feel that the police are prejudiced against them. The President's Commission on Campus Unrest (1970, p. 69) has commented that "to most Americans the development of the new youth

**Table 7.5**

Relationships between the Identification Indices and
Age for White, Black, and All Respondents
(gammas)

| Identification Index | | All Respondents | Whites | Blacks |
|---|---|---|---|---|
| Anti-Police | | -.15† | .03 | -.31§ |
| Positive Police | | .32§ | .38§ | .27‡ |
| Anti-Black Protesters | | .29§ | .48§ | -.07 |
| Positive Black Protesters | | -.13† | -.19† | .09 |
| | N | (283) | (145) | (133) |

†p < .05      ‡p < .005      §p < .001

culture is an unpleasant and often frightening phenomenon" and that "the emergence of this student perspective has led to confrontations, injuries, and death." It points out that when policemen are called to deal with disorders on university campuses they are threatening and unwelcome to many. The Commission also states that many policemen cherish established values and institutions and that they often equate unconventionality and eccentricity with disorderliness or even criminality (Report of the President's Commission on Campus Unrest 1970, p. 151). Students may taunt the police and, in turn, the police may take a dim view of the students. The youth counter-culture, which started on campus or among ex-students living in campus areas, has spread to many of today's young. Long hair, which was once confined largely to students or ex-students, has become prevalent among the young of every social class. Police dislike for members of the counter-culture has been ubiquitous. Young people, like blacks, often complain of police harassment. Consequently, it is not surprising to find the young more frequently expressing negative attitudes toward the police than do their elders.

The relationships between the identification indices and age among black and white respondents considered separately are also shown in Table 7.5. It can be seen that among black respondents younger people identify more negatively and less positively with the police than do older people. Among white respondents there is no relationship between age and anti-identification with the police, but there is a moderate relationship between age and positive identification with the police, older respondents being more favorably inclined.

Table 7.5 also shows that among white respondents, but not among black, negative feelings about black protesters increase with increasing age, and positive identification with black protesters decreases with increasing age. Both these findings are in keeping with the notion that young people have been turning toward more egalitarian principles. Whether or not this is a difference between cohorts or a function of age cannot be ascertained from these data, but it is a question of great interest. If the difference is one due to cohorts, one might hope that racial animosities will decline in the future. The lack of an association between age and the two Black Protesters Identification Indices among black respondents may be an indication of the commitment all blacks feel toward black protest. In any case, the relationships between the identification indices and age are generally what might have been expected on the basis of what appears to have been happening in the society at large.

**Education.** Among all respondents considered together there are relationships between two of the identification indices and education (Table 7.6). However, both relationships are greatly diminished within race, indicating that some of the association between identification and education found among all respondents is due to the educational differential between blacks and whites in the population studied. The only association between education and any identification index, which appears to be true for both white and black respondents, is with the Positive Police Identification Index. Here, among white and black

**Table 7.6**

Relationships between the Identification Indices
and Education for White, Black, and All Respondents
(gammas)

| Identification Index | | All Respondents | Whites | Blacks |
|---|---|---|---|---|
| Anti-Police | | -.18‡ | -.10 | .03 |
| Positive Police | | -.05 | -.22† | -.22† |
| Anti-Black Protesters | | .01 | -.20† | -.16 |
| Positive Black Protesters | | -.25§ | .01 | -.17 |
| | N | (283) | (145) | (133) |

†p < .05        ‡p < .005        §p < .001

respondents alike, the more educated the individual is the less apt he is
to be highly identified with the police. This may be a reflection of a
tendency on the part of more educated respondents to view the society
and the agents of society more critically than is true among less educated people. However, the relationships are small and should not
receive undue emphasis. Interestingly enough, the relationship between
the Positive Police Identification Index and education disappears
when blacks and whites are considered together, probably because
white respondents were both more educated and more inclined to view
the police favorably than were blacks in this study. Since the relationship between education and identification with the police is negative
within race, it vanishes when the two groups are combined.

The association between education and the Positive Black
Protesters Identification Index appears to be mainly due to racial
differences. Black respondents are both less educated and more likely
to score high on the Positive Black Protesters Index than are white.
When the two groups are combined, this difference leads to an apparent
association between the index and education. However, a small relationship between the Anti-Black Protesters Index and education among
white respondents remains, the less-educated being more apt than the
well-educated to score high on the Anti-Black Protesters Identification
Index. Overall, the relationships between education and the identification indices seem sufficiently small that they should not be a major
factor in subsequent analyses.

**Income.** Table 7.7 considers the relationships between family income and the identification indices. The table shows that family income
relates to the identification indices only when all respondents are
considered together. None of these relationships reach significant levels
when the two races are considered separately. Consequently, it may

**Table 7.7**

Relationships between the Identification Indices
and Family Income for White, Black, and All Respondents
(gammas)

| Identification Index | | All Respondents | Whites | Blacks |
|---|---|---|---|---|
| Anti-Police | | -.23‡ | -.14 | -.06 |
| Positive Police | | .16† | .06 | -.04 |
| Anti-Black Protesters | | .09 | -.12 | -.18 |
| Positive Black Protesters | | -.24‡ | -.06 | .08 |
| | N | (283) | (145) | (133) |

†p < .01      ‡p < .001

be assumed that the associations between income and the identification indices are largely due to income differences between the races. Black respondents were both poorer than white respondents and scored higher on the Anti-Police Identification Index, hence the association between this index and income when all respondents are considered together.

**Sex.** Sex showed only one significant association with the identification indices. Among black respondents, women were less positively identified with black protesters than were men (gamma = -.28; p < .05). These data are similar to the work of others (Brooks and Friedrich 1970) who have failed to find significant sex differences in relation to identification with the police.

*Assessment of the New Identification Indices
in Relation to the 1969 Items*

When new measures are created to replace older instruments, it is important to develop some sense of how the new instruments compare with the old. Ideally, all the old measures should be available for comparison with the new in the sama data collection. In the case of the identification indices, all the old and new items were not included in one interview because it was thought that the redundancy of the items would discourage the respondent and make the interviewing task too difficult. Consequently, only one of the old identification item stems, the one which had accounted for the largest part of the variance in the 1969 data, was included in the 1972 interview. Because a direct comparison of all the old and the new items is not possible, assessment of the new identification variables in relation to the old becomes complicated. Several conceptual and technical problems must be taken into account.

There are two main approaches to the problem of assessment: one is to explore the relationship of the old variables to the new indices, the other is to investigate how the two sets of measures compare with respect to their ability to predict the criterion variables. Both problems imply the use of some multivariate measure of association. The first problem in multivariate analysis arises from the limited number of cases in the 1972 data, and the second stems from the nature of the identification variables in the 1969 data. A Multiple Classification Analysis would have been the most desirable technique for analyzing the new identification indices in relation to the violence indices, since this analysis is most suitable for ordinal data (Andrews, Morgan, and Sonquist 1967). Such an analysis had originally been used to assess the predictive capacity of the measures in the 1969 national data. Unfortunately, the number of cases available in the 1972 dataset is too small to make such an analysis feasible. Consequently, it was necessary to use multiple regression.[1] As a first step in assessing the new identification variables, the results of a multiple classification analysis of the 1969 data will be compared with those of a multiple regression analysis. Next, details of the multiple regression analysis of the 1969 data will be presented, followed by a multiple regression analysis of the new identification indices and two of the old items in the 1972 data. Lastly, the few items available in both the 1969 and 1972 data will be compared.

Table 7.8 shows that when the violence indices are predicted by the identification items, results obtained in the 1969 data using a multiple classification analysis are roughly comparable to those found by using the multiple regression. There are differences between the two analyses when black respondents are considered separately; but when the population estimates of the statistics are utilized rather than the statistics themselves, the differences are not large. This is reassuring since the multiple classification technique is more appropriate to ordinal data than is multiple regression; and had the results of the two analyses diverged considerably, the results of the multiple regression would have had to be accepted with some reservation.

Table 7.9 presents the stepwise multiple regression predicting Violence for Social Control and Violence for Social Change from the eight 1969 identification items. It can be seen that the items "blacks

---

[1] For a detailed discussion of the relationship of the number of cases to multiple regression and multiple classification analysis, see Appendix C.

better R's life" and "police better R's life" are the two best predictors of Violence for Social Control when all respondents are considered separately.[2] "Blacks better R's life" is also the best predictor of Violence for Social Change among all respondents and among white

### Table 7.8

Identification Items in Relation to the
Violence for Social Control and Violence for Social Change Indices
(stepwise multiple regression and MCA)
(1969 study)

| VIOLENCE FOR SOCIAL CONTROL | All Respondents | Whites | Blacks |
|---|---|---|---|
| Stepwise Multiple Regression | | | |
| Variation Explained ($R^2$) | 17% | 16% | 12% |
| (Population Estimate) | 16 | 15 | 10 |
| Multiple Classification Analysis | | | |
| Variation Explained ($R^2$) | 17 | 16 | 20 |
| (Population Estimate) | 14 | 13 | 11 |
| VIOLENCE FOR SOCIAL CHANGE | | | |
| Stepwise Multiple Regression | | | |
| Variation Explained ($R^2$) | 18 | 10 | 17 |
| (Population Estimate) | 17 | 9 | 16 |
| Multiple Classification Analysis | | | |
| Variation Explained ($R^2$) | 21 | 15 | 21 |
| (Population Estimate) | 18 | 12 | 11 |
| N | (1,374) | (1,046) | (303) |

Note: The identification items in the 1969 study are presented in Table 7.9. A more complete wording of these items is given in Blumenthal et al. (1972, p. 140).

respondents considered separately. It is only the third best predictor among blacks with respect to the Violence for Social Change Index, and it does not make a significant independent contribution to the predictive power of the first two variables in the stepwise multiple regression. Nevertheless, the item does relate to the Violence for Social Change Index among blacks (Pearson r = .21) and, considering the items overall, the identification item "blacks better R's life" appears to be the best single predictor of the violence indices in the 1969 data.

---

[2] The complete wording of the "(police/blacks) better R's life" was: "If (police/black protesters) get the things they want, do you think *your* life will change? If "WILL CHANGE": Do you think *your* life will change for *better* or *worse?*"

## Table 7.9
### Identification Items in Relation to the
### Violence for Social Change and Violence for Social Control Indices
(stepwise multiple regression)
(1969 study)

| Predictor | Violence for Social Control Variation Explained ($R^2$) | | | Violence for Social Change Variation Explained ($R^2$) | | |
|---|---|---|---|---|---|---|
| | All Respondents | Whites | Blacks | All Respondents | Whites | Blacks |
| Blacks Better R's Life | 9%† **1** | 7%† **1** | 5%† **1** | 10%† **1** | 5%† **1** | 16% **3** |
| Police Better R's Life | 12† **2** | 11† **2** | 8† **2** | 18† **4** | 10 **4** | 18‡ **7** |
| Blacks Trustworthy | 14† **3** | 16† **5** | 12† **6** | 18‡ **6** | 10‡ **6** | 14‡ **2** |
| No Police Dislike R | 16† **4** | 15† **4** | 13‡ **7** | 17† **3** | 8† **2** | 8† **1** |
| Blacks Helpful | 16† **5** | 13† **3** | 13‡ **8** | 18‡ **7** | 10‡ **5** | 18‡ **6** |
| No Blacks Dislike R | 17 **6** | 16 **8** | 10 **3** | 18‡ **8** | 10‡ **7** | 18‡ **7** |
| Police Trustworthy | 17 **7** | 16 **7** | 12 **5** | 14‡ **2** | 9† **3** | 18‡ **5** |
| Police Helpful | 17 **8** | 16 **6** | 11 **4** | 18‡ **5** | 10‡ **8** | 17 **4** |
| Population estimate of variation explained. ($R^2$) utilizing entries with F level for entry of 1.0 or more | 16% | 15% | 10% | 17% | 9% | 16% |
| | (p < .01) | (p < .01) | (p < .01) | (p < .01) | (p < .01) | (p < .01) |
| N* | (1,374) | (1,046) | (303) | (1,374) | (1,046) | (303) |

Note: Numbers in boldface to the right of the percentage indicate the order in which the predictors entered into the analysis.
†Identification item makes a significant increment (p < .01) in explaining the variance in the criterion variable.
‡Did not enter regression; F level for entry below 1.0.

The data also show that "police better R's life" is the second best predictor of the Violence for Social Control Index. When considered in relation to the Violence for Social Change Index, the item enters the multiple regression as the fourth predictor among all respondents and among whites considered separately, but it is next to the last

### Table 7.10

### The Identification Indices and the Better R's Life Items in Relation to the Violence for Social Control Index
(stepwise multiple regression)
(1972 study)

| | ALL RESPONDENTS (N = 283) | | | |
|---|---|---|---|---|
| Variable Entered | Variation Explained (R²) | df | F Level of Entry | Pearson r |
| Anti-Black Protesters Identification Index | 15% | 1, 216 | 39.59†† | .39‡ |
| Anti-Police Identification Index | 18 | 1, 215 | 5.72† | -.22‡ |
| Positive Black Protesters Identification Index | 18 | 1, 214 | 1.64 | -.32‡ |

F Ratio for Full Regression Model (df = 3, 214) is 15.99§
Population estimate of variation explained (R²) is 18% (F = 15.12)§

| | WHITES (N = 145) | | | |
|---|---|---|---|---|
| Variable Entered | Variation Explained (R²) | df | F Level of Entry | Pearson r |
| Anti-Black Protesters Identification Index | 18% | 1, 111 | 24.72†† | .43‡ |
| Anti-Police Identification Index | 20 | 1, 110 | 2.80 | -.16 |
| Positive Black Protesters Identification Index | 22 | 1, 109 | 1.89 | -.32‡ |

F Ratio for Full Regresstion Model (df = 1, 100) is 2.99†††‡
Population estimate of variation explained (R²) is 20% (F = 9.08)††

| | BLACKS (N = 133) | | | |
|---|---|---|---|---|
| Variable Entered | Variation Explained (R²) | df | F Level of Entry | Pearson r |
| Anti-Black Protesters Identification Index | 3% | 1, 100 | 2.99 | .17 |

F Ratio for Full Regression Model (df = 1, 100) is 2.99†††‡

†p < .05        ‡p < .01        §p < .005        ††p < .001

item to enter the multiple regression among blacks. Both "better R's life" items were included in the multiple regression analysis of the violence indices in the 1972 data.

Tables 7.10 and 7.11 show the results of a stepwise multiple regression on the Violence for Social Control and Violence for Social Change Indices in the 1972 interview using the four new identification indices as well as the "blacks better R's life" and "police better R's life" items as predictors of Violence for Social Control and Violence for Social Change. The analysis was conducted for all respondents and for white and black respondents separately. Only those predictors which contributed to the regression with F levels of entry greater than 1.00 are shown in the table. It can be seen that when both the Violence for Social Control and the Violence for Social Change Indices are considered, all four identification indices contribute significantly to one or more of the regressions. Which index makes the largest independent contribution varies with the population on which the analysis is conducted and with the criterion variable predicted. Only once does either of the items which appeared to be so useful in the 1969 analysis of identification make a contribution over and above the contribution made by the new identification indices. Among white respondents, "police better R's life" enters as the last of three predictors of the Violence for Social Change Index. Consequently, it seems reasonable to conclude that, at a minimum, the new indices account for almost all the variance which can be explained by the two old items in the data.

The regression predicting Violence for Social Control from the identification indices does not reach significance among black respondents. However, it should be noted that neither of the identification items which were the first and second best predictors of the Violence for Social Control Index among blacks in the 1969 national survey was able to contribute significantly to the regression in the 1972 data. Thus, the failure of the new items to explain the variance in the Violence for Social Control Index among blacks does not indicate that they are less useful variables than are the old. The new identification indices do explain a significant amount of the variance in the Violence for Social Change Index among blacks; indeed, they appear to account for all of the variance which can be explained by the two old items.

Table 7.12 compares the variance in the Violence for Social Control Index explained by the new identification indices in the 1972 data and the variance explained by the items in the 1969 data. It can be seen that the new identification indices explain a slightly larger proportion of the variance in the Violence for Social Control Index in the 1972 data than the eight original items are able to explain in the 1969 data when the analysis is conducted among the population as a

**Table 7.11**

The Identification Indices and the Better R's Life Items
in Relation to the Violence for Social Change Index
(stepwise multiple regression)
(1972 study)

### ALL RESPONDENTS
### (N = 283)

| Variable Entered | Variation Explained ($R^2$) | df | F Level of Entry | Pearson r |
|---|---|---|---|---|
| Positive Black Protesters Identification Index | 18% | 1, 203 | 43.59†† | .42‡ |
| Positive Police Identification Index | 23 | 1, 202 | 15.19†† | -.37‡ |
| Anti-Police Indentification Index | 26 | 1, 201 | 6.39† | .40‡ |

F Ratio for Full Regression Model (df = 3, 201) is 23.29§
Population estimate of variation explained ($R^2$) is 24% (F = 21.64)§

### WHITES
### (N = 145)

| Variable Entered | Variation Explained ($R^2$) | df | F Level of Entry | Pearson r |
|---|---|---|---|---|
| Anti-Police Identification Index | 9% | 1, 108 | 10.46§ | .30‡ |
| Anti-Black Protesters Identification Index | 13 | 1, 107 | 5.34† | -.22† |
| Police Better R's Life Item | 15 | 1, 106 | 2.87 | -.25‡ |

F Ratio for Full Regression Model (df = 3, 106) is 6.46§
Population estimate of variation explained ($R^2$) is 14% (F = 5.57)‡

### BLACKS
### (N = 133)

| Variable Entered | Variation Explained ($R^2$) | df | F Level of Entry | Pearson r |
|---|---|---|---|---|
| Anti-Black Protesters Identification Index | 4% | 1, 90 | 3.89 | .20 |
| Positive Black Protesters Identification Index | 8 | 1, 89 | 3.43 | .14 |
| Positive Police Identification Index | 12 | 1, 88 | 3.80 | .17 |

F Ratio for Full Regression Model (df = 3, 88) is 3.82†
Population estimate of variation explained ($R^2$) is 10% (F = 3.14)†

†p < .05      ‡p < .01      §p < .005      ††p < .001

**Table 7.12**

The 1972 Identification Indices and the 1969 Identification Items
in Relation to the Violence for Social Control and
Violence for Social Change Indices
(stepwise multiple regression)

| | 1969 Data | | | 1972 Data | | |
|---|---|---|---|---|---|---|
| | N | Variation Explained (R²) | (Population Estimate) | N | Variation Explained (R²) | (Population Estimate) |
| Violence for Social Control Index | | | | | | |
| All Respondents | (1,374) | 17% | 16% | (283) | 18% | 18% |
| Whites | (1,046) | 16 | 15 | (145) | 22 | 20 |
| Blacks | (303) | 12 | 10 | (133) | 3 | 0 |
| Violence for Social Change Index | | | | | | |
| All Respondents | (1,374) | 18 | 17 | (283) | 26 | 24 |
| Whites | (1,046) | 10 | 9 | (145) | 15 | 14 |
| Blacks | (303) | 17 | 16 | (133) | 12 | 10 |

whole or among white respondents. When the multiple regression is considered among black respondents, the new identification variables cannot account for any of the variance in the 1972 Violence for Social Control Index.

The comparison of the predictive capacity of the old and new identification variables in relation to the Violence for Social Change Index gives results very similar to those found for the Violence for Social Control Index. The new identification indices account for a larger proportion of the variance in the index when all respondents are considered together, or when white respondents are considered separately. When results are calculated for black respondents alone, the indices are able to account for less of the variance than was true of the old items in the 1969 data.

It is not possible to say whether these differences in the amount of variance accounted for by the new identification indices in relation to the old items are due to the large differences in the populations investigated in the two studies, whether the differences are due to the lapse of time between 1969 and 1972, or whether the differences can be attributed to characteristics of the identification measures themselves. However, these questions are important and worthy of some consideration.

Table 7.13 serves as a guidepost in considering these issues. The table gives parallel data for 1969 and 1972 with respect to the two items which were included in both studies. When the two "better R's life" items are considered in relation to the Violence for Social Control Index, it can be seen that neither item correlates as highly in 1972 as in

**Table 7.13**

Relationships between the Better R's Life Items and the
Violence for Social Control and Violence for Social Change Indices
in the 1969 and 1972 Studies
(gammas)

|  | Violence for Social Control Index | | Violence for Social Change Index | |
|---|---|---|---|---|
| Blacks Better R's Life | 1969 | 1972 | 1969 | 1972 |
| All Respondents | -.32 | -.32 | .35 | .34 |
| Whites | -.30 | -.25 | .25 | .08 |
| Blacks | -.31 | -.07 | .24 | -.02 |
| Police Better R's Life |  |  |  |  |
| All Respondents | .20 | .11 | -.19 | -.18 |
| Whites | .17 | .15 | -.16 | -.21 |
| Blacks | .23 | .02 | -.17 | -.04 |

1969 among black respondents. Among all respondents, the "blacks better R's life" item correlates as well in 1972 as in 1969 with the Violence for Social Control and Violence for Social Change Indices. In addition, "blacks better R's life" does not correlate as well with the Violence for Social Change Index among either white or black respondents in 1972 as it did in 1969.

All in all, it seems as though the "blacks better R's life" item which was by far the best predictor of the violence indices in 1969, has somewhat less explanatory power in the 1972 data, particularly when attention is confined to results within race. It should be emphasized that results within race are the only results that are even remotely comparable across the two studies.[3] The "police better R's life" item also correlates less well with the Violence for Social Control Index in the 1972 than in the 1969 data. With respect to the Violence for Social Change Index, the "police better R's life" item correlates more

---

[3] In the 1969 national data, black respondents represent less than 11 percent of the total, while the 1972 population was selected in such a fashion that black respondents formed almost half the population. This difference in proportion of black respondents can exert a sizable influence on correlations computed for the entire population with respect to those variables where the differences between black and white respondents are substantial as they are in the case of the identification indices. It should be emphasized, however, that even when data are considered within race, the two samples are profoundly different and do not represent the same population.

among whites and less among blacks in 1972 than in 1969. All in all, one might speculate that the relationships between the 1969 identification items and the violence indices might have been somewhat smaller had all the 1969 items been available for analysis in 1972.

Generally, the 1969 identification items appear to have somewhat smaller associations with the violence indices in 1972 than in 1969. This allows us to reassess the comparative predictive power of the old and new identification measures shown in Table 7.12. The predictive capacity of the new identification indices in relation to the violence indices compares favorably with the predictive capacity of the eight 1969 items with respect to the 1969 violence indices. Since the few items which are available in both studies predict less well in 1972 than in 1969, one can feel reasonably certain that the predictive capacity of the new indices are at least as great as those of the old.

In summary, the new set of identification indices has statistical characteristics which are more desirable than was true for the eight original items used to measure identification. The indices appear to account for a larger part of the variance than was accounted for by the best of the old identification items, and the total variance explained by the new indices compares favorably to the explanatory power of the old measures.

### Identification in Relation to Violence for Social Change as Modified by the Avoid Problems Index

The construction of a new set of variables measuring identification raises substantive as well as methodological issues. The fact that the new measures predict the violence indices as well as did the old (at least among white respondents) can be taken as a second test of the hypothesis that identification with the protagonists in an act of violence is an important factor in determining the level of violence which is justified. This second test is more than a replication of the first since it involves a set of items which differ from the old items in both their wording and their response scale. The fact that the new measures yield the same results as the old represents a substantial verification of the hypothesis.

The current data also allow us to test additional hypotheses. Since we have previously shown that some relationships between the Violence for Social Change Index and other variables are modified by the respondent's valuation of remaining neutral and avoiding difficulty, it seemed reasonable to investigate such factors in relation to the extent to which identifications influence attitudes toward violence. Tables 7.14 and 7.15 show that among respondents who scored low on the Avoid

Problems Index, the identification indices predicted 31 percent of the variance in the Violence for Social Change Index; among respondents who scored high on the Avoid Problems Index, the identification indices accounted for only 21 percent. The difference in the amount of variance accounted for in the two groups is modest but suggests that the respondent's attitudes toward avoiding personal difficulties or problems may play a role in predicting attitudes toward violence from identification.

**Table 7.14**

The Identification Indices in Relation to the Violence for Social Change Index
for Respondents Scoring Low on the Avoid Problems Index
(all respondents scoring low, N = 144)
(stepwise multiple regression)

| Variable Entered | Variation Explained ($R^2$) | df | F Level of Entry | Pearson r |
|---|---|---|---|---|
| Anti-Police Identification Index | 24% | 1, 127 | 39.05‡ | .48† |
| Anti-Black Protesters Identification Index | 30 | 1, 126 | 11.19‡ | -.31† |
| Positive Police Identification Index | 32 | 1, 125 | 3.34 | -.48† |
| Positive Black Protesters Identification Index | 33 | 1, 124 | 2.27 | .41† |

F Ratio for Full Regression Model (df = 4, 124) is 15.14‡
Population estimate of variation explained ($R^2$) is 31% (F = 13.95)‡

†$p < .01$ ‡$p < .001$

**Table 7.15**

The Identification Indices in Relation to the Violence for Social Change Index
for Respondents Scoring High on the Avoid Problems Index
(all respondents scoring high, N = 137)
(stepwise multiple regression)

| Variable Entered | Variation Explained ($R^2$) | df | F Level of Entry | Pearson r |
|---|---|---|---|---|
| Positive Black Protesters Identification Index | 18% | 1, 114 | 25.35§ | .43‡ |
| Positive Police Identification Index | 20% | 1, 113 | 1.96 | -.24† |
| Anti-Black Protesters Identification Index | 22% | 1, 112 | 4.14† | -.16 |

F Ratio for Full Regression Model (df = 4, 112) is 10.81§
Population estimate of variation explained ($R^2$) is 21% (F = 9.73)§

†$p < .05$ ‡$p < .01$ §$p < .001$

The importance of the avoidance motive in relation to identification seems eminently comprehensible. Historically, people have allowed others to do violence to their friends and even their own families in circumstances where the odds were overwhelming. Anecdotal material from the time of the Nazi pursuit of the Jews in Germany prior to and during World War II testifies to the seeming indifference with which people were able to watch the kidnapping and destruction of their friends. It requires heroism to defend another at the possible expense of one's own life or well-being; and while heroism is often acknowledged and lauded, it is praised partly because it is rare. Most people are not naturally heroes. Heroism implies risk-taking on behalf of another; the converse of heroism is not taking such risks for someone else. But, life rarely calls for the kind of risk-taking which makes heroes; usually the stakes are not high enough, the dangers not great enough. Nevertheless, opportunities often present themselves where others can be benefited at some small expense to oneself. Many actions on behalf of others involve the possibility of some damage to the person who undertakes them. It seems reasonable to suppose that the willingness on the part of a person to involve himself in personal trouble might have profound effects on the positions individuals are willing to take on behalf of someone else. The data in this monograph seem to indicate that such may be the case.

### Identification and Protest Behaviors

We had previously shown that identification is a strong predictor of attitudes toward the use of violence for social change. One might also ask how strongly identification relates to what the respondent is prepared to do. To answer this question, the associations between the identification indices and the Protest Behaviors Index were examined (Table 7.16). The table shows that the expected relationship between the Protest Behaviors Index and the identification indices does exist, although the multiple R is somewhat smaller than is true when identification is examined in relation to the Violence for Social Change Index. This is not surprising. The Protest Behaviors Index is a measure which was constructed from responses to a question asking what the respondent would do to bring about a change that he thought was very important. In contrast, the Violence for Social Change Index is constructed from responses to two sets of questions, one asking what the respondent believes necessary to bring about changes needed for blacks and the other inquiring how much violence is necessary to bring about change in general. It seems obvious that questions asking about changes needed for blacks should relate more closely to

**Table 7.16**

The Identification Indices in Relation to the Protest Behaviors Index
(all respondents, N = 283)
(stepwise multiple regression)

| Variable Entered | Variation Explained ($R^2$) | df | F Level of Entry | Pearson r |
|---|---|---|---|---|
| Anti-Black Protesters Identification Index | 14% | 1, 269 | 43.26‡ | -.37† |
| Anti-Police Identification Index | 17 | 1, 268 | 11.52‡ | .25† |
| Positive Police Identification Index | 18 | 1, 267 | 2.40 | -.33† |
| Positive Black Protesters Identification Index | 19 | 1, 266 | 2.27 | .31† |

F Ratio for Full Regression Model (df = 4, 266) is 15.43‡
Population estimate of variation explained ($R^2$) is 18% (F = 14.50)‡

†p < .01      ‡p < .001

identification with black protesters than would anything in the explicit content of the questions comprising the Protest Behaviors Index. For example, some of the people who responded positively to the Protest Behaviors Index may have been thinking of abolishing busing as a change which was needed, an issue which might well be negatively related to identification with black protesters. Others may have been thinking of changes in specific working conditions. Protest to bring about such changes would probably be unrelated to identification with either black protesters or police but might be related to identification with labor or management. If the actions on which the Protest Behaviors Index is based had been solicited specifically in relation to black problems, the association with the identification indices might be somewhat higher.

## Summary

Four new identification indices were constructed to replace the eight items which had been used to measure identification in the 1969 study. The statistical characteristics of the indices represent an improvement over those of the items originally used to measure identification. It also seems probable that the new indices can account for a larger proportion of the variance than could be accounted for by the old items, although this conclusion should be regarded as speculative. The new indices are able to account for a substantial proportion of the variance in the Violence for Social Control Index when all respondents are considered together or when white respondents are considered separately. The new identification indices are not able to account for any of the variance in the Violence for Social Control Index when black respondents are considered separately. The reasons for this failure in explanatory power are not clear, however, it is true that two items which had explained variance in the Violence for Social Change Index among blacks in 1969 had no such explanatory power in the 1972 data. Whether this is a characteristic of the black respondents in this small sample, or whether theory will have to be revised after a more representative sample of blacks has been investigated, remains to be seen.

The new identification indices accounted for 10 to 24 percent of the variance in the Violence for Social Change Index, depending on whether blacks, whites, or all respondents were considered in the analysis. Since the new identification indices are based on items which are worded differently from the old items and have different response scales, these data can be taken as a second and independent verification of the hypothesis that identification with the contenders in violence is an important factor in determining the level of violence justified.

# Chapter 8

# VALIDATING MEASURES OF IDENTIFICATION

*Introduction*

The primary intention of the current set of studies has been to come to a better understanding of the measures used in our studies of violence, to develop some sense of their weaknesses and strengths, to determine where they might need improvement or revision, and to develop a more accurate concept of their essential meaning. The 1969 national survey showed that a substantial fraction of the variance in attitudes toward violence could be explained in terms of other variables such as the individual's values, what he defined as violence, and his identifications. Of these, identification was the single most powerful predictor of attitudes toward violence, both when violence is used as a means of social control and when it is used as a device for bringing about social change. Because of their centrality in the model used for predicting attitudes toward violence, it seemed desirable to investigate the validity of the measures used to assess identification and to develop a deeper understanding of the meaning of the measures.

Exploring the validity of measures of identification involves problems of definition and requires that attention be given to considering how identification relates to other constructs. In the monograph, *Justifying Violence*, the point was made that membership ought to be one important correlate of identification; one would suspect that a person who identifies himself as having membership in a group would be more identified with that group than nonmembers. It follows that college students should be more identified with student demonstrators than are others since, presumably, student demonstrators are most likely to be found among students. Similarly, blacks should be more identified with black protesters. In both cases, the 1969 data bore out the expectations. However, membership is only one test of identification, and it is perhaps not the best one. Many people are identified with groups and causes in the absence of specific membership ties. Thus, white liberals in the

219

1960's were strong proponents of civil rights for blacks, a stance which implies identification with black goals and issues irrespective of the race of the identifier. Furthermore, it is possible for members of a group, particularly if it is a group in which membership is attained by ascription, to be negatively identified with that group. For example, some women feel very negative toward women and toward groups promulgating women's rights. So, it is necessary to define identification and to specify the theoretical construct to which it ought to relate.

Identification may be defined as the extent to which an individual feels himself allied with the goals and aims of a group. Identification also includes the extent to which the individual sympathizes and empathizes with the membership of that group. It follows from this definition that it is not possible to discuss the validity of measures of identification in the abstract since the constructs to which the items ought to relate and the criterion groups which might assist in determining validity are different for each group for which identification is being measured. Consequently, the validity of the identification indices will be discussed first in relation to the police and next in relation to black protesters. Because the validity of an instrument is limited by its reliability, each discussion will begin with a consideration of the continuity correlations of the appropriate identification indices.

## THE POLICE IDENTIFICATION ITEMS

### Continuity Correlations of the Police Identification Items

Table 8.1 shows the available continuity correlations for the police identification items between the 1972 interview and 1972 reinterview. Since the list of identification items included in the 1972 interview was rather long, it was not practical to repeat the entire set in the second interview. Since it was not known at the time of the interview which items would show analytic characteristics that would allow their inclusion in indices, the selection of items included in the second interview was arbitrary. As luck would have it, not all the items which were finally found to be suitable for index construction were included in the 1972 reinterview. Consequently, it is not possible to calculate the continuity correlations of the indices. Instead, relationships between items are the only data available.

It can be seen in Table 8.1 that the continuity correlations are large, although they are somewhat smaller among black than among white respondents. We have previously seen that continuity correlations of indices tend to be higher than correlations between individual items. Thus, it seems reasonable to guess that the continuity correla-

**Table 8.1**

Test-Retest Reliability for Selected Police Identification Items
(gammas, tau$_b$'s)

| | All Respondents | | Whites | | Blacks | |
|---|---|---|---|---|---|---|
| | Gamma | Tau$_b$ | Gamma | Tau$_b$ | Gamma | Tau$_b$ |
| Anti-Police Identification Item Interview and Reinterview | | | | | | |
| The police are getting so much power that the average citizen has to worry. | .67 | .49 | .61 | .38 | .48 | .34 |
| Positive Police Identification Items Interview and Reinterview | | | | | | |
| Most policemen are trying to be helpful. | .81 | .56 | .81 | .46 | .61 | .39 |
| In general, there would be fewer problems if the police had more power. | .76 | .59 | .83 | .65 | .66 | .48 |
| Most policemen are interested in making the world a better place for all of us. | .78 | .57 | .79 | .53 | .66 | .47 |
| N | (283) | | (145) | | (133) | |

tions for the identification indices would be over .8 (gamma) among all respondents and among white respondents, and that they would probably be over .7 among black respondents. Indeed, multiple regression analysis shows that among all respondents the multiple R is .77 (corrected for shrinkage) when the Positive Police Identification Index in the 1972 interview is predicted from the three positive police identification items included in the 1972 reinterview; among blacks the multiple R is .67 (corrected for shrinkage). These high continuity correlations are helpful in examining the validity of the identification indices, since it is necessary to compare the indices in the 1972 interview with questions asked in the 1972 reinterview which relate to the validity of the indices.

## Validity of the Police Identification Indices

The validity of the Police Identification Indices can best be approached by examining the relationships between measures of identification and other constructs to which they ought to be related. In the 1972 reinterview a number of items were included which ought to be related to identification with the police if the indices are valid. The items were as follows:

*Now I want to talk about what some people have told us about the police. Some people have told us that they believe the police take bribes or pay-offs, others say they never do. Do you think that almost all policemen, some policemen, a few, hardly any, or none take pay-offs?*

*Some people say the police frisk or search people without good reason. Do you think this happens to people in this neighborhood?*

*Has this ever happened to you or anybody you know personally?*

*Some people say the police rough people up unnecessarily when they are arresting them. Do you think that happens to people in this neighborhood?*

*Has this ever happened to you or anybody you know personally?*

Questions similar to the four concerning the police frisking or using unnecessary roughness had been asked by Campbell and Schuman (1968, pp. 42-43) in their study of racial attitudes in fifteen cities. Their data demonstrated that substantially more blacks than whites believed that the police engaged in unnecessary roughness and frisked people without good reason. Moreover, Rossi and Berk (1972, p. 302) have demonstrated that black people's beliefs in police roughness (as elicited by the Campbell and Schuman questions) are correlated with police reports of abrasive practices. Since these data indicate that blacks are more likely to have had personal experiences with abrasive police practices than whites, one might expect that blacks would be less identified with the police than whites. It became a matter of interest to determine the extent to which the police identification indices related to beliefs about abrasive police practices. This association is of particular interest since it has been thought that attitudes toward the police were an important element in precipitating the riots in the late 1960's (Oberschall 1968). For example, as evidence that attitudes toward the police were an important factor in the riots, the Kerner Commission cited a Louis Harris Poll as finding that 51 percent of blacks interviewed thought police brutality was a major cause of the riots (Hyman 1972, p. 349).

Table 8.2 gives the responses to the 1972 reinterview questions about police practices for black and white respondents as well as the response distributions for all respondents. While both blacks and whites shared the belief that the police are liable to the corruption of bribery, the percentage of black respondents who believed that the police frisk and rough up people unnecessarily is substantially larger than the percentage of whites who gave such responses. Indeed, the percentage distributions are quite similar to those reported by Campbell andSchuman (1968).

**Table 8.2**

Percentage Responses to Items Inquiring about Police Behaviors
(1972 reinterview)

| | All Respondents | Whites | Blacks |
|---|---|---|---|
| Some people have told us that they believe the police take bribes or pay-offs, others say they never do. Do you think almost all policemen, some policemen, a few, hardly any, or none take pay-offs? | | | |
| Almost All | 3% | 2% | 4% |
| Some | 37 | 25 | 50 |
| A Few | 44 | 53 | 34 |
| Hardly Any | 13 | 20 | 5 |
| None | 3 | 0 | 7 |
| | 100% | 100% | 100% |
| Some people say the police frisk or search people without good reason. Do you think this happens to people in this neighborhood? | | | |
| Yes | 32 | 14 | 50 |
| Don't Know | 10 | 6 | 15 |
| No | 58 | 80 | 35 |
| | 100% | 100% | 100% |
| Has this ever happened to you or anybody you know personally? | | | |
| Yes | 34 | 24 | 44 |
| Don't Know | 0 | 1 | 0 |
| No | 66 | 75 | 56 |
| | 100% | 100% | 100% |
| Some people say the police rough people up unnecessarily when they are arresting them. Do you think that happens to people in this neighborhood? | | | |
| Yes | 34 | 14 | 54 |
| Don't Know | 12 | 7 | 18 |
| No | 54 | 79 | 28 |
| | 100% | 100% | 100% |
| Has this ever happened to you or anybody you know personally? | | | |
| Yes | 27 | 14 | 41 |
| Don't Know | 1 | 2 | 0 |
| No | 72 | 84 | 59 |
| | 100% | 100% | 100% |
| N | (240) | (120) | (116) |

Table 8.3 shows the relationship between the Police Identification Indices and the respondents' beliefs about how likely police are to
accept bribes. Both indices relate to the questions as would be expected if the indices were valid. Sixty-six percent of those who believed

**Table 8.3**

Percentage Responses to the Police Identification Indices
in Relation to the Respondent's Belief about
the Likelihood of the Police Taking Bribes
(1972 reinterview respondents, N = 240)

| | | Police Take Bribes | | |
|---|---|---|---|---|
| Anti-Police Identification Index | | Almost All / Some | A Few | Hardly Any/ None |
| Low  1-2 | | 30% | 53% | 66% |
| 3 | | 30 | 21 | 13 |
| High 4-5 | | 40 | 26 | 21 |
| | | 100% | 100% | 100% |
| | N* | (93) | (104) | (38) |
| Positive Police Identification Index | | Almost All/ Some | A Few | Hardly Any/ None |
| Low  1-2 | | 26 | 10 | 8 |
| 3 | | 25 | 26 | 10 |
| 4 | | 24 | 22 | 18 |
| High 5-6 | | 25 | 42 | 64 |
| | | 100% | 100% | 100% |
| | N* | (93) | (105) | (39) |

Note: Gamma for the Anti-Police Identification Index is -.29 (p < .001).
    Gamma for the Positive Police Identification Index is .38 (p < .001).

that "hardly any" or "none" of the police would accept bribes are low
on the Anti-Police Identification Index in contrast to 30 percent of those
who believed that "some" or "almost all" police accept bribes. In
other words, those who did not believe the police accept bribes did not
tend to think pejoratively of them. Similarly, 64 percent of those who
believed that "hardly any" or "none" of the police accept bribes scored
on the high end of the Positive Police Identification Index in contrast
to only 25 percent of those who believed that "almost all" or at least
"some" police accept bribes. This indicates that those who thought the
police don't take bribes tended to identify positively with the police. The
negative correlation of the Positive Police Identification Index with the
"police take bribes" item is slightly larger than the positive correlation
of the Anti-Police Identification Index; however, the validity of both
indices is supported by the association.

It is not possible to say on the basis of these data whether beliefs about the corruptibility of the police determine identification with police or whether those who form their identification with the police for other reasons naturally assume that the police function honestly. The question is of more than academic interest. Beliefs about police integrity may be causal in determining identification with the police. If this were true, scandals of the sort which have recently rocked the police departments in some of our major cities should lead to a decrease in identification with the police. Such decreased identification with the police could have a number of unintended consequences. Attitudes toward violence for social change are correlated with identification with the police—the lower the identification with the police the more likely the individual is to think violence necessary to bring about social change. It may be that identification with the police is related to attitudes toward violence in a causal way, so that a change in attitudes toward the police will generate changes in attitudes toward violence for social change. If this were so, a decrease in identification with the police could lead to more favorable attitudes toward violence for social change. If the number of people believing that violence is necessary increases, the change in social

**Table 8.4**

Percentage Responses to the Police Identification Indices
in Relation to Whether the Respondent Believes
Police Frisk without Reason
(1972 reinterview respondents, N = 240)

|  |  | Police Frisk Without Reason | | |
|---|---|---|---|---|
| Anti-Police Identification Index |  | Yes | Don't Know | No |
| Low  1-2 |  | 29% | 39% | 57% |
| 3 |  | 24 | 22 | 23 |
| High  4-5 |  | 47 | 39 | 20 |
|  |  | 100% | 100% | 100% |
|  | N* | (75) | (23) | (137) |
| Positive Police Identification Index |  | Yes | Don't Know | No |
| Low  1-2 |  | 31% | 25% | 7% |
| 3 |  | 29 | 38 | 17 |
| 4 |  | 20 | 8 | 25 |
| High  5-6 |  | 20 | 29 | 51 |
|  |  | 100% | 100% | 100% |
|  | N* | (75) | (24) | (138) |

Note: Gamma for the Anti-Police Identification Index is -.44 (p < .001).
    Gamma for the Positive Police Identification Index is .45 (p < .001).

climate may facilitate the occurrence of real violence in the name of social change. If police corruption lessens the identification the public has with them and if that lessened identification, in turn, contributes to positive attitudes toward violence, then it follows that police corruption may have consequences which are wider and more painful than might have been generally assumed.

Table 8.4 shows the Police Identification Indices in relation to whether or not the respondent believed that the police frisk people without reason. It can be seen that 47 percent of those who believed that the police frisk or search people without good reason fall in the highest two categories of the Anti-Police Identification Index in contrast to only 21 percent of those who believed the police do not engage in such procedures without good cause. Similarly, 51 percent of those who believed that the police do *not* search or frisk without good reason fall in the two highest categories of the Positive Police Identification Index in contrast to only 20 percent of those who believed that the police do engage in such practices. The size of the association is moderate and supports the validity of the indices.

**Table 8.5**

Percentage Responses to the Police Identification Indices
in Relation to Whether the Respondent Knows
Police Frisk without Reason
(1972 reinterview respondents, N = 240)

| | | Know Police Frisk Without Reason | |
|---|---|---|---|
| Anti-Police Identification Index | | Yes | No/Don't Know† |
| Low  1-2 | | 38% | 51% |
| 3 | | 19 | 25 |
| High  4-5 | | 43 | 24 |
| | | 100% | 100% |
| | N* | (81) | (155) |
| Positive Police Identification Index | | Yes | No/Don't Know† |
| Low  1-2 | | 27% | 10% |
| 3 | | 26 | 22 |
| 4 | | 18 | 25 |
| High  5-6 | | 29 | 43 |
| | | 100% | 100% |
| | N* | (80) | (158) |

Note: Gamma for the Anti-Police Identification Index is -.30 (p < .001).
    Gamma for the Positive Police Identification Index is .30 (p < .001).
†Only one respondent said "don't know."

Table 8.5 shows how the identification indices relate to the item which inquires whether the respondent or someone he knows personally has been frisked without good reason. It can be seen that 43 percent of those who had had such personal exposure to frisking fall into the two highest categories of the Anti-Police Identification Index while only 24 percent of those who had had no personal experience fall into these categories. Similarly, 53 percent of those who had either been frisked or knew someone who had been frisked without good reason fall into the three lowest categories of the Positive Police Identification Index, while only 32 percent of those who claimed no such knowledge do so. The associations are of modest size but in the predicted direction.

One would expect that persons who are identified with the police would tend to think well of them and to minimize or deny negative characteristics or behaviors. Consequently, one would expect that respondents who identified with the police would not be likely to believe the police use more physical force than necessary during arrests. Table 8.6 shows the relationships between the identification indices and one question regarding such behavior. The relationships between indices

**Table 8.6**

Percentage Responses to the Police Identification Indices
in Relation to Whether or Not the Respondent Believes
the Police Rough Up People Unnecessarily during Arrests
(1972 reinterview respondents, N = 240)

| Anti-Police Identification Index | | Police Rough People Up | | |
|---|---|---|---|---|
| | | Yes | Don't Know | No |
| Low  1-2 | | 25% | 34% | 62% |
| 3 | | 25 | 28 | 21 |
| High  4-5 | | 50 | 38 | 17 |
| | | 100% | 100% | 100% |
| | N* | (80) | (29) | (127) |
| Positive Police Identification Index | | Yes | Don't Know | No |
| Low  1-2 | | 31% | 21% | 5% |
| 3 | | 25 | 38 | 19 |
| 4 | | 24 | 24 | 20 |
| High  5-6 | | 20 | 17 | 56 |
| | | 100% | 100% | 100% |
| | N* | (80) | (29) | (129) |

Note: Gamma for the Anti-Police Identification Index is -.49 (p < .001).
Gamma for the Positive Police Identification Index is .50 (p < .001).

and the item are of moderate size and in the anticipated direction. It can be seen that 50 percent of those who believed that the police "rough up" people unnecessarily fall in the two highest categories of the Anti-Police Identification Index in contrast to only 17 percent of those who believed the police do not engage in such practices. Similarly, 56 percent of those who did not believe that the police use unnecessary roughness in their arrests fall in the two highest categories of the Positive Police Identification Index in contrast to only 20 percent of those who did hold such beliefs.

Table 8.7 shows the relationships between the Police Identification Indices and a question similar to the preceding, that is, whether or not the respondent himself, or someone he knows personally, has been

**Table 8.7**

Percentage Responses to the Police Identification Indices
in Relation to Whether the Respondent Knows
the Police Rough Up People Unnecessarily during Arrests
(1972 reinterview respondents, N = 240)

| | | Know of Police Roughing | |
| --- | --- | --- | --- |
| Anti-Police Identification Index | | Yes | No/Don't Know† |
| Low  1-2 | | 22% | 55% |
| 3 | | 25 | 23 |
| High  4-5 | | 53 | 22 |
| | | 100% | 100% |
| | N* | (64) | (173) |
| Positive Police Identification Index | | Yes | No/Don't Know† |
| Low  1-2 | | 30% | 11% |
| 3 | | 31% | 20 |
| 4 | | 20 | 23 |
| High  5-6 | | 19 | 46 |
| | | 100% | 100% |
| | N* | (64) | (175) |

Note: Gamma for the Anti-Police Identification Index is -.50 (p < .001).
    Gamma for the Positive Police Identification Index is .46 (p < .001).
†Only two respondents said "don't know."

subjected to unnecessary roughness during an arrest. The results are as expected. Fifty-three percent of those who had personal knowledge of unnecessary roughness used by police during arrests fall in the two highest categories of the Anti-Police Identification Index in contrast to only 22 percent of those who had no such personal knowledge. Similarly, 46 percent of those who had no personal knowledge of the police using unnecessary roughness during arrests fall into the two highest categories of the Positive Police Identification Index in contrast to only 19 percent of those who did have such personal knowledge.

One more set of relationships contributes to the construct validity of the Police Identification Indices. One might expect that people who were identified with the police would be less likely to regard police actions as forms of violence than are people who were not highly identified with the police. Table 8.8 shows the relationships between the Police Identification Indices and the Are Police Acts Violence? Index. The table shows that the relationships are as anticipated: 58 percent of those who believed police actions such as shooting looters, beating students, and frisking people to be acts of violence fall in the two highest categories of the Anti-Police Identification Index in contrast to only 23 percent of those who did not regard such police actions as violence. Similarly, 57 percent of those who scored low on the Are Police Acts Violence? Index fall in the two highest categories of the Positive Police Identification Index in contrast to only 22 percent of those who regarded police acts as violent. Again, these results support the construct validity of the Police Identification Indices.

**Table 8.8**

Percentage Responses to the Police Identification Indices
in Relation to the Are Police Acts Violence? Index
(1972 reinterview respondents, N = 240)

| | | Are Police Acts Violence? Index | | |
|---|---|---|---|---|
| Anti-Police Identification Index | | Not Violence 1-2 | 3 | Violence 4 |
| Low  1-2 | | 59% | 43% | 23% |
| 3 | | 18 | 30 | 19 |
| High  4-5 | | 23 | 27 | 58 |
| | | 100% | 100% | 100% |
| | N* | (121) | (107) | (52) |
| Positive Police Identification Index | | Not Violence 1-2 | 3 | Violence 4 |
| Low  1-2 | | 6% | 16% | 38% |
| 3 | | 11 | 32 | 23 |
| 4 | | 26 | 22 | 17 |
| High  5-6 | | 57 | 30 | 22 |
| | | 100% | 100% | 100% |
| | N* | (123) | (107) | (52) |

Note: Gamma for the Anti-Police Identification Index is .32 ($p < .001$).
Gamma for the Positive Police Identification Index is -.47 ($p < .001$).

Table 8.9 summarizes the relationships discussed above and provides the gammas for the identification indices in relation to the items for blacks and whites separately. It can be seen that the gammas within race are considerably smaller than the relationships when both groups are considered together. However, the gammas within race must be viewed with some skepticism since the bivariate distributions are often so skewed as to make the calculations somewhat dubious. This skew is hardly surprising in view of the known racial differences in attitudes toward the police. In spite of this difficulty all the associations within race are in the direction which is anticipated if the indices are valid, and among whites many of the associations reach moderate size and significant levels.

### Table 8.9

Relationships between the Police Identification Indices and
Variables Inquiring about Police Behaviors
(1972 reinterview)
(gammas)

| Anti-Police Identification Index | All Respondents | Whites | Blacks |
|---|---|---|---|
| Police Take Bribes | -.29†† | -.20 | -.08 |
| Police Frisk without Reason | -.44†† | -.38‡ | -.12 |
| Know Police Frisk without Reason | -.30§ | -.13 | -.28† |
| Police Rough People Up | -.49†† | -.40‡ | -.15 |
| Know of Police Roughing | -.50†† | -.29 | -.40§ |
| Are Police Acts Violence? Index | .32†† | .07 | .18 |
| Positive Police Identification Index | | | |
| Police Take Bribes | .38†† | .32‡ | .28† |
| Police Frisk without Reason | .48†† | .36† | .21 |
| Know Police Frisk without Reason | .30§ | .10 | .21 |
| Police Rough People Up | .50†† | .46†† | .14 |
| Know of Police Roughing | .46†† | .60†† | .10 |
| Are Police Acts Violence? Index | -.47†† | -.49†† | -.17 |
| N | (240) | (120) | (116) |

†$p < .05$      ‡$p < .01$      §$p < .005$      ††$p < .001$

One factor which may influence the relationships discussed above is that the identification indices are based on questions in the 1972 interview, while the questions with which the indices were correlated were in the 1972 reinterview. Since the continuity correlations of the identification items and, presumably, the indices are about .8 (gamma), the construct validity of the indices is probably being underestimated by correlations reported here. In any case, the results indicate that the police identification items have considerable construct validity.

## THE BLACK PROTESTERS IDENTIFICATION ITEMS

Having considered the validity of the identification items as they pertain to the police, we will now consider the same items in the context of their use as measures of identification with "black protesters." It is clear that in measuring identification with black protesters the goals of black protest may be a very salient issue. Thus, attention is directed toward examining the relationship between identification with black protesters and perception of the amount of political power held by blacks. In addition, the indices will be considered in relation to the respondent's perception of black protesters.

It is true of the Black Protesters Identification Indices, as it was of the Police Identification Indices, that the indices themselves are found in the 1972 interview, while the items that relate to their construct validity are found in the 1972 reinterview so that the measures must be correlated across a gap in time. For this reason the discussion will begin with an examination of the continuity correlations of the black protesters identification items.

### Continuity Correlations of the Black Protesters Identification Items

Table 8.10 gives the continuity correlations of selected items in the two Black Protesters Identification Indices. It can be seen that these continuity correlations are substantially smaller than were the analogous correlations of the police identification items. When all respondents are considered together the correlations are about .7 (gamma) with a multiple R of .68 (corrected for shrinkage). When the Positive Black Protesters Identification Index in the interview is predicted by the three items in the reinterview, the multiple R is only .41 (corrected for shrinkage) among blacks. The fact that the continuity correlations are low is a source of some concern. This is particularly the case since the questions designed to test the construct validity of the black protesters identification items appeared in the 1972 reinterview, while the questions on which the indices are based were asked during the 1972 interview which was conducted, on the average, seven weeks earlier. As a result of the time lag, one might expect that the correlations between the Black Protesters Identification Indices and items occurring in the reinterview would be somewhat lower than what might have been found had all the materials been available in a single interview.

**Table 8.10**

Test-Retest Reliability for Selected
Black Protesters Identification Items
(gammas, tau$_b$'s)

| | All Respondents | | Whites | | Blacks | |
|---|---|---|---|---|---|---|
| | Gamma | Tau$_b$ | Gamma | Tau$_b$ | Gamma | Tau$_b$ |
| Anti-Black Protesters Identification Items: Interview vs. Reinterview | | | | | | |
| Black protesters are getting so much power that the average citizen has to worry. | .70 | .54 | .69 | .52 | .55 | .38 |
| Positive Black Protesters Identification Items: Interview vs. Reinterview | | | | | | |
| Most black protesters are trying to be helpful. | .70 | .51 | .66 | .49 | .44 | .27 |
| In general, there would be fewer problems if black protesters had more power. | .69 | .52 | .53 | .32 | .46 | .32 |
| Most black protesters are interested in making the world a better place for all of us. | .67 | .52 | .58 | .42 | .31 | .20 |
| N | (283) | | (145) | | (133) | |

## Validity of the Black Protesters Identification Indices

Included in the second interview were a few questions which should shed some light on the validity of the Black Protesters Identification Indices. Among these was the following:

> Now we would like to ask your opinion about how much political power different groups of people have in the United States. I mean how much power they have to get laws passed in their favor. Do you think labor unions have **too much power, about the right amount of power,** or have **have too little power** in this country?

This question was followed by a list of groups including *blacks* and *black militants*.

The distribution of responses to the questions about the power of blacks and black militants is shown in Table 8.11. It can be seen that black respondents were far more likely than white respondents to believe that blacks have too little power. This is hardly surprising; the

**Table 8.11**

Percentage Responses to Items Inquiring about
the Power of Blacks and Black Militants
(1972 reinterview)

|  | All Respondents | Whites | Blacks |
|---|---|---|---|
| Do you think *blacks* have too much power, about the right amount of power, or have too little power in this country? | | | |
| Too Much | 8% | 12% | 4% |
| About Right | 36 | 59 | 14 |
| Too Little | 56 | 29 | 82 |
|  | 100% | 100% | 100% |
| Do you think *black militants* have too much power, about the right amount of power, or have too little power in this country? | | | |
| Too Much | 47 | 67 | 27 |
| About Right | 37 | 29 | 45 |
| Too Little | 16 | 4 | 28 |
|  | 100% | 100% | 100% |
| N | (240) | (120) | (116) |

most casual observer of the contemporary social scene can hardly fail to be aware that blacks feel they do not have sufficient political power (Aberbach and Walker 1970a). Moreover, it is clear that whites often fail to share the black perception of black powerlessness.

The responses are substantially different, however, with respect to the power of black militants. It is hardly surprising that two-thirds of the white respondents believed black militants have too much power. Previous work has shown that black power is viewed with apprehension among many whites (Aberbach and Walker 1970b). But, the vast majority of black respondents perceived black militants as having enough power, if not more than enough. Only 28 percent believed that black militants have too little power. Perhaps, black militancy raises some negative connotations among blacks as well as whites.

Table 8.12 shows the relationships between the Black Protesters Identification Indices and the respondents' perceptions of the amount of political power held by blacks. The relationships between the indices and the question are large. Indeed, they are so large as to suggest that the major issue involved in identification with black protesters is one of political power. Table 8.12 shows that 71 percent of those who thought blacks have enough power scored in the two highest categories of the Anti-Black Protesters Identification Index in contrast to only 31 percent of those who thought blacks have too little power. Similarly, 50 percent of those who thought blacks have too little power scored in the three highest categories of the Positive Black Protesters Identification Index in contrast to only 14 percent of those who felt blacks had enough or too much power. The high relationship between questions asking about power for black people generally and identification with black protesters suggests that the latter may very well be almost the same as identification with black people generally. This is an important point. It is virtually impossible to ask blacks questions which inquire about identification with other blacks. Such questions invariably sound offensive or abrasive. Nevertheless, the underlying issue in the struggle to generate social change for blacks is a black issue. It is reassuring that the paraphrase "black protesters," which was used to make asking

**Table 8.12**

Percentage Responses to the Black Protesters Identification Indices in Relation to the Amount of Power the Respondent Believes Blacks Have (1972 reinterview respondents, N = 240)

| | | | Power: Blacks | |
| --- | --- | --- | --- | --- |
| Anti-Black Protesters Identification Index | | | Too Little | About Right/ Too Much† |
| Low | 1 | | 15% | 4% |
| | 2 | | 37 | 11 |
| | 3 | | 17 | 14 |
| High | 4-5 | | 31 | 71 |
| | | | 100% | 100% |
| | | N* | (129) | (104) |
| Positive Black Protesters Identification Index | | | Too Little | About Right/ Too Much† |
| Low | 1 | | 10% | 41% |
| | 2 | | 15 | 28 |
| | 3 | | 25 | 17 |
| High | 4-6 | | 50 | 14 |
| | | | 100% | 100% |
| | | N* | (129) | (103) |

Note: Gamma for the Anti-Black Protesters Identification Index is .61 (p < .001).
  Gamma for the Positive Black Protesters Identification Index is -.57 (p < .001).
†Only 19 respondents said "too much."

blacks about blacks more feasible, does seem to be very closely linked with a general identification with blacks.

  Table 8.13 shows the relationships between the Black Protesters Identification Indices and the question about how much power the respondent believes is held by black militants. Again, the distribution of responses and the size of the association supports the essential validity of the indices. Thirty-nine percent of those who thought that black militants had too much power scored in the highest category of the Anti-Black Identification Index, in contrast to none of those who thought black militants had too little power. The relationship to the

**Table 8.13**

Percentage Responses to the Black Protesters Identification Indices
in Relation to the Amount of Power
the Respondent Believes Black Militants Have
(1972 reinterview respondents, N = 240)

| | | | Power: Black Militants | | |
|---|---|---|---|---|---|
| Anti-Black Protesters Identification Index | | | Too Little | About Right | Too Much |
| Low | 1-2 | | 77% | 38% | 18% |
| | 3 | | 11 | 20 | 15 |
| | 4 | | 12 | 30 | 28 |
| High | 5 | | 0 | 12 | 39 |
| | | | 100% | 100% | 100% |
| | | N* | (35) | (82) | (104) |
| Positive Black Protesters Identification Index | | | Too Little | About Right | Too Much |
| Low | 1 | | 0% | 15% | 43% |
| | 2 | | 17 | 20 | 20 |
| | 3 | | 14 | 25 | 18 |
| High | 4-6 | | 69 | 40 | 19 |
| | | | 100% | 100% | 100% |
| | | N* | (35) | (82) | (103) |

Note: Gamma for the Anti-Black Protesters Identification Index is .60 (p < .001).
Gamma for the Positive Black Protesters Identification Index is -.53 (p < .001).

Positive Black Protesters Identification Index shows 69 percent of those who felt that black militants had too little power fell in the three highest categories of this index, in contrast to only 19 percent of those who felt black militants had too much power.

The relationships between the Black Protesters Identification Indices and questions about political power held by blacks raise some interesting substantive issues in addition to the contribution that they make to understanding the validity of the indices. The data imply that a very large dimension in identification with black protesters is a political one, that is, the perceived need for power for black people. It is intuitively obvious that this should be so if one considers the nature of the civil liberties movement, which has placed a strong emphasis on equalizing political power for blacks. But, the notion of political power is not intrinisic to the stems in the identification items. Indeed, it would be very surprising if identification with other groups—the police, for example—should have such a close correlation with the perceived need for political power. These data imply that the identification stems measure a cognitive and affective set which can be derived from a variety of motives, a characteristic which implies that the indices are likely to show considerable flexibility.

One more question is available to shed some light on the validity of the Black Protesters Identification Indices. The question was as follows:

> *Now we want to talk about blacks who participate in protests. When we talk about **black protesters,** what kind of people do you have in mind?*

The question was coded in two ways. First, the coder was asked to code the "emotive content" of the answer—that is, the "feelings toward black protesters based on affective words." Secondly, the coder was asked to code the substantive content of the response. With respect to the emotive content of the responses, the coder could state that he believed the respondent had positive feelings toward black protesters, negative feelings, neutral feelings, or that the respondent's feelings could not be determined from the answer. It was not possible to develop a very high degree of accuracy in making these assessments: there was only 82 percent agreement among coders on this question. Nevertheless, the results in Table 8.14 are of interest. The table shows the relationship between responses to the above question and the Black Protesters Identification Indices. It can be seen that the affect displayed by the respondents is highly related to the Black Protesters Identification Indices. Fifty-three percent of those who were coded as having positive feelings toward black protesters on the open-ended question scored in the two lowest categories on the Anti-Black Protesters Identification Index, in contrast to only 17 percent of those who were coded as showing negative feelings toward black protesters. Similarly, 57 percent of those who were coded as showing positive feelings for black protesters on the open-ended question scored in the three highest categories on the Positive Black Protesters Identification Index in contrast to only 12 percent of those who were coded as having negative feelings toward black protesters.

A variety of substantive responses was obtained to the question asking the respondent what kind of people he had in mind when he

**Table 8.14**

Percentage Responses to the Black Protesters Identification Indices
in Relation to the Respondent's Feelings toward Black Protesters
(1972 reinterview respondents giving positive or negative responses, N = 148)

| Anti-Black Protesters Identification Index | | | Feelings Toward Black Protesters | |
|---|---|---|---|---|
| | | | Negative | Positive |
| Low | 1-2 | | 17% | 53% |
| | 3 | | 14 | 15 |
| | 4 | | 32 | 23 |
| High | 5 | | 37 | 9 |
| | | | 100% | 100% |
| | | N* | (95) | (53) |

| Positive Black Protesters Identification Index | | | Negative | Positive |
|---|---|---|---|---|
| Low | 1 | | 48% | 2% |
| | 2 | | 26 | 15 |
| | 3 | | 14 | 26 |
| High | 4-6 | | 12 | 57 |
| | | | 100% | 100% |
| | | N* | (95) | (53) |

Note: Gamma for the Anti-Black Protesters Identification Index is -.59 (p < .001).
Gamma for the Positive Black Protesters Identification Index is .80 (p < .001).

talked about "black protesters." Some of these responses could be used to evaluate the validity of the Black Protesters Identification Indices; others could not. For example, responses which did not contribute to this assessment were answers in terms of specific people such as Martin Luther King, Shirley Chisolm, or Malcolm X. Other nonusable responses redefined the question with answers such as "people who participate in protests." Responses couched in terms of the socioeconomic characteristics of protesters—such as young people, poor people, and so on—also could not be used.

However, some respondents did answer the question in terms which give some insight into the nature of their identification with black protesters. For example, a substantial number of respondents replied that they thought of black protesters as trouble-makers, while others described them as concerned people who wanted to increase equality and opportunity for black people. Responses such as these were used to assess the validity of the indices. Table 8.15 shows that the open-ended responses relate to the Black Protesters Identification Indices as would be expected if the indices were valid. Fifty-seven percent of those who thought of black protesters as concerned people who want equal rights fall in the two lowest categories of the Anti-Black Protesters Identification Index, in contrast to only 19 percent of those who thought of black protesters as "trouble-makers" or "wild people." Similar results are seen in relation to the Positive Black Protesters Identification Index. Forty-nine percent of those who regarded black protesters as "concerned people who want equal rights" fall in the upper three categories of the Positive Black Protesters Identification Index, in contrast to only 15 percent of those who thought of black protesters as "trouble-makers."

Table 8.16 gives the relationships between the Black Protesters Identification Indices and the items discussed previously for white, black, and all respondents. It can be seen that the relationships among white respondents are generally about as large as when the relationships are calculated for all respondents. Among black respondents they are substantially smaller and often fail to achieve significance; however, the direction of the relationship is always in the expected direction. Although the strength of the relationship within race is smaller than that among all respondents, the validity of the items is substantial when whites are considered separately or when all respondents are considered together. One factor that may contribute to the small size of the correlations when blacks are considered separately is the small continuity correlation obtained among blacks for these items. Since the items which are used to assess the construct validity of the identification indices are in the reinterview, while the indices themselves are in the initial interview, the correlations used to assess construct validity must be reduced by a factor which is proportionate to the change in the measures over time. Under the circumstances, it is surprising that we find any significant correlations between construct items and indices among black respondents considered separately.

The results described above, taken together, provide substantial support for the validity of the identification indices as they relate to black protesters. The evidence implies that identification with black protesters, while obviously not identical with identification with black people, is closely related to the latter. The data also indicate that a strong correlate of identification with black protesters is the respondent's assessment of the amount of political power that blacks ought to have but do not have. This political correlate of identification needs emphasis. Numerous social scientists have emphasized the meaningful nature of the urban disturbances of the late 1960's (Fogelson 1968, Grimshaw 1968). Others such as Banfield (1970, pp. 185-209) have contended that the outbursts were mainly for "fun and profit." In analyzing the meaning of the riots, much has been made of patterns

**Table 8.15**

Percentage Responses to the Black Protesters Identification Indices
in Relation to the Respondent's Description of Black Protesters
(1972 reinterview respondents, N = 240)

| Who Are Black Protesters? | Anti-Black Protesters Identification Index | | | | |
| --- | --- | --- | --- | --- | --- |
| | Number of Mentions | Low 1-2 | 3 | 4 | High 5 |
| Uneducated; lower class, unemployed people | (20) | 30% | 25 | 25 | 20 |
| Trouble-makers; wild people; radicals; violent people; ruthless people | (87) | 19% | 16 | 33 | 32 |
| Concerned people; people who want change, who want to help; people who want equal rights, opportunity, jobs, education, housing; people who act, go, and do what's necessary | (76) | 57% | 12 | 18 | 13 |
| Other | (104) | 35% | 15 | 26 | 24 |
| All responses combined | (287) | 35% | 15 | 27 | 23 |

| Who Are Black Protesters? | Positive Black Protesters Identification Index | | | | |
| --- | --- | --- | --- | --- | --- |
| | Number of Mentions | Low 1 | 2 | 3 | High 4-6 |
| Uneducated; lower class, unemployed people | (20) | 20% | 25 | 40 | 15 |
| Trouble-makers; wild people; radicals; violent people; ruthless people | (87) | 44% | 24 | 17 | 15 |
| Concerned people; people who want change, who want to help; people who want equal rights, opportunity, jobs, education, housing; people who act, go, and do what's necessary | (76) | 4% | 17 | 30 | 49 |
| Other | (104) | 25% | 25 | 16 | 34 |
| All responses combined | (287) | 25% | 23 | 22 | 30 |

Note: Respondents were allowed to give more than one answer so there are more
responses than respondents.

Percentages across each row total 100%.

**Table 8.16**

Relationships between the Black Protesters Identification Indices
and Variables Inquiring about Power of Blacks and Black Militants and
Feelings toward Black Protesters
(1972 reinterview)
(gammas)

| Anti-Black Protesters Identification Index | | All Respondents | Whites | Blacks |
|---|---|---|---|---|
| Power: Blacks | | .61†† | .66†† | .14 |
| Power: Black Militants | | .60†† | .47†† | .40†† |
| Feelings toward black protesters | | -.59†† | -.75†† | .15 |
| **Positive Black Protesters Identification Index** | | | | |
| Power: Blacks | | -.57†† | -.38‡ | -.14 |
| Power: Black Militants | | -.53†† | -.42§ | -.21 |
| Feelings toward black protesters | | .80†† | .79†† | .41† |
| | N | (240) | (120) | (116) |

†p < .05     ‡p < .01     §p < .005     ††p < .001

of looting and arson (Grimshaw 1968). These statements imply venge-
fulness and retribution rather than a struggle for political power. However, the riots can be viewed as a form of protest against the political
impotence which makes it so difficult to produce meaningful change.
Indeed, these views of riots are not incompatible. It is perfectly
possible for an individual to loot a store in order to revenge himself
for past business practices, and to find revenge may be both fun
and profitable under such circumstances. Moreover, there is no reason
to suppose that the coercive nature of the use of force as a political
bargaining chip is dependent on the political motive being the only one.
So, the motives of fun and profit, revenge, and the wish for political
power may coexist and may all have played a role in the urban riots.

We have previously demonstrated that identification is an important correlate of attitudes toward the use of violence for social
change, a finding which is replicated in the current data, and we have
suggested that the relationship is a causal one. The close association
between the perceived political powerlessness of blacks and identification with black protesters implies that a substantial motive in such
identification is political. We do not know that attitudes toward violence
cause violent behaviors, although the evidence in this monograph
implies that such is likely to be the case; nevertheless, the data support

the notion that the riots and protests of the 1960's were politically motivated. Moreover, the data collected in this study, while they were not collected from a representative sample and cannot be taken to be representative of the United States, suggest that there has not been any substantial change in such attitudes and perceptions since 1969. Since the underlying attitudes have not changed, the present ebbing of collective violence cannot be taken to indicate that the basic problems have been solved. Whether or not these unresolved problems will again flair into violence sometime in the future remains to be seen.

*Summary*

The construct validity of the identification indices has been investigated. Identification with the police was related to beliefs about whether or not the police were honest and whether they engaged in abusive practices. For example, personal knowledge of unnecessary roughness by the police was negatively related to identification with the police. The relationship between such items and the Police Identification Indices were moderate in size when all respondents were considered together in the analysis and suggested that the indices have substantial validity.

The construct validity of the Black Protesters Identification Indices was examined by exploring the relationship of the indices to the respondent's perception of the amount of political power held by blacks and black militants. The relationships were high and suggested that the theme of political power is a major component of identification with black protesters. In addition, responses to an open-ended question asking the respondent to describe black protesters related to the identification indices in the direction expected. Those that described black protesters in negative terms tended to score low on the Positive Black Protesters Indentification Index and high on the Anti-Black Protesters Identification Index. Those that described black protesters in positive terms on the open-ended question tended to score high on the Positive Black Protesters Identification Index and low on the Anti-Black Protesters Identification Index. These relationships suggest that the Black Protesters Identification Indices also have substantial validity.

The fact that both the Police and the Black Protesters Identification Indices show considerable validity is both interesting and important. It is interesting because the salient issues are quite different with respect to the police than in relation to black protesters. When one considers the police, integrity, fairness, and abrasive or brutal practices are particularly germane. These constructs are far less relevant when one considers black protesters for whom opinions about political power seem especially relevant. It is an interesting characteristic of the stems of the identification items that they can relate to such widely differing constructs when the subject of the identification is changed. These data suggest that the use of the identification stems allows measurement on commensurate dimensions of phenomena which have very different underlying motives. Such considerations suggest that the identification stems developed in the preceding chapter should prove to be exceedingly useful tools in future research.

# Chapter 9

# CONCLUSION

Every book, even a technical monograph, deserves an ending, a few words of summary, some graceful phrase to lay it all to rest. This work does not lend itself easily to such summary, perhaps because it raises more questions than it answers and unsettles more issues than it resolves.

The research described here was originally conceived as an effort to assess and improve the major measures which were used to study attitudes toward violence in 1969. The research was designed to serve an interim function. It was meant to explore and develop the measures so that the next study of attitudes toward violence could capitalize on a better understanding of the characteristics of the measures and how they could best be interpreted. Specifically, the study was designed as a response to two frequently repeated criticisms of attitudinal research: first, that measures are invented, used once, and never repeated, so that an understanding of their implications is often superficial; and second, that the behavioral concomitants of attitudes are assumed but rarely demonstrated.

Progress in complicated areas of social science is likely to be faster in proportion to the extent to which research is cumulative. So long as researchers insist on inventing a new set of measures for every study that is undertaken in a specific area of research, it is impossible to determine the degree of substantive agreement among them. Methodological effects leave such questions moot. Moreover, there is an unfortunate tendency among social scientists to engage in precisely this practice— the vast majority of instruments created to measure specific attributes are used once and never again (Chun et al. 1973).

In this work we have attempted to determine the quality of our measures. Their virtues and deficiencies are exposed here. In so doing we hope that others will use these measures, improve those that have failings, and integrate their work with our own. Thus, we hope that others will learn from our failures and benefit from our successes and consequently move knowledge forward.

Unfortunately, history has a way of moving quickly, and the character of the times exerts a profound effect on the kind of research which can be conducted. When our work on attitudes toward violence first began, collective violence in the United States was an unavoidable problem. Large scale riots were relatively frequent, several assassinations of major political figures had occurred, and ells of newspaper columns were devoted to these events. Since then the character of the times has changed. Few large scale riots have occurred since 1969, and these received relatively little attention from the communications media.

We were impressed in 1970 and afterwards that incidents of collective violence received far less newspaper space than they had been given in the late 1960's. In 1970 and 1971 we often heard of substantial episodes of collective violence from our interviewers, but these received almost no national coverage in the newspapers; and it seemed as though there was less collective violence, although we were not sure to what extent the decline was real or due to changes in reporting. Later, our interviewers reported progressively fewer episodes of collective violence, and it seems as though there has been a substantial decline in this type of violence in the United States in the last few years.

Not that violence has gone away altogether; recently truck drivers demonstrated for a "roll back" in gasoline prices and a change in speed restrictions. During that protest traffic was disrupted by blockades of major highways and in some instances shootings occurred. In Pennsylvania, the National Guard was called out to control the demonstrations. Interestingly enough, the truckers' activity did not seem to be generally regarded in the same light as were collective outbreaks which had so frightened the country five years earlier. As a general calm began to prevail, many agencies which had previously indicated interest in research on collective violence indicated diminished interest, and other research problems received higher priorities for research funding. So, it may be that, for the present at least, this methodologically oriented research will have to stand on its own rather than as a preliminary to a continuing series of national studies on violence.

It is a mistake, of course, to believe that collective violence is no longer a problem in the United States. A Staff Report to the National Commission on Causes and Prevention of Violence documented at length the ebb and flow of such activity in our country (Graham and Gurr 1969). It would be naive to suppose that we have come to the end of such cycles. It is also true that good research cannot be conducted in a vacuum. Knowledge of previous work in the field and a theoretical framework are all important to the research product. It would be unfortunate if all research on collective violence were to be dismantled now, only to be hastily resurrected with the next round of collective violence widespread enough to arouse attention, but such may come to be the case.

We believe that the study of attitudes toward violence is currently the best way of estimating the potentialities for violence in this country. It provides a set of measures which allow us to increase our knowledge of this important and painful social behavior even when we are not confronted by the behaviors themselves. It is also a complicated field of research which touches on a large number of separate fields of knowledge. Government, law enforcement, psychology, economics, psychiatry, and political science all have contributions to make to an understanding of attitudes toward violence and violent behaviors. Because of the way knowledge is organized in academic disciplines, progress on any problem that requires knowledge from a large number of fields is likely to be slow. It is easiest for the researcher to focus on those aspects of a phenomenon with which he is most familiar. But, the explanations for complicated social processes are not likely to lie within the domain of one particular scholar's expertise. So, researchers must follow the phenomenon wherever it leads them. Unfortunately, researchers are likely to make mistakes when they venture into areas which are not their primary area of endeavor and in which they have no training. In this monograph, for example, we failed to use the measure of political efficacy which is most commonly used by political scientists and which would have shed the most light on the problem—an error resulting from our combined ignorance of political science. Nevertheless, when an important social phenomenon has characteristics that border on several fields, its study should not be abandoned simply on account of the complexity of the endeavor. It should be recognized, however, that progress is likely to be slow until there has been an integration of the relevant specialties. On a practical level, such integration is difficult to establish and easy to destroy. All this is true of the study of collective violence and attitudes toward such violence.

There are some major lessons to be learned from the studies described here. The first deals with the issue of complexity. In almost every one of these investigations, and in many of the individual analyses, the questions that we posed were far more complicated than we had initially imagined. The Violence for Social Change Index provides a good example of this complexity. It seemed reasonable to suppose that attitudes toward violence for social change ought to be associated with predilections for behavior. Theory specifies they should and common sense affirms it. When attitudes toward violence for social change were explored in a series of groups chosen on the basis of specific behaviors, attitudes did relate to behaviors as had been hypothesized. Those groups that had been involved in episodes of violence for social change were more apt than their comparison groups to believe that violence was necessary to bring about change. However, among respondents who were not members of such criterion groups, there was only a small relationship between the extent to which people thought violence was necessary to bring about change and the extent to which they declared themselves willing to act to bring about change. Moreover, attitudes toward the necessity of using violence to bring about change showed virtually no relationship to protest behaviors when white respondents and black respondents were considered separately. One interpretation of this finding might be that the Violence for Social Change Index, our measure of attitudes toward the use of violence to bring about social change, has only very limited construct validity; but this is not the most persuasive interpretation of the data. Further analysis demonstrated a rather powerful variable which moderates the relationship between attitudes toward violence for social change and protest behaviors, namely, the respondent's need to avoid problems. The more he wishes to avoid difficulty, or so the data seem to indicate, the less likely his attitudes are to be reflected in his behaviors.

This seems reassuring and appeals to common sense. Motivation in everyday life is often complex, and people rarely act on the basis of single-minded propositions. The theory seems saved; attitudes tend to generate behavior, but counter-forces may inhibit or divert that tendency. But the solution proposed raises a number of other problems. One might very well wonder about the generality of the paradigm proposed. Is the relationship between attitudes and behaviors often modified by moderator variables which are themselves unrelated to the attitude in question? One might guess that this would be the case. But how are such moderating factors to be identified? The answers to such questions are not obvious and it seems unlikely that there will be any general solution to the problem. However, the data presented here indicate that variables which modify the relationship between attitudes and the behaviors to which they presumably predispose should play a crucial role in research which proposes to investigate the behavioral comcomitants of attitudes. The data indicate that moderating variables must be specified and measured before precise statements about the relationship between attitudes and behaviors can be made. The necessity for invoking statements about the role of moderating variables in describing attitudinal-behavioral relationships underlines the complexity of the phenomenon we wish to understand.

The fact that one variable, the need to avoid problems, has been found to modify the relationship between attitudes toward violence for social change and the respondent's willingness to undertake a variety of protest behaviors, raises the question of whether other variables serve the same function. For example, what is the role played by the individual's evaluation of the likelihood that a specific action will lead to the desired goal? If people believe that the probabilities for success are high, will they be more willing to act than if the chances are rated as low? It seems reasonable to speculate that such would be the case, and some theories of motivation do include an expectancy term (Atkinson and Feather, 1966; Vroom 1964). One could speculate, for example, that people who believe violence is necessary to bring about change at a reasonable rate and that success is just around the corner would be more likely to behave violently or disruptively than their more pessimistic colleagues. Clearly, the influence that the anticipated success of a particular line of action has on the relationship between attitudes and behavior should be studied.

If there are two moderating variables that influence the relationship between attitudes and behavior, the relationship between them must also be considered. For instance, the wish to avoid difficulty and the estimation of the likelihood of success might be relatively independent variables with interactive effects. Suppose, for example, that there exist in the real world groups of people who believe both that the chances for success are high and that there is little need to avoid problems and difficulties. Among such groups one would expect to find substantial relationships between attitudes and behavior. Among those who have a high need to avoid problems and who are pessimistic about the success of violence, one would expect little relationship between attitudes toward violence and violent behaviors. But, there are other possible combinations of the need to avoid problems and the estimation of the success of a violent action. For example, what would be the relationship between attitudes toward violence and behavior if the group was composed of people who believe not only that the chances of success are high if a certain line of protest action is undertaken, but also that they are likely to become entrapped in personal difficulties if such actions are undertaken? We do not know, and there is no clear cut theoretical guide to assist in predicting what the outcome should be. This line of reasoning suggests that in the case of attitudes toward violence for social change, a larger number of measurements than had originally been anticipated will have to be made before accurate evaluations can be made of the extent to which people are likely to behave in accordance with their beliefs.

The problems raised by our investigation of the construct validity of the Violence for Social Change Index are concerned with more than just pragmatic matters of measurements. Theoretical issues are raised as well, issues concerning the nature of the relationships between attitudes and behavior. If moderating factors which are a function of the individual's personality or philosophy of living exist, as these data seem to indicate, attention needs to be directed to the environmental circumstances which facilitate or inhibit the expression of such moderating variables. It is possible, for example, that those who have a need to avoid problems will be more likely to act on their beliefs if they find themselves in an environment where they perceive others as like-minded and less likely to act on their beliefs if they find themselves in a situation where others will disapprove. Other environmental factors may influence the relationship between attitudes and behaviors. For example, people may be inhibited by the presence of police or stimulated by the presence of reporters. Such speculations suggest that it is important for theory to specify the conditions which will modify relationships between attitudes and behaviors. Moreover, social policy makers can be wiser and more effective to the extent that they take into account such conditions.

The difficulties raised by the necessity of specifying the factors that moderate relationships between attitudes and behaviors is only one of the complications implicit in the data outlined in this monograph. A relationship between political cynicism and attitudes toward violence for social change was described in Chapter 3. This relationship existed only among those whose political orientation was toward the left. One might very well ask what effect political orientation has on other variables which we know to be important predictors of attitudes toward violence. For example, what is the relationship between identification and the Violence for Social Change Index among those who are politically oriented to the left? Would identification and political cynicism together predict more accurately to attitudes toward violence for social change if the political orientation were known? Unfortunately, the present sample is too small to allow us to answer such questions.

One can also ask whether other combinations of moderating variables affect the relationships between attitudes and behavior. Let us consider for a moment an imaginary group of people with the following characteristics: they share a specific political orientation, that is, they have certain common political goals which they wish to reach; they are profoundly cynical about the likelihood that the government will act in their behalf; they are highly identified with those whom they perceive as sharing their goals, and they are negatively identified with members of "the system"; they share a common optimism that disruptive or violent protest will force the government to act in their behalf; and they adhere to a philosophy of living that places little emphasis on avoiding difficulty. Moreover, their inability to reach their political goal engenders considerable frustration. Such a group begins to sound like real people who might engage in disruptive action. Such a description might be applicable to truckers who wish to roll back gasoline prices, blue collar workers who wish to unionize or increase their benefits, students who wish to change an unresponsive university administration, blacks who wish to share the good things in American life, or anxious white suburban parents who wish to prevent forced busing of their children. But, this model suggests that there are at least six variables which must be specified and measured: three independent variables—the extent of the cynicism about the effectiveness of using normal channels to produce the desired result, the level of identification with those involved in the conflict, and the level of frustration aroused; and three moderating variables—the desired political goal, the level of optimism that the result can be achieved by violent and disruptive means, and any personal predilection for avoiding difficulty.

Let us suppose for the sake of argument that half the population has a predilection for avoiding problems and the other half does not. Let us also suppose that half the population believes the chances for success through protest or disruption are high and the other half does not; and in addition, let us suppose that about one-fifth of the population under investigation shares the same political goal. It is among those who do not wish to avoid problems, who do believe that violence or disruption is likely to bring about success quickly, and who share one political goal that one would expect political cynicism, frustration, identification, and values to be especially powerful predictors of attitudes toward violence and protest behaviors (including violent protest). However, if the assumption is made that the moderator variables are not correlated, simple calculations will show that given these assumptions only one-twentieth of the population would fall into the category where attitudes are most likely to be influenced by factors such as frustration and cynicism and where attitudes in turn are most likely to be related to behaviors. If the further assumption were made that it would be desirable to have about 300 cases in this group so that an adequate multivariate analysis could be conducted, it would follow that a total sample of about 6,000 people would be needed. Of course, if the common political goal which is specified as one of the important moderating variables were more frequent or if one were willing to settle for a smaller number of cases in the relevant cell, the sample size could be reduced.

It has been suggested by political theorists that collective violence is likely to be a bargaining chip of a minority group which does not have other means of influencing the government. If this is the case, it is unlikely that a specific political goal which might serve as a moderating variable influencing the formation of attitudes toward violence would be a majority characteristic. Suppose such a goal were shared by as many as half the population; even if this were the case, a survey of 2,400 respondents would be required in order to have 300 cases in the low problem avoidance/high optimism about result/common political goal cell. Thus, a sample of about this size probably represents the lower limit of what is necessary to adequately study a phenomenon as complex as attitudes toward violence.

There are alternative approaches to this problem of sample size which is generated by the model proposed. One could study people who were known to have specific political goals or people who were known not to have a predilection for avoiding problems. The determinants of positive attitudes toward violence could be studied in such groups, thus avoiding the necessity of very large samples. However, whenever studies of specialized groups are undertaken, one foregoes the possibility of understanding how the characteristics which are being investigated are distributed in the larger population.

One of the difficulties in these methodological studies is the fact that the relationships we found cannot be taken as statements which are true for any general population. The group of respondents which was selected for the methodological studies had not been selected to be representative of the country. Instead, they were selected to increase the variance in the variables under consideration. It was clear in the data that many relationships varied greatly with race, and that the proportion of black respondents in the population under study had a profound effect on the size of the relationships obtained. Since much of the analysis was correlative in nature, and since correlations were influenced so strongly by race, it would have been helpful if we had been working with data from a representative population. Under those circumstances it would have been possible to describe relationships as they exist in the population, and the information obtained would give information about the phenomena as they exist in the United States. Such data would provide a better reference point in reality than can be gained from the arbitrary populations, no matter how ideal their characteristics for other research purposes.

Data obtained from specially selected groups have only very limited utility in describing social phenomena in the country at large. If the concern is with attitudes toward violence as a national problem, those attitudes and behaviors must be studied on a national level. Insights gained from limited and arbitrary populations must be tested in populations which have a literal social meaning. A phenomenon where interactions play a major role can be described accurately only in a population where the interactions are shaped by the real life distribution of the interacting variables.

The fact that interactions due to race play a prominent role in attitudes toward·violence has another implication. Blacks are not evenly distributed in the United States. Some urban areas are almost entirely populated by blacks; some suburbs consist exclusively of whites. The distribution of attitudes and behaviors and the relationships between independent and dependent variables will be profoundly different in different locations because of the differences in the populations inhabiting those areas. This does not mean that no general statements about attitudes toward violence or predilections toward collective violence can be made, but it does mean that statements of what constitutes the truth may vary profoundly from one place to another. Such variability based on interactions implies an additional complexity in the study of attitudes toward violence. It is only by learning to take such complexities into account that we can begin to come to a true understanding of how violence comes about.

# Appendix A

# SAMPLE DESIGN AND CHARACTERISTICS

Respondents for this study were interviewed in the Detroit metropolitan area[1] and in four southern sampling units: Montgomery, Alabama; East Carroll, Louisiana; Harris, Texas; and Atlanta, Georgia. The respondents, 283 in all, were chosen by two methods. The first method was a modified probability sample. Each interviewer was provided with six addresses on randomly selected blocks and was asked to complete only two interviews out of the six addresses provided, proceeding to each address in a specified manner. The decision of whether or not an interview was conducted at a particular address was made on the basis of quota constraints which specified that half the respondents were to be male and half female. The quota also specified an age distribution which was calculated on the basis of local census data, the youngest eligible respondents being 16. In some cases the interviewer was not able to meet the quota requirements by interviewing at only two addresses on a particular block. In these instances the interviewer was allowed to take one additional interview per block provided that all other blocks had been exhausted and that there were no eligible respondents at any address on a block where less than two interviews had been completed. A maximum of three interviews were taken per block. Interviews were completed with 192 respondents according to the requirements imposed by this procedure. The modified probability sampling procedure was followed in all sampling units included in the survey. In addition, a standard probability sampling procedure was used as a second method for selecting an additional 91 respondents (one per household) in Detroit.

The sampling units within which respondents were selected according to either standard probability or modified probability methods

---

[1] The Detroit area sampled corresponded only roughly to the standard metropolitan area. All housing units south of Detroit, Dearborn, and Dearborn Heights were excluded. Exact details of the sample are available in Working Memorandum No. 104, "Sample Design: Modified Probability and Standard Probability Samples," Institute for Social Research, The University of Michigan, Ann Arbor, 1973.

were initially selected to yield approximately one-half black respondents. Neither the modified probability nor the standard probability sample can be taken to be representative of anything other than the immediate geographic area in which they were located. However, the standard probability sample was drawn from the same Detroit blocks as was the modified probability sample so that the two samples could be compared. The response rate for the standard probability sample was 69 percent. Refusals accounted for 11 percent and noninterviews (interviews that were not completed because the respondent was not at home, or was senile, mentally retarded, or never available) accounted for 20 percent of the sample. It is not possible to give response rates for the modified probability sample since the interviewer was instructed to move on to the next address if the respondent was not at home or not available at the time of the first contact.

Respondents were interviewed and reinterviewed after a lapse of approximately seven weeks. The geographic units in which interviewing was conducted and the exact number of interviews are given in Table A.1.

**Table A.1**

Frequency Distribution for 1972 Respondents
by Location and Type of Sample

|  | Modified Probability Sample (Sample I) | Standard Probability Sample (Sample II) |
|---|---|---|
| Detroit Area | 98 | 91 |
| East Carroll, Louisiana | 30 | |
| Montgomery, Alabama | 16 | |
| Harris County, Texas | 26 | |
| Atlanta, Georgia | 22 | |
| Total | 192 | 91 |

Due to an error in interviewing instructions, the age distributions for the modified probability sample and the standard probability sample were not the same. The modified probability sample included respondents from 16 to 64 years of age. The standard probability sample included respondents who were at least 16 years of age but specified no upper age limit. Therefore, in the standard probability sample persons aged 65 and over were eligible respondents while they were not in the modified probability sample. Since the total number of respondents in the study was rather small, particularly in those instances when it was necessary to conduct analyses within selected subgroups, we had a vested interest in retaining in the analysis those respondents who were over 65. In order to justify this procedure, it was necessary to examine whether the inclusion of respondents over 65 made a noticeable difference in the demographic characteristics of the sample. Consequently, the standard probability sample was compared with itself including and excluding respondents over 65 years of age (Table A.2).

Table A.2 demonstrates that there were only minimal differences with respect to race and sex when the total Detroit standard probability sample was compared with the same sample with persons over 65 excluded. There were some small differences with respect to education and income. Among those respondents who were under 65 years of age only 21 percent had nine years of schooling or less, while when all respondents were considered 25 percent had nine years of schooling or less. The 4 percent difference was hardly large enough to be significant, but was in the direction one might have anticipated. Older respondents generally were less well educated than younger respondents. However, the number of respondents in the two groups who had finished college or at least attended college was almost identical, so it seems reasonable to ignore these very small differences in education. There were also some small differences with respect to income. In the group which included the oldest respondents there were 5 percent more who made less than $4,000 a year than in the group which included only those under 65. However, there were almost as many in the larger sample who made more than $16,000 a year as there were in the age restricted sample. The difference is in the direction which might have been expected— most studies show older people are more likely to be poor than are younger people; nevertheless, the difference between the two distributions is very small. The last characteristic given in Table A.2 is age. As might have been anticipated, there is a substantial difference in age between the two groups; among all respondents, 29 percent were 60 years or older, while in the population restricted to those who were under 65, only 15 percent were above 60. Age itself seems to be the only characteristic in which the age difference in the sampling instructions made a difference. Consequently, the 15 individuals who were 65 years of age or older were included in most of the analyses which constitute the substantive materials of this research.

Since the standard probability sample was based on dwelling units, individuals living in large households were less likely to be interviewed than individuals living in smaller households; consequently, it became necessary to consider the effect of weighting the data by the number of people in the household. Table A.3 shows a comparison of the Detroit standard probability sample when the data were weighted for the number of individuals living in the household and when the data were unweighted. It can be seen that weighting made only a small difference with respect to race and sex. There was, however, a considerable difference with respect to age. In the unweighted data 29 percent of the respondents were 60 years of age or older. In the weighted data only

### Table A.2

Selected Demographic Characteristics
of All Detroit Respondents in the Standard Probability Sample
Compared with Those Under 65 Years of Age
(percentage distribution)

|  | All Detroit Respondents | Those Under 65 Years |
|---|---|---|
| **Race** | | |
| Whites | 57% | 54% |
| Blacks | 42 | 45 |
| Other | 1 | 1 |
|  | 100% | 100% |
| **Sex** | | |
| Men | 41 | 40 |
| Women | 59 | 60 |
|  | 100% | 100% |
| **Education** | | |
| 9 Years or Less | 25 | 21 |
| 10-11 Years | 32 | 34 |
| High School Graduate | 21 | 21 |
| At Least Some College | 12 | 15 |
| B.A. or Graduate Degree | 10 | 9 |
|  | 100% | 100% |
| **Income** | | |
| $3,999 or Less | 23 | 18 |
| $4,000-$7,999 | 22 | 20 |
| $8,000-$11,999 | 19 | 21 |
| $12,000-$15,999 | 15 | 18 |
| $16,000 or More | 21 | 23 |
|  | 100% | 100% |
| **Age** | | |
| 16-19 Years | 10 | 12 |
| 20-29 Years | 15 | 18 |
| 30-39 Years | 15 | 18 |
| 40-49 Years | 13 | 16 |
| 50-59 Years | 18 | 21 |
| 60 Years or Older | 29 | 15 |
|  | 100% | 100% |
| N | (91) | (76) |

18 percent of the respondents fell in this category. This is probably due to the fact that many older people live alone, and in the weighting process those who lived alone received less weight in comparison to those who lived in families with other persons.

One might think that if the weighting affected age substantially, which it did, that education might also have been affected. According to

**Table A.3**

Selected Demographic Characteristics
of the Detroit Standard Probability Sample
for Unweighted and Weighted Data
(percentage distribution)

|  | Unweighted | Weighted |
|---|---|---|
| **Race** | | |
| Whites | 57% | 54% |
| Blacks | 42 | 45 |
| Other | 1 | 1 |
|  | 100% | 100% |
| **Sex** | | |
| Men | 41 | 42 |
| Women | 59 | 58 |
|  | 100% | 100% |
| **Education** | | |
| 9 Years or Less | 25 | 23 |
| 10-11 Years | 32 | 35 |
| High School Graduate | 21 | 21 |
| Some College | 12 | 12 |
| B.A. or Graduate Degree | 10 | 9 |
|  | 100% | 100% |
| **Age** | | |
| 16-19 Years | 10 | 15 |
| 20-29 Years | 15 | 17 |
| 30-39 Years | 15 | 19 |
| 40-49 Years | 13 | 14 |
| 50-59 Years | 18 | 17 |
| 60 Years or Older | 29 | 18 |
|  | 100% | 100% |
| **Income** | | |
| $3,999 or Less | 23 | 18 |
| $4,000-$7,999 | 22 | 19 |
| $8,000-$11,999 | 19 | 23 |
| $12,000-$15,999 | 15 | 17 |
| $16,000 or More | 21 | 23 |
|  | 100% | 100% |
| N | (91) | (91) |

Table A.3, it was not. However, there was a small effect on income, although this effect was not as large as that on age. When the data were not weighted, 45 percent of respondents fell into a category of people with incomes of less than $8,000 a year. When the data were weighted, only 37 percent fell in this category. Thus, weighting did make some difference, particularly with respect to age and income. Consequently, the comparisons between the modified and the standard probability samples were made with the standard probability sample data weighted. Weights were not applied in analyses which were conducted on data combining the modified probability and standard probability samples since these data cannot be regarded as representative in any case.

Table A.4 compares the Detroit modified probability and the standard probability samples when the latter was weighted for the number of respondents in the household. It can be seen that there were essentially no differences in the percentages of white and black respondents in the two samples. There appears to be a small difference with respect to sex; slightly more men appeared in the modified than in the standard probability sample. This may be because the former was designed to require that half the sample be men. There were also somewhat fewer black men in the standard probability sample than in the modified probability sample, although black men formed the smallest race-sex category in both cases. It is not clear why there should have been fewer black men in the standard than in the modified probability sample, although it may have been due to the modified probability sample's quota requirements that more black men be located; that is, black men were overrepresented because of arbitrary decision rules. However, it is also true that black men are notoriously underrepresented in standard probability samples. Both the census and our sampling section estimate that black men are less likely to be located by sampling methods than any other type of respondent. In any case it seems clear that, if one does not require a representative sample, the modified probability sample is a slightly better mechanism for finding black men than the standard probability sample.

There was a small difference in education between the two samples; slightly more people with high school diplomas were interviewed in the modified than in the standard probability sample. This might be a function of the fact that interviewers have slightly more discretion in the modified probability sampling procedure. One might think that since interviewers had some option in selecting respondents for the modified probability sample, the interviewers might have had a bias in favor of the more educated. However, this bias was demonstrated only weakly in the data by the slightly higher percentage of high school graduates in the modified probability sample.

**Table A.4**

Selected Demographic Characteristics for Respondents in
the Detroit Modified Probability Sample
and Standard Probability (Weighted) Sample
(percentage distribution)

| | Modified Probability | Standard Probability (Weighted) |
|---|---|---|
| **Race** | | |
| Whites | 53% | 54% |
| Blacks | 46 | 45 |
| Other | 1 | 1 |
| | 100% | 100% |
| **Sex** | | |
| Men | 48 | 42 |
| Women | 52 | 58 |
| | 100% | 100% |
| **Sex and Race** | | |
| White Men | 27 | 26 |
| Black Men | 21 | 16 |
| White Women | 27 | 28 |
| Black Women | 24 | 29 |
| Other | 1 | 1 |
| | 100% | 100% |
| **Education** | | |
| 9 Years or Less | 18 | 23 |
| 10-11 Years | 33 | 35 |
| High School Graduate | 29 | 21 |
| Some College | 11 | 12 |
| B.A. or Graduate Degree | 9 | 9 |
| | 100% | 100% |
| **Income** | | |
| $3,999 or Less | 14 | 18 |
| $4,000-$7,999 | 27 | 19 |
| $8,000-$11,999 | 21 | 23 |
| $12,000-$15,999 | 20 | 17 |
| More than $16,000 | 18 | 23 |
| | 100% | 100% |
| **Age†** | | |
| 16-19 Years | 15 | 17 |
| 20-29 Years | 24 | 18 |
| 30-39 Years | 23 | 21 |
| 40-49 Years | 16 | 15 |
| 50-59 Years | 13 | 18 |
| 60-64 Years | 9 | 11 |
| | 100% | 100% |
| N | (98) | (91) |

†Standard probability sample excluded respondents 65 years or older.

There were also small differences in income between the modified and the standard probability samples; however, the income discrepancies were not consistent. While there was a slightly greater percentage of individuals with incomes below $4,000 in the standard than in the modified probability sample, there was also a slightly higher percentage of individuals earning more than $16,000 in the standard than in the modified probability sample. Thus, the modified probability sample seems to have "missed" people at both ends of the income distribution.

The last section of Table A.4 shows the differences in the distribution of ages between the respondents in the modified and standard probability samples. For purposes of this comparison, only data from respondents under 65 years of age were utilized in the analysis. The percentage distributions show that there were only very minor differences with respect to age between these two populations.

The largest difference between the standard and the modified probability samples relates to the percentage of reinterviews which were completed. In the modified probability sample only 12 percent of the respondents did not complete a second interview (Table A. 5). In the standard probability sample 21 percent of the respondents did not complete the second interview. The difference between the two figures is

**Table A.5**

Percentage Responses to Questions Measuring Whether or Not
the Respondent was Reinterviewed, Respondent Cooperation,
and Respondent Understanding on the Modified Probability
and Standard Probability (Unweighted) Samples

|  | Modified Probability | Standard Probability (Unweighted) |
|---|---|---|
| Reinterview Taken |  |  |
| Not Reinterviewed | 12% | 21% |
| Reinterviewed | 88 | 79 |
|  | 100% | 100% |
| Cooperation |  |  |
| Fair and Poor Cooperation | 12 | 14 |
| Good Cooperation | 88 | 86 |
|  | 100% | 100% |
| Understanding |  |  |
| Fair and Poor Understanding | 33 | 33 |
| Good Understanding | 67 | 67 |
|  | 100% | 100% |
| N | (192) | (91) |

too small to be of statistical significance, but the difference is large enough to raise questions as to the comparability of the two types of samples. It seems reasonable to suppose that this is a reflection of a true difference. People in the modified probability sample presumably were somewhat more accessible on the first interview than those in the standard probability sample. This is likely because in the standard probability sample interviewers often make a substantial number of callbacks to locate a respondent. For the modified probability sample interviewers were instructed not to make more than three callbacks; indeed, they were urged to make as few callbacks as possible. It appears that factors leading to the original accessibility of the respondents also carried over into willingness to cooperate with the reinterviewing procedure. However, there were no apparent differences with respect to respondent cooperation or understanding as far as the interviewers were concerned (Table A.5).

# Appendix B

# INTERVIEW SCHEDULE

The interview and reinterview forms used in the survey on attitudes toward violence conducted in the winter of 1972 are reproduced here.

**1**

Project 462140
January 1972

## Interview

SOCIAL PROBLEMS

| | |
|---|---|
| **SURVEY RESEARCH CENTER**<br>INSTITUTE FOR SOCIAL RESEARCH<br>THE UNIVERSITY OF MICHIGAN<br>ANN ARBOR, MICHIGAN 48106 | |
| | *(Do not write in above space)* |

*1.* Interviewer's Label

2. **P S U** _____

3. Your Interview No. _____

4. Date _____

5. Length of Interview _____
(Minutes)

6. Type of Cover Sheet _____
(Color)

COPY INFORMATION FROM LISTING BOX ON COVER SHEET

| (a)<br>Relationship to, or<br>connection with Head | (b)<br>Sex | (c)<br>Age | (d)<br>Race | (e)<br>√R |
|---|---|---|---|---|
| HEAD OF HOUSEHOLD | | | | |
| | | | | |
| | | | | |
| | | | | |
| | | | | |
| | | | | |
| | | | | |
| | | | | |

263

**2**

INTRODUCTION

This survey is part of a national study of social problems.  We are interested in how people feel about problems in society nowadays, particularly problems involving violence.  There has been a lot of talk lately about how life in this country is changing, and we are interested in finding out how you feel about some of the things that have been going on.

SECTION A:

A1. What things going on in this community worry or concern you?

_____

_____

_____

A2. What other things in this community worry you?

_____

_____

_____

A3. Can you think of a violent event over the last year or so that happened in this community that really upset you?  (PROBE: What was that?)

_____

_____

_____

A4. Here are some words that have been used to describe violence. (HAND R RING CARD A.) The first words are necessary and unnecessary. Do you think violence belongs at the <u>necessary end</u> or at the <u>unnecessary end</u> or <u>in between</u>? Please tell me where you think it belongs. ('X' NUMBER NEAREST R'S POSITION. REPEAT INSTRUCTION FOR SECOND ITEM AND OTHERS IF NEEDED.)

A4a. NECESSARY     1   2   3   4   5   6   7    UNNECESSARY

A4b. AVOIDABLE     1   2   3   4   5   6   7    UNAVOIDABLE

A4c. VALUABLE     1   2   3   4   5   6   7    WORTHLESS

A4d. GOOD     1   2   3   4   5   6   7    BAD

A5. Here are six questions about things that have been in the news. Tell me if you think of these as violence. I don't mean if they lead to violence, but if you think about them <u>as violence in themselves</u>.

A5a. Do you think of <u>student protest</u> as violence?

    1. YES        3. NO        2. BOTH OR DEPENDS

A5b. Do you think of <u>police beating students</u> as violence?

    1. YES        3. NO        2. BOTH OR DEPENDS

A5c. Do you think of <u>police shooting looters</u> as violence?

    1. YES        3. NO        2. BOTH OR DEPENDS

A5d. Do you think of <u>sit-ins</u> as violence?

    1. YES        3. NO        2. BOTH OR DEPENDS

A5e. Do you think of <u>draft card burning</u> as violence?

    1. YES        3. NO        2. BOTH OR DEPENDS

A5f. Do you think of <u>police stopping to frisk people</u> as violence?

    1. YES        3. NO        2. BOTH OR DEPENDS

3
1

1:6-10

11

12

13

14

15

16

17

18

19

20

**4**

A6.  Here are some things people have told us about violence. (HAND R RING
CARD B.)  We would like to know how much you agree or disagree with each
of these opinions.  Do you <u>agree a great deal</u>, <u>agree somewhat</u>, <u>disagree
somewhat</u>, or <u>disagree a great deal</u> that poverty helps cause violence?

|  |  | AGREE<br>GREAT DEAL | AGREE<br>SOMEWHAT | DISAGREE<br>SOMEWHAT | DISAGREE A<br>GREAT DEAL |  |
|---|---|---|---|---|---|---|
| A6a. | Poverty helps cause violence. | 4 | 3 | 2 | 1 | 21 |
| A6b. | A poor education is one cause of violence. | 4 | 3 | 2 | 1 | 22 |
| A6c. | Discrimination helps cause violence. | 4 | 3 | 2 | 1 | 23 |
| A6d. | There would be less violence if our present laws were always enforced. | 4 | 3 | 2 | 1 | 24 |
| A6e. | One cause of violence is that punishments for breaking the law are not tough enough. | 4 | 3 | 2 | 1 | 25 |
| A6f. | There would be less violence if more people had good jobs. | 4 | 3 | 2 | 1 | 26 |

A7.  Some people tell us that new laws giving more severe punishments for violence
are needed to reduce violence; others say such new laws are not needed.  Do
you think that such new laws are needed or not?

| 3. NEW LAWS NEEDED |     | 2. NOT SURE |     | 1. NEW LAWS NOT NEEDED |    27 |

A8.  Some people tell us that the police can't deal with violence because the
law interferes with their work; others say the law does not interfere.  What
do you think?

| LAW INTERFERES | 2. NOT SURE | 1. LAW DOES NOT INTERFERE |    28 |
|  | (GO TO B1) | (GO TO B1) | |

A8a.  Do you think the law interferes a great deal or
just somewhat?

| 4. GREAT DEAL | 3. SOMEWHAT |

### SECTION B

B1.  **There have been many** different kinds of disturbances in the United
     States, and we would like to know what people think the police
     should do in these ·situations.

     There have been times when gangs of hoodlums have gone into a town,
     terrified people, and caused a lot of property damage. How do you
     think the police should handle this situation?  (HAND R PASTE CARD
     #1 AND INSTRUCT R TO FILL OUT THE CARD BY CHECKING ONE ANSWER FOR
     EACH STATEMENT.)

B1a.  The police should let it go,    [4] Almost always
      not do anything.                [3] Sometimes
                                       [2] Hardly ever          □
                                       [1] Never               1:29

B1b.  Police should make arrests      [4] Almost always
      without using clubs or guns.    [3] Sometimes
                                       [2] Hardly ever          □
                                       [1] Never                30

B1c.  Police should use clubs,        [4] Almost always
      but not guns.                   [3] Sometimes
                                       [2] Hardly ever          □
                                       [1] Never                31

B1d.  The police should shoot,        [4] Almost always
      but not to kill.                [3] Sometimes
                                       [2] Hardly ever          □
                                       [1] Never                32

B1e.  The police should shoot         [4] Almost always
      to kill.                        [3] Sometimes
                                       [2] Hardly ever          □
                                       [1] Never                33

*Note: In an earlier version of this interview schedule, these items appeared in a horizontal format.*

INTERVIEWER CHECK

    [1] R FILLED OUT CARD
    [2] INTERVIEWER FILLED OUT CARD FOR R          □
                                                   34

**6**

B2. Now we have some questions about policemen.  People have different opinions about policemen.  We would like to know how much you agree or disagree with each of these statements.  (HAND R RING CARD B.)

|  | | AGREE A GREAT DEAL | AGREE SOMEWHAT | DISAGREE SOMEWHAT | DISAGREE A GREAT DEAL | |
|---|---|---|---|---|---|---|
| B2a. | Most policemen are trying to be helpful. | 4 | 3 | 2 | 1 | 1:35 |
| B2b. | The police are getting more than their share of the tax dollar. | 4 | 3 | 2 | 1 | 36 |
| B2c. | Most policemen are trustworthy. | 4 | 3 | 2 | 1 | 37 |
| B2d. | Policemen should feel satisfied with their position nowadays. | 4 | 3 | 2 | 1 | 38 |
| B2e. | In general, there would be fewer problems if the police had more power. | 4 | 3 | 2 | 1 | 39 |
| B2f. | Most policemen are interested in making the world a better place for all of us. | 4 | 3 | 2 | 1 | 40 |
| B2g. | Most policemen are people who use bad language and are disrespectful. | 4 | 3 | 2 | 1 | 41 |
| B2h. | The police are getting so much power that the average citizen has to worry. | 4 | 3 | 2 | 1 | 42 |
| B2i. | More money should be spent to help the police get the things they need. | 4 | 3 | 2 | 1 | 43 |

B3. If the police get the things they want, do you think your life will change?

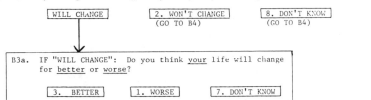

| WILL CHANGE | 2. WON'T CHANGE (GO TO B4) | 8. DON'T KNOW (GO TO B4) |

B3a. IF "WILL CHANGE": Do you think <u>your</u> life will change for <u>better</u> or <u>worse</u>?

| 3. BETTER | 1. WORSE | 7. DON'T KNOW |

144

**8**

B4.  Did you happen to hear about the prison riot at Attica?

| 1. YES | | 2. NO<br>(TURN TO<br>SECTION C) | 3. DON'T KNOW<br>(TURN TO<br>SECTION C) |
|---|---|---|---|

`[ 1:45 ]`

B4a.  Were you very interested in what happened at Attica at the time, or were you not too interested?

| 1. VERY INTERESTED | 2. NOT TOO INTERESTED<br>(TURN TO SECTION C) |
|---|---|

`[ 46 ]`

B4b.  You may remember, the authorities called in troops to put down the riot.  On the whole, do you think the authorities handled the riot well or not?

| 1. WELL | 2. DON'T KNOW | 3. NOT WELL |
|---|---|---|

`[ 47 ]`

B4c.  Do you think that troops should have been called in sooner than they were, later -- were they called in just about the right time, or should they not have been called at all?

| 1. SOONER | 2. JUST RIGHT | 3. LATER | 4. SHOULDN'T<br>HAVE BEEN<br>CALLED |
|---|---|---|---|

`[ 48 ]`

B4d.  Some think Governor Rockefeller should have talked to the prisoners to try to end the riot; others think not.  What do you think?

| 1. SHOULD NOT<br>HAVE TALKED | 2. DON'T KNOW | 3. SHOULD HAVE<br>TALKED |
|---|---|---|

`[ 49 ]`

B4e.  If the prisoners at Attica got what they demanded, like better food, medical care, and vocational training, do you think the prison system would improve or get worse?

| 3. IMPROVE | 2. WON'T CHANGE | 1. GET WORSE |
|---|---|---|

`[ 50 ]`

B4f.  Do you think the deaths of the hostages and prisoners could have been prevented or not?

| 1. NOT PREVENTABLE | 2. DON'T KNOW | 3. PREVENTABLE |
|---|---|---|

`[ 51 ]`

SECTION C:

Next, we have a different kind of question.  I will read you a short story without an ending.  Then I will ask how you think the story will end. Just tell me what you think will probably happen next.

C1.  STORY 1:  Joe is hurrying to get to the bank before it closes.  A little man with a gun suddenly blocks his way, threatens him, and demands his money.  There is no policeman in sight and Joe is scared at first.  Then he sees the gun is a toy.
What does Joe do then?

_____

_____

_____

C2:  STORY 2:  Pete is wearing his new suit to go to a party with his wife after supper.  He wants everyone to hurry up and eat, as it's almost time to go. Suddenly his young son knocks over his milk and it spills all over Pete's new suit.
What does Pete do then?

_____

_____

_____

C3.  STORY 3:  It's hot and Jim has been waiting and waiting in a long line.  Suddenly a man rudely pushes ahead of him in line.
What does Jim do then?

_____

_____

_____

C4.   STORY 4:  Bob needs to get some back pay his company owes him because he has promised to pay off a large debt by 6:00 o'clock that night.  Every person he goes to see refers him to someone else.  It is almost closing time when he finds the right clerk and he is nervous and says he needs the money right away.  The clerk says, "I don't like your attitude and I don't think I'll give you this check until tomorrow."
What does Bob do then?

_____

_____

_____

C5.   STORY 5:  Bill is sitting in his brand new car.  He is just about to start it when his neighbor, Mary, backs her old car up and bangs into Bill's car, denting it.  Mary's husband runs over and yells at Bill, "I saw you ram into my car!  I'll sue you, you jerk!"
What does Bill do then?

_____

_____

_____

C6.   STORY 6:  Nancy tells her two-year-old child that it's past his bed time and he must go to bed.  The child throws himself on the floor, kicking and screaming, "NO I WON'T!"
What does Nancy do then?

_____

_____

_____

SECTION D:

D1.  Here is a situation that sometimes occurs with young children.  Think how you
would handle this situation if you had a child about <u>five or six years old</u>:

> You have something <u>very</u> important that you want your child to do
> for you <u>right away</u>.  He is watching television.  You tell him what
> you want done and ask him to do it <u>right away</u>.  He says he'll do it
> when the program is over, in about an hour.

What would you do if something like that happened?

_____

_____

_____


D2.  This is a list of things that some parents we've talked with say they do
when such things happen.  (HAND R RING CARD C.)  When he says he will do
something later and you want it done <u>right away</u>, how often would you do
each of the following?

|  |  | USUALLY | SOMETIMES | RARELY | NEVER |  |
|---|---|---|---|---|---|---|
| D2a. | Hit or spank him | 4 | 3 | 2 | 1 | 1:52 |
| D2b. | Tell him he ought to be ashamed of himself | 4 | 3 | 2 | 1 | 53 |
| D2c. | Tell him that you're hurt or disappointed | 4 | 3 | 2 | 1 | 54 |
| D2d. | Tell him that if he doesn't do it right away he won't be able to have something or do something he wants | 4 | 3 | 2 | 1 | 55 |

**12**

|  | | USUALLY | SOMETIMES | RARELY | NEVER |  |
|---|---|:---:|:---:|:---:|:---:|---|
| D2e. | Spank him until he can't sit down | 4 | 3 | 2 | 1 | ☐ 56 |
| D2f. | Not say a word, just go and do it yourself | 4 | 3 | 2 | 1 | ☐ 57 |
| D2g. | Go over and turn off the television set | 4 | 3 | 2 | 1 | ☐ 58 |
| D2h. | Tell him that he'll have to miss the program, and explain the reason why it must be done right away | 4 | 3 | 2 | 1 | ☐ 59 |
| D2i. | Tell him you will hit or spank him if he doesn't do it right away | 4 | 3 | 2 | 1 | ☐ 60 |
| D2j. | Hit him with a belt or paddle | 4 | 3 | 2 | 1 | ☐ 61 |

D3.  Now please tell me the one thing that you would probably do most often.

Question Letter _____

☐ 62-63

D4.  Please tell me the one thing that you would probably do second most often.

Question Letter _____

☐ 64-65

D5.  Now tell me the one thing that you think is the worst way of handling this situation.

Question Letter _____

☐ 66-67

SECTION E:

2

E1. Over the last few years there has been a lot of protest by blacks (Negroes/colored people). Do you think these protests are happening <u>more</u> or <u>less</u> often than they used to?

_____

_____

_____

2:6-10

E2. What do you think causes these protests?

_____

_____

_____

E3. Here are some things people have told us about black (Negro/colored) protesters. We would like to know whether you <u>agree a great deal</u>, <u>agree somewhat</u>, <u>disagree somewhat</u>, or <u>disagree a great deal</u>. (HAND R RING CARD B.)

|  |  | AGREE A GREAT DEAL | AGREE SOMEWHAT | DISAGREE SOMEWHAT | DISAGREE A GREAT DEAL |  |
|---|---|---|---|---|---|---|
| E3a. | Most black protesters are trying to be helpful. | 4 | 3 | 2 | 1 | |
| E3b. | Black protesters are getting more than their share of the tax dollar. | 4 | 3 | ? | 1 | |
| E3c. | Most black protesters are trustworthy. | 4 | 3 | 2 | 1 | |

11

12

13

**14**

|  | AGREE A GREAT DEAL | AGREE SOMEWHAT | DISAGREE SOMEWHAT | DISAGREE A GREAT DEAL |
|---|---|---|---|---|
| E3d. Black protesters should feel satisfied with their position nowadays. | 4 | 3 | 2 | 1 |
| E3e. In general, there would be fewer problems if black protesters had more power. | 4 | 3 | 2 | 1 |
| E3f. Most black protesters are interested in making the world a better place for all of us. | 4 | 3 | 2 | 1 |
| E3g. Most black protesters are people who use bad language and are disrespectful. | 4 | 3 | 2 | 1 |
| E3h. Black protesters are getting so much power that the average citizen has to worry. | 4 | 3 | 2 | 1 |
| E3i. More money should be spent to help black protesters get the things they need. | 4 | 3 | 2 | 1 |

2:14

15

16

17

18

19

E4. If black (Negro/colored) protesters get what they want, do you think your life will change?

| WILL CHANGE | 2. WON'T CHANGE (GO TO E5) | 8. DON'T KNOW (GO TO E5) |
|---|---|---|

20

E4a. IF "WILL CHANGE": Do you think your life will change for _better_ or _worse_?

| 3. BETTER | 1. WORSE | 7. DON'T KNOW |
|---|---|---|

P A S T E   C A R D   #2   H E R E

**15c-d**

E5. Many blacks (Negroes/colored people) feel changes are needed in our society. Some people think violence is needed to bring about the changes which would make life better for blacks (Negroes/colored people). We would like to know how much you agree or disagree with each of these opinions about how much violence is necessary for blacks (Negroes/colored people) to bring about changes. (HAND R PASTE CARD #2 AND INSTRUCT R TO CHECK ONE ANSWER FOR EACH STATEMENT.)

E5a. Changes can be made fast enough without action involving property damage or injury.

- 4 Agree a Great Deal
- 3 Agree Somewhat
- 2 Disagree Somewhat
- 1 Disagree a Great Deal

2:21

E5b. Protest in which some people are hurt is necessary for changes to come fast enough.

- 4 Agree a Great Deal
- 3 Agree Somewhat
- 2 Disagree Somewhat
- 1 Disagree a Great Deal

22

E5c. Protest in which there is some property damage is necessary for changes to be brought about fast enough.

- 4 Agree a Great Deal
- 3 Agree Somewhat
- 2 Disagree Somewhat
- 1 Disagree a Great Deal

23

E5d. Protest in which there is much property damage is necessary before changes can be brought about fast enough.

- 4 Agree a Great Deal
- 3 Agree Somewhat
- 2 Disagree Somewhat
- 1 Disagree a Great Deal

24

E5e. Protest in which some people are killed is necessary before changes will take place fast enough.

- 4 Agree a Great Deal
- 3 Agree Somewhat
- 2 Disagree Somewhat
- 1 Disagree a Great Deal

25

*Note: In an earlier version of this interview schedule, these items appeared in a horizontal format.*

INTERVIEWER CHECK

- 1 R FILLED OUT CARD
- 2 INTERVIEWER FILLED OUT CARD FOR R

26

16c          P A S T E   C A R D   #3   H E R E

E6. When you think about inner-city disturbances (big city riots) involving blacks (Negroes/colored people) and police, how do you think the police should handle the situation? (HAND R PASTE CARD #3 AND INSTRUCT R TO CHECK ONE ANSWER FOR EACH STATEMENT.)

E6a. The police should let it go, not do anything.

[4] Almost always
[3] Sometimes
[2] Hardly ever
[1] Never

☐ 2:27

E6b. Police should make arrests without using clubs or guns.

[4] Almost always
[3] Sometimes
[2] Hardly ever
[1] Never

☐ 28

E6c. Police should use clubs, but not guns.

[4] Almost always
[3] Sometimes
[2] Hardly ever
[1] Never

☐ 29

E6d. The police should shoot, but not to kill.

[4] Almost always
[3] Sometimes
[2] Hardly ever
[1] Never

☐ 30

E6e. The police should shoot to kill.

[4] Almost always
[3] Sometimes
[2] Hardly ever
[1] Never

☐ 31

*Note: In an earlier version of this interview schedule, these items appeared in a horizontal format.*

INTERVIEWER CHECK

[1] R FILLED OUT CARD
[2] INTERVIEWER FILLED OUT CARD FOR R

☐ 32

SECTION F:

F1. Some high schools and even junior high schools have been having trouble with violence. Some schools have had disturbances and have had to be shut down. Have you heard about this kind of trouble in any school that you know about?

| YES | 3. NOT SURE | 4. NO |
|-----|-------------|-------|
|     | (TURN TO PAGE 19, Q G1) | (TURN TO PAGE 19, Q G1) |

2:35

F2. Were you interested in the disturbance at the school, or didn't you pay too much attention to it?

| 1. WAS INTERESTED | 2. DIDN'T PAY ATTENTION |
|-------------------|-------------------------|
|                   | (TURN TO PAGE 19, Q G1) |

F3. What was the disturbance you heard about? _____

_____

_____

F4. What do you think causes disturbances like the one you were talking about?

_____

_____

_____

**18**

F5.   Some people tell us that the reason schools have disturbances is because
      school authorities refuse to listen to the students and the community.
      Others say that has nothing to do with it.  Do you think disturbances
      are caused by the school authorities not listening, or do you think that
      has nothing to do with it?

| 1. AUTHORITIES REFUSE TO LISTEN | 2. NOT SURE | 3. NOTHING TO DO WITH IT |

2:34

F6.   Some schools have set up councils where school officials, community
      members, parents, students, and teachers can all talk about school
      problems together.  Some say such councils might reduce violence.  Others
      say not.  Do you think such councils will reduce violence or not?

| 1. WILL REDUCE VIOLENCE | 2. NOT SURE | 3. WILL NOT REDUCE VIOLENCE |

35

F7.   Some people tell us that the way to handle school problems is to have a
      much stricter discipline code.  Others say the discipline codes are
      unfair and cause more trouble than they cure.  Do you think stricter
      discipline codes will reduce violence, or do you think they will cause
      more trouble?

| 3. STRICTER CODES REDUCE VIOLENCE | 2. NOT SURE | 1. STRICTER CODES CAUSE TROUBLE |

36

F8.   Some people have told us that having policemen in the schools will help
      reduce violence.  Others say having policemen in the schools helps cause
      the trouble.  What do you say?

| 3. POLICEMEN WILL REDUCE VIOLENCE | 2. NOT SURE | 1. POLICEMEN WILL CAUSE TROUBLE |

37

SECTION G

ASK EVERYONE

G1.    (HAND R RING CARD D .)  We would like you to list these in the order you
       feel is most important for the kind of world you want to live in.  Please
       tell me which you think is <u>most</u> important.  Now which do you think is the
       next most important?  (INTERVIEWER:  CONTINUE ASKING UNTIL R HAS ORDERED
       ALL ITEMS.  MARK THE NUMBER 1 IN FRONT OF THE ITEM WHICH IS <u>MOST</u> IMPORTANT,
       <u>2</u> IN FRONT OF THE ITEM WHICH IS NEXT MOST IMPORTANT, AND SO ON UNTIL ALL
       ITEMS HAVE BEEN ASSIGNED A NUMBER FROM ONE TO SIX.)

       A.    (  )    EQUALITY

       B.    (  )    HUMAN DIGNITY

       C.    (  )    RESPECT FOR PROPERTY

       D.    (  )    RESPECT FOR LAW

       E.    (  )    FREEDOM

       F.    (  )    FINANCIAL SECURITY FOR SELF AND LOVED ONES

G2.    Here are some things people have told us.  We would like to know whether
       you <u>agree a great deal</u>, <u>agree somewhat</u>, <u>disagree somewhat</u>, or <u>disagree a</u>
       <u>great deal</u>.  (HAND R RING CARD B .  READ STATEMENTS TO R.)

| | | AGREE A GREAT DEAL | AGREE SOMEWHAT | DISAGREE SOMEWHAT | DISAGREE A GREAT DEAL | |
|---|---|---|---|---|---|---|
| | When a person harms you, you should turn the other cheek and forgive him. | 4 | 3 | 2 | 1 | 2:38 |
| G3. | People who commit murder deserve capital punishment. | 4 | 3 | 2 | 1 | 39 |
| G4. | Violence deserves violence. | 4 | 3 | 2 | 1 | 40 |
| G5. | "An eye for an eye and a tooth for a tooth" is a good rule for living. | 4 | 3 | 2 | 1 | 41 |

**20**

| | | AGREE A GREAT DEAL | AGREE SOMEWHAT | DISAGREE SOMEWHAT | DISAGREE A GREAT DEAL | |
|---|---|---|---|---|---|---|
| G6. | It is best to stay neutral on things others have strong feelings about. | [4] | [3] | [2] | [1] | ▫ 2:42 |
| G7. | It is often necessary to use violence to prevent violence. | [4] | [3] | [2] | [1] | ▫ 43 |
| G8. | When someone does wrong, he should be punished for it. | [4] | [3] | [2] | [1] | ▫ 44 |
| G9. | People should stand up for themselves even if it leads to trouble. | [4] | [3] | [2] | [1] | ▫ 45 |
| G10. | Even if you don't like a person, you should still try to help him. | [4] | [3] | [2] | [1] | ▫ 46 |
| G11. | A man has a right to kill another man in a case of self-defense. | [4] | [3] | [2] | [1] | ▫ 47 |
| G12. | A man has the right to kill a person to defend his family. | [4] | [3] | [2] | [1] | ▫ 48 |
| G13. | A man has the right to kill a person to defend his house. | [4] | [3] | [2] | [1] | ▫ 49 |
| G14. | Nothing will ever get done if people just wait for the government to act. | [4] | [3] | [2] | [1] | ▫ 50 |

**21**

| | AGREE A GREAT DEAL | AGREE SOMEWHAT | DISAGREE SOMEWHAT | DISAGREE A GREAT DEAL | |
|---|---|---|---|---|---|

G15. People who make
speeches stirring
people up should
be put in prison
before they cause
serious trouble.    4    3    2    1    ☐ 2:51

G16. It is better to
avoid a fight
than to take a
chance on getting
hurt.    4    3    2    1    ☐ 52

G17. There is no point in
individual citizens
trying to do anything
about social problems,
such as poverty.    4    3    2    1    ☐ 53

G18. Sometimes a person
has to take the
law into his own
hands to see that
justice gets done.    4    3    2    1    ☐ 54

G19. When police don't
stop crime in a
neighborhood,
people should set
up their own
patrols.    4    3    2    1    ☐ 55

**22**

SECTION H:

H1. Do you think people in the government waste <u>a lot</u> of the money we pay in taxes, waste <u>some</u> of it, or <u>don't waste very much of it</u>?

| 3. A LOT | | 2. SOME | | 1. NOT VERY MUCH |

2:56

H2. How much of the time do you think you can trust the government in Washington to do what is right--<u>just about always</u>, <u>most of the time</u>, or only <u>some of the time</u>?

| 1. JUST ABOUT ALWAYS | | 2. MOST OF THE TIME | | 3. SOME OF THE TIME |

57

H3. Would you say the government is pretty much run by a <u>few big interests</u> looking out for themselves, or that it is run for the <u>benefit of all</u> the people?

| 2. FEW BIG INTERESTS | | 1. BENEFIT OF ALL |

58

H4. Do you feel that almost all of the people running the government are smart people who usually <u>know what they are doing</u>, or do you think that quite a few of them <u>don't seem to know what they're doing</u>?

| 1. KNOW WHAT THEY'RE DOING | | 2. DON'T KNOW WHAT THEY'RE DOING |

59

H5. Do you think that <u>quite a few</u> of the people running the government are a little crooked, <u>not very many</u> are, or do you think <u>hardly any</u> of them are crooked at all?

| 3. QUITE A FEW | | 2. NOT VERY MANY | | 1. HARDLY ANY |

60

PASTE CARD #4 HERE _____ **23**c-d

H6.   Some people feel that important changes can be brought about only
      through violence; others say violence is not necessary.  What do you
      think?  (HAND R PASTE CARD #4 AND INSTRUCT R TO CHECK ONE ANSWER FOR
      EACH STATEMENT.)

H6a.   Changes can be made fast enough            4 Agree a Great Deal
       without action involving property          3 Agree Somewhat
       damage or injury.                          2 Disagree Somewhat
                                                  1 Disagree a Great Deal
                                                                              2:61

H6b.   Protest in which some people are           4 Agree a Great Deal
       hurt is necessary for changes to           3 Agree Somewhat
       come fast enough.                          2 Disagree Somewhat
                                                  1 Disagree a Great Deal
                                                                              62

H6c.   Protest in which there is some             4 Agree a Great Deal
       property damage is necessary               3 Agree Somewhat
       for changes to be brought about            2 Disagree Somewhat
       fast enough.                               1 Disagree a Great Deal
                                                                              63

H6d.   Protest in which there is much             4 Agree a Great Deal
       property damage is necessary               3 Agree Somewhat
       before changes can be brought              2 Disagree Somewhat
       about fast enough.                         1 Disagree a Great Deal
                                                                              64

H6e.   Protest in which some people               4 Agree a Great Deal
       are killed is necessary before             3 Agree Somewhat
       changes will take place fast               2 Disagree Somewhat
       enough.                                    1 Disagree a Great Deal
                                                                              65

*Note:  In an earlier version of this interview schedule, these items appeared in a horizontal format.*

INTERVIEWER CHECK

1 R FILLED OUT CARD
2 INTERVIEWER FILLED OUT CARD FOR R

66

**24**

H7.  Here are some political actions people have taken to bring about change.
(HAND R RING CARD E.)  We would like to know how violent you think each of
these is, in and of itself.  Do you think being in a sit-in is at the violent
end or at the not-violent end or in between?  Using the line at the top of
the card, please point  to where you think it belongs.  You may use any number
on the line.  (REPEAT INSTRUCTIONS FOR SECOND ITEM AND OTHERS IF NEEDED.)

```
┌─┐
│3│
├─┤
│ │
├─┤
│ │
├─┤
│ │
└─┘
3:6-10
```

H7a.  Being in a sit-in       NOT VIOLENT_____VIOLENT
                                         1    2    3    4    5    6    7
□ 11

H7b.  Signing a petition      NOT VIOLENT_____VIOLENT
                                         1    2    3    4    5    6    7
□ 12

H7c.  Holding a protest       NOT VIOLENT_____VIOLENT
      meeting                            1    2    3    4    5    6    7
□ 13

H7d.  Holding a march         NOT VIOLENT_____VIOLENT
      without a permit                   1    2    3    4    5    6    7
      from city officials
□ 14

H7e.  Filing a Federal        NOT VIOLENT_____VIOLENT
      lawsuit in court                   1    2    3    4    5    6    7
□ 15

H7f.  Interfering with work   NOT VIOLENT_____VIOLENT
      in an office building              1    2    3    4    5    6    7
□ 16

H7g.  Holding a march         NOT VIOLENT_____VIOLENT
      with a permit from                 1    2    3    4    5    6    7
      city officials
□ 17

H7h.  Blocking traffic as     NOT VIOLENT_____VIOLENT
      a protest                          1    2    3    4    5    6    7
□ 18

H7i.  Holding a protest       NOT VIOLENT_____VIOLENT
      meeting without                    1    2    3    4    5    6    7
      a permit
□ 19

H8. Which of the following things would you be willing to do to bring about <u>a</u> <u>change you felt was very important</u>? Would you sign a petition?

|  |  | YES | NOT SURE | NO |  |
|---|---|---|---|---|---|
| H8a. | Sign a petition | 3 | 2 | 1 | ☐ 3:20 |
| H8b. | Hold a protest meeting with a permit | 3 | 2 | 1 | ☐ 21 |
| H8c. | Be in a sit-in | 3 | 2 | 1 | ☐ 22 |
| H8d. | Block traffic | 3 | 2 | 1 | ☐ 23 |
| H8e. | Interfere with work in an office building | 3 | 2 | 1 | ☐ 24 |

## SECTION I:

I1. Now we would like to know a few things about you. Here are some things that come up in a person's life. Some people want to talk about these with relatives or friends; others prefer not to talk about such things. If these things came up in your life, how likely would you be to talk about them with someone other than your (wife/husband)? (HAND R RING CARD F .) How about:

|  |  | LIKELY | SOMEWHAT LIKELY | SOMEWHAT UNLIKELY | UNLIKELY |  |
|---|---|---|---|---|---|---|
| I1a. | Difficulties at work with your supervisor | 4 | 3 | 2 | 1 | ☐ 25 |
| I1b. | Whether to change jobs | 4 | 3 | 2 | 1 | ☐ 26 |
| I1c. | A serious personal medical problem | 4 | 3 | 2 | 1 | ☐ 27 |
| I1d. | How to handle a problem involving your child | 4 | 3 | 2 | 1 | ☐ 28 |
| I1e. | Troubles between you and your (wife/husband) | 4 | 3 | 2 | 1 | ☐ 29 |

**26** PASTE CARD #5 HERE

I2. Here is a list of statements about the way some people may feel. Please read each statement and check the way you feel. (HAND R PASTE CARD #5 . INSTRUCT R TO FILL OUT CARD.)

|  | TRUE | FALSE |  |  |
|---|---|---|---|---|
| I2a. | 2 | 1 | I don't seem to get what's coming to me. | 5.30 |
| I2b. | 2 | 1 | At times I feel I get a raw deal out of life. | 31 |
| I2c. | 2 | 1 | I tend to be on my guard with people who are somewhat more friendly than I expected. | 32 |
| I2d. | 2 | 1 | I commonly wonder what hidden reason another person may have for doing something nice for me. | 33 |
| I2e. | 2 | 1 | I used to think most people told the truth, but now I know otherwise. | 34 |

INTERVIEWER CHECK

1 R FILLED OUT CARD
2 INTERVIEWER FILLED OUT CARD FOR R

35

SECTION J:

J1.  STORY 7: Paul is visiting the parents of his steady girl friend for the first time. He wants to make a good impression. After a while the father says to him, "What makes you think you're good enough for my daughter?"
What does Paul do then?

_____

_____

_____

J2.  STORY 8: John has worked a double shift and is very tired. His neighbor is playing the radio so loud he can't sleep. He knocks on the neighbor's door and asks him to be more quiet. The neighbor gives John a shove and yells, "I'll be as loud as I want!"
What does John do then?

_____

_____

_____

J3.  STORY 9: Ron has worked at his job for about five years and likes it fine. One day he gets a new supervisor who says to him, "I expect everybody to work hard around here and you'll have to prove to me that you should stay on."
What does Ron do then?

_____

_____

_____

**28**

J4.   STORY 10: Tom's younger sister is going with a guy with no job who runs around and borrows money from her. One day Tom tells the kid he should get a job. The kid laughs at him and says, "Why should I work? Your sister's working for me."
What does Tom do then?

_____

_____

_____


J5.   STORY 11:  Lee is walking past a bar when suddenly a drunken man bumps into him.  The man grabs Lee's collar, insults him, and says, "Are you man enough to fight?"
What does Lee do then?

_____

_____

_____

SECTION K

K1.  In this last section, I'd like to ask some questions about you.
     In what country were you born?

     _____

K2.  Where was your father born?

     | 1. U.S.A. |     | 2. OTHER |

K3.  Where was your mother born?

     | 1. U.S.A. |     | 2. OTHER |

K4.  In what state did you live longest during the first ten years of your life?

     STATE (OR COUNTRY IF NOT U.S.A.): _____

K5.  Was that in a large city (over 100,000 people), a suburb, a small city, a
     small town, or on a farm?

     | 5. LARGE CITY |   | 4. SUBURB |   | 3. SMALL CITY |   | 2. SMALL TOWN |   | 1. FARM |

INTERVIEWER CHECK:

     ☐ R MENTIONED SOUTHERN STATE IN K4   (GO TO K7)
     ☐ R DID NOT MENTION SOUTHERN STATE IN K4

              (SOUTHERN STATES:  ALA., ARK., FLA., GA., KY., LA., MD., MISS.,
                                 N.C., OKLA., S.C., TENN., VA., WASH. D.C.)

K6.  Have you ever lived for six months or more in the South?

              | 1. YES |          | 3. NO |

**30**

K7. What month and year were you born?

_____     _____
(MONTH)                    (YEAR)

K8. Is your religious preference Protestant, Roman Catholic, Jewish, or something else?

| PROTESTANT | | 200. ROMAN CATHOLIC | | 300. JEWISH | | OTHER |

What denomination?

_____

(SPECIFY)

_____

ASK IF R IS OTHER THAN QUAKER

K9. Have you ever been a Quaker or attended Quaker meetings or activities?

| 1. YES, QUAKER | | 2. YES, ONLY ATTENDED MEETINGS AND ACTIVITIES | | 3. NO |

3:39

ASK IF R IS OTHER THAN JEHOVAH'S WITNESS

K10. Have you ever been a Jehovah's Witness?

| 1. YES | | 2. NO |

40

K11. Are you married, single, divorced, widowed, or separated?

| 1. MARRIED | | 2. SINGLE (GO TO K12) | | 3. DIVORCED (GO TO K12) | | 4. WIDOWED | | 5. SEPARATED |

41

K11a. (Is/Was) this your first marriage?

| 1. YES (GO TO K12) | | NO |

42

K11b. Did your previous marriage end through divorce or death?

| 2. DIVORCE | | 3. DEATH |

K12. We would like to know if you are working now, looking for work, retired, (a housewife,) a student, or what?

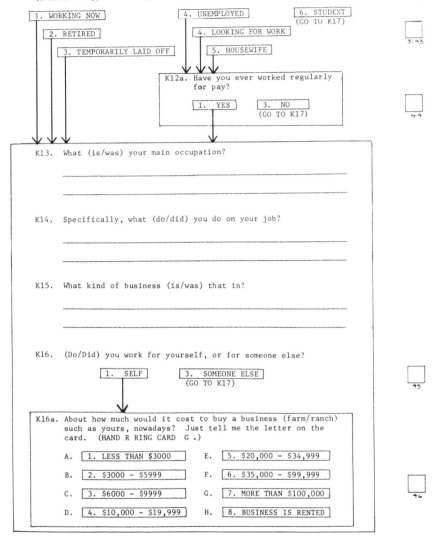

K12a. Have you ever worked regularly for pay?

    1. YES     3. NO (GO TO K17)

K13. What (is/was) your main occupation?

_____

_____

K14. Specifically, what (do/did) you do on your job?

_____

_____

K15. What kind of business (is/was) that in?

_____

_____

K16. (Do/Did) you work for yourself, or for someone else?

    1. SELF     3. SOMEONE ELSE (GO TO K17)

K16a. About how much would it cost to buy a business (farm/ranch) such as yours, nowadays? Just tell me the letter on the card. (HAND R RING CARD G.)

A. 1. LESS THAN $3000     E. 5. $20,000 - $34,999

B. 2. $3000 - $5999     F. 6. $35,000 - $99,999

C. 3. $6000 - $9999     G. 7. MORE THAN $100,000

D. 4. $10,000 - $19,999     H. 8. BUSINESS IS RENTED

**32**

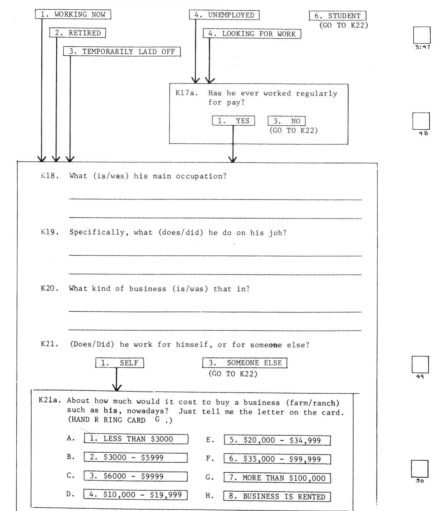

ASK MARRIED WOMEN RESPONDENTS ONLY -- OTHERS GO TO K22

K17.   Now we would like to know if your husband is working now, looking for
       work, retired, a student, or what?

| 1. WORKING NOW | | 4. UNEMPLOYED | 6. STUDENT |
|---|---|---|---|

2. RETIRED

4. LOOKING FOR WORK

(GO TO K22)

3. TEMPORARILY LAID OFF

K17a.   Has he ever worked regularly
        for pay?

        1. YES    3. NO
                  (GO TO K22)

K18.    What (is/was) his main occupation?

_____

_____

K19.    Specifically, what (does/did) he do on his job?

_____

_____

K20.    What kind of business (is/was) that in?

_____

_____

K21.    (Does/Did) he work for himself, or for someone else?

        1. SELF       3. SOMEONE ELSE
                      (GO TO K22)

K21a.   About how much would it cost to buy a business (farm/ranch)
        such as his, nowadays?  Just tell me the letter on the card.
        (HAND R RING CARD G .)

        A.  1. LESS THAN $3000       E.  5. $20,000 - $34,999

        B.  2. $3000 - $5999         F.  6. $35,000 - $99,999

        C.  3. $6000 - $9999         G.  7. MORE THAN $100,000

        D.  4. $10,000 - $19,999     H.  8. BUSINESS IS RENTED

3:47

48

49

50

K22.  What is the highest grade of school or year of college you have finished?

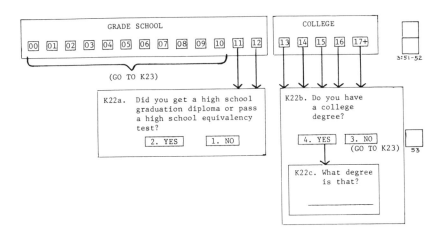

```
┌──────────────── GRADE SCHOOL ────────────────┐    ┌──────── COLLEGE ────────┐
│ 00  01  02  03  04  05  06  07  08  09  10  11  12 │ 13  14  15  16  17+ │
└──────────────────────────────────────────────┘    └─────────────────────┘
                                                                            3:51-52
```

(GO TO K23)

K22a.  Did you get a high school graduation diploma or pass a high school equivalency test?

2. YES     1. NO

K22b. Do you have a college degree?

4. YES     3. NO (GO TO K23)     53

K22c. What degree is that?

_____

K23.  Are you going to school now?

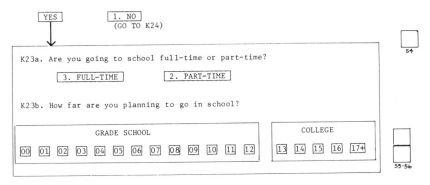

YES        1. NO (GO TO K24)

54

K23a. Are you going to school full-time or part-time?

3. FULL-TIME     2. PART-TIME

K23b. How far are you planning to go in school?

```
┌──────────────── GRADE SCHOOL ────────────────┐    ┌──────── COLLEGE ────────┐
│ 00  01  02  03  04  05  06  07  08  09  10  11  12 │ 13  14  15  16  17+ │
└──────────────────────────────────────────────┘    └─────────────────────┘
                                                                            55-56
```

**34**

ASK MARRIED WOMEN RESPONDENTS ONLY -- OTHERS GO TO K25

K24.  How about your husband's education?  What is the highest grade of school
or year of college he has finished?

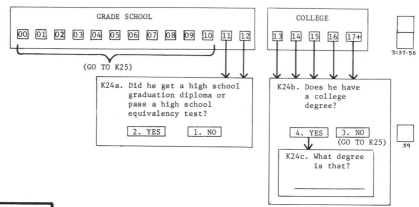

3:57-58

(GO TO K25)

K24a. Did he get a high school
graduation diploma or
pass a high school
equivalency test?

2. YES     1. NO

K24b. Does he have
a college
degree?

4. YES     3. NO
(GO TO K25)     59

K24c. What degree
is that?

_____

ASK EVERYONE

K25.  In this study we are trying to get a clear picture of people's financial
situations.  Taking into consideration all sources of income for all
your family living here, what was your total family income before taxes
in 1971?  Just tell me the letter on the card.    (HAND R RING CARD H.)

A.  1. UNDER $2000            E.  5. $8000 - $9999

B.  2. $2000 - $3999          F.  6. $10,000 - $11,999

C.  3. $4000 - $5999          G.  7. $12,000 - $15,999

D.  4. $6000 - $7999          H.  8. $16,000 AND OVER

60

K25a.  Does that include the income of everyone in the family?

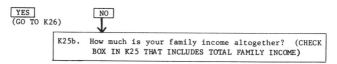

YES                NO
(GO TO K26)

K25b.  How much is your family income altogether?  (CHECK
BOX IN K25 THAT INCLUDES TOTAL FAMILY INCOME)

K26.  How many people depend on this income for their support?

```
[ 1 ]  [ 2 ]  [ 3 ]  [ 4 ]  [ 5 ]  [ 6 ]  [ 7 ]  [ 8+ ]
```

K27.  Were you ever in any of the armed services, including the national guard?

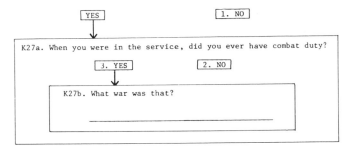

| YES | | 1.  NO |

K27a. When you were in the service, did you ever have combat duty?

| 3.  YES | | 2.  NO |

K27b. What war was that?

_____

ASK ONLY OF R WITH LILAC OR ORANGE COLOR COVER SHEET

K28.  We may want to make another call on you in about a month to see how you are
getting along and to ask you a few more questions.  Just so we will be sure
to get the right person, would you please give me your name?  Can I have
your telephone number too, so we can make an appointment ?

| 1.  GIVEN | | 2.  REFUSED |

INTERVIEWER:  PUT INFORMATION ON PAGE 3 OF COVER SHEET

SECTION Z

F O R   I N T E R V I E W E R   O N L Y

Z1.  This interview was taken in a:

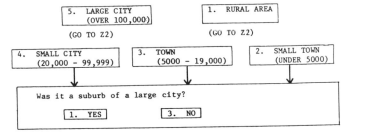

| 5.  LARGE CITY<br>(OVER 100,000) | | 1.  RURAL AREA |

(GO TO Z2)                    (GO TO Z2)

| 4.  SMALL CITY<br>(20,000 - 99,999) | 3.  TOWN<br>(5000 - 19,000) | 2.  SMALL TOWN<br>(UNDER 5000) |

Was it a suburb of a large city?

| 1.  YES | | 3.  NO |

**36**

Z2.    Sex of Respondent:

| 1. MALE |          | 2. FEMALE |

☐
65

Z3.    Race of Respondent

| 1. WHITE |    | 2. BLACK |    | 3. MEXICAN-AMERICAN |    | 4. OTHER |

☐
66

↓
(SPECIFY)

_____

Z4.    Cooperation of respondent:

| 3.  VERY COOPERATIVE |    | 2.   SOMEWHAT COOPERATIVE |    | 1.   NOT COOPERATIVE |

☐
67

Z5.    Respondent's understanding of questions:

| 3.  GOOD UNDERSTANDING |    | 2.   FAIR UNDERSTANDING |    | 1.   POOR UNDERSTANDING |

☐
68

THUMBNAIL SKETCH

Project 46214
Winter 1972

1

# Re-Interview

SOCIAL PROBLEMS

**SURVEY RESEARCH CENTER**
INSTITUTE FOR SOCIAL RESEARCH
THE UNIVERSITY OF MICHIGAN
ANN ARBOR, MICHIGAN 48106

*(Do not write in above space)*

*1.* Interviewer's Label

2. Date of Original Interview

_____

3. Interviewer No. - Original Interview

_____

4. Questionnaire Form - Original Interview

|A|  |B|  |C|  |D|

(Use same form for Re-Interview)

5. P.S.U. _____

6. Your Interview No. _____

7. Date _____

8. Length of Interview _____
   (Minutes)

**2**

INTRODUCTION

This is a continuation of last month's interview.  I will be asking how you feel <u>now</u> about some of the same problems we talked about last time, as well as some new questions.  This interview will be shorter.

1:6-10

SECTION A:

A1.  Has anything happened in this community during the last month that you were particularly worried or concerned about?

| 1. YES | | 2. NO |
|---|---|---|
| | | (GO TO A2) |

11

A1a.  What was that? _____

_____

_____

_____

A2.  Were there any violent events that happened in the last month or so that you were especially concerned about?

| 1. YES | | 2. NO |
|---|---|---|
| | | (GO TO A3) |

12

A2a.  What were they? _____

_____

_____

_____

**3**

A3.  Here are some things people have told us about violence. We would like
to know how much you agree or disagree with each of these opinions. Do
you <u>agree a great deal</u>, <u>agree somewhat</u>, <u>disagree somewhat</u>, or <u>disagree
a great deal</u> that drug abuse helps cause violence? (HAND R RING CARD B.)

|  |  | AGREE A<br>GREAT DEAL | AGREE<br>SOMEWHAT | DISAGREE<br>SOMEWHAT | DISAGREE A<br>GREAT DEAL |  |
|---|---|---|---|---|---|---|
| A3a. | Drug abuse helps<br>cause violence. | 4 | 3 | 2 | 1 | ☐ |
| A3b. | A poor education is<br>one cause of violence. | 4 | 3 | 2 | 1 | ☐ |
| A3c. | There would be less<br>violence if there was<br>more gun control. | 4 | 3 | 2 | 1 | ☐ |
| A3d. | Discrimination helps<br>cause violence. | 4 | 3 | 2 | 1 | ☐ |
| A3e. | There would be less<br>violence if more<br>people had good jobs. | 4 | 3 | 2 | 1 | ☐ |

A4.  Some people tell us that the police can't deal with violence because
laws interfere with their work; others say laws do not interfere. What
do you think?

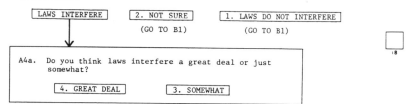

| LAWS INTERFERE | 2. NOT SURE | 1. LAWS DO NOT INTERFERE |
|---|---|---|
|  | (GO TO B1) | (GO TO B1) |

A4a.  Do you think laws interfere a great deal or just
somewhat?

| 4. GREAT DEAL | 3. SOMEWHAT |
|---|---|

☐

**4a**

P A S T E  C A R D  # 1  H E R E

SECTION B

B1.  There have been many different kinds of disturbances in the United
States, and we would like to know what people think the police
should do in these situations.

There have been times when gangs of hoodlums have gone into a town,
terrified people, and caused a lot of property damage.  How do you
think the police should handle this situation?  (HAND R PASTE CARD
#1 AND INSTRUCT R TO FILL OUT THE CARD BY CHECKING ONE ANSWER FOR
EACH STATEMENT.)

| | | Almost always | Some-times | Hardly ever | Never | |
|---|---|---|---|---|---|---|
| B1a. | The police should let it go, not do anything. | [4] | [3] | [2] | [1] | 19 |
| B1b. | Police should make arrests without using clubs or guns. | [4] | [3] | [2] | [1] | 20 |
| B1c. | Police should use clubs, but not guns. | [4] | [3] | [2] | [1] | 21 |
| B1d. | The police should shoot, but not to kill. | [4] | [3] | [2] | [1] | 22 |
| B1e. | The police should shoot to kill. | [4] | [3] | [2] | [1] | 23 |

B2.  INTERVIEWER CHECK

[1]  R FILLED OUT CARD
[2]  INTERVIEWER FILLED OUT CARD FOR R

24

B3. Here are some things people have told us about policemen. We would like to know how much you agree or disagree with each of these statements. (HAND R RING CARD B.)

|  | AGREE A GREAT DEAL | AGREE SOMEWHAT | DISAGREE SOMEWHAT | DISAGREE A GREAT DEAL |
|---|---|---|---|---|
| B3a. Most policemen are trying to be helpful. | 4 | 3 | 2 | 1 |
| B3b. The police are getting so much power that the average citizen has to worry. | 4 | 3 | 2 | 1 |
| B3c. Most policemen are interested in making the world a better place for all of us. | 4 | 3 | 2 | 1 |
| B3d. The police are just looking for trouble. | 4 | 3 | 2 | 1 |
| B3e. In general, there would be fewer problems if the police had more power. | 4 | 3 | 2 | 1 |

1:25

26

27

28

29

B4. If the police get the things they want, do you think your life will change?

| WILL CHANGE | 2. WON'T CHANGE (GO TO B5) | 8. DON'T KNOW (GO TO B5) |

30

B4a. IF "WILL CHANGE": Do you think your life will change for better or worse?

| 3. BETTER | 1. WORSE | 7. DON'T KNOW |

B5. What do you think the police want?

_____

_____

_____

**6**

B6.   Now I want to talk about what some people have told us about the
      police.

B6a.   Some people have told us that they believe the police take
       bribes or pay-offs, others say they never do.  Do you think
       almost all policemen, some policemen, a few, hardly any, or
       none take pay-offs?

| 1. ALMOST ALL | 2. SOME | 3. A FEW | 4. HARDLY ANY | 5. NONE |
|---|---|---|---|---|

1:31

B6b.   Some people say the police frisk or search people without good
       reason.  Do you think this happens to people in this neighborhood?

| 1. YES | 2. DON'T KNOW | 3. NO |
|---|---|---|

32

B6c.   Has this ever happened to you or anybody you know personally?

| 1. YES | 2. DON'T KNOW | 3. NO |
|---|---|---|

33

B6d.   Some people say the police rough people up unnecessarily when
       they are arresting them.  Do you think that happens to people
       in this neighborhood?

| 1. YES | 2. DON'T KNOW | 3. NO |
|---|---|---|

34

B6e.   Has this ever happened to you or anybody you know personally?

| 1. YES | 2. DON'T KNOW | 3. NO |
|---|---|---|

35

B7.   How safe do you feel it is for you to go out alone at night in
      this neighborhood?  Do you feel it is completely safe, somewhat safe,
      not too safe, or not safe at all?

| 4. COMPLETELY SAFE | 3. SOMEWHAT SAFE | 2. NOT TOO SAFE | 1. NOT SAFE AT ALL |
|---|---|---|---|

36

ASK MALE RESPONDENTS ONLY -- OTHERS GO TO B9

B8.    How safe do you feel it is for women to go out alone at night in this
       neighborhood? Do you feel it is completely safe, somewhat safe, not
       too safe, or not safe at all?

| 4. COMPLETELY SAFE | 3. SOMEWHAT SAFE | 2. NOT TOO SAFE | 1. NOT SAFE AT ALL |
|---|---|---|---|

□ 37

ASK EVERYONE

B9.    Do you think this neighborhood is safer now than it was five years
       ago, or is it less safe now?

| 1. SAFER NOW | 2. ABOUT THE SAME | 3. LESS SAFE NOW |
|---|---|---|

□ 38

B10.   Do you think that local crime changes the way people live or how
       they feel about their lives?

| 1. YES | 2. NO |
|---|---|
|  | (GO TO B11) |

□ 39

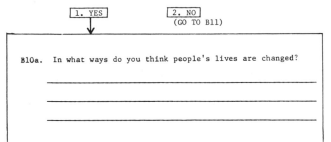

B10a.  In what ways do you think people's lives are changed?

_____

_____

_____

B11.   During the last year or so, **were** you or someone you know personally,
       the victim of a crime?

| 1. YES | 2. NO |
|---|---|
|  | (GO TO SECTION C) |

□ 40

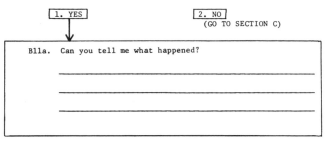

B11a.  Can you tell me what happened?

_____

_____

_____

**8**

SECTION C

We have been talking about crime. Now we would like to talk about another problem. We are interested in what people think about racial problems in this country.

C1.  Do you think the problems of race in this country are generally getting better or worse?

| 1. GETTING BETTER | 2. STAYING THE SAME | 3. GETTING WORSE | 4. BOTH OR NOT SURE |
|---|---|---|---|
| | (GO TO C2) | | (GO TO C2) |

⌐1.41

C1a.  In what ways do you think they are getting (better/worse)?

_____

_____

_____

C2.  What do you think causes racial problems in this country?

_____

_____

_____

C3.  Now we want to talk about blacks who participate in protests. When we talk about black protesters, what kind of people do you have in mind?

_____

_____

_____

C4. Here are some things people have told us about black (Negro/colored) protesters. We would like to know whether you <u>agree a great deal</u>, <u>agree somewhat</u>, <u>disagree somewhat</u>, or <u>disagree a great deal</u>. (HAND R RING CARD B.)

|  |  | AGREE A GREAT DEAL | AGREE SOMEWHAT | DISAGREE SOMEWHAT | DISAGREE A GREAT DEAL |  |
|---|---|:---:|:---:|:---:|:---:|---|
| C4a. | Most black protesters are trying to be helpful. | 4 | 3 | 2 | 1 | ☐ 1:42 |
| C4b. | Black protesters are getting so much power that the average citizen has to worry. | 4 | 3 | 2 | 1 | ☐ 43 |
| C4c. | Most black protesters are interested in making the world a better place for all of us. | 4 | 3 | 2 | 1 | ☐ 44 |
| C4d. | Black protesters are just looking for trouble. | 4 | 3 | 2 | 1 | ☐ 45 |
| C4e. | In general there would be fewer problems if black protesters had more power. | 4 | 3 | 2 | 1 | ☐ 46 |

C5. If black (Negro/colored) protesters get what they want, do you think your life will change?

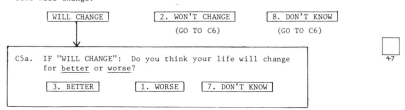

| WILL CHANGE | 2. WON'T CHANGE | 8. DON'T KNOW |
|---|---|---|
| | (GO TO C6) | (GO TO C6) |

C5a. IF "WILL CHANGE": Do you think your life will change for <u>better</u> or <u>worse</u>?

| 3. BETTER | 1. WORSE | 7. DON'T KNOW |

☐ 47

C6. Many blacks (Negroes/colored people) feel changes are needed in our society. Some people think violence is needed to bring about the changes which would make life better for blacks (Negroes/colored people). We would like to know how much you agree or disagree with each of these opinions about how much violence is necessary for blacks (Negroes/colored people) to bring about changes. (HAND R PASTE CARD #2 AND INSTRUCT R TO CHECK ONE ANSWER FOR EACH STATEMENT.)

| | | | | |
|---|---|---|---|---|
| C6a. Changes can be made fast enough without action involving property damage or injury. | Agree a Great Deal ⬜4 | Agree Somewhat ⬜3 | Disagree Somewhat ⬜2 | Disagree a Great Deal ⬜1 |
| C6b. Protest in which some people are hurt is necessary for changes to come fast enough. | Agree a Great Deal ⬜4 | Agree Somewhat ⬜3 | Disagree Somewhat ⬜2 | Disagree a Great Deal ⬜1 |
| C6c. Protest in which there is <u>some</u> property damage is necessary for changes to be brought about fast enough. | Agree a Great Deal ⬜4 | Agree Somewhat ⬜3 | Disagree Somewhat ⬜2 | Disagree a Great Deal ⬜1 |
| C6d. Protest in which there is <u>much</u> property damage is necessary before changes can be brought about fast enough. | Agree a Great Deal ⬜4 | Agree Somewhat ⬜3 | Disagree Somewhat ⬜2 | Disagree a Great Deal ⬜1 |
| C6e. Protest in which some people are killed is necessary before changes will take place fast enough. | Agree a Great Deal ⬜4 | Agree Somewhat ⬜3 | Disagree Somewhat ⬜2 | Disagree a Great Deal ⬜1 |

C7. INTERVIEWER CHECK

⬜1 R FILLED OUT CARD
⬜2 INTERVIEWER FILLED OUT CARD FOR R

PASTE CARD #3 HERE     11a

C8.     When you think about inner-city disturbances (big city riots) involving blacks (Negroes/colored people) and police, how do you think the police <u>should</u> handle the situation?  (HAND R PASTE CARD #3 AND INSTRUCT R TO CHECK ONE ANSWER FOR EACH STATEMENT.)

C8a.   The police should let it go, not do anything.

Almost always [4]     Some- times [3]     Hardly ever [2]     Never [1]

1:54

C8b.   Police should make arrests without using clubs or guns.

Almost always [4]     Some- times [3]     Hardly ever [2]     Never [1]

55

C8c.   Police should use clubs, but not guns.

Almost always [4]     Some- times [3]     Hardly ever [2]     Never [1]

C8d.   The police should shoot, but not to kill.

Almost always [4]     Some- times [3]     Hardly ever [2]     Never [1]

56

C8e.   The police should shoot to kill.

Almost always [4]     Some- times [3]     Hardly ever [2]     Never [1]

57

58

C9.   INTERVIEWER CHECK

[1] R FILLED OUT CARD
[2] INTERVIEWER FILLED OUT CARD FOR R

59

**12**

SECTION D

D1.  Are you or your family affected by school desegregation?

| 1. YES |     | 3. NO |
(GO TO D2)

☐ 1:60

> D1a.  Are these changes for the better or worse?
>
> | 1. BETTER |   | 2. DON'T KNOW |   | 3. WORSE |
>
> D1b.  What kinds of changes are these?
>
> _____
>
> _____
>
> _____

☐ 61

---

ASK WHITE RESPONDENTS ONLY -- OTHERS GO TO D4

D2.  Have you ever been concerned about what would happen to property values
in your neighborhood because of blacks moving into this area?

| 1. YES |     | 3. NO |
(GO TO D3)

☐ 62

> D2a.  What happened to make you think about this?
>
> _____
>
> _____
>
> _____

D3.   Have you ever thought that you might lose your job or miss a promotion because blacks (Negroes/colored people) are pushing for better jobs?

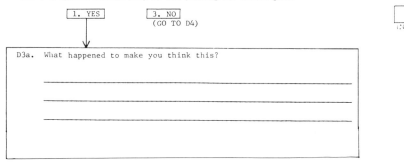

| 1. YES | | 3. NO |
| --- | --- | --- |
| | | (GO TO D4) |

D3a.   What happened to make you think this?

_____

_____

_____

(:63

D4.   (HAND R RING CARD D .)  We would like you to list these in the order you feel is most important for the kind of world you want to live in.  Please tell me which you think is <u>most</u> important.  Now which do you think is the next most important?  (INTERVIEWER:  CONTINUE ASKING UNTIL R HAS ORDERED ALL ITEMS.  MARK THE NUMBER 1 IN FRONT OF THE ITEM WHICH IS <u>MOST</u> IMPORTANT, <u>2</u> IN FRONT OF THE ITEM WHICH IS NEXT MOST IMPORTANT, AND SO ON UNTIL ALL ITEMS HAVE BEEN ASSIGNED A NUMBER FROM ONE TO SIX.)

A.   (   )   EQUALITY

B.   (   )   HUMAN DIGNITY

C.   (   )   RESPECT FOR PROPERTY

D.   (   )   RESPECT FOR LAW

E.   (   )   FREEDOM

F.   (   )   FINANCIAL SECURITY FOR SELF AND LOVED ONES

**14**

2

D4a. Are there other things that are important for the kind of world you want to live in?

| 1. YES | | 2. NO |
(GO TO D5)

> D4b. What are they? _____
>
> _____
>
> _____

D5. Here are some things people have told us. We would like to know whether you <u>agree a great deal</u>, <u>agree somewhat</u>, <u>disagree somewhat</u>, or <u>disagree a great deal</u> with these opinions. (HAND R RING CARD B. READ STATEMENTS TO R.)

|  | AGREE A GREAT DEAL | AGREE SOMEWHAT | DISAGREE SOMEWHAT | DISAGREE A GREAT DEAL |
|---|---|---|---|---|
| People who commit murder deserve capital punishment. | 4 | 3 | 2 | 1 |
| D6. Most people try to apply the Golden Rule. | 4 | 3 | 2 | 1 |
| D7. Violence deserves violence. | 4 | 3 | 2 | 1 |
| D8. Most people will be "Good Samaritans" if given the chance. | 4 | 3 | 2 | 1 |
| D9. "An eye for an eye and a tooth for a tooth" is a good rule for living. | 4 | 3 | 2 | 1 |

|  | | AGREE GREAT DEAL | AGREE SOMEWHAT | DISAGREE SOMEWHAT | DISAGREE A GREAT DEAL | |
|---|---|---|---|---|---|---|
| D10. | Most people go out of their way to help someone in trouble. | 4 | 3 | 2 | 1 | 2:17 |
| D11. | It is often necessary to use violence to pre-vent violence. | 4 | 3 | 2 | 1 | 18 |
| D12. | The typical person is concerned about the problems of others. | 4 | 3 | 2 | 1 | 19 |
| D13. | When someone does wrong, he should be punished for it. | 4 | 3 | 2 | 1 | 20 |
| D14. | Most people would stop and help a person whose car has broken down on the road. | 4 | 3 | 2 | 1 | 21 |
| D15. | A man has a right to kill another man in a case of self-defense. | 4 | 3 | 2 | 1 | 22 |
| D16. | A man has the right to kill a person to defend his family. | 4 | 3 | 2 | 1 | 23 |
| D17. | A man has the right to kill a person to defend his house. | 4 | 3 | 2 | 1 | 24 |

## 16

E1. Now we would like to ask your opinion about how much political power different groups or people have in the United States. I mean how much power they have to get laws passed in their favor. Do you think labor unions have <u>too much power</u>, <u>about the right amount of power</u>, or have <u>too little power</u> in this country?

|  |  | TOO MUCH | ABOUT RIGHT | TOO LITTLE |  |
|--|--|----------|-------------|------------|--|
| E1a. | Labor Unions | 3 | 2 | 1 | 2:25 |
| E1b. | Poor People | 3 | 2 | 1 | 26 |
| E1c. | The Military | 3 | 2 | 1 | 27 |
| E1d. | Young People | 3 | 2 | 1 | 28 |
| E1e. | Blacks | 3 | 2 | 1 | 29 |
| E1f. | Women | 3 | 2 | 1 | 30 |
| E1g. | Black Militants | 3 | 2 | 1 | 31 |
| E1h. | Senior Citizens | 3 | 2 | 1 | |
| E1i. | Big Business | 3 | 2 | 1 | 33 |

E2. How much political power do you think people like you have? <u>A great deal</u>, <u>some</u>, <u>not very much</u>, or <u>none</u>?

| 4. A GREAT DEAL | 3. SOME | 2. NOT VERY MUCH | 1. NONE |

34

E3. Do you think that people like you have <u>too little</u> political power, or <u>just about the right amount</u>?

| 1. TOO LITTLE |                    | 2. ABOUT THE RIGHT AMOUNT |

35

E3a. Could you tell me more about that? Why do you think that people like you have (too little/about the right amount of) power?

_____

_____

_____

E4.   Suppose a law was being considered by the Congress in Washington, and
      you thought the law was **very unjust or harmful.** What do you think you
      could do about it?

      _____

      _____

      _____

E5.   If you made an effort to change this law, how likely is it that you
      would succeed:  very likely, somewhat likely, not very likely, or not
      likely at all?

      | 4. VERY LIKELY | 3. SOMEWHAT LIKELY | 2. NOT VERY LIKELY | 1. NOT LIKELY AT ALL |

                                                                                          2:56

E6.   Have you ever done anything to try to influence a national decision?

      | 2. YES |                    | 1. NO |
                                     (GO TO E7)

                                                                                          37

      ┌─────────────────────────────────────────────────────────────┐
      │  E6a.   What was that? _____       │
      │                                                               │
      │         _____         │
      │                                                               │
      │         _____         │
      │                                                               │
      └─────────────────────────────────────────────────────────────┘

**18**

E7.    Do you feel that almost all of the people running the government are smart
people who usually <u>know what they are doing</u>, or do you think that quite a
few of them <u>don't seem to know what they're doing</u>?

| 1. KNOW WHAT THEY'RE DOING |        | 2. DON'T KNOW WHAT THEY'RE DOING |

2:38

E8.    Do you think that <u>quite a few</u> of the people running the government are a
little crooked, <u>not very many</u> are, or do you think <u>hardly any</u> of them are
crooked at all?

| 3. QUITE A FEW |        | 2. NOT VERY MANY |        | 1. HARDLY ANY |

39

PASTE CARD #4 HERE

E9.   Some people feel that important changes can be brought about only
      through violence; others say violence is not necessary. What do you
      think? (HAND R PASTE CARD #4 AND INSTRUCT R TO CHECK ONE ANSWER FOR
      EACH STATEMENT.)

2:40

| | | Agree a Great Deal | Agree Somewhat | Disagree Somewhat | Disagree a Great Deal |
|---|---|---|---|---|---|
| E9a. | Changes can be made fast enough without action involving property damage or injury. | 4 | 3 | 2 | 1 |

41

| | | Agree a Great Deal | Agree Somewhat | Disagree Somewhat | Disagree Great Deal |
|---|---|---|---|---|---|
| E9b. | Protest in which some people are hurt is necessary for changes to come fast enough. | 4 | 3 | 2 | 1 |

42

| | | Agree a Great Deal | Agree Somewhat | Disagree Somewhat | Disagree Great Deal |
|---|---|---|---|---|---|
| E9c. | Protest in which there is some property damage is necessary for changes to be brought about fast enough. | 4 | 3 | 2 | 1 |

43

| | | Agree a Great Deal | Agree Somewhat | Disagree Somewhat | Disagree a Great Deal |
|---|---|---|---|---|---|
| E9d. | Protest in which there is much property damage is necessary before changes can be brought about fast enough. | 4 | 3 | 2 | 1 |

44

| | | Agree a Great Deal | Agree Somewhat | Disagree Somewhat | Disagree a Great Deal |
|---|---|---|---|---|---|
| E9e. | Protest in which some people are killed is necessary before changes will take place fast enough. | 4 | 3 | 2 | 1 |

E10.  INTERVIEWER CHECK

      ┌─────────────────────────────────────┐
      │ 1 R FILLED OUT CARD                  │
      │ 2 INTERVIEWER FILLED OUT CARD FOR R  │
      └─────────────────────────────────────┘

45

**20**

SECTION F

F1.  In each of the next questions, I'm going to read you two sentences.  Would
     you tell me the one that comes closest to the way you feel things <u>actually</u>
     are in life.  Be sure it's the way things <u>actually</u> <u>are</u> in life, <u>not</u> the way
     you'd like them to be.  (HAND R RING CARD E.)

     Which of these first two statements is closest to the way you feel things
     actually are?

     1 Becoming a success is a matter of hard work; luck has little or
       nothing to do with it.  -- or --

     3 Getting a good job depends mainly on being in the right place at          2:46
       the right time.

F2.  Which of these two?

     1 When I make plans, I am almost certain that I can make them work.
       -- or --

     3 It is not always wise to plan too far ahead because many things           47
       turn out to be a matter of good or bad luck anyhow.

F3.  Which of these is closest to the way you feel things actually are?

     1 What happens to me is my own doing.  -- or --

     3 Sometimes I feel that I don't have enough control over the                48
       direction my life is taking.

F4.  And these?

     1 Knowing the right people is important in deciding whether a
       person will get ahead.  -- or --

     3 People will get ahead in life if they have the skills and do a            49
       good job; knowing the right people has nothing to do with it.

F5.  How about these?

     1 People who don't do well in life often work hard, but the breaks
       just don't come their way.  -- or --

     3 Some people just don't use the breaks that come their way;  if           50
       they don't do well, it's their own fault.

F6.  And these?

    ☐1☐  I've usually felt pretty sure my life would work out the way I wanted it to.  -- or --

    ☐3☐  There are times when I haven't been very sure that my life would work out the way I wanted it to.

☐<br>2:5:

F7.  Now I have a few questions concerning poverty and unemployment.  People have different ideas about poverty and unemployment -- I'd like to ask you about your ideas.

    Which of these two statements is closest to the way you feel?

    ☐1☐  People who are born poor have less chance to get ahead than other people.  -- or --

    ☐3☐  People who have the ability and work hard have the same chance as anyone else, even if their parents were poor.

☐<br>52

F8.  Which of these two statements is closest to the way you feel?

    ☐1☐  It's the lack of skills and abilities that keep most unemployed people from getting a job; if they had the skills most of them could get a job.  -- or --

    ☐3☐  Many people with skills can't get a job; there just aren't any jobs for them.

☐<br>53

F9.  Which of these?

    ☐1☐  Most people who are unemployed just haven't had the right breaks in life.  -- or --

    ☐3☐  Most people who are unemployed have had the opportunities; they haven't made use of the opportunities that came their way.

☐<br>54

**22**

F10.   All of us want certain things out of life.  When you think about what
       really matters in your own life, what are your wishes and hopes for the
       future?  In other words, if you imagine your future in the <u>best</u> possible
       light, what would your life be like then, if you are to be happy?
       Take your time in answering; such things aren't easy to put into words.

       PERMISSIBLE PROBES:  What are your hopes for the future?  What would
       your life have to be like for you to be completely happy?  What is
       missing for you to be happy?  (Use also, if necessary, the words "dreams"
       and "desires.")

       _____

       _____

       _____

F11.   Now, taking the other side of the picture, what are your fears and worries
       about the future?  In other words, if you imagine your future in the
       <u>worst</u> possible light, what would your life be like then?  Again, take
       your time in answering.

       PERMISSIBLE PROBE:  What would make you unhappy?  (Stress the words
       "fears" and "worries.")

       _____

       _____

       _____

F12.   SHOW R RING CARD F.  Here is a picture of a ladder.  Suppose we say
       that the top of the ladder (POINTING) represents the best possible
       life for you and the bottom (POINTING) represents the worst possible
       life for you.

       Where on the ladder (MOVING FINGER RAPIDLY UP AND DOWN LADDER) do
       you feel you personally stand at the <u>present</u> time?  Step number _____.    2:55-56

F13.   Where on the ladder would you say you stood five years ago?  Step
       number _____.                                                                  57-58

F14.   And where do you think you will be on the ladder five years from now?
       Step number _____.                                                            59-60

F15. This is the last question of the interview.
Here is a list of clubs and organizations that some people belong to.
Please look at this list and tell me which of these organizations you
belong to, if any. (HAND R RING CARD G.) IF R ANSWERS "OTHER" PLEASE
ASK R TO SPECIFY WHICH ONE OR ONES.

|  | YES | NO |  |
|---|---|---|---|
| F15a. | 3 | 1 | Labor Unions |
| F15b. | 3 | 1 | Political Clubs or Organizations |
| F15c. | 3 | 1 | Church Connected Groups |
| F15d. | 3 | 1 | Neighborhood Associations |
| F15e. | 3 | 1 | Business or Civic Groups |
| F15f. | 3 | 1 | Other (SPECIFY) _____ |

2:61

62

63

64

65

66

F16. That finishes the interview. Is there anything you would like to add to
any of the subjects we've discussed?

_____

_____

_____

THUMBNAIL SKETCH

# Appendix C

# STATISTICAL TECHNIQUES

## Adjustment of the Multiple R² for the Appropriate Degrees of Freedom in MCA and Multiple Regression

The following tables have been prepared to illustrate one of the practical differences between Multiple Regression and Multiple Classification Analysis (MCA). To minimize the capitalization on random associations, the multiple $R^2$ in the data must be adjusted for the appropriate degrees of freedom. The procedure is similar for both regression and MCA, but the extent of the actual shrinkage between the unadjusted $R^2$ and the adjusted $R^2$ is much greater for MCA. The reason for this greater shrinkage lies in the use of categorical predictors in the MCA. This point is illustrated by two differing formulae for the adjustment factor. For multiple regression the adjustment factor equals

$$\frac{N - 1}{(N - 1) - P}$$

where N equals the number of cases and P equals the number of predictor variables. The adjustment factor for MCA equals

$$\frac{N - 1}{(N - 1) - (C - P)}$$

where N equals the number of cases, C equals the total number of categories across all predictors, and P equals the number of predictor variables. It is clear that (C − P) will always be larger than P when any of the predictor variables has more than two categories. Consequently, when parallel analyses are conducted using both MCA and multiple regression on the same dataset and with the same variables, the shrinkage between the unadjusted $R^2$ and the adjusted $R^2$ will be much greater for the model developed by MCA. Tables C.1 and C.2 illustrate this point.

For practical reasons we have found it advisable to establish a limit on the acceptable degree of shrinkage between the unadjusted and adjusted $R^2$. Our 1969 research had demonstrated that many of the

## Table C.1

### Multiple Classification Analysis:
### Assessment of Shrinkage from $R^2$ in Data to $R^2$
### Adjusted for Degrees of Freedom

$$R^2_{adj} = 1 - \left\{(1 - R^2_{un}) \cdot A\right\} \quad \text{where A} = \frac{N - 1}{(N - 1) - (C - P)}$$

Conditions:

$$N > (C - P) + 1$$

$$A > \frac{1}{1 - R^2_{un}}$$

N = Number of cases
P = Number of predictors†
C = Number of categories
    across all predictors
df = (C − P)†

### Adjusted $R^2$ for Given Sample Sizes

| | | | 2,400 | 1,200 | 600 | 300 | 150 | 75 |
|---|---|---|---|---|---|---|---|---|
| Sample Size = | | | | | | | | |
| $R^2_{un}$ | P | df‡ | $R^2_{adj}$ | $R^2_{adj}$ | $R^2_{adj}$ | $R^2_{adj}$ | $R^2_{adj}$ | $R^2_{adj}$‡ |
| $R^2_{un} = .80$ | 20 | (80) | .793 | .786 | .769 | .729 | .568 | — |
| | 15 | (60) | .795 | .789 | .778 | .750 | .665 | — |
| | 10 | (40) | .797 | .793 | .786 | .769 | .727 | .565 |
| | 5 | (20) | .798 | .797 | .793 | .786 | .769 | .726 |
| | 2 | ( 8) | .799 | .798 | .797 | .795 | .789 | .776 |
| $R^2_{un} = .60$ | 20 | (80) | .586 | .572 | .538 | .454 | .136 | — |
| | 15 | (60) | .590 | .579 | .556 | .500 | .330 | — |
| | 10 | (40) | .593 | .586 | .571 | .538 | .453 | .130 |
| | 5 | (20) | .597 | .593 | .586 | .571 | .538 | .452 |
| | 2 | ( 8) | .599 | .597 | .594 | .589 | .577 | .552 |
| $R^2_{un} = .40$ | 20 | (80) | .380 | .357 | .308 | .181 | — | — |
| | 15 | (60) | .384 | .368 | .333 | .249 | — | — |
| | 10 | (40) | .390 | .379 | .357 | .308 | .180 | — |
| | 5 | (20) | .395 | .390 | .379 | .357 | .307 | .178 |
| | 2 | ( 8) | .398 | .396 | .392 | .384 | .366 | .327 |
| $R^2_{un} = .20$ | 20 | (80) | .173 | .143 | .077 | — | — | — |
| | 15 | (60) | .179 | .158 | .111 | — | — | — |
| | 10 | (40) | .186 | .172 | .142 | .077 | — | — |
| | 5 | (20) | .194 | .186 | .172 | .142 | — | — |
| | 2 | ( 8) | .198 | .194 | .189 | .178 | .154 | .103 |

†Assume each P has 5 categories.
‡df = (C − P)

**Table C.2**

Multiple Regression:
Assessment of Shrinkage from $R^2$ in Data to $R^2$
Adjusted for Degrees of Freedom

$$R^2_{adj} = 1 - \left\{(-R^2_{un}) \cdot A\right\} \text{ where } A = \frac{N-1}{(N-1)-P}$$

Conditions:

$$N > (P + 1)$$

$$A > \frac{1}{1 - R^2_{un}}$$

$N$ = Number of cases
$P$ = Number of predictors

Adjusted $R^2$ for Given Sample Sizes

| Sample Size = | | 2,400 | 1,200 | 600 | 300 | 150 | 75 |
|---|---|---|---|---|---|---|---|
| $R^2$ in data | P† | $R^2_{adj}$ | $R^2_{adj}$ | $R^2_{adj}$ | $R^2_{adj}$ | $R^2_{adj}$ | $R^2_{adj}$ |
| $R^2_{un} = .80$ | 20 | .798 | .797 | .793 | .786 | .769 | .726 |
| | 15 | .799 | .797 | .795 | .789 | .778 | .749 |
| | 10 | .799 | .798 | .797 | .793 | .786 | .769 |
| | 5 | .800 | .799 | .798 | .797 | .793 | .786 |
| $R^2_{un} = .60$ | 20 | .597 | .593 | .586 | .571 | .538 | .452 |
| | 15 | .598 | .595 | .590 | .579 | .555 | .498 |
| | 10 | .598 | .597 | .593 | .586 | .571 | .538 |
| | 5 | .599 | .598 | .597 | .593 | .586 | .571 |
| $R^2_{un} = .40$ | 20 | .395 | .390 | .379 | .357 | .307 | .178 |
| | 15 | .396 | .392 | .384 | .368 | .333 | .248 |
| | 10 | .398 | .395 | .390 | .379 | .357 | .306 |
| | 5 | .399 | .398 | .395 | .390 | .379 | .357 |
| $R^2_{un} = .20$ | 20 | .194 | .186 | .172 | .142 | .076 | — |
| | 15 | .195 | .190 | .179 | .158 | .110 | — |
| | 10 | .197 | .194 | .186 | .172 | .142 | .075 |
| | 5 | .198 | .197 | .194 | .186 | .172 | .142 |

†P = df

bivariate relationships which were of interest to us were relatively small eta's on the order of .3 or less; nevertheless, their combined explanatory power was substantial. However, the number of independent predictors required was large. With a large dataset the shrinkage is small, but with a small dataset shrinkage reduces the multiple R in many multivariate analyses to zero if MCA is used. Since we wished to reduce the possibility that we were making errors of inference by rejecting multivariate relationships which were in fact true, we used a limitation on the percentage shrinkage as a guideline in our analysis.

The guideline adopted for this study required that the adjusted $R^2$ must be at least 80 percent of the magnitude of the unadjusted $R^2$. Because the formula for the adjustment factor involves the number of cases (for survey data this would mean the sample size in a typical analysis operation), the limitation on the acceptable degree of shrinkage acts as a parameter on the minimum number of cases which must be involved in the analyses. Turning again to Tables C.1 and C.2, it can be seen that the degree of shrinkage from the unadjusted to the adjusted $R^2$ is positively related to the number of predictors in the model, inversely related to the sample size, and inversely related to the level of explanation in the model. Taking these factors into account, it is possible to construct a table which estimates the minimum ratio between cases and degrees of freedom necessary to prevent a shrinkage greater than 20 percent. Table C.3 presents the results of such an effort.

**Table C.3**

Estimates of Minimum Factor Ratio Required to Limit Shrinkage
between $R^2$ in Data and $R^2$ Adjusted for Degrees of Freedom†

| $R^2$ in Data | $R^2$ Adjusted for Maximum Allowable Shrinkage | Minimum Factor‡ Ratio Required |
|---|---|---|
| .80 | .64 | 3 |
| .60 | .48 | 5 |
| .40 | .32 | 10 |
| .20 | .16 | 20-23 |

†For MCA, df = (number of categories minus the number of predictors).
   For Multiple Regression, df equals the number of predictors.
‡Factor ratio equals the number of cases divided by the degrees of freedom.

Table C.3 is derived from Tables C.1 and C.2. For each level of explanation postulated in Tables C.1 and C.2, Table C.3 presents the multiple adjusted $R^2$ at the maximum degree of acceptable shrinkage. The third column in Table C.3 presents the estimated minimum ratio between the number of cases in the analysis and the degrees of freedom. It is interesting to note that both the similarity and the differences between the two techniques are evident in this table. The similarity is that the same ratio between cases and degrees of freedom applies for both techniques. However, there is a difference in the calculation of the degrees of freedom for multiple regression and MCA. For multiple regression, df = P, that is, the degrees of freedom equal the number of predictor variables. For MCA, df = (C − P), i.e., the degrees of freedom equal the total number of categories across all predictor variables minus the number of predictor variables. Referring back to the two formulae for the adjustment factor "A," it can be seen that MCA will require far more cases than multiple regression to perform the same analysis without exceeding an arbitrary limit on the shrinkage between the adjusted and unadjusted correlation.

# Appendix D

# DEVELOPMENT AND CONSTRUCTION OF THE IDENTIFICATION MEASURES

*Items*

One of the important predictors of attitudes toward violence was identification with the persons or groups involved in the violence. The original model of attitudes toward violence proposed that an individual's identification with the victim of violence would act as a force diminishing the justification of violence to be used against the group. Similarly, the model specified that an individual's identification with the aggressor in an act of violence would serve to increase the level of violence which was thought to be justified by that individual or group. This general hypothesis was supported by the data collected in the 1969 national study with respect to both attitudes toward violence for social change and violence for social control. It was concluded that the hypothesis and concepts were of major importance in explaining attitudes toward violence and probably violent behaviors.

In the 1969 study, identification with police, black protesters, and white student demonstrators were all measured. The original items consisted of the following stems:

*(1) On the whole, would you say that **most** (white student demonstrators/black protesters/police) are **trying to be helpful**, or that they are **looking for trouble**, or that they aren't one way or the other?*

*(2) Think of how (white student demonstrators/black protesters/police) think of people like yourself. Do you think that **none** dislike people like yourself, only **a few, many**, or **almost all** dislike people like yourself?*

*(3) Would you say that most (white student demonstrators/ black protesters/police) **can be trusted**, or that you **can't be too careful** in dealing with them?*

*(4) If (white student demonstrators/black protesters/police)
get the things they want, do you think **your** life will
change? (If "WILL CHANGE": Do you think **your** life
will change for **better** or **worse?**)*

These stems were asked three times during the interview—once in relation to white student demonstrators, once in relation to black protesters, and once in relation to the police.

The statistical characteristics of the 1969 items caused considerable technical difficulty. The original intention had been to combine the items into indices in order to reduce the number of variables in the analysis and to increase the stability and generally improve the statistical properties of the variables. However, the relationships between items were not sufficiently consistent to allow for the construction of such indices. The result was that all analyses relating to identification involved twelve separate items which were exceedingly cumbersome. In addition, it was unsatisfying to work with items which, although they appeared to be closely related, apparently were viewed differently by different subgroups in the population.

In order to develop a better set of items for use in the 1972 study, a new item pool was generated. The stems, which were meant to be useful for measuring identification with a variety of groups including black protesters and police (the two groups which were the focus of the 1972 study), are given in Figure D.1. These stems were first used in the study of the California arrestees and then in a pretest of forty white and twenty black Detroit respondents.

The data gathered in the preliminary studies cited above allowed us to make some estimate of the validity of the items on the following basis: It was known that the California arrestees were negatively oriented toward the police; the disturbance in which these respondents were arrested had occurred after an anti-police rally failed to materialize. In addition, the arrestees had made many negative comments about police in response to open-ended questions in the interview (see Chapter 1). The 1969 data on identification had shown that blacks were likely to regard the police more negatively than whites. Consequently, it was thought that a reasonable test of the validity of the police identification items would be if the California arrestees responded most negatively to the items, black pretest respondents next most negatively, and white pretest respondents most positively.

The data available in the preliminary studies also allowed some examination of the validity of the items as they related to black protesters. It had been observed in the California interviews that, although the arrestees had presumably been acting in the interest of

**Figure D.1**

Identification Item Pool by Interview in Which Used

| Interview | | | | |
|---|---|---|---|---|
| 1 | 2 | 3 | 4 | |

| Interview 1 2 3 4 | Item |
|---|---|
| X X X X | Black protesters/police are getting so much power that the average citizen has to worry. |
| X X | Black protesters/police may feel they don't get what's coming to them, but they really are doing as well as anybody else. |
| X X | Black protesters/police often have moral standards that are lower than most people's. |
| X X | Black protesters/police are generally treated the same as everybody else. |
| X X X | Most black protesters/police are trustworthy. |
| X X X | Black protesters/police are getting more than their share of the tax dollar. |
| X X X X | Most black protesters/police are interested in making the world a better place for all of us. |
| X X X X | In general, there would be fewer problems if black protesters/police had more power. |
| X X | In general, most black protesters/police get a fair deal nowadays. |
| X X | You can't be too careful in dealing with black protesters/police. |
| X X | Black protesters/police still have a long way to go before they get what they really need. |
| X X | Most black protesters/police really mean well. |
| X X X | Black protesters/police should feel satisfied with their position nowadays. |
| X X X | Most black protesters/police are people who use bad language and are disrespectful. |
| X X X X | Most black protesters/police are trying to be helpful. |
| X X X | More money should be spent to help black protesters/police get the things they need. |
| X X X | In general, black protesters/police are just looking for trouble. |
| X X | If the police/black protesters get the things they want, do you think your life will change? If "WILL CHANGE": Do you think your life will change for better or worse? |

1 = California arrestees
2 = 60 Detroit respondents
3 = 1972 interview
4 = 1972 reinterview

social change—that is, the thrust of the movement had been to change the relations between the police and the Spanish-American Community—many of the California arrestees had made negative comments about blacks. Thus, it appeared that many of the California arrestees were negative in their orientation toward blacks. Nevertheless, the arrestees were protesters and might be expected to be more identified with protesters of any color than people who were not actively involved in protest. Consequently, it was thought that a reasonable test of the validity of the items measuring identification with black protesters implied that black respondents should give the most positive responses, the California arrestees the next most positive responses, and the white Detroit respondents the least positive responses. Items that were not valid according to these criteria were not included in the 1972 interview.

Additional criteria were used in selecting items for the 1972 interview. For example, distributions on items were inspected for their skew. The distributions of both black protester and police identification stems were considered separately among black and white respondents, and those stems which showed the most skew were discarded. Interviewer comments on how the respondents viewed the clarity and applicability of the items were noted and some stems were discarded on this basis. In addition, a Smallest Space Analysis and an examination of inter-item relationships comparing the matrix for the police identification items with that of black protesters were used to make the final selection of items.[1] The items selected for the 1972 interview on the basis of the combined criteria are indicated in Figure D.1.

## DEVELOPMENT OF NEW IDENTIFICATION INDICES

Table D.1 shows the distribution of responses to the identification items as they occurred in the 1972 interview. It can be seen that the responses of white respondents tended to be more skewed with respect to both the police and black protesters. Moreover, in the case of white respondents the skew is in opposite directions for items about the police and items about black protesters. For example, 77 percent of white respondents answered "agree a great deal" that police were helpful, while only 6 percent responded "agree a great deal" that blacks were helpful. In spite of these problems of distribution, the items were retained for inter-item analyses since, on the basis of past experience, it seemed unlikely that other items would be less skewed when tested in these two disparate groups.

---

[1] Details of these procedures are available in Working Memorandum No. 42, "Further Work on Identification," by Monica D. Blumenthal, 1972.

## Table D.1

### Percentage Responses to the Police and the Black Protesters
### Identification Items
(all respondents, N = 283; whites, N = 145; blacks, N = 133)

| | Agree a Great Deal | Agree Somewhat | Disagree Somewhat | Disagree a Great Deal |
|---|---|---|---|---|
| **POLICE IDENTIFICATION ITEMS** | | | | |
| Police get too much taxes | | | | |
| All Respondents | 8% | 17 | 46 | 29 |
| Whites | 3% | 9 | 48 | 40 |
| Blacks | 14% | 26 | 45 | 15 |
| Police use bad language | | | | |
| All Respondents | 4% | 16 | 36 | 44 |
| Whites | 0% | 11 | 27 | 62 |
| Blacks | 9% | 22 | 46 | 23 |
| Police too powerful | | | | |
| All Respondents | 8% | 11 | 39 | 42 |
| Whites | 3% | 4 | 31 | 62 |
| Blacks | 13% | 19 | 47 | 21 |
| Police try to be helpful | | | | |
| All Respondents | 56% | 35 | 7 | 2 |
| Whites | 77% | 19 | 3 | 1 |
| Blacks | 34% | 52 | 11 | 3 |
| Police trustworthy | | | | |
| All Respondents | 40% | 38 | 15 | 7 |
| Whites | 60% | 34 | 5 | 1 |
| Blacks | 19% | 42 | 26 | 13 |
| Police need more power | | | | |
| All Respondents | 30% | 24 | 26 | 20 |
| Whites | 37% | 27 | 21 | 15 |
| Blacks | 21% | 20 | 32 | 27 |
| Police make world better | | | | |
| All Respondents | 41% | 40 | 14 | 5 |
| Whites | 56% | 35 | 7 | 2 |
| Blacks | 25% | 46 | 22 | 7 |
| Police need more money | | | | |
| All Respondents | 29% | 40 | 20 | 11 |
| Whites | 39% | 41 | 16 | 4 |
| Blacks | 18% | 37 | 27 | 18 |
| Police should be satisfied | | | | |
| All Respondents | 21% | 29 | 37 | 13 |
| Whites | 18% | 25 | 41 | 16 |
| Blacks | 25% | 33 | 33 | 9 |
| | (Better) | (Won't Change) | (Worse) | |
| Police better R's life | | | | |
| All Respondents | 40% | 53 | 7 | |
| Whites | 46% | 49 | 5 | |
| Blacks | 33% | 57 | 10 | |

**Table D.1** (continued)

Percentage Responses to the Police and the Black Protesters
Identification Items
(all respondents, N = 283; whites, N = 145; blacks, N = 133)

| | Agree a Great Deal | Agree Somewhat | Disagree Somewhat | Disagree a Great Deal |
|---|---|---|---|---|
| **BLACK PROTESTERS** **IDENTIFICATION ITEMS** | | | | |
| Blacks get too much taxes | | | | |
| All Respondents | 14% | 22 | 35 | 29 |
| Whites | 28% | 29 | 32 | 11 |
| Blacks | 1% | 13 | 38 | 48 |
| Blacks use bad language | | | | |
| All Respondents | 11% | 21 | 42 | 26 |
| Whites | 17% | 26 | 41 | 16 |
| Blacks | 4% | 16 | 43 | 37 |
| Blacks too powerful | | | | |
| All Respondents | 19% | 22 | 32 | 27 |
| Whites | 31% | 26 | 33 | 10 |
| Blacks | 5% | 18 | 32 | 45 |
| Blacks try to be helpful | | | | |
| All Respondents | 21% | 42 | 20 | 17 |
| Whites | 6% | 33 | 31 | 30 |
| Blacks | 38% | 49 | 9 | 4 |
| Blacks trustworthy | | | | |
| All Respondents | 10% | 40 | 32 | 18 |
| Whites | 4% | 27 | 35 | 34 |
| Blacks | 18% | 54 | 27 | 1 |
| Blacks need more power | | | | |
| All Respondents | 11% | 21 | 33 | 35 |
| Whites | 3% | 8 | 31 | 58 |
| Blacks | 20% | 36 | 35 | 9 |
| Blacks make world better | | | | |
| All Respondents | 23% | 35 | 24 | 18 |
| Whites | 5% | 24 | 37 | 34 |
| Blacks | 43% | 46 | 9 | 2 |
| Blacks need more money | | | | |
| All Respondents | 20% | 29 | 23 | 28 |
| Whites | 8% | 12 | 29 | 51 |
| Blacks | 33% | 47 | 16 | 4 |
| Blacks should be satisifed | | | | |
| All Respondents | 17% | 24 | 32 | 27 |
| Whites | 25% | 28 | 29 | 18 |
| Blacks | 8% | 19 | 35 | 38 |
| | (Better) | (Won't Change) | | (Worse) |
| Blacks better R's life | | | | |
| All Respondents | 38% | 34 | | 28 |
| Whites | 14% | 35 | | 51 |
| Blacks | 65% | 33 | | 2 |

Note: Percentages across each row total 100%.

**Table D.2**

Relationships between the Police and Black Protesters Identification Items

(all respondents, N = 283)

(gammas)

| | V29 / V60 | V34 / V65 | V35 / V66 | V28 / V59 | V30 / V61 | V32 / V63 | V33 / V64 | V36 / V67 | V37 / V68 |
|---|---|---|---|---|---|---|---|---|---|
| V29 Police Get Too Much Taxes | | | | | | | | | |
| V60 Blacks Get Too Much Taxes | | | | | | | | | |
| V34 Police Use Bad Language | .5 | | | | | | | | |
| V65 Blacks Use Bad Language | .5 | | | | | | | | |
| V35 Police Too Powerful | .6 | .6 | | | | | | | |
| V66 Blacks Too Powerful | .6 | .6 | | | | | | | |
| V28 Police Try to be Helpful | -.6 | -.5 | -.7 | | | | | | |
| V59 Blacks Try to be Helpful | -.5 | -.3 | -.4 | | | | | | |
| V30 Police Trustworthy | -.5 | -.5 | -.6 | .8 | | | | | |
| V61 Blacks Trustworthy | -.5 | -.5 | -.6 | .8 | | | | | |
| V32 Police Need More Power | -.2 | -.3 | -.5 | .6 | .5 | | | | |
| V63 Blacks Need More Power | -.5 | -.3 | -.5 | .7 | .7 | | | | |
| V33 Police Make World Better | -.4 | -.4 | -.6 | .8 | .7 | .6 | | | |
| V64 Blacks Make World Better | -.6 | -.5 | -.5 | .8 | .7 | .7 | | | |
| V36 Police Need More Money | -.5 | -.4 | -.5 | .5 | .5 | .4 | .5 | | |
| V67 Blacks Need More Money | -.6 | -.4 | -.6 | .6 | .6 | .7 | .7 | | |
| V37 Police Better R's Life | -.3 | -.3 | -.4 | .5 | .5 | .5 | .6 | .7 | |
| V68 Blacks Better R's Life | -.6 | -.5 | -.6 | .7 | .7 | .7 | .7 | .8 | |
| V31 Police Should Be Satisfied | .4 | .2 | .3 | -.2 | -.1 | .0 | -.1 | -.3 | -.3 |
| V62 Blacks Should Be Satisfied | .5 | .5 | .6 | -.4 | -.4 | -.4 | -.5 | -.4 | -.5 |

## Table D.3
### Relationships between the Police and Black Protesters Identification Items for Selected Subgroups
(gammas)

| | All Respondents | Whites | Blacks | Men | Women | 25 Years or Younger | Education† Low | Education† High | Low Income† Whites | Low Income† Blacks | South |
|---|---|---|---|---|---|---|---|---|---|---|---|
| **3-Item Cluster** | | | | | | | | | | | |
| 1 Get too much taxes vs. | .5 | .4 | .3 | .5 | .4 | .6 | .3 | .4 | .2 | .3 | .6 |
| Use bad language | .5 | .3 | .4 | .4 | .5 | .4 | .4 | .5 | .4 | .3 | .6 |
| 2 Get too much taxes vs. | .6 | .5 | .4 | .5 | .7 | .7 | .4 | .8 | .4 | .4 | .7 |
| Too powerful | .6 | .5 | .4 | .6 | .6 | .4 | .6 | .7 | .5 | .2 | .5 |
| 3 Use bad language vs. | .6 | .6 | .5 | .5 | .7 | .7 | .7 | .5 | .4 | .4 | .6 |
| Too powerful | .6 | .6 | .6 | .7 | .6 | .6 | .5 | .6 | .4 | .5 | .8 |
| **6-Item Cluster** | | | | | | | | | | | |
| 4 Try to be helpful vs. | .8 | .9 | .6 | .8 | .8 | .8 | .8 | .9 | .8 | .6 | .8 |
| Trustworthy | .8 | .7 | .6 | .8 | .7 | .8 | .8 | .8 | .6 | .5 | .7 |
| 5 Try to be helpful vs. | .6 | .6 | .5 | .6 | .5 | .5 | .6 | .8 | .6 | .3 | .4 |
| Need more power | .7 | .5 | .5 | .7 | .6 | .6 | .7 | .7 | .6 | .4 | .7 |
| 6 Try to be helpful vs. | .8 | .7 | .7 | .8 | .8 | .8 | .8 | .8 | .8 | .6 | .8 |
| Make world better | .8 | .7 | .5 | .8 | .8 | .8 | .8 | .6 | .8 | .3 | .7 |
| 7 Try to be helpful vs. | .5 | .6 | .3 | .5 | .5 | .5 | .6 | .5 | .3 | .5 | .5 |
| Need more money | .6 | .6 | .3 | .7 | .6 | .7 | .6 | .7 | .7 | .3 | .6 |
| 8 Try to be helpful vs. | .5 | .3 | .5 | .5 | .4 | .6 | .5 | .3 | .6 | .4 | .3 |
| Better R's life | .7 | .6 | .3 | .7 | .7 | .6 | .7 | .6 | .5 | .3 | .7 |
| 9 Trustworthy vs. | .5 | .5 | .4 | .5 | .5 | .4 | .7 | .7 | .4 | .6 | .5 |
| Need more power | .7 | .5 | .6 | .7 | .6 | .6 | .7 | .6 | .5 | .7 | .7 |

|  |  | (283) | (145) | (133) | (131) | (152) | (84) | (104) | (63) | (49) | (68) | (94) |
|---|---|---|---|---|---|---|---|---|---|---|---|---|
| 10 | Trustworthy vs. | .7 | .7 | .6 | .7 | .8 | .8 | .8 | .6 | .7 | .5 | .7 |
|  | Make world better | .7 | .7 | .5 | .7 | .8 | .7 | .8 | .6 | .7 | .5 | .7 |
| 11 | Trustworthy vs. | .5 | .5 | .3 | .5 | .5 | .5 | .4 | .5 | .1 | .4 | .5 |
|  | Need more money | .6 | .5 | .5 | .6 | .6 | .6 | .6 | .6 | .7 | .6 | .7 |
| 12 | Trustworthy vs. | .5 | .3 | .5 | .5 | .4 | .6 | .5 | .3 | .2 | .6 | .5 |
|  | Better R's life | .7 | .5 | .4 | .6 | .7 | .6 | .8 | .5 | .5 | .4 | .7 |
| 13 | Need more power vs. | .6 | .6 | .5 | .5 | .6 | .4 | .6 | .5 | .6 | .5 | .5 |
|  | Make world better | .7 | .6 | .5 | .7 | .8 | .5 | .7 | .8 | .6 | .4 | .7 |
| 14 | Need more power vs. | .4 | .5 | .3 | .6 | .3 | .4 | .5 | .5 | .4 | .4 | .3 |
|  | Need more money | .7 | .6 | .6 | .7 | .7 | .6 | .6 | .8 | .8 | .6 | .7 |
| 15 | Need more power vs. | .5 | .5 | .5 | .6 | .5 | .7 | .5 | .5 | .4 | .6 | .4 |
|  | Better R's life | .7 | .6 | .5 | .8 | .7 | .5 | .7 | .9 | .3 | .6 | .7 |
| 16 | Make world better vs. | .5 | .5 | .4 | .5 | .6 | .5 | .7 | .3 | .4 | .7 | .6 |
|  | Need more money | .7 | .7 | .3 | .7 | .7 | .6 | .7 | .8 | .9 | .3 | .7 |
| 17 | Make world better vs. | .6 | .6 | .6 | .7 | .5 | .7 | .6 | .6 | .7 | .5 | .5 |
|  | Better R's life | .7 | .5 | .3 | .7 | .7 | .5 | .7 | .7 | .6 | .3 | .7 |
| 18 | Need more money vs. | .7 | .7 | .6 | .7 | .6 | .7 | .7 | .7 | .8 | .8 | .7 |
|  | Better R's life | .8 | .6 | .5 | .8 | .8 | .7 | .8 | .6 | .6 | .8 | .8 |
| | N | (283) | (145) | (133) | (131) | (152) | (84) | (104) | (63) | (49) | (68) | (94) |

6-Item Cluster

Note: Top:     Police Identification Items
      Bottom: Black Identification Items

†See Appendix E for an explanation of these groups.

**Inter-item Relationships among All Respondents.** The gamma matrix of all identification items for the total population appears in Table D.2. The table is arranged to show the two main clusters which emerge from this analysis. A three-item cluster appears in the upper left corner; a six-item cluster appears in the lower right corner. The variables in the three-item cluster center on negative identification with the contenders, while those in the six-item cluster center on positive identification. The relationships for items within the two clusters range from .44 to .76, with more gammas toward the upper end of the range than the lower. Relationships between items falling in the two different clusters tend to be smaller in magnitude.

The stem which reads "should be satisfied" is shown at the bottom of Table D.2. It can be seen that the item shows low positive relationships to the cluster which contains the negatively worded items and low negative relationships to the cluster which contains the positively worded items, especially when the stem is applied to the police. Consequently, the "should be satisfied" stem was eliminated from further consideration for inclusion in the identification indices.

**Relationships between Items in Selected Subgroups.** Table D.3 shows relationships between items within the two clusters as they occur in selected demographic subgroups. Gammas between items are generally high. When the two sexes, the two races, those under 26, and those living in the South are considered, gammas are almost always .4 or more and, with very few exceptions, reach significant levels. Among those with low incomes, whether white or black, gammas tend to be lower, and a fair number fail to reach statistical significance even when their apparent magnitude seems reasonable enough. The failure of these gammas to reach significance is probably partly a function of the fact that these subgroups contain a relatively small number of cases and partly due to the skewed distribution of the items in some of these subgroups. Nevertheless, the generally low magnitude of these relationships does raise some questions as to the meaning of combined measures in low income groups. Similar remarks can be made about relationships in the highly educated group: the numbers are small; the responses are often very skewed among such people; and some of the gammas fail to achieve significance, although relationships between items are generally higher than is true for the low income groups.

Table D.4 summarizes the relationships between item pairs presented in Table D.3. The table is arranged so that the number of gammas of each size generated by all the inter-item relationships of a particular item are listed next to the item in question. Because each gamma reflects a relationship between two items, every gamma in

**Table D.4**

Summary of Relationships (gammas) for Item Pairs Presented in Table D.3
(all respondents, N = 283)

| | Number of Associations According to Size of the Gamma | | | | | | | | |
|---|---|---|---|---|---|---|---|---|---|
| | .1 | .2 | .3 | .4 | .5 | .6 | .7 | .8 | .9 |
| **NEGATIVE 3-ITEM CLUSTER** | | | | | | | | | |
| Get too much taxes† | | | | | | | | | |
|   Police | | 1 | 3 | 7 | 4 | 3 | 3 | 1 | |
|   Black Protesters | | 1 | 2 | 7 | 6 | 5 | 1 | | |
| Use bad language† | | | | | | | | | |
|   Police | | 1 | 3 | 5 | 5 | 5 | 3 | | |
|   Black Protesters | | | 2 | 6 | 5 | 7 | 1 | 1 | |
| Too Powerful† | | | | | | | | | |
|   Police | | | | 6 | 5 | 4 | 6 | 1 | |
|   Black Protesters | | 1 | | 3 | 5 | 10 | 2 | 1 | |
| **POSITIVE 6-ITEM CLUSTER** | | | | | | | | | |
| Try to be helpful | | | | | | | | | |
|   Police | | | 6 | 3 | 14 | 12 | 2 | 16 | 2 |
|   Black Protesters | | | 5 | 1 | 5 | 14 | 19 | 11 | |
| Trustworthy† | | | | | | | | | |
|   Police | 1 | 1 | 3 | 6 | 18 | 7 | 7 | 10 | 2 |
|   Black Protesters | | | | 2 | 10 | 16 | 19 | 8 | |
| Need more power | | | | | | | | | |
|   Police | | | | 4 | 11 | 22 | 14 | 3 | 1 |
|   Black Protesters | | | 1 | 2 | 8 | 16 | 22 | 5 | 1 |
| Make world better† | | | | | | | | | |
|   Police | | 1 | | 3 | 13 | 15 | 12 | 11 | |
|   Black Protesters | | | 5 | 1 | 7 | 6 | 24 | 11 | 1 |
| Need more money | | | | | | | | | |
|   Police | 1 | 1 | 6 | 8 | 21 | 7 | 9 | 2 | |
|   Black Protesters | | | 4 | | 3 | 21 | 17 | 9 | 1 |
| Better R's life | | | | | | | | | |
|   Police | | 1 | 5 | 5 | 18 | 13 | 11 | 2 | |
|   Black Protesters | | | 5 | 2 | 9 | 11 | 19 | 8 | 1 |

†These items were included in the Identification Indices.

Table D.2 is counted twice in Table D.3—once for each of the items with which it is associated. It can be seen that there are very few gammas below .3, although there are more in the six- than in the three-item cluster. For example, there is a gamma of .1 associated with the item pair "trustworthy" versus "need more money." Of the two, more low gammas are associated with the latter stem than with the former. In addition, the gammas on this item pair differ more between the police identification item and the black protesters identification item for the "need for money" stem than for the "trustworthy" stem. Consequently, it was decided not to include the "need more money" stem in the indices. The "better R's life" item also generated a relatively large number of low gammas (.3 or less) and few very high gammas (.8 or more). In addition, this item is worded in such a way that it generates a fairly large amount of missing data; therefore, it was also deleted from the indices.

**Index Construction.** On the basis of these analyses two indices were constructed from the item pool, an Anti-Identification Index and a Positive Identification Index. The former contained the items "(Black protesters/Police) are getting more than their share of the tax dollar," "Most (black protesters/policemen) are people who use bad language and are disrespectful," and "(Black protesters/Police) are getting so much power that the average citizen has to worry." The index was scored by summing responses to constituent items according to a

**Table D.5**

Construction of the Anti-Identification Indices
(all respondents, N = 283)

**Anti-Police**
**Identification Index**

|  | Low |  |  |  | High | Total |
|---|---|---|---|---|---|---|
| Original Score | 3 | 4-5 | 6 | 7-8 | 9-12 | |
| Recoded Score | 1 | 2 | 3 | 4 | 5 | |
| Percent | 17 | 29 | 23 | 21 | 10 | 100% |

(Missing Data = 1.0%)

**Anti-Black Protesters**
**Identification Index**

|  | Low |  |  |  | High | Total |
|---|---|---|---|---|---|---|
| Original Score | 3 | 4-5 | 6 | 7-8 | 9-12 | |
| Recoded Score | 1 | 2 | 3 | 4 | 5 | |
| Percent | 11 | 23 | 16 | 27 | 23 | 100% |

(Missing Data = 1.0%)

simple additive model, so that the more negative the feelings the respondent expressed toward the group in question, the higher the score on the Anti-Identification Index. The index was constructed in parallel form for police and for black protesters. Details of index construction are given in Table D.5.

The Positive Identification Index contains the following items: "Most (police/black protesters) are trying to be helpful," "Most (police/black protesters) are trustworthy," "In general, there would be fewer problems if (black protesters/police) had more power," and "Most (policemen/black protesters) are interested in making the world a better place for all of us." As in construction of the Anti-Identification Indices, scores on constituent items were summed. The index was constructed in parallel form for police and black protesters, so that the more positive feelings the respondent expressed about the group in question, the higher the score on the index. Details of index construction are given in Table D.6.

**Table D.6**

Construction of the Positive Identification Indices
(all respondents, N = 283)

**Positive Police Identification Index**

|                | Low |     |       |       |       | High | Total |
|----------------|-----|-----|-------|-------|-------|------|-------|
| Original Score | 4-7 | 8-9 | 10-11 | 12-13 | 14-15 | 16   |       |
| Recoded Score  | 1   | 2   | 3     | 4     | 5     | 6    |       |
| Percent        | 4   | 12  | 21    | 22    | 23    | 18   | 100%  |

(Missing Data = 0.0%)

**Positive Black Protesters Identification Index**

|                | Low |     |       |       |       | High | Total |
|----------------|-----|-----|-------|-------|-------|------|-------|
| Original Score | 4-7 | 8-9 | 10-11 | 12-13 | 14-15 | 16   |       |
| Recoded Score  | 1   | 2   | 3     | 4     | 5     | 6    |       |
| Percent        | 25  | 20  | 22    | 20    | 9     | 4    | 100%  |

(Missing Data = 0.1%)

Any of the four identification indices was scored as missing data if more than one of the constituent items had missing data. If only one constituent item had missing data, it was assigned a value equal to the average for the valid items.

# Appendix E

# DERIVED MEASURES

*Introduction*

Index construction in this study was based on specific criteria similar to those used in the 1969 national study of attitudes toward violence (Blumenthal et al. 1972, p. 301). Four principles were utilized in the construction of the indices:

1) Constituent items must be statistically related.

2) Structural relationships between items must be stable across heterogeneous subgroups of the population.

3) The final result of combining several items was to be a three to seven category scale with an approximately rectangular distribution.

4) In general, a high score on the index implies a high amount of the characteristic being measured.

This section describes the procedure used to combine various items into indices. First the constituent items will be presented in the format in which they appeared in the interview schedule, then the interrelationships between all items will be presented for the total population, and next, the stability of item interrelationships within specific subgroups of the population will be examined. Finally, the items selected for index construction will be given. The results of combining the items will be shown in tables giving the summed scores, recoded scores, and percentage distribution for each index.

The following population subgroups were defined and used to examine the stability of interitem relationships:

1) Race
   a) Black respondents
   b) White respondents
2) Sex
   a) Men
   b) Women

3) Age
   a) Age 25 years or younger
   b) Age 40 years or older
4) Education
   a) Low education respondents (tenth grade education or less)
   b) High education respondents (one year of college or more)
5) Income[1]
   a) Low income whites (whites earning less than or equal to $7,999 per year)
   b) Low income blacks (blacks earning less than or equal to $5,999 per year)
6) Interview Region
   South (respondents sampled in Harris County, Texas; East Carroll, Louisiana; Atlanta, Georgia; and Montgomery, Alabama).

## THE ALTRUISM INDEX

The original items considered for inclusion in the Altruism Index are presented in Table E.1. For each item the respondent was asked to respond to a Likert-type, four point response scale: "disagree a great deal," coded 1; "disagree somewhat," coded 2; "agree somewhat," coded 3; and "agree a great deal," coded 4.

The relationships among the items shown above are given in Table E.2 for the total population and selected subgroups. Even though the items interrelate reasonably well for the total population, there is considerable variation across the different subgroups with a number of low gammas, including a negative relationship. Table E.3 shows that a disproportionate number of the low relationships are associated with the items on the "Golden Rule," being a "Good Samaritan," and "concern

### Table E.1
#### Items Measuring Altruism
##### (1972 reinterview)

Most people try to apply the Golden Rule.
Most people will be "Good Samaritans" if given the chance.
Most people go out of their way to help someone in trouble.
The typical person is concerned about the problems of others.
Most people would stop and help a person whose car has broken down on the road.

Note: These items were taken from Wrightman's Philosophy of Human Nature Scales (L. Wrightman, "Measurement of Philosophies of Human Nature," *Psychological Reports* 14:743-775) and also appear in John Robinson and P. R. Shaver, *Measures of Social Psychological Attitudes* (Ann Arbor: Survey Research Center, Institute for Social Research, The University of Michigan, 1969), pp. 517-525.

[1] Blacks and whites were skewed in opposite directions on income. Far fewer whites than blacks earned an income below $5,999; likewise, far fewer blacks than whites earned an income above $7,999.

**Table E.2**

Relationships between Items Measuring Altruism for All Respondents and Selected Subgroups
(1972 reinterview)
(gammas)

| | All Respondents | Whites | Blacks | Men | Women | 25 Years or Younger | 40 Years or Older | Low Education | High Education | Low Income Whites | Low Income Blacks | South |
|---|---|---|---|---|---|---|---|---|---|---|---|---|
| **Golden Rule vs.** | | | | | | | | | | | | |
| Good Samaritan | .4 | .5 | .3 | .4 | .4 | .3 | .4 | .1 | .5 | .5 | .2 | .1 |
| Go out of way | .4 | .4 | .4 | .3 | .4 | .3 | .4 | .2 | .6 | .6 | .5 | .3 |
| Concerned with others | .4 | .3 | .5 | .5 | .3 | .5 | .4 | .4 | .4 | .5 | .5 | .4 |
| Help with car | .3 | .4 | .4 | .3 | .3 | .3 | .4 | .3 | .3 | .4 | .3 | .2 |
| **Good Samaritan vs.** | | | | | | | | | | | | |
| Go out of way | .5 | .6 | .6 | .5 | .6 | .6 | .4 | .4 | .7 | .4 | .5 | .6 |
| Concerned with others | .5 | .5 | .4 | .5 | .5 | .5 | .5 | .3 | .9 | .6 | -.2 | .4 |
| Help with car | .5 | .4 | .6 | .4 | .5 | .4 | .4 | .4 | .6 | .3 | .6 | .5 |
| **Go out of way vs.** | | | | | | | | | | | | |
| Concerned with others | .4 | .3 | .5 | .4 | .4 | .5 | .5 | .5 | .4 | .5 | .4 | .3 |
| Help with car | .5 | .4 | .7 | .6 | .5 | .7 | .4 | .5 | .4 | .2 | .7 | .4 |
| **Concerned with others vs.** | | | | | | | | | | | | |
| Help with car | .4 | .3 | .5 | .3 | .5 | .5 | .5 | .2 | .5 | .7 | .3 | .3 |
| N | (240) | (120) | (116) | (115) | (125) | (72) | (110) | (85) | (54) | (39) | (60) | (82) |

**Table E.3**

Summary of Relationships (gammas) for Items Measuring Altruism
Presented in Table E.2
(1972 reinterview respondents, N = 240)

| | Number of Associations According to Size of the Gamma | | | | | | | | |
| | -.2 | .1 | .2 | .3 | .4 | .5 | .6 | .7 | .8 | .9 |
|---|---|---|---|---|---|---|---|---|---|---|
| Golden Rule | | | 2 | 3 | 14 | 18 | 9 | 2 | | |
| Good Samaritan | 1 | | 2 | 1 | 4 | 14 | 15 | 9 | 1 | 1 |
| Go out of way | | | | 2 | 5 | 17 | 12 | 8 | 4 | |
| Concern with others | 1 | | | 1 | 9 | 13 | 21 | 1 | 1 | 1 |
| Help with car | | | | 3 | 12 | 14 | 11 | 4 | 4 | |

with others." However, if the items pertaining to "Golden Rule" and "concern with others" are eliminated most of the low gammas are also eliminated. Consequently, these items were not included in the index. Using an additive model the values on the three remaining items were summed to form the Altruism Index:

Most people will be "Good Samaritans" if given the chance.

Most people go out of their way to help someone in trouble.

Most people would stop and help a person whose car has broken down on the road.

Respondents who failed to answer one of the three items were given a score on that item equal to the averaged value of the remaining two valid scores. A respondent with missing data on two or more items was scored as missing data. The summed scores, recoded scores, and percentage distribution for the Altruism Index are presented in Table E.4. The higher the score on the index, the more the respondent felt that others would act altruistically.

**Table E.4**

Construction of the Altruism-Index
(1972 reinterview respondents, N = 240)

| Altruism Index | Low | | | | High | |
|---|---|---|---|---|---|---|
| Summed Score | 3-6 | 7 | 8 | 9 | 10-12 | |
| Recoded Score | 1 | 2 | 3 | 4 | 5 | |
| Percent | 20 | 17 | 25 | 21 | 17 | 100% |
| (Missing Data = 0.8%) | | | | | | |

## THE AVOID PROBLEMS INDEX

The items considered for inclusion in the Avoid Problems Index (Neutrality Continuum) are listed in Table E.5. The respondent was asked to answer each item on a Likert-type four point scale: "disagree a great deal," coded 1; "disagree somewhat," coded 2; "agree somewhat," coded 3; "agree a great deal," coded 4.

**Table E.5**

Items Measuring the Neutrality Continuum

---

It is best to stay neutral on things others have strong feelings about.

People who make speeches stirring people up should be put in prison before they cause serious trouble.

It is better to avoid a fight than to take a chance on getting hurt.

There is no point in individual citizens trying to do anything about social problems, such as poverty.

---

Table E.6 shows moderate relationships between the above items. Interitem relationships for the various subgroups are less stable. The item expressing the powerlessness of citizens seems to relate to the others at lower levels, particularly among low income blacks and those with low education. There were other low relationships among low income blacks. Low relationships in this subgroup have been characteristic of these data as a whole. The subgroup is very small and index construction becomes virtually impossible if low relationships among low income blacks are made the basis of exclusion. Consequently, it was decided to proceed with index construction, excluding only the item referring to the powerlessness of citizens. However, the low gammas do indicate that caution must be exercised in interpreting data on the Avoid Problems Index for low income blacks. The following items were included in the Avoid Problems Index.

*It is best to stay neutral on things others have strong feelings about.*

*People who make speeches stirring people up should be put in prison before they cause serious trouble.*

*It is better to avoid a fight than to take a chance on getting hurt.*

Values on the above items were summed to form the Avoid Problems Index. The summed scores, recoded scores, and percentage distribution to the index are presented in Table E.7. The higher the score on the index, the more the respondent believed in remaining neutral or avoiding problems.

**Table E.6**

Relationships between Items Measuring the Neutrality Continuum
for All Respondents and Selected Subgroups
(gammas)

| | All Respondents | Blacks | Men | Women | 25 Years or Younger | Low Education | Low Income Whites | Low Income Blacks | South |
|---|---|---|---|---|---|---|---|---|---|
| **Best to stay neutral vs.** | | | | | | | | | |
| Imprison agitators | .3 | .3 | .3 | .4 | .6 | .3 | .3 | .1 | .3 |
| Better to avoid fight | .4 | .4 | .5 | .3 | .5 | .4 | .7 | .3 | .5 |
| Citizens' powerlessness | .4 | .4 | .4 | .5 | .2 | .2 | .7 | .0 | .4 |
| **Imprison agitators vs.** | | | | | | | | | |
| Better to avoid fight | .4 | .4 | .5 | .4 | .4 | .5 | .5 | .2 | .5 |
| Citizens' powerlessness | .3 | .3 | .2 | .4 | .2 | .1 | .3 | .1 | .2 |
| **Better to avoid fight vs.** | | | | | | | | | |
| Citizens' powerlessness | .4 | .4 | .5 | .2 | .3 | .3 | .5 | .4 | .4 |
| N | (283) | (133) | (131) | (152) | (84) | (104) | (49) | (68) | (94) |

**Table E.7**

Construction of the Avoid Problems Index
(all respondents, N = 283)

| Avoid Problems Index | Low | | | | | High | |
|---|---|---|---|---|---|---|---|
| Summed Score | 3-6 | 7 | 8 | 9 | 10 | 11-12 | |
| Recoded Score | 1 | 2 | 3 | 4 | 5 | 6 | |
| Percent | 17 | 15 | 20 | 20 | 17 | 11 | 100% |

(Missing Data = 0.7%)

A respondent who failed to answer one item was given a score on that item based on the average of the two valid responses. Respondents with missing data on two of the three items were reported as missing data on the index.

## THE INTERNAL-EXTERNAL CONTROL INDICES

The item pool for the three internal-external control indices is presented in Table E.8. As can be seen, the items are grouped under headings denoting the specific dimension of internal-external control. Preceding the items in the reinterview was this statement:

*In each of the next questions, I'm going to read you two sentences. Would you tell me the one that comes closer to the way you feel things **actually** are in life. Be sure it's the way things actually **are** in life, not the way you'd like them to be.*

The interviewer continued inquiring of the respondent which of the two items came closest to the way he felt things actually were in life until all the items had been read. It should be noted that the internal-external dimension in the items "work hard for success" (control ideology set) and "skills vs. no job" (system blame set) are opposite that of the other items. This is reflected in several negative interrelationships in the tables below.

It was our intent to replicate scales among the internal-external control items originally produced by Gurin et al. (1969). However, gammas among the items for the total population (Tables E.9-E.11) show some relationships are very weak between items in the control ideology and system blame sets. As can be seen in Table E.10, the control ideology item "work hard for success" has a low relationship to "people don't get breaks." Likewise, among the system blame items "born poor: less chance" has a low relationship to "skills vs. no jobs."

## Table E.8

### Items Measuring the Internal-External Control Dimension
(1972 reinterview)

Personal Control Items

When I make plans, I am almost certain that I can make them work.

It is not always wise to plan too far ahead because many things turn out to be a matter of good or bad luck anyhow.

What happens to me is my own doing.

Sometimes I feel that I don't have enough control over the direction my life is taking.

I've usually felt pretty sure my life would work out the way I wanted it to.

There are times when I haven't been very sure that my life would work out the way I wanted it to.

System Blame Items

People who are born poor have less chance to get ahead than other people.

People who have the ability and work hard have the same chance as anyone else, even if their parents were poor.

It's the lack of skills and abilities that keep most unemployed people from getting a job; if they had the skills most of them could get a job.

Many people with skills can't get a job; there just aren't any jobs for them.

Most people who are unemployed just haven't had the right breaks in life.

Most people who are unemployed have had the opportunities; they haven't made use of the opportunities that came their way.

Control Ideology Items

Becoming a success is a matter of hard work; luck has little or nothing to do with it.

Getting a good job depends mainly on being in the right place at the right time.

Knowing the right people is important in deciding whether a person will get ahead.

People will get ahead in life if they have the skills and do a good job; knowing the right people has nothing to do with it.

People who don't do well in life often work hard, but the breaks just don't come their way.

Some people just don't use the breaks that come their way; if they don't do well, it's their fault.

Note: Items were taken from P. B. Gurin, G. Gurin, R. Lao, and M. Beattie, "Internal-External Control in the Motivational Dynamics of Negro Youth," *Journal of Social Issues* 25 (1969):29-54.

## Table E.9

### Relationships between Items Measuring-Personal Control
(1972 reinterview respondents, N = 240)
(gammas)

|  | I Control My Life | My Life Works Out O.K. |
|---|---|---|
| I can make plans work | .6 | .4 |
| I control my life |  | .5 |
| My life works out o.k. |  |  |

**Table E.10**

Relationships between Items Measuring Control Ideology
(1972 reinterview respondents, N = 240)
(gammas)

|  | Knowing the Right People | People Don't Get Breaks |
|---|---|---|
| Work hard for success | -.5 | -.1 |
| Knowing the right people |  | .4 |
| People don't get breaks |  |  |

**Table E.11**

Relationships between Items Measuring System Blame
(1972 reinterview respondents, N = 240)
(gammas)

|  | Skills vs. No Jobs | Unemployed: No Breaks |
|---|---|---|
| Born poor: less chance | .1 | .6 |
| Skills vs. no jobs |  | -.4 |
| Unemployed: no breaks |  |  |

Tables E.12-E.14 show the interrelationships among items in the personal control set, the control ideology set, and the system blame set within population subgroups. It can be seen that, in general, relationships are not maintained across subgroups. In particular, relationships between items in the control ideology set and the system blame set are often low or nonexistent.

In spite of the failure of the internal-external control items to meet most criteria established as rules for index construction in this study, we proceeded to construct indices based on earlier scales described by Gurin et al. (1969) in order to replicate their internal-external dimension. Three indices consisting of three items were constructed. A respondent scoring missing data on any one of the items in these three indices was coded missing data on the index.

The Personal Control Index is detailed in Table E.15. The higher the score on the index, the more the individual believed himself in control of his fate. The Control Ideology Index is summarized in Table E.16. The higher the score on the index, the more the individual believed that people generally have control over their lives. Table E.17 presents a summary of the System Blame Index. The higher the score on the index, the more the individual attributed responsibility for failure to the system.

**Table E.12**

Relationships between Items Measuring Personal Control for Selected Subgroups
(1972 reinterview respondents, N = 240)
(gammas)

| | Whites | Blacks | Men | Women | 25 Years or Younger | 40 Years or Older | Low Education | High Education | Low Income Whites | Low Income Blacks | South |
|---|---|---|---|---|---|---|---|---|---|---|---|
| I can make plans work vs. | | | | | | | | | | | |
| I control my life | .7 | .5 | .7 | .6 | .2 | .8 | .4 | .7 | .6 | .2 | .4 |
| My life works out o.k. | .5 | .3 | .3 | .5 | .2 | .5 | .2 | .7 | .3 | .4 | .3 |
| I control my life vs. | | | | | | | | | | | |
| My life works out o.k. | .6 | .5 | .5 | .6 | .7 | .2 | .3 | .7 | .0 | .1 | .4 |
| N | (120) | (116) | (115) | (125) | (72) | (110) | (85) | (54) | (39) | (60) | (82) |

## Table E.13

Relationships between Items Measuring the Control Ideology for Selected Subgroups
(1972 reinterview respondents, N = 240)
(gammas)

| | Whites | Blacks | Men | Women | 25 Years or Younger | 40 Years or Older | Low Education | High Education | Low Income Whites | Low Income Blacks | South |
|---|---|---|---|---|---|---|---|---|---|---|---|
| **Work hard for success vs.** | | | | | | | | | | | |
| Knowing the right people | -.7 | -.3 | -.4 | -.6 | -.7 | -.5 | -.4 | -.3 | -.7 | -.6 | -.6 |
| People don't get breaks | -.3 | -.1 | .0 | -.3 | -.4 | .2 | .0 | -.2 | -.4 | -.3 | -.1 |
| **Knowing the right people vs.** | | | | | | | | | | | |
| People don't get breaks | .1 | .6 | .2 | .5 | .5 | .3 | .6 | -.2 | .4 | .6 | .2 |
| N | (120) | (116) | (115) | (125) | (72) | (110) | (85) | (54) | (39) | (60) | (82) |

## Table E.14

Relationships between Items Measuring System Blame for Selected Subgroups
(1972 reinterview respondents, N = 240)
(gammas)

| | Whites | Blacks | Men | Women | 25 Years or Younger | 40 Years or Older | Low Education | High Education | Low Income Whites | Low Income Blacks | South |
|---|---|---|---|---|---|---|---|---|---|---|---|
| **Born poor: less chance vs.** | | | | | | | | | | | |
| Skills vs. no jobs | .1 | .1 | -.2 | .3 | -.2 | .0 | .0 | .6 | .0 | .6 | .1 |
| Unemployed: no breaks | .7 | .6 | .7 | .6 | .3 | .9 | .7 | .8 | .5 | .8 | .7 |
| **Skills vs. no jobs vs.** | | | | | | | | | | | |
| Unemployed: no breaks | -.5 | -.3 | -.4 | -.4 | -.5 | -.3 | -.3 | -.2 | -.4 | -.3 | -.1 |
| N | (120) | (116) | (115) | (125) | (72) | (110) | (85) | (54) | (39) | (60) | (82) |

### Table E.15

Construction of the Personal Control Index
(1972 reinterview respondents, N = 240)

| Personal Control Index | Low | | | High | |
|---|---|---|---|---|---|
| Summed Score | 9 | 7 | 5 | 3 | |
| Recoded Score | 1 | 2 | 3 | 4 | |
| Percent | 24 | 32 | 28 | 16 | 100% |
| (Missing Data = 0.1%) | | | | | |

### Table E.16

Construction of the Control Ideology Index
(1972 reinterview respondents, N = 240)

| Control Ideology Index | Low | | | High | |
|---|---|---|---|---|---|
| Summed Score | 3 | 5 | 7 | 9 | |
| Recoded Score | 1 | 2 | 3 | 4 | |
| Percent | 12 | 25 | 36 | 27 | 100% |
| (Missing Data = 0.3%) | | | | | |

### Table E.17

Construction of the System Blame Index
(1972 reinterview respondents, N = 240)

| System Blame Index | Low | | | High | |
|---|---|---|---|---|---|
| Summed Score | 3 | 5 | 7 | 9 | |
| Recoded Score | 1 | 2 | 3 | 4 | |
| Percent | 37 | 34 | 23 | 6 | 100% |
| (Missing Data = 0.4%) | | | | | |

## THE IS DISSENT VIOLENCE? AND
## IS DISRUPTION VIOLENCE? INDICES

Table E.18 presents the original items considered for inclusion in the Is Dissent Violence? and Is Disruption Violence? Indices as they appeared on a card on which the respondent was asked to indicate his responses. The card was presented to the respondent after the following was read:

*Here are some political actions people have taken to bring about change. We would like to know how violent you think each of these is, in and of itself. Do you think being in a sit-in is at the violent end or at the not-violent end or in between? Using the line at the top of the card, please point to where you think it belongs. You may use any number on the line.*

**Table E.18**

Items Considered for Inclusion in the Is Dissent Violence? and
Is Disruption Violence? Indices

|  | Not Violent | | | | | | Violent |
|---|---|---|---|---|---|---|---|
| Being in a sit-in | | | | | | | |
|  | 1 | 2 | 3 | 4 | 5 | 6 | 7 |
| Signing a petition | | | | | | | |
|  | 1 | 2 | 3 | 4 | 5 | 6 | 7 |
| Holding a protest meeting | | | | | | | |
|  | 1 | 2 | 3 | 4 | 5 | 6 | 7 |
| Holding a march without a permit from city officials | | | | | | | |
|  | 1 | 2 | 3 | 4 | 5 | 6 | 7 |
| Filing a Federal lawsuit in court | | | | | | | |
|  | 1 | 2 | 3 | 4 | 5 | 6 | 7 |
| Interfering with work in an office building | | | | | | | |
|  | 1 | 2 | 3 | 4 | 5 | 6 | 7 |
| Holding a march with a permit from city officials | | | | | | | |
|  | 1 | 2 | 3 | 4 | 5 | 6 | 7 |
| Blocking traffic as a protest | | | | | | | |
|  | 1 | 2 | 3 | 4 | 5 | 6 | 7 |
| Holding a protest meeting without a permit | | | | | | | |
|  | 1 | 2 | 3 | 4 | 5 | 6 | 7 |

The interitem relationships for the total population are presented in Table E.19. The relationships suggest two sets of item clusters. One cluster includes "sit-in," "petition," "protest meeting," "filing lawsuit," and "march with a permit." The second cluster includes "protest meeting without a permit," "march without a permit," "interfering with work," and "blocking traffic." The first cluster had gammas ranging from .3 to .6. The second cluster had a large number of small and inconsistent gammas ranging from .1 to .7. The item "interfering with work" did not relate well to the other items but was retained for subgroup analysis.

**Table E.19**

Relationships between Items Considered for Inclusion in the
Is Disruption Violence? and Is Dissent Violence? Indices
(all respondents, N =283)
(gammas)

|  | V117 | V118 | V120 | V122 | V124 | V119 | V121 | V123 |
|---|---|---|---|---|---|---|---|---|
| V116 Sit-in | .6 | .5 | .4 | .3 | .3 | .4 | .2 | .2 |
| V117 Petition |  | .5 | .6 | .4 | .3 | .4 | .1 | .2 |
| V118 Protest meeting |  |  | .5 | .4 | .4 | .4 | .1 | .3 |
| V120 Filing Lawsuit |  |  |  | .4 | .2 | .3 | .2 | .3 |
| V122 March with a permit |  |  |  |  | .2 | .3 | .1 | .3 |
| V124 Protest meeting<br>without a permit |  |  |  |  |  | .7 | .4 | .5 |
| V119 March without<br>a permit |  |  |  |  |  |  | .4 | .6 |
| V121 Interfering with work |  |  |  |  |  |  |  | .5 |
| V123 Blocking traffic |  |  |  |  |  |  |  |  |

Table E.20 shows the interitem relationships among selected subgroups for the items in the first cluster, the Is Dissent Violence? cluster. "Filing lawsuit" and "march with a permit" showed a number of low relationships in this analysis. Consequently, these items were not included in the index. The items "sit-in," "petition" and "protest meeting" showed relationships of moderate size. There is one gamma of .0 between "petition" and "protest meeting" in the high education subgroup. This relationship is associated with a highly skewed distribution of responses and should be regarded with some caution. There are also a number of relatively low gammas among low income blacks. Nevertheless, the Is Dissent Violence? Index was constructed by summing scores on "sit-in," "petition," and "protest meeting."

Details of the index construction are given in Table E.21. The higher the score on the Is Dissent Violence? Index, the more the respondent believed dissent to be violent.

Interitem relationships for the second cluster, the Is Disruption Violence? cluster, are presented in Table E.22 for selected subgroups in the population. The item "interfering with work" did not show consistent relationships to "protest meeting without a permit." The interviewers had raised doubt as to the suitability of the item about holding a protest meeting without a permit. Respondents were apparently confused by the item, and several stated that they didn't know one needed a permit to hold a protest meeting. Consequently this item was excluded from index construction.

The Is Disruption Violence? Index was formed by summing the

## Table E.20

### Relationships between Items Inquiring Whether Dissent Is Violence for Selected Subgroups
(all respondents, N = 283)
(gammas)

| | Whites | Blacks | Men | Women | 25 Years or Younger | 40 Years or Older | Low Education | High Education | Low Income Whites | Low Income Blacks | South |
|---|---|---|---|---|---|---|---|---|---|---|---|
| **Sit-in vs.** | | | | | | | | | | | |
| Petition | .7 | .5 | .6 | .6 | .7 | .6 | .5 | .3 | .5 | .3 | .4 |
| Protest meeting | .5 | .5 | .5 | .5 | .4 | .5 | .5 | .6 | .6 | .3 | .4 |
| Filing lawsuit | .3 | .4 | .2 | .4 | .4 | .6 | .5 | .3 | .5 | .4 | .2 |
| March with a permit | .4 | .2 | .4 | .2 | .1 | .4 | .3 | .5 | .4 | .0 | .2 |
| **Petition vs.** | | | | | | | | | | | |
| Protest meeting | .6 | .4 | .5 | .5 | .6 | .5 | .5 | .0 | .7 | .3 | .6 |
| Filing lawsuit | .6 | .7 | .5 | .7 | .4 | .7 | .7 | .6 | .6 | .7 | .5 |
| March with a permit | .4 | .5 | .4 | .3 | .2 | .4 | .3 | .7 | .4 | .0 | .2 |
| **Protest meeting vs.** | | | | | | | | | | | |
| Filing lawsuit | .5 | .5 | .6 | .5 | .6 | .6 | .5 | .3 | .7 | .5 | .4 |
| March with a permit | .5 | .2 | .5 | .2 | .3 | .3 | .2 | .5 | .3 | .0 | .3 |
| N | (145) | (133) | (131) | (152) | (84) | (129) | (104) | (63) | (49) | (68) | (94) |

values on "march without a permit," "interfering with work," and "blocking traffic." Details of the index construction for the Is Disruption Violence? Index are shown in Table E.23. The higher the score on the index, the more the respondent believed disruptive activities to be violent.

**Table E.21**

Construction of the Is Dissent Violence? Index
(all respondents, N = 283)

| Is Dissent Violence? Index | Low | | | | High | |
|---|---|---|---|---|---|---|
| Summed Scores | 3 | 4-5 | 6-7 | 8-9 | 10-18 | |
| Recoded Scores | 1 | 2 | 3 | 4 | 5 | |
| Percent | 29 | 18 | 21 | 16 | 16 | 100% |
| (Missing Data = 4.0%) | | | | | | |

**Table E.23**

Construction of the Is Disruption Violence? Index
(all respondents, N = 283)

| Is Disruption Violence? Index | Low | | | | High | |
|---|---|---|---|---|---|---|
| Summed Score | 3 | 4-5 | 6-7 | 8-9 | 10-18 | |
| Recoded Score | 1 | 2 | 3 | 4 | 5 | |
| Percent | 17 | 19 | 21 | 21 | 22 | 100% |
| (Missing Data = 1.0%) | | | | | | |

Missing data were handled on both the Is Dissent Violence? and Is Disruption Violence? Indices in the following manner. A respondent with one missing data score had his score replaced by an average score derived from the two valid codes. If data were missing on two of the three items, the index was coded as missing data for that respondent.

## THE PHYSICAL PUNISHMENT INDEX

The items inquiring about physical punishment were introduced by the following question:

*Here is a situation that sometimes occurs with young children. Think how you would handle this situation if you had a child about five or six years old.*

*You have something very important that you want your child to do for you right away. He is watching television. You tell him what you want done and ask him to do it right away. He says he'll do it when the program is over, in about an hour.*

*What would you do if something like that happened?*

**Table E.22**

Relationships between Items Inquiring Whether Disruption Is Violence for Selected Subgroups

(all respondents, N = 283)

(gammas)

| | Whites | Blacks | Men | Women | 25 Years or Younger | 40 Years or Older | Low Education | High Education | Low Income Whites | Low Income Blacks | South |
|---|---|---|---|---|---|---|---|---|---|---|---|
| **March without a permit vs.** | | | | | | | | | | | |
| Interfering with work | .4 | .5 | .4 | .4 | .3 | .4 | .5 | .4 | .3 | .5 | .4 |
| Blocking traffic | .5 | .6 | .6 | .5 | .5 | .5 | .6 | .7 | .4 | .6 | .6 |
| Protest meeting without a permit | .6 | .8 | .6 | .7 | .7 | .6 | .7 | .6 | .6 | .7 | .5 |
| **Interfering with work vs.** | | | | | | | | | | | |
| Blocking traffic | .5 | .5 | .5 | .6 | .3 | .6 | .6 | .6 | .3 | .4 | .4 |
| Protest meeting without a permit | .3 | .5 | .3 | .4 | .2 | .3 | .4 | .3 | .1 | .5 | .2 |
| **Blocking traffic vs.** | | | | | | | | | | | |
| Protest meeting without a permit | .5 | .6 | .6 | .5 | .4 | .5 | .6 | .5 | .5 | .7 | .5 |
| N | (145) | (133) | (131) | (152) | (84) | (129) | (104) | (63) | (49) | (68) | (94) |

The respondent was given a chance to respond to this open-ended question. He was then asked to respond to a series of items indicating a variety of ways of handling the situation. The items were introduced by the following stem:

> *This is a list of things that some parents we've talked with say they do when such things happened. When he says he will do something later and you want it done **right away**, how often would you do each of the following?*

To each of the items (Table E.24) the respondent could answer "never," "rarely," "sometimes," or "usually."

### Table E.24

#### Items Measuring Physical Punishment

Hit or spank him.
Spank him until he can't sit down.
Tell him you will hit or spank him if he doesn't do it right away.
Hit him with a belt or paddle.

Interrelationships between the items above are presented in Table E.25 for all respondents. The items were moderately to highly related, with the exception of the relationship between "spank—can't sit down" and "threaten to hit." Table E.25 also shows relationships among the physical punishment items in a variety of subgroups. The item "threaten to hit" produced a number of low relationships in several subgroups. Relationships between the other items showed moderate to high interitem correlations except for one low gamma among southern respondents.

The Physical Punishment Index was formed by summing the values on the following items:

> *Hit or spank him.*
> *Spank him until he can't sit down.*
> *Hit him with a belt or paddle.*

A respondent with missing data on one of the three items in the Physical Punishment Index had his score replaced with a value derived from the average of his two valid scores. Missing data on two of the three items were scored as missing data on the Physical Punishment Index. Details of the index construction for the Physical Punishment Index are outlined in Table E.26. The higher the score on the index, the more the respondent believed it necessary to use physical punishment in the situation described.

**Table E.25**

**Relationships between Items Measuring Physical Punishment
for All Respondents and Selected Subgroups**

(gammas)

| | All Respondents | Whites | Blacks | Men | Women | 25 Years or Younger | Low Education | Low Income Whites | Low Income Blacks | South |
|---|---|---|---|---|---|---|---|---|---|---|
| **Hit or spank vs.** | | | | | | | | | | |
| Spank—can't sit down | .5 | .5 | .5 | .6 | .5 | .6 | .4 | .5 | .5 | .4 |
| Threaten to hit | .7 | .7 | .5 | .8 | .6 | .7 | .6 | .7 | .4 | .5 |
| Hit with belt | .7 | .7 | .7 | .7 | .7 | .8 | .8 | .8 | .9 | .7 |
| **Spank—can't sit down vs.** | | | | | | | | | | |
| Threaten to hit | .3 | .3 | .2 | .5 | .1 | .4 | .0 | .4 | .0 | .0 |
| Hit with belt | .5 | .6 | .4 | .4 | .5 | .6 | .4 | .6 | .4 | .1 |
| **Threaten to hit vs.** | | | | | | | | | | |
| Hit with belt | .5 | .5 | .3 | .7 | .4 | .6 | .5 | .7 | .1 | .5 |
| N | (283) | (145) | (133) | (131) | (152) | (84) | (104) | (49) | (68) | (94) |

**Table E.26**

Construction of the Physical Punishment Index
(all respondents, N = 283)

| Physical Punishment Index | Low | | | | High | |
|---|---|---|---|---|---|---|
| Summed Score | 3-4 | 5 | 6 | 7 | 8-12 | |
| Recoded Score | 1 | 2 | 3 | 4 | 5 | |
| Percent | 24 | 17 | 17 | 17 | 25 | 100% |

(Missing Data = 0.3%)

## THE POLITICAL CYNICISM INDEX

Items measuring political cynicism are listed in Table E.27. Interrelationships among the political cynicism items show a reasonable degree of consistency, with gammas ranging from .4 to .8 (Table E.28). Relationships between items within selected population subgroups are also presented in Table E.28. The table shows that the item which asks whether or not people in government are smart people who know what they are doing had a number of low relationships with other items.

**Table E.27**

Items Measuring Political Cynicism

Do you think people in the government waste *a lot* of money we pay in taxes, waste *some* of it, or *don't waste very much of it?*
Not very much                Some                                    A lot

How much of the time do you think you can trust the government in Washington to do what is right—*just about always, most of the time,* or only *some of the time?*
Just about always            Most of the time                    Some of the time

Would you say the government is pretty much run by a *few big interests* looking out for themselves, or that it is run for the *benefit of all* the people?
Benefit of all               Few big interests

Do you feel that almost all of the people running the government are smart people who usually *know what they are doing,* or do you think that quite a few of them *don't seem to know what they're doing?*
Know what they're doing                  Don't know what they're doing

Do you think that *quite a few* of the people running the government are a little crooked, *not very many* are, or do you think *hardly any* of them are crooked at all?
Hardly any                   Not very many                       Quite a few

Note: Items were taken from J. P. Robinson, J. G. Rusk, and K. B. Head, *Measures of Political Attitudes* (Ann Arbor: Center for Political Studies, The Institute for Social Research, The University of Michigan, 1972), pp. 643-648.

## Table E.28

### Relationships between Items Measuring Political Cynicism for All Respondents and Selected Subgroups
(gammas)

| | All Respondents | Whites | Blacks | Men | Women | 25 Years or Younger | 40 Years or Older | Low Education | High Education | Low Income Whites | Low Income Blacks | South |
|---|---|---|---|---|---|---|---|---|---|---|---|---|
| **Government wastes taxes vs.** | | | | | | | | | | | | |
| Distrust in government | .6 | .8 | .5 | .4 | .8 | .7 | .7 | .6 | .6 | .9 | .6 | .6 |
| Government run for big interests | .6 | .7 | .6 | .6 | .6 | .6 | .7 | .8 | .3 | .7 | .7 | .7 |
| Government people smart | .4 | .3 | .5 | .4 | .3 | .4 | .3 | .4 | .5 | .4 | .4 | .3 |
| Government people crooked | .5 | .6 | .4 | .4 | .6 | .6 | .4 | .5 | .6 | .7 | .5 | .6 |
| **Distrust in government vs.** | | | | | | | | | | | | |
| Government run for big interests | .8 | .8 | .7 | .7 | .9 | .7 | .8 | .8 | .8 | .8 | .6 | .8 |
| Government people smart | .5 | .3 | .5 | .4 | .5 | .5 | .5 | .6 | .6 | .6 | .7 | .5 |
| Government people crooked | .7 | .7 | .6 | .7 | .8 | .9 | .7 | .8 | .7 | .6 | .6 | .7 |
| **Government run for big interests vs.** | | | | | | | | | | | | |
| Government people smart | .4 | .5 | .4 | .4 | .4 | .1 | .5 | .5 | .4 | .6 | .3 | .3 |
| Government people crooked | .7 | .8 | .7 | .7 | .7 | .8 | .7 | .7 | .8 | .7 | .6 | .8 |
| **Government people smart vs.** | | | | | | | | | | | | |
| Government people crooked | .4 | .2 | .3 | .3 | .4 | .4 | .3 | .5 | .5 | .5 | .3 | .5 |
| N | (283) | (145) | (133) | (131) | (152) | (84) | (129) | (104) | (63) | (49) | (68) | (94) |

Table E.29 summarizes the interitem relationships for the subgroups detailed in Table E.28 and shows clearly that the item "government people smart" shows more relationships of .3 or below than any other item. Consideration of the item makes it quite clear that responses to

**Table E.29**

Summary of Relationships (gammas) for Items Measuring Political
Cynicism Presented in Table E.28
(all respondents, N = 283)

| | | | Number of Associations According to Size of the Gamma | | | | | | |
| --- | --- | --- | --- | --- | --- | --- | --- | --- | --- |
| | .1 | .2 | .3 | .4 | .5 | .6 | .7 | .8 | .9 |
| Government wastes taxes | | | 5 | 10 | 6 | 15 | 8 | 3 | 1 |
| Distrust in government | | | 1 | 2 | 7 | 12 | 12 | 11 | 3 |
| Government run for big interests | 1 | | 3 | 5 | 3 | 8 | 15 | 12 | 1 |
| Government people smart | 1 | 1 | 11 | 15 | 15 | 4 | 1 | | |
| Government people crooked | | 1 | 3 | 6 | 7 | 9 | 14 | 6 | 1 |

the question may have quite different meanings depending on the frame of reference of the respondent. On the one hand, if a respondent is trusting he may say that people in government know what they are doing. On the other hand, a very cynical respondent may give the same response ("Of course, they know what they are doing, the bastards!"). Consequently, the item "government people smart" was not included in the index.

The following items were used to construct the Political Cynicism Index:

> *Do you think people in the government waste **a lot** of the money we pay in taxes, waste **some** of it, or **don't waste very much of it?***

> *How much of the time do you think you can trust the government in Washington to do what is right—**just about always, most of the time,** or only **some of the time?***

> *Would you say the government is pretty much run by a **few big interests** looking out for themselves, or that it is run for the **benefit of all** the people?*

> *Do you think that **quite a few** of the people running the government are a little crooked, **not very many** are, or do you think **hardly any** of them are crooked at all?*

Before summing the values for the above items, variance was equalized in the following manner. Each item with three code categories was increased by twice the value of the original code (i.e., respondents scoring "1," "2," or "3" received scores of "2," "4," and "6" respectively). A two code category item had each of its categories increased by three times the value of the original code (i.e., respondents scoring "1" or "2" received scores of "3" or "6" respectively). The derived values were summed to combine the items into the Political Cynicism Index.

A respondent scoring missing data on three or more of the Political Cynicism Index items was coded as having missing data on the index. Individuals scoring missing data on only one or two of the four items had their scores replaced with an average score derived from the two or three valid responses.

The construction of the Political Cynicism Index is outlined in Table E.30. The higher the score on the index, the more cynically the respondent viewed the government.

**Table E.30**

Construction of the Political Cynicism Index
(all respondents, N = 283)

| Political Cynicism Index | Low | | | High | |
|---|---|---|---|---|---|
| Summed Score | 9-15 | 16-19 | 20-22 | 24 | |
| Recoded Score | 1 | 2 | 3 | 4 | |
| Percent | 22 | 23 | 30 | 25 | 100% |
| (Missing Data = 1.0%) | | | | | |

## THE PROTEST BEHAVIORS INDEX

Items considered for inclusion in the Protest Behaviors Index inquire about the willingness of the respondent to engage in specific

**Table E.31**

Items Measuring Protest Behaviors

Sign a petition.
Hold a protest meeting with a permit.
Be in a sit-in.
Block traffic.
Interfere with work in an office building.

**Table E.32**

Relationships between Items Measuring Protest Behaviors
for All Respondents and Selected Subgroups
(gammas)

| | All Respondents | Men | Women | 25 Years or Younger | Low Education | Low Income Whites | Low Income Blacks | South |
|---|---|---|---|---|---|---|---|---|
| **Sign a petition vs.** | | | | | | | | |
| Protest meeting with permit | .7 | .9 | .5 | .9 | .6 | 1.0 | .5 | .7 |
| Be in a sit-in | .7 | 1.0 | .6 | .8 | .5 | 1.0 | .7 | .7 |
| Block traffic | 1.0 | 1.0 | 1.0 | 1.0 | 1.0 | 1.0 | 1.0 | 1.0 |
| Interfere with work | .4 | 1.0 | .2 | 1.0 | .1 | 1.0 | .0 | 1.0 |
| **Protest meeting with permit vs.** | | | | | | | | |
| Be in a sit-in | .8 | .9 | .8 | .9 | .8 | .6 | .8 | .6 |
| Block traffic | .8 | .8 | .8 | .6 | .7 | 1.0 | 1.0 | .6 |
| Interfere with work | .5 | .3 | .6 | .4 | .5 | .8 | .3 | .3 |
| **Be in a sit-in vs.** | | | | | | | | |
| Block traffic | 1.0 | .9 | 1.0 | .9 | .9 | 1.0 | 1.0 | .9 |
| Interfere with work | .8 | .7 | .9 | .7 | .6 | 1.0 | .7 | .8 |
| **Block traffic vs.** | | | | | | | | |
| Interfere with work | .9 | .8 | .9 | .9 | .9 | .9 | .8 | .9 |
| N | (283) | (131) | (152) | (84) | (104) | (49) | (68) | (94) |

behaviors to bring about change. The items were preceded by the following stem:

> *Which of the following things would you be willing to do to bring about a* **change you felt was very important?** *Would you . . .*

Then the respondent was asked the items which appear in Table E.31. The respondent was given a choice of replying "no," "not sure," or "yes" when asked whether or not he would be willing to perform each of the above actions to bring about a change he felt was very important.

Table E.32 presents the interitem relationships among all respondents and within selected subgroups. With the exception of the item refering to interfering with work, the items measuring protest behaviors showed strong interrelationships. "Interfere with work" produced a number of low relationships, particularly in relation to the items "protest meeting with a permit" and "sign a petition." In fact, "interfere with work" was so highly correlated with "block traffic" that it seemed that the two items were redundant.

Consequently, the item "interfere with work" was not included in the index construction. Because of its very skewed distribution among both blacks and whites, "sign a petition" was also excluded.

The following items were combined to form the Protest Behaviors Index:

> *Hold a protest meeting with a permit.*
> *Be in a sit-in.*
> *Block traffic.*

Individuals with missing data on two or more of the three items in the Protest Behaviors Index scored missing data on the index. Individuals with one missing data score had their scores calculated by averaging the values on the two valid items. Details of the index construction are presented in Table E.33. A high score on the Protest Behaviors Index indicates a high degree of willingness on the part of the respondent to participate in behaviors described in the three protest behaviors items above.

**Table E.33**

Construction of the Protest Behaviors Index
(all respondents, N = 283)

| Protest Behaviors Index | Low | | | High | |
|---|---|---|---|---|---|
| Summed Score | 3-4 | 5-6 | 7 | 8-9 | |
| Recoded Score | 1 | 2 | 3 | 4 | |
| Percent | 30 | 31 | 27 | 12 | 100% |

(Missing Data = 1.0%)

## THE PUNITIVE LAW ENFORCEMENT INDEX

Those items which measure the respondent's attitude toward stricter laws, tougher punishment, and law enforcement as a means of reducing violence are presented in Table E.34. Examination of the inter-item relationships for all respondents showed many low gammas between the punitive law enforcement items (Table E.35). The items

**Table E.34**

Items Measuring Attitudes toward Punitive and Stricter Laws
and Stricter Law Enforcement

---

There would be less violence if our present laws were always enforced.

| Disagree a great deal | Disagree somewhat | Agree somewhat | Agree a great deal |

One cause of violence is that punishments for breaking the law are not tough enough.

| Disagree a great deal | Disagree somewhat | Agree somewhat | Agree a great deal |

Some people tell us that new laws giving more severe punishments for violence are needed to reduce violence; others say such laws are not needed. Do you think that such new laws are needed or not?

New laws not needed            Not sure            New laws needed

Some people tell us that the police can't deal with violence because the law interferes with their work; others say the law does not interfere. What do you think? Do you think the law interferes a great deal or just somewhat?

| Law does not interfere | Not sure | Law interferes somewhat | Law interferes a great deal |

Some people tell us that the way to handle school problems is to have a much stricter discipline code. Others say the discipline codes are unfair and cause more trouble than they cure. Do you think stricter discipline codes will reduce violence, or do you think they will cause more trouble?

Stricter codes cause trouble            Not sure            Stricter codes reduce violence

Some people have told us that having policemen in the schools will help reduce violence. Others say having policemen in the schools helps cause the trouble. What do you say?

Policemen will cause trouble            Not sure            Policemen will reduce violence

**Table E.35**

Relationships between Items Measuring Attitudes toward
Punitive and Stricter Laws and Stricter Law Enforcement
(all respondents, N = 283)
(gammas)

|  | Not Tough Enough Punishments Cause Violence | Tougher Punishments Reduce Violence | Laws Interfere with Police | Stricter Codes Reduce Violence | Police in Schools Reduce Violence |
|---|---|---|---|---|---|
| Enforcing laws lessens violence | .6 | .2 | .3 | .4 | .2 |
| Not tough enough punishments cause violence |  | .4 | .4 | .6 | .3 |
| Tougher punishments reduce violence |  |  | .2 | .3 | .1 |
| Laws interfere with police |  |  |  | .3 | .2 |
| Stricter codes reduce violence |  |  |  |  | .4 |
| Police in schools reduce violence |  |  |  |  |  |

"tougher punishments reduce violence" and "police in schools reduce violence" had especially low relationships with other items. Consequently, these items were excluded from further consideration for index construction.

Interrelationships among the remaining items measuring attitudes toward punitive and stricter laws and law enforcement are presented for various subgroups in Table E.36. The table shows that the only items which relate consistently to each other in a variety of subgroups are:

*There would be less violence if our present laws were always enforced.*

*One cause of violence is that punishments for breaking the law are not tough enough.*

**Consequently, the Punitive Law Enforcement Index was formed by summing the values on these two items. A respondent scoring missing data on one item received a score equal to the value of his valid score on the other item. A respondent scoring missing data on both items was scored missing data on the index.**

## Table E.36

### Relationships between Items Measuring Attitudes toward Punitive and Stricter Laws and Law Enforcement for Selected Subgroups
(gammas)

| | Whites | Blacks | Men | Women | 25 Years or Younger | 40 Years or Older | Low Education | High Education | Low Income Whites | Low Income Blacks | South |
|---|---|---|---|---|---|---|---|---|---|---|---|
| **Enforcing laws lessens violence vs.** | | | | | | | | | | | |
| Not tough enough punishments cause violence | .7 | .5 | .6 | .6 | .4 | .7 | .6 | .7 | .7 | .4 | .4 |
| Laws interfere with police | .5 | .1 | .3 | .3 | .3 | .5 | .6 | .4 | .4 | .2 | .4 |
| Stricter codes reduce violence | .4 | .2 | .4 | .3 | .2 | .2 | .3 | .5 | .3 | .3 | .4 |
| **Not tough enough punishments cause violence vs.** | | | | | | | | | | | |
| Laws interfere with police | .6 | .1 | .4 | .3 | .0 | .5 | .5 | .5 | .2 | .1 | .3 |
| Stricter codes reduce violence | .7 | .3 | .6 | .5 | .3 | .4 | .6 | .6 | .0 | .1 | .5 |
| **Laws interfere with police vs.** | | | | | | | | | | | |
| Stricter codes reduce violence | .4 | .1 | .3 | .3 | .3 | .2 | .3 | .3 | .4 | .4 | .0 |
| N | (145) | (133) | (131) | (152) | (84) | (129) | (104) | (63) | (49) | (68) | (94) |

Table E.37 shows the summed values, recoded scores, and percentage distributions to the Punitive Law Enforcement Index. A high score on the index indicates a strong belief in the need for punitive measures and law enforcement.

### Table E.37

Construction of the Punitive Law Enforcement Index
(all respondents, N = 283)

| Punitive Law Enforcement Index | Low | | | | High | |
|---|---|---|---|---|---|---|
| Summed Score | 2-4 | 5 | 6 | 7 | 8 | |
| Recoded Score | 1 | 2 | 3 | 4 | 5 | |
| Percent | 16 | 16 | 18 | 17 | 33 | 100% |

(Missing Data = 0.0%)

## THE RESPONDENT'S POLITICAL POWER INDEX

Those items in the reinterview of the 1972 study which we describe as measuring the respondent's perception of his own political power are presented in Table E.38. Interrelationships among the respondent's political power items for the total population are presented in Table E.39. As can be seen, the item "influence national decision" does not relate well to two of the other remaining three items; hence, this item was eliminated from further analysis.

Further examination of relationships between the three remaining items, "political power of people like you," "power too little/just right," and "how likely to change (unjust or harmful) law," was conducted in a number of population subgroups (Table E.40). It can be seen that the item "how likely to change (unjust or harmful) law" relates weakly to the other two items in a number of subgroups. The two items "political power of people like you" and "power too little/just right" correlate with moderate gammas except there is no relationship among low income whites. This lack of relationship must be considered in light of the small number of respondents in this group. Consequently, it was decided to combine the two items into an index in spite of the weak association among low income whites.

The Respondent's Political Power Index is based on the summation of values on these items:

*How much political power do you think people like you have?*

*Do you think that people like you have too little political power, or just about the right amount?*

## Table E.38

### Items Measuring the Respondent's Political Power
(1972 reinterview)

How much political power do you think people like you have?

|  |  |  |  |
|---|---|---|---|
| A great deal | Some | Not very much | None |

Do you think that people like you have *too little* political power, or *just about the right amount*?

| Too little | About the right amount |
|---|---|

If you made an effort to change this (unjust or harmful) law, how likely is it that you would succeed?

|  |  |  |  |
|---|---|---|---|
| Very likely | Somewhat likely | Not very likely | Not likely at all |

Have you ever done anything to influence a national decision?

| Yes | No |
|---|---|

## Table E.39

### Relationships between Items Measuring the Respondent's Political Power
(1972 reinterview respondents, N = 240)
(gammas)

|  | Power Too Little/ Just Right | Change (Unjust/ Harmful) Law | Influence National Decision |
|---|---|---|---|
| Political power of people like you | .4 | .4 | .1 |
| Power too little/just right |  | .2 | .1 |
| How likely to change (unjust or harmful) law |  |  | .4 |

Variance was equalized on the original value of each item in this manner. A respondent's original score on "political power of people like you" was "1," "2," "3," and "4." This score was multipled by 2, thus giving derived values of "2," "4," "6," and "8" respectively. The item "power too little/just right" was originally scored "1" and "2." Each original score for this item was multiplied by 3, thus giving derived values of "3" and "6" respectively. The derived values were summed on the two items to form the Respondent's Political Power Index. A respondent scoring missing data on one of the two

**Table E.40**

**Relationships between Items Measuring the Respondent's Political Power for Selected Subgroups**

(1972 reinterview respondents, N = 240)

(gammas)

| | Whites | Blacks | Men | Women | 25 Years or Younger | 40 Years or Older | Low Education | High Education | Low Income Whites | Low Income Blacks | South |
|---|---|---|---|---|---|---|---|---|---|---|---|
| **Political power of people like you** | | | | | | | | | | | |
| Power too little/just right | .4 | .4 | .5 | .4 | .7 | .4 | .4 | .6 | .0 | .6 | .5 |
| How likely to change (unjust or harmful) law | .6 | .2 | .3 | .4 | .3 | .4 | .1 | .4 | .4 | .2 | .3 |
| **Power too little/just right** | | | | | | | | | | | |
| How likely to change (unjust or harmful) law | .2 | .1 | .2 | .2 | .3 | .3 | .0 | .5 | .1 | .2 | .2 |
| N | (120) | (116) | (115) | (125) | (72) | (110) | (85) | (54) | (39) | (60) | (82) |

items in this index received a score equal to the value of the valid score on the other item. A respondent scoring missing data on both items was assigned a missing data score on the index.

Table E.41 presents a summary of the Respondent's Political Power Index. The higher the score on the index, the more politically efficacious the respondent perceived himself.

**Table E.41**

Construction of the Respondent's Political Power Index
(1972 reinterview respondents, N = 240)

| Respondent's Political Power Index | Low | | | | High | |
|---|---|---|---|---|---|---|
| Summed Score | 5-6 | 7 | 8-9 | 10-11 | 12-14 | |
| Recoded Score | 1 | 2 | 3 | 4 | 5 | |
| Percent | 13 | 34 | 18 | 16 | 19 | 100% |

(Missing Data = 0.2%)

# BIBLIOGRAPHY

Aberbach, J. D., and Walker, J. L. "Political Trust and Racial Ideology." *The American Political Science Review* 64(1970a): 1199-1219.

Aberbach, J. D., and Walker, J. L. "The Meanings of Black Power: A Comparison of White and Black Interpretations of a Political Slogan." *The American Political Science Review* 64(1970b): 367-388.

Andrews, F. M., Morgan, J. N., and Sonquist, J. A. *Multiple Classification Analysis*. Ann Arbor: Survey Research Center, Institute for Social Research, The University of Michigan, 1967.

Atkinson, J. W., and Feather, N. T. *A Theory of Achievement Motivation*. New York: Wiley and Sons, 1966.

Banfield, E. C. *The Unheavenly City*. Boston: Little, Brown and Co., 1970.

Berkowitz, L. *The Psychology of Aggression*. New York: Wiley and Sons, 1961.

Berkowitz, L. *Aggression: A Social Psychological Analysis*. New York: McGraw-Hill, Inc., 1962.

Berkowitz, L. "Frustrations, Comparisons, and Other Sources of Emotional Arousals as Contributors to Social Unrest" *Journal of Social Issues* 28(1972): 77-92.

Blalock, H. M., Jr. *Social Statistics*. New York: McGraw-Hill, Inc., 1970.

Blumenthal, M. D. "The Belief Systems of Protesting College Students." *Journal of Youth and Adolescence* 2(1973a): 103-123.

Blumenthal, M. D. "Resentment and Suspicion Among American Men." *American Journal of Psychiatry* 130(1973b): 8-12.

Blumenthal, M. D. "Further Work on Identification." Working Memorandum No. 42. Ann Arbor: Survey Research Center, Institute for Social Research, The University of Michigan, 1972.

Blumenthal, M. D., Kahn, R. L., Andrews, F. M., and Head, K. B. *Justifying Violence: Attitudes of American Men*. Ann Arbor: Survey Research Center, Institute for Social Research, The University of Michigan, 1972.

Bowen, D. R., Bowen, E., Gawiser, S., and Masotti, L. H. "Deprivation, Mobility and Orientation toward Protest of the Urban Poor." *The American Behavioral Scientist* 11(1968): 20-24.

Brooks, W., and Friedrich, G. "Police Image: An Exploratory Study." *Journal of Communications* 20(1970): 370-374.

Campbell, A., Converse, P. E., Miller, W., and Stokes, D. *The American Voter*. New York: Wiley and Sons, 1960.

Campbell, A., Gurin, G., and Miller, W. *The Voter Decides*. Evanston: Row, Peterson and Co., 1954.

Campbell, A., and Schuman, H. "Racial Attitudes in Fifteen American Cities." In *Supplemental Studies for the National Advisory Commission on Civil Disorders*. Washington, D. C.: United States Government Printing Office, July, 1968.

Cannell, C., and Robison, S. "Analysis of Individual Questions." In *Working Papers on Survey Research in Poverty Areas*, edited by J. B. Lansing, S. B. Withey, and A. C. Wolfe. Ann Arbor: Institute for Social Research, The University of Michigan, 1971.

Cantril, A., and Roll, C. W., Jr. *Hopes and Fears of the American People*. New York: Universe Books, 1971.

Cantril, H. *The Patterns of Human Concerns*. New Brunswick: Rutgers University Press, 1965.

Caplan, N. "Identity in Transition: A Theory of Black Militancy." In *The New American Revolution*, edited by R. Aya and N. Miller. New York: The Free Press, 1971.

Cash, W. J. *The Mind of the South*. London: Thames and Hudson, 1941.

Chun, K., Cobb, S., French, J., Jr., and Seashore, S. "Storage and Retrieval of Information on Psychological Measures." *American Psychologist* 28(1973): 592-599.

Converse, P. E. "Changes in the American Electorate." In *The Human Meaning of Social Change*, edited by A. Campbell and P. E. Converse. New York: Russell Sage Foundation, 1972.

Converse, P. E., and Schuman, H. " 'Silent Majorities' and the Vietnam War." *Scientific American* 222(1970): 17-25.

Crawford, T. J., and Naditch, M. "Relative Deprivation, Powerlessness, and Militancy: The Psychology of Social Protest." *Psychiatry* 33(1970): 208-223.

Davies, J. C. "Toward a Theory of Revolution." In *Anger, Violence and Politics: Theories and Research*, edited by I. K. Feierabend, R. L. Feierabend, and T. Gurr. Englewood Cliffs: Prentice-Hall, Inc., 1972.

Dollard, J., Doob, L., Miller, N., Mowrer, O., and Sears, R. *Frustration and Aggression*. New Haven: Yale University Press, 1939.

Easton, D. *A Systems Analysis of Political Life*. New York: Wiley and Sons, 1965.

Feierabend, I. K., and Feierabend, R. L. "Systemic Conditions of Political Aggression: An Application of Frustration-Agression Theory." In *Anger, Violence and Politics: Theories of Research*, edited by I. K. Feierabend, R. L. Feierabend, and T. Gurr. Englewood Cliffs: Prentice-Hall, Inc., 1972.

Feierabend, I. K., Feierabend, R. L., and Nesvold, B. A. "Social Change and Political Violence: Cross National Patterns." In *Anger, Violence and Politics: Theories and Research*, edited by I. K. Feierabend, R. L. Feierabend, and T. Gurr. Englewood Cliffs: Prentice-Hall, Inc., 1972.

Ferdinand, T., and Luchterhand, E. "Inner City Youth, the Police, the Juvenile Court and Justice." *Social Problems* 17(1970): 510-527.

Flax, M. J. *Blacks and Whites: An Experiment in Racial Indicators*. Washington, D. C.: The Urban Institute, 1971.

Fogelson, R. M. "Violence as Protest: An Interpretation of the 1960's Riots." *Proceedings of the Academy of Political Science* 29(1968): 25-42.

Fogelson, R. M., and Hill, R. B. "Who Riots? A Study of Participation in the 1967 Riots." In *Supplemental Studies for the National Advisory Commission on Civil Disorders*. Washington, D. C.: United States Government Printing Office, July, 1968.

Forward, J., and Williams, J. "Internal-External Control and Black Militancy." *Journal of Social Issues* 26(1970): 75-94.

Frideres, J. S., Warner, L. G., and Albrecht, S. L. "The Impact of Social Constraints on the Relationship between Attitudes and Behavior." *Social Forces* 50(1971): 102-112.

Gamson, W. A. *Power and Discontent*. Homewood, Ill.: Dorsey Press, 1968.

Geller, J. D., and Howard, G. "Some Sociopsychological Characteristics of Student Political Activists." *Journal of Applied Social Psychology* 2(1972): 114-137.

Goodman, L. A., and Kruskal, W. H. "Measures of Association for Cross Classification III: Approximate Sampling Theory." *Journal of the American Statistical Association* 58(1963): 310-364.

Graham, H. D., and Gurr, T. *Violence in America: Historical and Comparative Perspectives.* Staff Report to the National Commission on the Causes and Prevention of Violence. Washington, D. C.: United States Government Printing Office, July, 1969.

Grimshaw, A. D. "Three Views of Urban Violence: Civil Disturbance, Racial Revolt, Class Assault." *American Behavioral Scientist* 2(1968): 2-7.

Grofman, B., and Muller, E. N. "The Strange Case of Relative Gratification and Potential for Political Violence: The V-Curve Hypothesis." *American Political Science Review* 67(1968): 514-539.

Guilford, J. P. *Psychometric Methods.* New York: McGraw-Hill, Inc., 1954.

Gurin, P., Gurin, G., Lao, R. C., and Beattie, M. "Internal-External Control in the Motivation Dynamics of Negro Youth." *Journal of Social Issues* 25(1969): 29-53.

Gurr, T. "Psychological Factors in Civil Strife." *World Politics* 20(1968a): 245-278.

Gurr, T. "A Causal Model of Civil Strife: A Comparative Analysis Using New Indices." *American Political Science Review* 62(1968b): 1104-1124.

Gurr, T. *Why Men Rebel.* Princeton: Princeton University Press, 1970.

Hackney, S. "Southern Violence." In *Violence in America: Historical and Comparative Perspectives,* edited by H. D. Graham and T. Gurr. Staff Report to the National Commission on the Causes and Prevention of Violence. Washington, D. C.: United States Government Printing Office, July, 1969.

Hopkins, P., and Feierabend, R. L. "Correlates of United States Riots, 1965-1967: A Cross City Comparison." *The Proceedings of the Annual Convention of the American Psychological Association* 6(1971): 311-312.

Hyman, H. "Dimensions of Social-Psychological Change in the Negro Population." In *The Human Meaning of Social Change,* edited by A. Campbell and P. E. Converse. New York: Russell Sage Foundation, 1972.

Kamii, C. K., and Radin, N. I. "Class Differences in the Socialization Practices of Negro Mothers." *Journal of Marriage and the Family* 29(1967): 307-317.

Kohn, M. "Social Class and Parent-Child Relationships: An Interpretation." *The American Journal of Sociology* 68(1963): 471-480.

Lipset, S. M. "The Activists: A Profile." In *Confrontation: The Student Rebellion and the Universities,* edited by D. Bell and I. Kristol. New York: Basic Books, Inc., 1969.

McConochie, D., Jayaratne, T. E., and Blumenthal, M. D. "Reduction of Criterion Variables." Unpublished manuscript. Ann Arbor: Survey Research Center, Institute for Social Research, The University of Michigan, 1973.

Miller, A. H. 1972. Political Issues and Trust in Government: 1964-1970. Paper read at the 1972 Annual Meeting of the American Political Science Association Convention, September, 1972, in Washington, D. C.

Miller, A. H., Brown, T. A., and Raine, A. S. 1973. Social Conflict and Political Estrangement: 1958-1972. Paper read at the Midwest Political Science Association, May, 1973, in Chicago, Illinois.

Miller, A. H., Miller, W. E., Raine, A. S., and Brown, T. A. 1973. A Major Party in Disarray: Policy Polarization in the 1972 Election. Paper read at the Annual Meeting of the American Political Science Association, September, 1973, in New Orleans, Louisiana.

Mirels, H. "Dimensions of Internal versus External Control." *Journal of Consulting and Clinical Psychology* 34(1970): 226-228.

Muller, E. N. "A Test of a Partial Theory of Potential for Political Violence." *American Political Science Review* 66(1972): 928-959.

Nunnally, J. C. *Psychometric Theory.* New York: McGraw-Hill, Inc., 1967.

Oberschall, A. "The Los Angeles Riot of August 1965." *Social Problems* 15(1968): 322-341.

Pettigrew, T. F. *A Profile of the Negro American.* Princeton: D. Van Nostrand, Inc., 1964.

Pettigrew, T. F. "Social Evaluation Theory: Convergences and Applications." *Nebraska Symposium on Motivations* 15(1967): 241-311.

Reiss, A. J. "How Common is Police Brutality?" *Transaction* 5(1968): 10-20.

*Report of the National Advisory Commission on Civil Disorders.* New York: Bantam Books, 1968.

*Report of the President's Commission on Campus Unrest.* Washington, D. C. United States Government Printing Office, September, 1970.

Robinson, J. P. 'Public Reaction to Political Protest: Chicago, 1968." *Public Opinion Quarterly* 34(1970): 1-9.

Robinson, J. P., Rusk, J. G., and Head, K. B. *Measures of Political Attitudes.* Ann Arbor: Center for Political Studies, Institute for Social Research, The University of Michigan, 1972.

Robinson, J. P., and Shaver, P. R. *Measures of Social Psychological Attitudes.* Ann Arbor: Survey Research Center, Institute for Social Research, The University of Michigan, 1969.

Rokeach, M. "The Nature of Attitudes." In the *International Encyclopedia of the Social Sciences.* New York: Macmillan Company and the Free Press, 1968.

Rosenthal, R., and Jacobson, L. F. "Teacher Expectations for the Disadvantaged." *Scientific American* 218(1968): 19-23.

Rossi, P., and Berk, R. "Local Political Leadership and Popular Discontent in the Ghetto." In *Collective Violence,* edited by J. F. Short and M. W. Wolfgang. Chicago: Aldine-Atherton Press, 1972.

Rotter, J. B. "Generalized Expectancies for Internal versus External Control of Reinforcement." *Psychological Monographs* 80(1966): 1-28.

Runkel, P. J., and McGrath, J. E. *Research on Human Behavior.* New York: Holt, Rinehart, and Winston, Inc., 1972.

Sampling Section, Survey Research Center. Sample Design: Modified Probability and Standard Probability Samples. Working Memorandum No. 104. Ann Arbor: Institute for Social Research, The University of Michigan, 1973.

Schuman, H. "Attitudes vs. Actions versus Attitudes vs. Attitudes." *Public Opinion Quarterly* 36(1972): 347-354.

Singer, B. D., Osborn, R. W., and Geschwender, J. A. *Black Rioters.* Lexington, Mass.: Heath Lexington Books, 1970.

Stevenson, W. C. *Year of Doom, 1975.* London: Hutchinson and Co., Ltd., 1967.

Toch, H. *Violent Men.* Chicago: Aldine Publishing Co., 1969.

*To Establish Justice, To Insure Domestic Tranquility.* Final Report of the National Commission on the Causes and Prevention of Violence. Washington, D. C.: United States Government Printing Office, December, 1969.

Vroom, V. *Work and Motivation.* New York: Wiley and Sons, 1964.

Walker, D. *Rights in Conflict.* New York: New American Library, Inc., 1968.

*Webster's Seventh New Collegiate Dictionary.* Springfield, Mass.: G. & C. Merriam Co., 1969.

Weinstein, A. G. "Predicting Behavior from Attitudes." *Public Opinion Quarterly* 36(1972): 355-360.

Zellman, G. L., and Sears, D. O. "Childhood Tolerance of Dissent." *Journal of Social Issues* 27(1971): 109-136.

Zygmunt, J. F. "Prophetic Failure and Chiliastic Identity: The Case of Jehovah's Witnesses." *American Journal of Sociology* 75(1970): 926-948.

# LIST OF TABLES

# INDEX